D0455731

TIME AND CHANCE

The Political Memoirs of Canada's First Woman Prime Minister

Kim Campbell

Doubleday Canada Limited

TORONTO NEW YORK LONDON SYDNEY AUCKLAND

Canadian Cataloguing in Publication Data

Campbell, Kim, 1947–

Time and chance : the political memoirs of Canada's first woman prime minister

Includes index. ISBN 0-385-25527-5

1. Campbell, Kim, 1947– . 2. Canada – Politics and government – 1984–1993.* 3. Canada – Politics and government – 1993– .* 4. Prime ministers – Canada – Biography. 5. Cabinet ministers – Canada – Biography.* 6. Women in politics – Canada – Biography. 7. Progressive Conservative Party of Canada – Biography. I. Title.

FC631.C34A3 1996 971.064'7'092 C95-932383-8 FL034.3.C34A3 1996

Jacket photo by Denise Grant
Jacket design by Tania Craan
Text design by Heidy Lawrance Associates
Printed and bound in the USA

Published in Canada by
Doubleday Canada Limited
105 Bond Street
Toronto, Ontario
M5B 1Y3

To all the people (too
numerous to name) who
were part of this story, and
especially to my family
and the people in the
pink hats.

Contents

ACKNOWLEDGMENTS

Writing this book was, for the most part, a happy experience, thanks largely to the support and encouragement provided by many people. In fact, it is these Acknowledgments that cause me anxiety since I'm afraid of leaving out any of the names of those who have helped me so much.

I began writing in the summer of 1994 but the ground was prepared during the spring of 1994, when I was a fellow at the Institute of Politics at the John F. Kennedy School of Government at Harvard. There I taught a study group in comparative Canadian/American political processes, which enabled me to return to a number of the contentious issues — abortion, gun control, gay rights, women's rights, pornography — that I had dealt with as minister of justice. I am grateful to the staff and other fellows at the institute for creating a stimulating and supportive environment. The interest of the students, not just at Harvard but at the other universities I spoke to that year in New England and Texas, encouraged me in the belief that there was genuine interest in my experiences both as a policy maker and as a woman in politics.

When my former policy adviser John Dixon, a computer aficionado, arrived in Cambridge as a guest in my study group, he insisted that I "bite the bullet" and buy a computer. I did so, and between John and Peter Lugli, also of my ministerial staff, I was launched into the world of word processing and cyberspace. It is no exaggeration to say that without this prompting, I would not have been able to write this book myself.

I returned to the Kennedy School in the fall of 1994 as a fellow of the Joan Shorenstein Center on the Press, Politics and Public Policy. There, instead of teaching, fellows write papers on some aspect of the press and politics. I used this opportunity to examine the press coverage of the 1993 federal election. I am grateful to Michael Ferrabee for making available to me the archive he kept:

for each day of the campaign he preserved the collection of national press clippings prepared by the Privy Council Office as well as the verbatim transcripts of all my media interviews, scrums, open-line appearances, and speeches. Going through these to prepare my paper, "Honour Among Scribes: When Journalists Think They've Crossed the Fairness Line," was as depressing as it was enlightening, but it was crucial preparation for writing the election chapter of this book. Again, the staff and faculty of the Shorenstein Center, especially our research directors Fred Schauer and Pippa Norris, and the other fellows, especially Betty Hanson and Geoffrey Smith, were wonderfully supportive and helped me to step back and look somewhat objectively at the relationship between the press and the political process.

In the fall of 1994 I was invited to speak in the Donahue Lecture series at Suffolk University Law School in Boston. My talk, "Post Conviction Review in Canada: Politics and the Law," provided an opportunity to return to the details of the Milgaard case. Although the version in this book is much less technical, I am grateful for the feedback of the faculty and students to that earlier discussion. Two Canadian students at Harvard Law School — Adam Dodek and Victoria Donaldson — did valuable research for me on aspects of the law related to this topic, as did Peter Lugli, who already knew the case well from his days as a lawyer on my ministerial staff.

I benefitted enormously from discussions with many people who were not part of the events of this book but who believed it important for me to tell this story. In addition to those already mentioned, Florrie Darwin and Paul Weiler in Cambridge, Mass., were warm in their encouragement, generous in their hospitality, and astute in their advice.

Reconstructing the events of this memoir was made possible by the efforts of many people. Wendy Waite and Cathy Buck, who remained as staff in the transitional office graciously provided to me by Prime Minister Chrétien for a year after the election, organized an enormous volume of papers in preparation for sending them to the National Archives. National Archivist Jean-Pierre Wallot and his staff were wonderfully cooperative in giving me access to my papers and photographs in Ottawa, Montreal, and Vancouver. However, many important issues were clarified and memories refreshed by personal interviews with people who have shared these events. I wish to thank Cindy Boucher, Libby Burnham, David Camp, Ray Castelli, Marianne Campbell, Susan Campbell, Susan Christie, Bea Cleary, Pamela Divinsky, John Dixon, Michael Ferrabee, Robert Foster, Alain Gourd, Catherine Kane, Patrick Kinsella, Myles Kirvan, Diana Lam, Senator Marjory LeBreton, Peter Lugli, Dan Macdonald, Hon. Shirley Martin, Ian McPhail, Rick Mosley, Senator Lowell Murray, Bill Neville, Marlie Oden, Ian Potter, Virginia Richards, Steven Sharzer, Brian Smith, Bud Smith, Norman Spector, John Tait, and Eugene Williams for their cheerful willingness to check facts or, in most cases, spend considerable time reviewing past adventures.

A number of people read and responded to the manuscript, in whole or in part. My sister, Alix Campbell, read an early draft of the first part of the book. Gregory Lekhtman was also a willing reader of early parts of the manuscript and a source of encouragement. He also provided important feedback on the 1993 portions. John Dixon and Peter Lugli looked at the early stages of the Justice chapters and Eugene Williams reviewed the discussion of the Milgaard case. Pamela Divinsky and Virginia Richards gave me early feedback on the election chapter.

The entire manuscript was reviewed by a number of people: David Camp, Florrie Darwin, John Dixon, Michael Ferrabee, Diana Lam, Scott McIntyre, Prof. Kristin Monroe, University of California at Irvine, and John Tait. Their comments were perceptive and helpful. None of the people who reviewed the book bear responsibility for its shortcomings or errors.

In setting out to write this book, I wanted to write a one-volume memoir, accessible to the general reader, that would explain not only how I saw my time in federal politics but who I was when I arrived in Ottawa in 1988. The choice of that whole-life, autobiographical approach has meant that I have treated some areas of policy perfunctorily in order not to impede the narrative flow of an already long book. I have also been constrained by my desire to respect the privacy of those who of necessity figure in this story but who have not chosen to be in public life. In speaking of my early family life and my marriages, I have tried to say no more than is essential to explain my actions. (I know what the French writer Guizot meant when he said that all memoirs are written either too early or too late.)

Until I began this book, I had no idea of the pleasures of working with really good editors. John Pearce, editor-in-chief of Doubleday Canada, kept a watchful eye on the entire project and, towards the end, helped with paring a very long manuscript. I owe to John's persistence the opportunity to work with Rick Archbold. As structural editor, Rick made time from his many commitments to see me through the first draft. I learned a great deal from Rick, including the lesson that, even when writing non-fiction, one should think like a novelist. With Rick's constant urging and encouragement, I found my voice and the way to tell a complex story. Laurie Coulter then attacked the problem of a too-long manuscript. It is a reflection of her skill and persuasiveness that she persuaded me to hack out large quantities of my first draft. She was right — less is more. Barbara Czarnecki and I were able to agree on how to fine-tune the manuscript, and our occasional discussions of matters political were certainly lively. To John, Rick, Laurie, and Barbara I give my heartfelt thanks not only for their care and professionalism but also for their support in helping me to write the book I wanted to write — controversial but not scandalous, personal but not indiscreet, and acerbic but not mean-spirited. If I have failed to achieve those goals, it is not their fault.

Maggie Reeves, Robert Mackwood, and Dara Rowland at Doubleday gave me great confidence in the quality of the production and marketing of the book and were a pleasure to deal with. Also, thanks to the staff at Doubleday Canada in Toronto for their kindness during my periods in residence over the fall of 1995, and to my stepdaughter Pamela Divinsky for her hospitality and encouragement during the final rewriting process, and for her excellent taste in movies when inspiration fizzled. Special thanks as well to my agent, Perry Goldsmith.

I'm grateful to the many people who have told me, over the past two years, "I'm looking forward to reading your book."

I returned, and saw under the sun,
that the race is not to the swift,
nor the battle to the strong, neither
yet bread to the wise, nor yet
riches to men of understanding, nor
yet favour to men of skill; but
time and chance happeneth to them all.

Ecclesiastes, 9:11

PROLOGUE

Australian aborigines believe that having your photograph taken robs you of your soul. A political career, I believe, robs you of your persona. People you have never met feel at perfect liberty to describe and explain you. Family and friends pick up their newspapers and read descriptions of a person bearing your name whom they don't recognize at all. If you become really well known, every person who ever disliked or held a grudge against you is now an eager interpreter of the "real" you. One thing is certain, in seeking public office, you were up to no good!

An exaggeration, you say? Well, perhaps, just a little. Sometimes the errors go the other way — attributing fine qualities to you that you would never claim for yourself. (You are, however, fully responsible for the inevitable disillusionment.) In my observation, politicians are like people anywhere: complex, multidimensioned, and difficult to explain in twenty-five words or less. The experiences of my life have led me to be non-judgmental about people. Most people are capable of both good and bad, and behaviour that disappoints is often the reflection of qualities that are simply human. The portraits in this book are written in that spirit.

Recently, I was taken with an observation by the Czech writer Milan Kundera that life is not something we go through with a clear view of the path ahead. Rather, the experience is more like travelling through a fog. Looking back, however, the observer sees good visibility and judges people's actions accordingly. "He sees their mistakes but not the fog." It isn't just in the writing of distant history that we assume a certainty and clarity that weren't present. In our time of rapid and profound change, the fog is thicker and closer than it has been for some time, both in Canada and the world.

In choosing the title of this book and the epigraph from which it is drawn, I was not thinking only of my own life, but of politics in general. Like all ambitious people, I have worked hard to make my own luck, but perhaps in no other endeavour are timing and circumstance as important to success as they are in politics.

Few exercises are more fraught with peril than the attempt to explain how people become who they are. In early 1993, my candidacy for the leadership of the governing Progressive Conservative Party of Canada generated an explosion of such efforts. Magazines, newspapers, and no fewer than five books set out to explain how I had arrived at a point where I might become the first woman to hold the office of prime minister of Canada. They ranged from the most extravagant leaps of psychobiography, focussing on the absence of my mother, to one astonishing attempt to demonstrate that I could be explained by three men in my life: my first husband, my thesis adviser at graduate school, and the philosopher Edmund Burke!

My becoming prime minister of Canada represented a number of firsts for that office: first woman, first British Columbian, first member of the post-war baby-boom generation, first to be divorced at the time of taking office. These factors alone suggest the limitations of a simplistic explanation of who I am. And so I decided upon an attempt to reclaim my own persona. This book, however, is not a definitive autobiography: it is a political memoir — my story of how "a nice girl like me wound up in a place like that."

1

Formative Years

> Her poor heart must be broken, people say, but it isn't true. Her heart was merely squeezed and wrung dry for a time, like an old rag.
>
> Yet wherever she goes, her story marches ahead of her.
>
> Carol Shields, *The Stone Diaries*

THE STORY THAT used to march ahead of me began in the fall of 1959 when I was twelve and a half years old. My sister Alix and I had been enrolled at St. Anne's Academy, a Roman Catholic boarding school in Victoria, British Columbia. On the day my mother took us to St. Anne's, I remember looking forward to what promised to be an exciting adventure, beginning with my first ride in an airplane. Unfortunately, because of unusual turbulence, the normally short hop from Vancouver took over an hour and both my mother and sister became ill. Alix's discomfort went beyond airsickness. Mum believed that all girls should have the chance of experiencing at least a year at boarding school. But Alix was going into grade eleven and greatly resented being separated from her friends. She was going through a decidedly rebellious stage and regarded our going to St. Anne's as being "sent to jail."

By October, when Mum and Dad came to visit us for the Thanksgiving holiday, Alix and I had settled into a routine. Shortly after that weekend, when I arrived in the boarders' lounge after school one day for the customary snack and mail check, Alix whispered that she had something to tell me and took me up to her room.

"Mum's gone," she said.

"You mean she's dead?" I asked incredulously. Mum had been crippled two years before, and so I assumed something awful had happened to her.

"No," said my sister, "she's just left."

St. Anne's was a convent and in those pre–Vatican II days, the nuns believed they had a right and a duty to supervise all aspects of the lives of their young charges. This included reading our mail before we received it. In the case of Dad's letter to Alix telling her of Mum's departure, the letter had been given to her in private, which was probably kinder than allowing her to open it in the midst of the other girls. However, in the following months, the nuns also took it upon themselves to hold back the letters Mum wrote to us, with the result that we were in a state of shock with no idea where our mother was or if she was all right.

Mum had sent us to St. Anne's calculating that we would be well looked after while she attempted to leave what had become for her an intolerable marriage. It would be many years before I could appreciate how she viewed her position, in those days when divorce was virtually impossible to obtain from an unwilling spouse, and could comprehend the powerlessness of women in her situation at that time. It would be ten years before she and I would see each other again.

In reading about the impact on girls of the loss through death, physical abandonment, or emotional abandonment of their mothers, I see myself in descriptions of girls who become highly self-reliant, who reject the standard definitions of appropriate gender roles, and who feel "different" from their friends after the loss of their mothers. But it is hard for me to attribute these characteristics solely to my motherless adolescence, although they may well have been reinforced by that experience. I think these qualities were part of who I was long before my mother left. Whenever

I try to draw a causal link between my childhood and adult lives, I'm reminded of research done on identical twins separated at birth that shows an uncanny similarity in their life patterns, even in markedly different social environments, and suggests that much of who we are is a function of our genes. So, while the peculiar circumstances of my personal and family life no doubt help to explain how I arrived at Canada's highest political office and who I was when I got there, like anyone else, I am a product of many forces and experiences, not least of which is that ineffable quality we know as individuality.

I was born in Port Alberni on the west coast of Vancouver Island. My mother's family, which traces its roots to Scotland and Ireland, had been pioneers on the Island. Elizabeth Hill Gardiner, my grandmother, was teaching school in Nanaimo when she met and fell in love with my grandfather, Carlyle Edward Cook. Since women teachers weren't allowed to continue teaching if they married, my grandparents had to postpone their wedding until Carl had graduated from dental college and was able to support them. They married in 1921 and had four children — Shirley, Phyllis (my mother, who is called Lissa), Douglas, and Marjorie (who died in early childhood). My grandfather decided that small towns were great places to raise children and moved his family from Nanaimo to Port Alberni, where he set up his dental practice. A much-loved member of his community, Carl Cook taught all the kids in town how to swim. He was both a hunter and a conservationist. My grandmother used to describe canning the venison that he would bring back from hunting trips. My grandfather died suddenly of a heart attack in 1939 while on a hiking trip. His death at the age of forty-four was devastating for his wife and for his children, who were then only fifteen, fourteen, and nine.

My mother was a beautiful young woman, highly intelligent, with a love of literature and language. After graduating from high school in 1941, she worked briefly at a bank before horrifying her mother by enlisting in the Women's Royal Naval Service (WRNS). She had met my father by this time but was determined to be part of the war effort before she became a bride. Shortly after enlisting, Mum was posted to Halifax. She and a friend made several trips to the Halifax archives, where they learned the origins of all the street and place names and revelled in what, to them, coming from Vancouver Island, seemed like an ancient city.

Later that year, the Navy posted Mum to Saint-Hyacinthe, Quebec, to train as a signals operator. This was a new unit that would eventually number 200; their training was in radio telegraphy, and their job was to listen in on radio bands to detect and identify transmissions from German submarines in the north Atlantic and the Gulf of St. Lawrence. It was exacting work because the U-boats surfaced for only a short time to send their messages. If more than one of the Canadian or English stations detected the same signal, it was possible to determine the location of the U-boat and send planes or ships out after it. My mother served in Moncton, New Brunswick, and Gloucester, Ontario, locations where there were no steel-reinforced buildings to interfere with the reception of radio signals.

In May of 1943 my mother married George Campbell while on leave in Port Alberni. Dad was born in Montreal in 1920, the youngest of three sons of Scottish immigrant parents. His father abandoned the family when Dad was still a toddler, and he and his brothers were raised largely by a series of foster parents. After graduating from high school, Dad enlisted in the Canadian Army in 1939. He then spent several years trying to persuade the army to send him overseas. First attached to the Army Dental Corps, he was posted to Port Alberni, where he met my mother. Finally, in July 1944, he was sent to Italy with the Seaforths. In December, Mum received word that her husband had been seriously wounded. She was pregnant and had retired from the navy to return to her mother's home to await the birth of my sister. (Alix likes to describe herself as having been born "after a brief career in the Royal Canadian Navy.") On March 2, 1945, my sister was born.

Dad was injured in the same burst of fire that killed his best friend, Leo Charbonneau of Gravelbourg, Saskatchewan. He was evacuated to a military hospital in England. Thanks to the "wonder drug" sulpha, he survived his abdominal wound, but the experience of seeing his best friend cut in half left other scars. After returning home, he would sometimes wake up screaming from nightmares about horrors my mother could only guess at.

While Dad was convalescing, my parents lived with my grandmother in her Port Alberni house. Dad commuted weekly to his studies at Victoria College (now University of Victoria) at its original campus in Craigdarroch Castle. In the summer of 1946 my parents lived and worked in the Alberni Forest lookout as forest fire wardens. The lookout was on top of a mountain and consisted of an elevated structure with living accommodations on one level and the watchtower above. It was an idyllic and romantic setting for two people who loved nature. I came along on March 10, 1947.

After Dad received his B.A. in 1949, my parents bought their first house, a tiny bungalow in what was still the fairly rural municipality of Burnaby. It was a wonderful environment for young children. Although we weren't well off, it certainly didn't feel that way. Our lot was covered with fruit trees, and we grew vegetables and raised chickens. There was a field with horses next door. Because many of the houses on our street were still being completed, usually by their owners, hammers, nails, and other tools were common playthings. We ran wild in that baby-boom neighbourhood with the other kids, most of whose fathers were also returning veterans.

Mum worked at a variety of jobs while Dad was a student and after he graduated. She also pursued art studies at the Vancouver School of Art when she could. Sometimes she was able to put her artistic talents to use in her various jobs, but she was never able to do as much as she would have liked.

One of the first lessons I remember learning at my mother's knee was not to be afraid to be different. My sister and I confronted the sense of being "different" at an early age, if only because of our unusual names. Hers was Alix Paula Bernadette and mine was Avril Phaedra Douglas. The "A" in our first names is pronounced to rhyme with the "A" in April. My sister's name lent itself to nicknames such as Ajax or Ex-lax, which were the bane of her youthful existence. We were also unusual in that *both* our parents had been in uniform during World War II.

I have no recollection at all of feeling neglected by a working mother. Our maternal grandmother — a short, slightly plump, still attractive and energetic woman whom we called Nana — often came to stay, and she loved to look after us. In the early 1950s, as the baby-boomers started to hit the schools, there was a shortage of teachers. Nana decided to sell her house in Port Alberni and return to the teaching she had been required to leave when she married. After a brief refresher course, my sixty-year-old grandmother launched into her second teaching career. She eschewed the comforts of urban schools and instead took on the adventure of teaching in rural schools, many in remote areas. I remember her wonderful stories of teaching in places like Burns Lake, where she had to board in a farmhouse and share the outhouse with the odd porcupine. Nana was an important role model and source of love in our childhood.

Our paternal grandmother we called Nannie. She lived in Montreal, so we got to know her on her visits to Vancouver. Nannie was a very intelligent woman who, in another time, might have been able to benefit more from her talents. But she had had a difficult life and was, as a result, rather difficult herself. Her stories were not, to put it mildly, always on the most intimate terms with reality. I admired my father's patience with her. She had hardly been an ideal mother, and his upbringing by foster parents had been truly awful in many respects. However, both my parents included her in the family whenever she appeared, and Alix and I were fond of her.

My childhood impressions of Canada came from Mum's accounts of the war, including her "adoption" by a French-speaking family in Saint-Hyacinthe; Dad's reminiscences of his childhood spent in Montreal and his adolescence on the prairies; and Nannie's identity as a Montrealer. Nannie was proud of being from Montreal, which was, during my youth, Canada's pre-eminent city. She always took great care to look stylish, despite her limited means, and it was from her that I learned expressions such as "chic." Dad also took pride in his Montreal roots. Although many years later he told me about fights with the "French kids" when he was growing up in Rosemount, I never heard any anti-French views expressed as a child. In fact, Dad liked to demonstrate his rudimentary French and often signed his birthday cards to us, "*Ton père qui t'aime.*"

My father graduated from law school in 1953, and as a result of a special program for returning veterans that allowed them to article in the summers, he was called to the bar that autumn. He set up practice on the busy thoroughfare of Kingsway, where he was soon busy enough to employ two secretaries. In May of 1954 we moved from Burnaby to Vancouver, into what my junior-high classmate Vicki Gabereau has described as "the relentlessly middle-class area of Kerrisdale." Mum set about decorating our new house with murals. On one wall of my bedroom, she copied a wonderful Miró painting. I was the only one of my friends who had a mural, much less a Miró, on her bedroom wall.

My sister and I were both happy children. Up to that time, there hadn't been any major crises in our young lives. Those that did occur had to do with medical problems. Alix suffered from strabismus, a hereditary eye condition in which the eyes do not move together. She underwent two painful operations as a child, one at four years of age and the other at eight.

When I was about two, I had an emergency tracheotomy. I had begun to cough and was gradually turning blue as my throat closed and my breathing became constricted. Dad was playing golf at the time and suddenly had an irresistible urge to return home, the only time he has ever had such a premonitory experience. He rushed to the closest telephone, at the end of the street, and called an ambulance. According to Mum, I was practically black from lack of oxygen. My family doctor assumed that I had bulbar polio — the kind that paralyzes the respiratory tract. Mum was falsely encouraged by his comment that "at least there will be no paralysis of the limbs." I say falsely, because when it didn't prove lethal, bulbar polio condemned its victims to life in an iron lung. Happily, the polio team at the hospital immediately recognized that I had septic laryngitis, and an emergency tracheotomy was quickly performed, leaving me with the still prominent scar characteristic of that procedure.

I remained in the hospital for ten days, during which time I was in considerable pain. Mum came to the hospital every day, but I wasn't allowed to see her. The medical staff were afraid that I would cry when she left and that this would cause me to choke to death. When Mum was finally allowed to stand where I could see her, I just sighed and turned away. She was furious that I hadn't been allowed to know she was there.

It's tempting to assume that I sought to compensate for the later loss of my mother by seeking public attention and acclaim. However, the theory doesn't stand up because I loved to perform right from the start. One Christmas when I was almost three, Alix prepared a concert of poems and songs to entertain Nana. After she had sung the first song, I stood up and performed the second one, much to everyone's surprise. Clearly I wasn't inclined to stay in the background.

In our Vancouver house we had a large rec room in the basement, which had a slightly elevated floor in one half. Alix and I wasted no time in making it into a stage and Mum made a curtain for it. We dragooned the neighbourhood kids into taking part in various performances or watching ours. Years later, one of those kids, Peter Insley, by then a lawyer working for the provincial government in Victoria, would express surprise that I was going to marry his colleague, the somewhat quiet and retiring Howard Eddy. As he explained to a co-worker, "The Campbell sisters were ... well, so theatrical!"

We also shared a somewhat off-the-wall sense of humour. In the early 1950s, we were given two books, one of jokes and the other of riddles. We had always loved funny things, but these books sent us over the moon. Jokes like: "Q: Why did the ant run back and forth across the cereal box? A: Because it says, 'Tear along dotted line'" set a pattern for us from which we have never recovered. Alix was the best wit in the family, and I often find myself using her quirky expressions such as "thinking you're a poached egg" for being crazy.

In grade five I had my first experience as a television performer. The CBC was planning a children's show to run for nine weeks in the spring of 1957. The producers canvassed the Vancouver schools for students who might be promising participants. I was one of the students selected from my school, and after auditioning, I was offered one of the regular places on *Junior TV Club*. I interviewed guests on the talent segment and moderated a panel discussion at the end of each program on such important issues as how much allowance kids our age should be getting. I learned a lot about television during those nine weeks. This early experience allowed me to be more comfortable with the medium than many.

It was also in grade five that an event occurred that would have a dramatic impact on our family. After a day of sleighing on the hills of the local golf course during an untypically snowy winter, Mum slipped and fell on the way home, smashing her right hip. The efforts to put her back together with metal plates and nails didn't work, and in 1959 she had the first titanium hip replacement in Canada. The artificial hip joint never worked well and was removed in 1970. She has functioned without one ever since.

My mother's crippling accident at the age of only thirty-three was devastating. She was in excruciating pain and forced herself to walk before she should have, further damaging her body. One effect of this terrible event was to further exacerbate the strains that had already arisen in my parents' marriage. I can remember sitting in school that year trying to hide my uncontrollable weeping because my father had left home. The marriage had been troubled for some time. While no child can fully understand the dynamics of her parents' marriage, with hindsight, I can see that no two people could have had more opposite experiences of family life. It was a recipe for disaster. In the mid-1950s divorce was a relatively uncommon and difficult process. Mum's accident added not only to the problems of the marriage but also to her own powerlessness in an era of general powerlessness among women.

Lissa Campbell was a loving mother, and I owe a great deal of my strength and positive attitude to her, not to mention my love of poetry and language. She used to delight in expanding her children's vocabularies with what she would call "good fifty-cent words." Alix and I relished word games and jokes that turned on twists of language. The comic strip "Pogo" was a wonderful source of these and we grew up speaking Pogo-ese. We still say things like "finger of speech" and other Pogo-isms that perplex our younger, post-Pogo friends.

I can't remember my mother ever telling us that we were too young to discuss something or to learn it. We learned to cook at an early age, and when I expressed an interest in sewing at the age of nine or ten, Mum bought a pattern and material for a skirt and blouse. She made the blouse and I made the skirt. After I sat down at the piano as a toddler and began to pick out tunes by ear, she decided that I would take piano lessons as soon as I was old enough. And when Alix showed a particular interest in ballet, Mum started her at the Kay Armstrong School in Vancouver. Piano and dancing lessons were no mean feat given our family's modest income.

My mother claims it was Alix and I who were curious and asked to be taught things. At the age of four, Alix stomped into the house in an absolute froth, declared indignantly, "Johnny Cliff can tie his own shoes!" and demanded to be taught how to tie hers then and there. Because Mum readily obliged in these situations, we were both self-sufficient and confident about taking on new tasks. I can remember making breakfast in bed for our parents when we couldn't have been more than five and seven.

Many years later, in 1972, I was living in London with my husband, Nathan Divinsky, and two of my three stepdaughters, Pamela, then thirteen, and Mimi, nineteen. Pamela's school curriculum included needlework, a course that the other girls had already taken for a year. To help her catch up, I sat down with her one day to teach her some rudiments, including how to use a thimble. I suddenly had an eerie sensation as I heard myself speaking in Mum's patient voice.

In the 1950s it was uncommon for women to teach their daughters to be advocates for women's equality. I'm not sure if my mother even used the word "feminism," but one of the first fifty-cent words I can remember being taught was "misogynist." (I should say that what I call "feminism" reflects the usage of an earlier time. To me, it means a commitment to equality for women. It has unfortunately taken on a connotation of hostility to men in the minds of some people. For that reason, many young women don't like to identify themselves with feminism today. I continue to use the term because I have yet to find an adequate alternative.) From Mum, Alix and I learned that women can do anything, but from her we also understood that this was not a universally accepted proposition. We were exposed at an early age to examples of women who had done extraordinary things, to women's poetry, and to sayings such as the wonderful comment by Ottawa mayor Charlotte Whitton, "Whatever women do they must do twice as well as men to be thought half as good. Luckily, this is not difficult."

My Uncle Doug's first wife was a doctor. I can remember telling my family physician when I was about twelve that I wanted to be a doctor.

"Women can't be doctors," he said.

"But my Aunt Alice is one," I replied. He had no response, and I wonder now what I would have thought had I not had a handy female doctor in the family to counterbalance that sort of prejudice.

Although Mum was unable to attend university, my sister and I grew up assuming that we would. We thought of our future selves as doctors or veterinarians. Unlike many of our friends, we were never presented with the either/or approach to family and career. Both my grandmothers had jobs for part of the time I knew them, and both took pride in what they did and saw it as a reflection of their independence and skill. Mum was a competent domestic manager who took pride in her cooking, but she never made a fetish out of domesticity. She always had other interests and, except when she was too ill to do so, worked outside the home.

Losing my mother at the age of twelve and a half meant losing my female role model and losing the person who did most to encourage and validate me in life. But, in the words of Carol Shields that began this story, my heart was not irrevocably broken, just squeezed and wrung dry for a time. I was strong and resilient as a child — a result perhaps of the survivors' genes that came my way from both sides of my family. I would survive the loss of my mother, wounded in some ways but strengthened in others. The knowledge that I could survive this pain formed part of the emotional armament that would make it possible for me as an adult to face down the fear of other losses.

2

My Own Person

NEITHER DAD NOR Alix dealt well with Mum's departure and it fell to me, almost by default, to be the one in the family who didn't come apart. My sister's anguish was compounded by two factors. In the two years preceding the separation, Mum had confided to Alix some of her difficulties with the marriage. I can remember being aware of their suddenly changing the subject when I entered a room. I resented this secrecy but put some of it down to my sister's adolescence. Alix had not, however, been privy to Mum's decision to leave. Her sense of being shut out of such an important deliberation, given the other confidences she had shared with my mother, was particularly hurtful. My complete exclusion from what had been going on was perhaps a blessing. The second factor that increased Alix's vulnerability during this crisis was the fact that she was experiencing a particularly troublesome adolescence. She had skipped two grades in school and hadn't had the luxury of maturing at her own pace. Alix was forced to deal with the pressures of teenage life before she was ready. I think Mum's decision to send us to St. Anne's was partly motivated by a desire to put Alix in an all-girl environment that would reduce some of those stresses.

Years later, when I became a trustee on the Vancouver School Board, I worked hard to expand programs for gifted children. There is a misapprehension that gifted students don't need any special treatment. If nothing is done for them at school, however, they often become bored and drop out. In Alix's case, it would have been unthinkable not to respond to her intellectual precocity when she entered school. But in those days the only approach was to put children ahead, with results that were often socially damaging.

Alix and I left St. Anne's after that year, and my enrolment at Prince of Wales Secondary School near our home in Vancouver for grade nine was the beginning of the compensatory overachieving that marked my teenage years. The inclination to do the kinds of things that won approval and recognition from my teachers and classmates was not new for me, but no doubt it now provided a substitute for the lack of support at home. Dad was emotionally absent and Nana had moved to Ontario to be with my Aunt Shirley. Beyond the fact that my mother lived in Europe and that I corresponded with her, my family situation was something I didn't discuss with even my closest friends.

One obvious reaction to Mum's departure was my desire to change my name. I decided that henceforth I would be known as Kim, a name my mother had actually considered for me but rejected when a friend with the same surname had chosen it for her son. I was baptized and confirmed in the Anglican church in 1960 and insisted on adding to my name several others, all names from my mother's family. In hindsight, the desire to flee from a name so closely associated with Mum on the one hand, but to reinforce my attachment to her on the other, indicates my natural emotional confusion towards her at that time.

It has surprised me to learn that even women who have lost their mothers through the perfectly respectable mechanism of death feel the same sense of shame and freakishness as I did. The truth is that girls without mothers *are* freaks. There are a thousand and one ways in which not having a mother marks you as "different" and denies you experiences that other girls take for granted. Alix remembers her resentment on hearing a girl complain about "having to go shopping with my mother."

The self-reliance that characterizes such girls is a necessary result of there not being anyone you can count on. Developing the habit of doing things for yourself reduces the pain of acknowledging that fact. What was a positive tendency when Mum was present became a necessity for survival once she had left. I believe my inclination to keep negative feelings to myself dates from this period. I was an outwardly happy and well-adjusted young woman. The happiness was real enough; it just wasn't the whole story.

Many people's teenage years are the period when they develop a social conscience. In my case, from about the age of ten, I had become increasingly interested in the history of World War II and the Holocaust. The war was recent history and the involvement of both my parents had made it very immediate to me. The voice of Sir Laurence Olivier narrating *The World at War* on television would draw me from wherever I was to watch. Books such as Leon Uris's novel *Mila 18*, about the Warsaw Ghetto, both fascinated and disturbed me. Lying on my bed reading, I would try to imagine what the numbers of dead meant — that each one was someone like me with a consciousness, a life, parents. I admired Winston Churchill and was inspired by his memoir of his early life. My own parents' service to their country was a strong influence on me; I believed that I, too, would have to find some way to contribute to world peace or the betterment of society.

During the 1993 leadership campaign, I was amused to see that an enterprising reporter had tracked down some of my high school poetry. What it lacks in literary merit it certainly makes up for in earnestness. Most, if not all, of the poems were on social themes. The early sixties were the years of the folk music revival. When I was sixteen, I bought a second-hand guitar and taught myself to play. Like so many of my generation, I sang the socially conscious songs of the time and wrote a few of my own (now consigned to a well-deserved musical oblivion).

My teenage years were also a period of active religious searching. At my thirty-year high school reunion in 1994, my classmate Jim Patterson reminded me that in grade eleven I would drag him along to various church services, including Catholic mass. Dad had been raised Catholic by his foster parents but had left the Church before he met my mother. Mum, whose family was Scots Presbyterian, had taught Sunday school at the United Church when she was a teenager. However, neither of my parents was a churchgoer when Alix and I were children, although they did encourage us to attend Sunday school at a variety of Protestant denominations. In grade school, I happily accompanied one of my friends, Elizabeth Stevenson, to the song-filled services of the Kitsilano Gospel Hall and to a Pentecostal summer camp on Anvil Island near Vancouver. Another year I sang in the Knox United Church choir, which had a wonderful choirmistress who would ensure attendance at practice by supplying a basketful of buttered Scottish tea pancakes. I was introduced to Jewish family life and religious observances in the home of another good friend, Shelley Hanson. And at St. Anne's I attended mass two mornings a week and on Saturdays, and trooped off on Sundays with the other Protestant boarders to Christ Church Cathedral, the Anglican church where I was baptized and confirmed.

The result of my exposure to these various religions was that I absorbed much of the ethic but none of the dogma. I would have liked the comfort and security of finding a home in one particular church but, as I grew older, I felt less and less comfortable with the exclusivity this entails. I also became impatient with the extent to which organized religions take moral and ethical concepts and turn them into complicated codes of behaviour that become ends in themselves. The secondary role that many religions assign to women was another problem for me. In my view, the soul has no gender.

In 1964 I graduated from Prince of Wales Secondary School. I gave the valedictory speech and accepted the prize for English and the Girls' Merit Award for best all-round girl student. In my final year, I had been student council president, the first girl to be elected in the school's forty-three-year history. In the early sixties, this earned a write-up in the Vancouver *Sun* as "news"! It was my involvement in student politics that first made me aware of my ability to move people when I spoke. I began to think in vague terms of fulfilling my desire to "change the world" in the political arena. Unlike most other politicians' families, however, mine wasn't particularly interested in politics, so I knew very little about it. In fact, I don't recall ever having a political discussion with either of my parents before becoming an adult.

I enrolled at the University of British Columbia in the fall of 1964. Because I had been student council president of my high school, I was invited to attend Frosh Retreat. An election for the Frosh Council was to be held later that fall, and, for reasons that escape me now, I decided to run for president. For reasons that also escape me now, I was elected. The Frosh presidency also gave me a seat on the Alma Mater Society (AMS) Council, UBC's student council.

I was UBC's first woman Frosh president, which created some problems for the engineering students. The engineering-Frosh rivalry was a long-standing tradition on the campus, and one of the fall rituals was to throw the Frosh president into the library pond. There was great consternation when I was elected because they knew they could not "tank" a woman. How to keep up the tradition? One morning a group of first-year engineers came to the Frosh office and escorted me to the engineering building. I was presented with some old clothes and shown the ladies' room; it was suggested that I get changed. Then they marched me to the front of the library, where I was elevated in a hammock between two trees. I guess I went along with the stunt because it was a tradition and the engineers had shown considerable ingenuity in finding an acceptable way of fulfilling it. At the time I was going out with Steve Whitelaw, who happened to be the president of the engineering students. He came along and after a few minutes told them to let me down, to much good-natured ribbing.

My first year of university, 1964–65, was the end of an era. University campuses changed dramatically over the remainder of the 1960s. Campus pranks gave way to demonstrations against the war in Vietnam, the military-industrial complex, and the Americanization of Canadian universities. During those undergraduate years, I wasn't attracted to any one political party. Many of the young male activists I knew on the AMS council were Liberals. It always seemed to me that they were there as much for their careers as for any other reason. Given the virtual stranglehold that the Liberals had on Ottawa, perhaps this was not surprising. Although I sympathized with the anti-war movement, I was repelled by many of the other positions taken by the left on campus, particularly their apologies for the Communist regimes in China and the Soviet Union. The women's movement had also begun to build steam during my undergraduate years, and like many of my classmates I read Simone de Beauvoir's *The Second Sex* and Betty Friedan's *The Feminine Mystique*, both feminist classics, and, later, Kate Millett's *Sexual Politics*.

The summer after my first year of university I travelled a

thousand miles north and west to the small fishing community of Prince Rupert, to work at the Royal Fish Plant. One of my sister's friends had convinced the owner, Al Fletcher, to give me a job. He did so out of the kindness of his heart, and I'm grateful to him because the job not only gave me much-needed income but also contributed significantly to my education. It was the first of several jobs that I took to pay my university expenses. I was touched by my father's recognition of the extent to which I had relied on myself when he told me on my university graduation day, "Well, there's one thing no one can take away from you, that you did it on your own."

Royal Fish was primarily a halibut packing plant. After the enormous fish were unloaded from the boats, each one was hauled up against a board and a worker called a fletcher would cut it into four giant fillets, or fletches. These were placed at the end of a long table where six or seven women trimmed the pieces and cut them into the sizes in which they would be frozen for sale. The smallest pieces and trimmings were passed to my group. We packed them into small boxes, which were first closed by a machine and then frozen under pressure. The final blocks were cut into fish sticks.

When I wasn't working on the fish-stick line, I would be out in the main work area scrubbing the freezer shelves, using a hose and a long-handled brush. Although it was harder work physically than the fish-stick line, I preferred it because I could look out at the wonderful view of the Prince Rupert harbour. Eagles were as plentiful as starlings there. So were ravens, which I had never seen before. My comment that "the crows up here are as big as chickens!" was greeted with considerable amusement and identified me immediately as a southerner.

The women and the men worked in separate units in the plant, and the women were always the first to be laid off when there weren't any fish. Some of the women had been working there for twenty years, but it was just accepted that even men with far less experience had first call on the jobs. Similarly, it was accepted that women earned less than men. In most plants the job of fletcher was done by a man because of the strength needed to make those first cuts in the giant fish, some of which weighed well in excess of three hundred pounds. In our plant the job was done by an enormous Scandinavian woman named Helga. Not only was she strong, she was fast. The man who used to help her by carrying the fletches to the cutting table could hardly keep up with her. Yet Helga was paid according to the women's scale.

Even in those days I was angered by the double standard of the workplace. I had no personal complaint because I was paid the then princely sum of $1.82 per hour, a handsome wage for a university student. But it bothered me that the women I worked with, many of whom had given years to the industry, had so little seniority. This didn't appear to bother the plant's union — the United Fishermen and Allied Workers Union — and may explain why the women workers were rather lukewarm to the union reps.

My first two years of university were difficult for me and among the most troubled of my life. I had no study habits — I had never needed them — and my home life was very unhappy. High school had provided a stable environment, which made it easier to deal with the pain of my personal life. In first year, university activities on the student council and my relationship with Steve provided support and a focus. I was uncertain about what I wanted to do in the future, however, and this added to my lack of commitment to my studies. Second year brought me to a crisis point. Steve had graduated and gone off to work in Ontario, I was only marginally involved in campus activities, and I was still feeling at a loss about what direction to take.

When I was fifteen, my father had remarried. My stepmother, Ginny Vessey, was twenty years younger than Dad, which was regarded as faintly scandalous by some of my friends' parents. But Ginny was mature for her years and a good person. In spite of the fact that she was not much older than we were, Alix and I both liked her and hoped the marriage would last. Unfortunately, within three years, it was in the process of disintegration. Although I still lived at home, I tried to minimize the time I needed to be there because of the tension between Dad and Ginny. I spent a lot of time with friends, much of it drinking and partying. The result was predictable. When I received my second-year marks, I found I had failed my year.

Looking back, I think that failing the second year of university was the best thing that could have happened to me. It made me confront my own mixed-up emotions and realize just what was important in my life. I was extremely fortunate that the university allowed me to re-enrol the following year. I settled down and took my courses seriously, and by Christmas I had good enough marks to qualify for a student loan. The loan allowed me to move in with two friends from high school, Marilyn and Julie Wallach. Our one-bedroom apartment seemed like heaven to me. Marilyn, who was a close friend of my sister, was completing her master's degree in English. She had been the top student in her graduating year at high school and was an extremely good influence on me. That year was a turning point, and I settled into academic life.

By the end of my repeat second year, my marks were good enough to enable me to run for student council again, and I became second vice-president of the Alma Mater Society in the last election I would contest for thirteen years. At the same time, I applied for the honours program in political science. I had decided that if I wanted to pursue my interest in international relations or work for the United Nations, perhaps political science would give me the education I needed. To my delight and relief, I was accepted.

It was now 1967, Canada's Centennial Year and the year of Expo 67. In the summer, the Canadian Union of Students held its annual seminar in Vancouver, to be followed by its annual conference at the University of Western Ontario in London. As a member of the AMS executive, I was a delegate to both. One of the friends I made at the seminar, who remains a friend to this day, was Alphonse Morrissette, the student council president of what was then Canada's only bilingual university, the University of Ottawa. He arranged for me to stay with some friends of his in Montreal so that I could see Expo 67 on my trip east. Expo was a magical experience. The world came to our doorstep and Montreal was in its glory. I then travelled by train to Toronto to stay with my Aunt Shirley and Nana before going on to London.

At the conference in London the discussions focussed largely on student finances and the Americanization of Canadian universities. I can remember being surprised at the number of French-speaking delegates from New Brunswick. My first trip east made me realize how little I knew about Canada. I don't think I was atypical of my generation; our schooling had left us woefully ignorant about Canadian history. In the years that followed, I tried to read and learn more about my country.

It was during my third year of university that I became friends with the man who would become my first husband. Nathan Divinsky was a professor of mathematics at UBC, and I had first met him at Frosh Retreat in 1964. He participated in the program and was well liked by the students for his sense of humour. In 1966 I was asked to participate in a humorous debate at Frosh Retreat, and when asked which faculty member I would like as my debate partner, I remembered the short, plump, good-natured math prof and suggested him. I can't even remember now exactly how our friendship developed. Nathan Divinsky was known to his friends as Tuzie (a family nickname resulting from his inability as a young child to pronounce his Hebrew nickname, Tula). My first reaction on hearing this name was to ask, "Does he have a brother called Threezie?" Tuzie was separated from his wife. I remember visiting him with a boyfriend after a date and meeting his two younger daughters, Pamela and Mimi.

My premature growing up made me feel out of sync with my contemporaries and so I tended to gravitate towards older people. Certainly, my university friends had tended to be older than I was; Steve Whitelaw had been five years my senior. But age was only one of the reasons that Tuzie was the first man with whom I felt completely comfortable. We shared many of the same interests and I enjoyed the company of his friends as well. Later I realized how much I learned from his friends' wives that I hadn't been able to learn from my mother.

There have been numerous attempts to characterize my relationship with my first husband as some sort of Svengali-Trilby, professor-student one. Being twenty-one years older, he was obviously more knowledgeable than I was. But what attracted us to each other was the similarity of our interests and tastes, particularly in music and theatre. I started seeing Tuzie the same year I decided to take control of my life. His scholarly habits were a great influence on me and his respect for my mind boosted my self-confidence. When we began to date, I quizzed him seriously about the possibility of a reconciliation in his marriage. He had three daughters and I wasn't about to contribute to giving anyone else the kind of miserable adolescence I had experienced.

The year 1969 — ten years after my mother left — was a landmark in my life and in my relationships with both my parents.

After graduating in honours political science with straight first-class marks, I was accepted to do the year of graduate work at UBC that I needed to qualify for the Canada Council Doctoral Fellowship. This would take me in the fall of 1970 to the London School of Economics and Political Science (LSE) in England. The honours program had been a godsend for me, giving me both intellectual challenge and the companionship of a small and talented group of fellow students.

My mother was determined to be at my graduation. She and my stepfather, Bill Vroom, were living in the West Indies but made arrangements to return to Vancouver for the occasion. I had mixed emotions about this. Of course I wanted to see Mum again, but since my father would also be attending, I felt awkward. I had never before had to deal with the major-event manoeuvrings that arise for the children of unamicably divorced parents. I also had very mixed feelings about my parents' using my successful completion of university to let them off the hook for their inadequacies in the parenting department over the past decade.

The reunion with my mother went well, but it would take more than one visit to rebuild a relationship. Although the fact that they lived in Europe and the West Indies led some people to conclude they were wealthy, in fact Mum and Bill had left Canada with virtually nothing. Bill Vroom had been offered a job delivering a boat to England. Knowing that my mother could not leave on her own, he invited her to join him.

Like Mum, Bill hoped by leaving to convince his unwilling spouse to end their marriage. Her response was to put liens on all his Canadian property, leaving him without resources. Making use of the only skills they had, Mum and Bill worked as professional yacht crew, trying to put together enough money to start again. What had begun as a mutually supportive friendship grew into love, and eventually, when they were legally able to do so, they married. Within a year after my graduation Mum and Bill had bought property on Vancouver Island with their savings and moved back to Canada. There was no way that life could continue as if Mum had never left, but gradually, over the years, we have built a relationship that is gratifying to us both.

My relationship with my father also took a turn for the better that year. I have good memories of times spent with Dad before

Mum left. He took Alix and me several times to a dude ranch in the Cariboo, where we learned to ride. He had a small boat capable of towing waterskiers, and we spent several summer vacations on Shuswap Lake in the interior of B.C., where Alix and I both learned to waterski. But after Mum left, life at home became erratic. In the course of his own difficult upbringing, Dad had had no role models for how to be a good husband or father. It isn't surprising, then, that he was unable to meet the emotional needs of his daughters or that his second marriage ended in divorce. However, in the fall of 1969 my father married Marguerite Parkinson. Marg's mother, Freda, and her father, Ernie (Parkie) Parkinson, provided Dad with a family that brought out the best in him. At their twenty-fifth wedding anniversary celebration in 1994 Marg declared that her marriage to my father was the best thing that had ever happened to her, and this was certainly true for Dad as well. Ernie has since died, but both my sister and I continue to have a warm relationship with Dad, Marg, and Freda.

If neither of my parents was able to provide the role models Alix and I needed in our teenage years, we both feel that they are an inspiration for later life. Both are young in their outlook and enjoy life to the fullest. Since 1969 they have become not only parents whom we love, but also our friends. For myself, the need to encompass both the good and the bad in my parents and their behaviour has helped me appreciate the complexity of human beings and the lives they lead.

By the time I started my year of graduate work at UBC, Tuzie and I had been together for three years. As my plans to go to London began to firm up, he broached the idea of my staying in Vancouver to get married. I was tempted but had seen too many academic wives sacrifice their own careers, only to reproach their husbands later or feel betrayed when their marriages ended. I didn't want ever to say to him, "If it weren't for you, I could have gone to the LSE!" If our relationship was strong, I believed it would survive the separation of my going to London. Not even a stable relationship could overcome my deep-seated need for self-reliance.

3

A Canadian Abroad

During the 1970s I would come to have a clearer sense of my own political identity. But in other ways I was moving in the opposite direction to the conventional career path for an aspiring politician, through my choice of Soviet studies as an academic field, my unconventional relationship with Tuzie, and my total lack of partisan political involvement. I was intrigued, then, by a conversation I had during the first course I taught at UBC in the spring of 1975. One of my students was Andy Stark. At only eighteen, he was the national president of the Young Progressive Conservatives. By that time I had come to think of myself as a political conservative, but I had never belonged to a political party. Andy gave me copies of some speeches by Tory leader Robert Stanfield, and I was impressed by their thoughtfulness. One day I told Andy that I thought I might like to go into politics at some time in the future. "But," I said, "I've never been involved in a party. I guess I should join one." Surprisingly, he shook his head. "If you want to run for politics, don't get involved in a party. Become a star."

The only kind of stardom I aspired to in 1970 was of the academic kind. I was looking forward to attending the LSE in the fall. Political science as a discipline was dominated at that time by American scholars, and since most of my undergraduate professors were American-educated, going overseas to get a different perspective on the world seemed like a good idea. I can't deny that I was also tempted by the prospect of spending several years in a city where I could indulge my passion for music and the theatre.

The emphasis of my honours and graduate studies had been on international politics. Branching out linguistically after four years of high school French, I decided to study Russian for three years, which seemed like a sensible choice for someone with my interests. By the end of my first year of graduate work, I had found myself thinking more and more about the question of how people and nations form their political views and whether it is possible to create a particular type of political mentality in a society. The place where it seemed to make most sense to examine this question was the Soviet Union, where the effort to create the New Soviet Man had been under way for some decades. After I arrived at the LSE, I made an appointment to see the leading Soviet scholar there, Professor Leonard Schapiro. He agreed to take me on as a student.

Leonard Schapiro was a wonderful man and a truly great scholar. Although he died in 1983, his name still evokes reverent responses from scholars in the field. He was already in his late sixties when I met him. He liked to use snuff, and would hold an audience transfixed during a seminar while he put a bit into each nostril and then pulled out a large paisley handkerchief to wipe his impressive nose. His craggy face (one scholar told him he should be on Mount Rushmore) was usually host to a benign and interested expression. Leonard Schapiro was one of the sweetest-souled individuals I have ever met. He was involved in a number of liberal causes, including the Society for the Unwed Mother and Her Child, which is why I was amused to see him described by one of my biographers during the leadership campaign as a "rightwinger." His criticism of the Soviet regime stemmed from his straightforward criteria for judging a state, including the rule of law and the presence of an independent judiciary, reflecting his early career as a lawyer.

Soviet studies was a fascinating area because it invited so much wishful thinking or projection of personal views by its participants. Professor Schapiro, on the other hand, was a scrupulous man who refused to be moved by ideological fashion. His impact on his students came from the example he set of scholarly rigour and intellectual honesty, rather than his insistence that they follow a particular set of views.

When I arrived at the LSE at the end of the tumultuous sixties, I was hardly an advocate of the status quo, but I still didn't buy the vision of the political left. Underlying the facile call for "relevance" in education was an arrogant denial of the value of the classic thinkers, and the idealization of Communist countries just left me cold. In the case of China, I saw the admiration of Maoism as a reflection of the distaste some people had for the complexity and moral ambiguity of modern Western society. It seemed to me that they wanted to believe that somewhere there was a simpler, purer society where happy peasants sang as they carried out the night soil. But in my opinion this view of China was fundamentally racist. Here was an ancient and rich culture being subjected to a regime dedicated to obliterating that culture and putting every aspect of life at the service of the state.

The LSE has an undeserved reputation as a radical left-wing institution. It is true that there had been major political disturbances at the school in 1968, but by 1970 the campus was much calmer. While the well-known Labourite Harold Laski had taught many generations of LSE students (including Pierre Trudeau), the LSE's faculty had also included such luminaries as Friedrich von Hayek (an inspiration to the young Margaret Thatcher) and Karl Popper, neither of whom could be called left-wing. Perhaps some of the school's reputation as a hotbed of sedition was simply a reflection of the fact that it's entirely devoted to the social sciences. This, plus the fact that its student body is international, means that there are always reasons for LSE students to be up in arms about one thing or another.

I began my studies of the Soviet Union with the goal of finding a research topic for my thesis. Professor Schapiro hosted a seminar every Tuesday evening where presentations in the area of Soviet and Russian studies were made by leading scholars from all over the world. In other seminars, the students gave papers. I also sat in on classes in political philosophy and particularly enjoyed listening to Michael Oakeshott, a leading conservative philosopher who held the chair in political philosophy. Oakeshott is a modern exponent of some of the ideas of Edmund Burke and echoes Burke in his critiques of what he calls "bookishness" in politics.

Since the eighteenth century, there has been a powerful movement in favour of rationalism, the notion that reason should be the ultimate authority in life and that it is the most reliable basis on which to construct a society. But, as Burke so clearly saw at the beginning of the French Revolution, rationalism leads to abstraction, and that is the seedbed of fanaticism. It was Burke who accurately predicted in the first year of the French Revolution that it would degenerate into terror and dictatorship. In one of the most significant observations of modern times, he said that the French Revolutionaries saw men as abstractions, and in seeing them as abstractions, they forgot that they were human.

While I was in London, former Labour cabinet minister Richard Crossman published his diaries. One of the stories he relates from his time as minister of housing in Harold Wilson's government reveals the dilemma of abstraction as a basis of policy. In the period after World War II, in the great vogue of "planning," thousands of council flats were built by the British government, most of them in highrise developments that — despite the intentions of their designers — quickly became social deserts. Crossman writes about visiting a particular community where, instead of razing the old housing stock and building new buildings, the local authorities had renovated the existing houses and equipped them with indoor plumbing and other amenities they had lacked. The residents were happy with this arrangement. The neighbourhood had been preserved and people felt a powerful sense of attachment to it, in contrast to the new housing estates, which were constantly plagued by vandalism.

I had decided to study social engineering in Soviet society because of my scepticism that such engineering was, in fact, possible. But the lessons of Soviet failure were equally applicable to the non-Communist world. The difference between philosophical conservatives and liberals, it seemed to me, was that the latter believed in the possibility of remaking human nature. I certainly thought that there was a great deal one could do to make society better. I didn't for a moment advocate an attitude of laissez-faire or non-involvement on the part of governments. Rather, I differed from the liberal (and Marxist) tradition in my belief that because human nature is complex, and capable of good and evil, one should bring a certain humility to the task of public policy, a certain modesty with regard to what governments can achieve. People are not infinitely manipulable, and too much evil has been done in the ostensible cause of "perfecting" society. Abstract theorizing in government can tempt us to forget that at the end of the day, it is flesh-and-blood human beings who have to live with the results. Both Burke and Oakeshott recognized the kind of wisdom that comes from experience and argued for the participation of people in the making of policy that will affect them.

The early 1970s were a fascinating time to be studying politics because so many assumptions, especially about power, were being challenged. The war in Vietnam had put into serious question the conventional military power of the United States while at the same time demonstrating the power of public will. The question of "consciousness," whether related to race, gender, or another form of identity, had become central to understanding political power. In 1965 Ralph Nader published *Unsafe at Any Speed*, which warned of the design flaws of the Chevrolet Corvair. This frontal attack on the power of General Motors was the opening salvo in a war against corporations by consumers. The power that flowed from people's recognition of their shared interests was exactly what Marx had been talking about when he spoke of the necessity for the working class to move from being a class "in itself" to being a class "for itself."

Consciousness-raising became a key part of the political movements of that time. The women's movement was particularly active in this area, and as a result, my own views underwent a transformation. Although I had always believed strongly in the equality of women, I had tended to see this simply in terms of my own ability to do whatever I wanted to do. The sense of a solidarity with other women developed as I came to have a better sense of how deeply rooted the barriers to women were and of how much my own aspirations were tied to the opportunities for all women. Shortly after my arrival in London, one of the women students who was working in the Soviet area invited me to participate in a march for women's liberation. It was a cold autumn day when we gathered at Hyde Park Corner for the march to Trafalgar Square. It was the first demonstration I had ever participated in. A huge, good-natured crowd of both women and men took part. Not long ago I read an account of this march and its historical significance for the British women's movement. The snide coverage in the British press — one reporter wrote of "bra-less breasts swinging under heavy coats in the cold weather" — was an unintentional demonstration of the need for the march in the first place.

Consumerism, feminism, anti-war and civil rights movements — all these developments reflected the growing importance of political consciousness. In fact, I think it would be fair to argue that democratic politics today is largely a struggle not for the hearts and minds of voters so much as for their sense of self-identification. In the Soviet Union, where the structure of power was just the opposite of that in the Western democracies, the regime was determined to prevent the growth of this type of political consciousness.

The Soviet model of government had its origins in the period following the Russian Revolution. While Vladimir Lenin, as leader of the Bolshevik Party, created the strategy of the revolution, another dramatic personality, Leon Trotsky, was out in the country leading the Red Army. Someone had to stay home in Moscow to do the boring business of running the party. The job fell to an uninspiring Georgian, Josef Vissarionovich Dzhugashvili, whose revolutionary nom de plume was Stalin (Man of Steel). Given the official title of general secretary of the party, Stalin set about establishing the party bureaucracy and filling its posts. By 1923, when Lenin was seriously ill and his death seemed imminent, it was clear that Stalin, far from being a grey non-entity, had become extremely powerful. The people he had put into positions of authority owed their allegiance to him as their patron. After that time it was recognized that the position of general secretary of the Communist Party was the most powerful in the Soviet Union, more powerful than president, prime minister, or any other government post. The pattern of political power would reflect this, and for almost seventy years, Soviet scholars would trace the rise and fall of individuals in the Communist hierarchy by whose patron was being promoted or demoted.

This model of party rule was characteristic of all the Marxist-Leninist states, and in those days, I regarded it as the complete antithesis of Western democratic systems. I knew, of course, that there was such a thing as patronage in Canada, but what I didn't realize then was that my perspective on it was peculiar to my region. According to Jeffrey Simpson's study of patronage, *The Spoils of Power*, British Columbia has one of the least patronage-oriented political cultures in the country. In Brian Mulroney's Ottawa I would come to see that patronage is a much more important, if contentious, element of democratic politics than I had recognized, and that the use of the power of appointment to secure a position of political leadership was not confined to the practitioners of Marxism-Leninism.

The thesis topic I chose was "The Role of Political Socialization in Legitimizing Political Change in the U.S.S.R.: The Case of Destalinization." I wanted to examine how a state such as the Soviet Union deals with a complete about-face in one of the most important tenets of the state's claim to legitimacy. In this case I would be looking at the situation following Khrushchev's "secret speech" in 1956, when he began the process of denouncing Stalin. Although the kind of direct opinion research that one would use today wasn't possible then, I wanted to experience Soviet society at first hand. I was able to obtain a travel grant from the Canada Council and set off in April 1972 for a three-month study trip to the U.S.S.R.

My trip was organized according to an agenda that I had negotiated with Intourist, the Soviet tourism department. You couldn't simply go where you wanted in the U.S.S.R., nor could you spend your entire trip in one or two of the more desirable places, such as Moscow or Leningrad (today St. Petersburg). Even so, I was struck by the reaction of my Intourist guide in the Ukrainian city of Kharkhov. "Six days in Kharkhov!" she exclaimed. "Whoever gave you six days in Kharkhov?" But in general, I had no complaints with my itinerary. I started out with a week in Moscow and then headed southwest to Central Asia: Samarkand, Tashkent, and Alma-Ata. Then back to Moscow for two weeks, followed by eight days each in Kiev and Odessa and the infamous six days in Kharkhov. After a final two weeks in Moscow, I spent eight days in Riga and two more weeks in Leningrad. As a bonus, I discovered that as a tourist I could indulge my love of culture with the preference given to me as a foreigner, able to pay in hard currency. Tickets to the Bolshoi Theatre in Moscow and the Kirov in Leningrad would be mine when they were unavailable to Soviet citizens.

I arrived in Moscow on April 1, in some ways unprepared for

what awaited me in the weeks to come. Although I had been studying Russian for five years, my classes had been for scholarly, not conversational, purposes. My fluency improved dramatically over the three months, but it was tiring to speak a foreign language all day long. I was also experiencing culture shock. Some Soviet ways were amusing: I discovered that I could set off something approaching an international incident by entering a restaurant with my overcoat on (one was supposed to use the coat check). But others were frustrating; I had to elbow my way if I ever wanted to reach the front of a line (or get my coat back from the coat check). The latter, after almost two years among the strict, queue-respecting British, took some getting used to.

There were constant reminders that, however much the regime wanted to put on a good face for foreigners, this was a police state. In Moscow a young woman graduate student in English whom I'd met through a professor at the LSE wasn't allowed into my hotel to meet me. In Kiev two women befriended me. They both invited me to a meal in their homes — in each case, one room in a communal apartment. But when I wanted to return their hospitality at a restaurant, they refused. They were afraid to go with me. Moreover, neither had ever eaten in a restaurant in her life. I had been in Cuba in 1968, so this wasn't the first time I had been in a country where people were afraid of the government, but during this trip I was struck by the many ways such a society undermines human dignity. For example, in a Soviet store, the customer was always wrong. There was no question of taking your business elsewhere if the service was bad. So over and over I watched the ritual of people trying to size up the person behind the counter in an attempt to figure out the best way of getting what they wanted. The overwhelming sense I came away with was one of waste — wasted resources, wasted time, wasted human potential.

I was obviously interested in the position of women in Soviet life and what I saw wasn't encouraging. Soviet women, virtually all of whom held full-time jobs, would spend hours each week standing in line for food, clothing, and other goods. That and the absence of labour-saving devices, not to mention the macho attitude of Soviet men, made their lives extremely onerous.

In the area of birth control the U.S.S.R. really let its women down. In the early 1970s, birth control pills were scarcely available. I visited a clinic in Odessa and was shown the contraceptive diaphragms, which resembled B.F. Goodrich retreads and were, I suspect, of a one-size-fits-all variety. Poor-quality condoms were available as well, but many men refused to use them. The upshot, I was told, was that abortion had become the chief method of birth control for Soviet women. A woman in her mid-thirties who worked at the Intourist office at the National Hotel in Moscow told me she had had fourteen abortions. Her experience was not unusual. Aside from the health implications of having so many abortions, the procedure was usually performed without anaesthetic under the generally unhygienic conditions found in most Soviet health care facilities. Post-operative infection was a major cause of death. Not surprisingly, people with connections could obtain better health care.

Western apologists for the Soviet regime liked to point to the economic success of Soviet society. The reality I observed didn't support this view, except perhaps in Moscow. I had no idea then of the extraordinary environmental degradation that was one of the costs of this "economic miracle," but there were signs everywhere of scarcity. A common Soviet comment was that because goods were so scarce and of such limited quantity, when you saw a queue, you got in it and then inquired what it was for.

Two examples of the underdevelopment of the Soviet economy stand out in my mind. Riding on a Moscow bus, it seemed to me that the bus driver hadn't the foggiest idea of how the clutch worked. At first I thought it was just the nature of the transmission that resulted in the grinding sound every time he changed gears, but I was told by a Muscovite that Moscow Transit had to replace the transmissions on its buses regularly because of misuse by the drivers. This suggested a society where very few people had access to technology in their daily lives. For instance, few people had private cars. A Russian joke from that time tells of a man who finally earns enough money to put in an order on a small car. It is 1972. He goes to the sales office with his deposit and is told that the car will be ready to be picked up on June 22, 1984. "Is that the morning or the afternoon of June 22, 1984?" asks the prospective car owner. "Why do you need to know?" asks the salesman. "Because the plumber is coming that morning."

On my last stop in Moscow I took a tour to Zagorsk, an old village north of Moscow with a famous monastery. Driving north through the outskirts of the city, I was struck by the charming wooden houses that lined the road. Many had the gingerbread carving characteristic of traditional Russian dwellings. They were a welcome change from the huge highrise apartments in Moscow. It wasn't until the return journey that I realized that they didn't have running water. It was about 5 p.m. and people were coming out of their houses with buckets to draw water from roadside wells or taps. If they didn't have running water, then obviously they didn't have indoor plumbing.

Since the founding of the Soviet Union, the "nationalities question" had been one of the central dilemmas of state life. The expression of nationalist sentiment by any of its more than a hundred constituent nationalities was strictly forbidden. Nationalist poets, writers, and artists had been ruthlessly repressed. On the other hand, ethnicity was an important part of one's official identity in the Soviet Union. Soviet adults all carried an internal passport that specified their nationality. This approach to official nationalities resulted on more than one occasion in humorous exchanges with Soviet citizens. "Where are you from?" I would be asked.

"I'm from Canada."

"What is your nationality?"

"I'm a Canadian."

"Yes, but what is your nationality?"

"I am Canadian."

At this point the questioner would determine that my Russian just wasn't up to grasping the subtlety of the question.

"But what does your passport say?"

"It says I am Canadian," I would answer, leaving my interlocutor either confused, amazed, or convinced that the right question would have elicited a different response.

Leningrad was my last stop, and I was there during the famous White Nights at the end of June. One evening I was lying on my bed reading. I looked out the window and thought it was about 9 o'clock. When I checked, it was 3 o'clock in the morning! I stayed at the beautiful Aurora Hotel across from St. Isaac's Cathedral. The Aurora was where Hitler had planned to have his victory celebration after the fall of Leningrad. By the time I arrived in the city, I was thoroughly frustrated at the difficulties of dealing with various Soviet bureaucracies. I had my worst confrontation while trying to change my travel plans for the return to London. I was booked to go by boat and decided I just couldn't face five days on a Soviet ship. I arranged for money to be wired to me so that I could buy a plane ticket. The complications of negotiating a draft of the Bank of Foreign Trade–U.S.S.R.–Moscow at the Bank of Foreign Trade–U.S.S.R.–Leningrad were more than even three months in the country had prepared me for. I stormed back to the hotel, fuming. "What's more," I muttered to myself, "if one more person elbows me on the street or offers to buy my clothes, I'll scream!"

That evening, sitting in the hotel dining room, I heard a couple at the next table speaking English. I took little notice until I heard the woman mention Cowichan. I turned around, practically in tears. "You must be from Canada," I cried. And indeed they were. Sharon Van Raalte worked for the Canadian Eskimo Arts Council, and George Moore was a museum consultant. They were in Leningrad to set up an exhibit of Inuit art at the Hermitage. I hadn't realized until then how homesick I was. The sound of those Canadian voices had a powerful emotional impact on me. Later Sharon and George took me behind the scenes at the Hermitage and shared their precious stock of powdered orange Tang. I had found the Soviet soft drinks much too sweet and the mineral water too minerally. That Tang tasted wonderful!

I flew home from Leningrad at the end of June on a British plane. Never had economy class seemed so luxurious. The positive and negative experiences of the past three months had been intense. I fell in love with the people I met, and confirmed my strong attraction to the Russian soul, which had made Russian writers among my favourites, but the physical beauty and cultural richness of the U.S.S.R. had been in vivid contrast to the waste and inefficiency that made life for its citizens so bleak. I consider myself enormously fortunate to have had the opportunity to see up close the alternative to democracy. It would take me a number of years to reflect upon my experiences there. As for now, Tuzie was waiting for me in London, where he would spend the year on sabbatical, and we turned our attention to planning our wedding.

4

VANCOUVER

ON SEPTEMBER 15, 1972, Nathan Divinsky and I were married in London at the Hampstead Registry Office. Mimi and Pamela, who would be living with us for the year, were in attendance, as was Nana. If Nana's presence was important to my sense of "family past," having Mimi and Pamela living with us that year laid the foundation for "family future."

That first year of our marriage in London was very important for my relationship with my stepdaughters, particularly Pamela. That the bond with Pamela has remained strong is not, however, simply a result of my being there to nurture her. It is also a reflection of the healing effect her willingness to allow me to "mother" her had on me. Mimi and her older sister, Judy, then an undergraduate in Vancouver, needed friendship rather than mothering. But when I married her father, Pamela was roughly the same age I was when my mother left. In the following years, we would create together many of the mother-daughter activities that I had not had with my own mother, and that was as important to my emotional well-being as to hers.

Since the girls usually lived with their mother in Vancouver, I knew that year in London would be our only chance to be a family together for any extended time, and so I threw myself into making a home. We had rented the main floor of a large house not far from Hampstead Heath, and I enjoyed having my first real home in years, as opposed to student's digs. Cooking for a family of four was much more fun than cooking for one or two, and I managed to fatten us all up over the year. The challenges of adjusting to my new marriage did take a toll on my own work, and when I went back to Vancouver in August of 1973, I was worried about being so far from my thesis adviser.

Not long after our return, Tuzie and I found a house to buy. It was in an area known as the University Endowment Lands, within easy walking distance of UBC. The location was ideal for Tuzie and he happily returned to his teaching duties in the UBC mathematics department that fall. I began to think about my own career. Being in Vancouver meant that there were a limited number of teaching possibilities for me: UBC and Simon Fraser or the local college system. So I was thrilled when I saw an advertisement for a Soviet specialist for the political science department at Simon Fraser University. I knew there was hot competition for academic jobs, but I was certain that a student of one of the world's great authorities in the area, and a Canadian to boot, would at least be a strong candidate. I sent off my curriculum vitae and rushed over to UBC to talk to Ole Holsti, a well-known scholar who had been my adviser during my graduate studies year at UBC. I told him I had given his name as a reference, and he wrote a letter for me right away.

I was very discouraged when I received no reply to my application. Tuzie consoled me with the thought that perhaps they hadn't received the funding necessary for the position. However, not long after Christmas, Mark Zacher, head of the Institute of International Relations at UBC and a former professor of mine, called to tell me of a strange telephone conversation he had just had. In speaking to a member of the Simon Fraser political science department, he remarked casually that it was too bad they couldn't find a position for me in their department. "Who is Kim Campbell?" came the reply. "She's the student of Schapiro who applied for your Soviet position," answered Mark. "What! You mean a student of Schapiro applied? That's the first I've heard of it. We just met yesterday and appointed a man from Columbia."

When I phoned the department to find out what had happened to my application, no one, it appears, could find it or the letter from Ole Holsti. This seemed rather strange to me. I went to see the head of the department, who could offer no explanation, and I left feeling frustrated and dissatisfied. I had no recourse. If I had been interviewed for the position and not been hired, I would have accepted the situation. The injustice of not even being considered, though, was upsetting. It is standard practice at universities to hire faculty before their doctorates are finished. Like me, the successful applicant had not yet completed his Ph.D. I hated to admit it, but I felt I had just been staring discrimination in the face. The following autumn, Pauline Jewett became Simon Fraser's president, but that spring, there was no one I could turn to.

In the fall of 1974 UBC invited me to teach a course in the spring term. A visiting professor from England was unable to come and I was asked at the last moment to fill in. I started to teach in January 1975 and continued until the summer of 1978. The courses I taught included Contemporary Ideologies, Comparative Soviet and American Government, International Politics, and Soviet Government, as well as Urban Studies. This was a much wider variety of subjects than I would have taught as a regular faculty member and resulted in my having less time to do my own doctoral work. Although I enjoyed teaching and had a good rapport with my students, the university already had a Soviet specialist and wasn't interested in hiring another.

In 1978 I came to the end of the time I could teach at UBC; the limit for sessional lecturers was three years. Irrespective of the quality of my work, I had to find another job. I was able to obtain a sessional lectureship at the Langara campus of Vancouver Community College and began there in the fall of 1978. A year later, when I received my course assignments, I found that I had been given only three to teach, rather than a full load of four. Although eventually I was given the full complement, I realized that I didn't want to be forty years old, waiting to see how many courses I would be given each term. It was time to consider another career.

Alix, who had gone to law school in the late seventies, had graduated in 1979 and was enjoying her new career. In the absence of any possibility of an academic career, I decided to follow in her footsteps, although it meant making the difficult decision to abandon my thesis. I wanted not so much to practise law as to retrain myself in a profession that had a variety of applications. Also in the back of my mind was the idea that law was a useful discipline if I wanted to enter politics. I applied to UBC Law School. In the spring of 1980 I received word that I had been accepted, and I arranged to teach two courses at Langara, in the evenings, once school started.

That summer another opportunity arose that was to signal a change of direction for me. Tuzie had served as a trustee on the Vancouver School Board since 1974 and was at that time chairman of the board. Rather than seek a fourth term on the board in the upcoming fall civic election, he decided to run for city council. His party, the Civic Nonpartisan Association (known as the NPA), was looking for new candidates for the school board and asked me if I would consider running. I was interested for two reasons. First, by this time I had been teaching for five years and had some definite opinions about how my students, almost all products of the Vancouver school system, were prepared for university work. Second, it seemed to be a chance to determine if I had any talent for politics. I didn't know if I had the temperament for it. Could I take the pressure that inevitably goes with putting yourself on the line in the public arena? Dealing with issues that really mattered to me would be a good way to find out. So I agreed to let my name stand for nomination. There was just one problem: I insisted on using my own name. I had always used Campbell professionally and it made no sense to me to change now. However, the other trustees in the NPA were certain that I would have a better chance of getting elected if I used my married name because my husband was strongly identified with the school board. Despite this "error," in the November election we were both successful.

I started law school in the fall of 1980 and found right away that I enjoyed the study of law. It was a natural extension of my work in political science, and coming to it with an already well-developed world view gave it both context and significance. Like me, a number of students in the class were retraining after other professional careers. However, the school was also full of my former students, including my first-year moot partner, Les Armitstead.

Shortly after school started, a notice went up inviting people to participate in the Law Revue, a show of legal and political satire put on by the students every spring. The usual format was to have a variety of skits in the first half followed by a musical. At the first meeting we were asked to think up ideas. I came back with a proposal for a musical play, which I called *Westcoast Story*, based on the difference between big downtown law firms and public-interest "storefront" firms. Since mine was the only plot idea put forward, it won by default. One of my classmates, June Forrester, volunteered to write lyrics. This would be the beginning of a three-year collaboration in which I would come up with the plot line and dialogue, and both of us would write the lyrics and perform. Although rather shy in everyday life, June was a different person on stage. Those present will never forget her hilarious "strip-tease" to her own brilliant lyrics in "My Heart Belongs to Bora" in our second-year production, *How to Succeed in Law School Without Really Trying*. In third year June played Madam Justice Bertha Wilson to my Justice Sandra Day O'Connor in *Best Little Courthouse in Canada*. I directed the Law Revue in each of the three years and was always amazed at how much talent there was in the school. Many of the people we sent up would later be sitting around the cabinet table with me in Ottawa, a fact that caused me no small amount of retrospective guilt.

After the civic election, the NPA formed a minority on a school board dominated by the Committee of Progressive Electors (COPE). COPE was a civic party considerably to the left of the NDP. The NPA was called nonpartisan because it was based on the idea that civic politics should not be dominated by provincial and federal parties. In Vancouver, there is no ward system and civic politicians are elected city-wide.

The COPE board was chaired by Pauline Weinstein, a professor of mathematical education at UBC. She was a nice woman but obviously predisposed towards the teachers who were our main employee group. Another teacher on the board avoided the legal problem of conflict of interest by teaching in Burnaby, while another COPE trustee was a paid employee of the B.C. Teachers' Federation. One of the brightest but also most irritating members of the COPE team was Philip Rankin. A lawyer and the son of a well-known Vancouver alderman, Harry Rankin, Philip appeared to be following in the footsteps of his father, who was known for his irascibility and crude remarks. Although Philip could get my goat as few could, I respected his intelligence. What annoyed me most about him was his rabid partisanship.

Over the years, any journalist writing about my political career has always found a willing interviewee in Philip Rankin. One of his criticisms of me is that I am an "elitist" because I promoted programs for gifted children. After the 1982 election, when my party formed a majority of the board and I became its chairperson, I did work to have the International Baccalaureate program introduced into Vancouver schools. This program, originally designed to provide a curriculum for the children of diplomats, consisted of enriched high-school courses that gave highly motivated students a chance to move beyond the standard curriculum and provided its graduates an extra boost in applying to the best colleges. In addition, it allowed teachers, many of whom had advanced degrees, a greater professional challenge, which they welcomed. The program was finally established at Sir Winston Churchill Secondary School, where it continues to this day to be one of the best in the world, I'm told.

Elitism has nothing to do with my reasons for supporting programs for gifted children. From my sister's experience, I knew how important it was for children to stay with their own age group. Similarly, I supported programs for developmentally handicapped students that maximized their interaction with students of their own age. Intelligence is no respecter of class or income. Like the families of other special-needs students, families with higher incomes or where the parents have higher education can often provide the extra stimulation and opportunities that gifted children require, but most parents are completely dependent on the public school system. Philip managed to use the rhetoric of Marxist class analysis to suggest that these programs had some nefarious agenda. However, the countries of the Soviet bloc, which he visited and admired, far exceeded any scheme I was trying to put into place in attempting to identify and foster the talents of their best and brightest. My suspicion that his position was motivated primarily by partisan considerations was confirmed a few years later when I read in a Vancouver newspaper that school trustee Philip Rankin was complaining that on the east side of the city, where he lived, there were not enough programs for gifted children.

School board politics are an excellent way to get your feet wet in public life. Aside from exposing me to an enormous range of issues, from capital planning to labour relations, they honed my political instincts and reflexes. At the municipal level, a politician works in close proximity with the people she serves. The meetings are open and the public certainly attends. You have instant feedback on the effects of your decisions. This intimacy is very rewarding in personal terms when all is going well, but there is no buffer between you and any "dissatisfied customers."

I found that I was able to deal with controversy. It is not so much that I grew a thick skin, but rather that I developed a sense of perspective. Since one can't always make decisions that are universally popular, I came to realize that the most important thing is to have decision-making processes that, on the one hand, give the decisionmaker the best information and input possible and, on the other hand, reassure those who are affected by the decision that they were heard and that the process was fair.

French immersion was a contentious issue in Vancouver school politics, not because no one wanted it but rather because the demand was higher than could be met by the available native French-speaking teachers. Many young Quebeckers have travelled to other parts of Canada to teach French, but at that time, there just weren't enough of them. French immersion has been an enormous success not just in Vancouver but throughout B.C. Students start as early as kindergarten being taught entirely in French. By the end of elementary school, their studies are half in English, half in French. It is a great pity that few Quebeckers have any idea of the lengths to which people will go to support the notion of a Canada where English and French are official languages. Most parents simply accepted the fact that French would be required for certain types of employment in a country committed to preserving the official status of French. Other parents thought in terms not so much of employment as of nationhood. I remember Jean Charest telling me once about visiting students in a French immersion program in Regina. He expected that their French would be rather crude, because he believed that one could not acquire a true facility in the language without a cultural ambience to support it. He was astonished to find that, on the contrary, the students spoke excellent French and peppered him with questions. French immersion is a story of good will, of people "voting with their feet" (or their children's feet) to support the continuance of French culture and language in North America. It is a story that needs to be told.

English as a second language was also a major challenge in Vancouver. In some elementary schools, as many as 80 per cent of the students didn't speak English at home. The number of languages represented was often as high as sixty or seventy. There was a strong sentiment that the federal government, which sets immigration policy, should contribute resources to teaching English as a second language in the schools. Because the vast majority of immigrants settle in the metropolitan areas of Vancouver, Toronto, and Montreal, the effects of immigration are not felt evenly across the country. Thus the costs borne by school districts vary considerably. Later, when serving in the federal government, I came to appreciate Ottawa's point of view that each level of government has its own responsibilities, but at the time I was annoyed by the lack of appreciation for the very real difficulties created at other levels of government by Ottawa's decisions regarding issues like immigration. Although it is true that, especially in the fiscal area, provincial actions may affect the federal government, in general the impact is in the other direction. The answer is not to muddy the definitions of responsibilities held by the various levels of government, but to promote greater cooperation in making policy in areas that have an impact beyond the federal government itself. English as a second language was the first issue to alert me to this problem; it would not be the last.

Cutting my political teeth at the municipal level was also a way to learn some important lessons in a protected environment of relative obscurity. Some lessons are harder to learn than others; the danger of unguarded comments to the media is a good example. In the spring of 1983, Vancouver's teachers went on strike. At that time, such strikes were prohibited by law. As chairperson of the Vancouver School Board, I instructed the board's lawyers to seek an injunction. Although I always got on well with the teachers I met in the schools, I found their political organizations less appealing. When it suited them, they would argue for the professionalism of teachers, but when it served their purposes they weren't above acting in the tradition of the most radical trade unionists. This was a difficult time in British Columbia, since our economy was badly hit by the recession of the early eighties, but rampant inflation made it very difficult to hold the line on public-sector spending. Wage settlements of 15, 18, and even 21 per cent were not uncommon in school districts around the province. We were under enormous pressure from the provincial government, and much of our time was spent in haggling with the province.

One Saturday morning during the strike, I was awakened early by a telephone call from a reporter at the Vancouver *Province*. It was evident from her questions about the strike that she was completely ignorant of the issues. I spent about half an hour taking her through the events and the law and explaining the position the board would be taking in court, namely, that the strike was illegal. I remarked that I hoped the court would not only grant the injunction but also make it clear that the teachers' position was illegal; I said I hoped the teachers would get "kicked in the ass." I didn't think much of this (my instincts were clearly undeveloped then!) because I had spent so much time explaining the issue to her and assumed the issue would be the thrust of her story. I was horrified to see the headline in the next day's *Province*: "Campbell Hopes Teachers Get Kicked in the Ass."

I was embarrassed, to say the least. Throwaway lines that seem innocuous in the context of a conversation can look very different in the cold black and white of a newspaper headline. The irony was that while I did receive a number of critical letters, I got just as many calls and letters telling me that I was "right on." I was uncomfortable with the praise because, although I certainly didn't disavow the sentiment, my choice of words had been inappropriate. In granting the injunction to the school board, the court delivered the desired message, but in much more judicious language.

Perhaps the most significant aspect of my political beginnings is that I started my career as an elected person in a context where party was relatively unimportant. Later, when I went on to serve provincially and federally, I happily recognized my responsibility to my party, since at those levels parties are important vehicles for mobilizing political support. They offer the voters choices on election day by drawing together like-minded people around a core group of ideas. But because I didn't come up through a party organization, my primary point of reference has always been the voter, not the party. In the years to come I found this gave me a different perspective on the nature and uses of political power from that of some of the people I met.

In the middle and late seventies two other experiences gave

me insights that I would draw on later in my political career. The first was my involvement in property development, and the second was in starting a small business. Tuzie and I became involved in forming the University Non-Profit Building Society, which developed nineteen condominium units on a piece of property in the district of Kerrisdale, and later fifty more on an excellent site in False Creek. Tuzie, who really enjoyed the challenge of making it all work, was more involved in these projects than I was. However, I did learn a lot about property development and the impact that government decisions can have on the economic viability of projects. For example, once our society took out an option on the property for the first project, the financial clock began ticking. Delays in obtaining decisions regarding rezoning or permits added to the cost. The problem was not so much getting no for an answer, as getting no answer at all.

Sometime in 1977 or 1978, we also jumped at the chance of a 10 per cent share in a partnership that would knock down the old Arrow Transfer building on Granville Island and rebuild it in its original industrial form as a restaurant/pub complex. This was part of a federal government plan to redevelop the whole island. Our proposal was for a restaurant upstairs in the enormous second-floor area, and a bistro or wine bar sharing the ground floor with the pub. Our design proposal won, and in 1980 Bridges Pub was opened, to be followed the next year by Bridges Bistro and Bridges Restaurant. The restaurant business is a difficult one. You are only as good as your last meal. Again, my involvement was marginal, but I learned a lot about business. When I became a cabinet minister I sold my shares because Granville Island is federal government land. I can now enjoy my visits there without worrying whether everyone is happy with the food.

By the early 1980s, my marriage to Tuzie was in trouble. We separated in January 1982 after nine years together. It was a very painful period for me. I felt enormous guilt at wanting to leave the marriage. My close relationships with my stepdaughters compounded those feelings. Judy was now married, Mimi was practising medicine in Toronto, and Pamela, with whom I was especially close, had left in the fall of 1981 to study for her Ph.D. at the University of Chicago. I think Pamela's departure made it possible for me to make the painful decision to end the marriage.

Disillusionment in marriage is probably inevitable, and I'm sure Tuzie could identify a number of ways I disappointed him. For my part, I began to feel that my willingness to adjust to the realities of a marriage to an older man with children was not reciprocated in ways that were important to me. Oddly enough, politics also played a role in pulling us apart. Once Tuzie moved on from the school board to the broader challenges of city council, I found myself out of sympathy with his political values, although many people automatically attributed them to me. In our case, politics made estranged bedfellows. I have great respect for Nathan Divinsky and no regrets about the time we spent together.

In February 1983 I was approached by Peter Hyndman, whom I had known at UBC, and Patrick Kinsella, the principal secretary to Premier Bill Bennett, to run as a Social Credit candidate in the upcoming provincial election in the riding of Vancouver Centre. It was considered a safe NDP riding but, they both assured me, my winning here was not an impossibility. Vancouver Centre was a two-member riding, and my running mate would be parks commissioner Philip Owen.

I wasn't uninterested because it seemed a natural progression to move to the level of legislature that had a significant say in educational policy. Did the thought cross my mind that if I won I might wind up as minister of education? Of course it did. There was only one problem: I was in my last year of law school and would be starting my final exams in April. The election had not yet been called, and neither Peter nor Patrick was at liberty to tell me when it would be, except that it would be sooner rather than later. I remember that Patrick looked a little uncomfortable when I told him that I had to write final exams in April.

Their offer raised other concerns as well. Until that time I had not allied myself with any of the mainstream parties. In British Columbia in those days there were only two provincial parties, Social Credit and the NDP. The B.C. Socred party was unlike similarly named parties elsewhere in Canada. It was, for all intents and purposes, an umbrella party that made it possible for federal Liberals and Conservatives to support the same party provincially. British Columbians tended to see provincial elections as a choice between free enterprise and socialiasm. There was a general belief that unless the free-enterprise votes supported one party, their vote would be divided and the "socialists" would get in. If I declared myself as a Socred candidate, it would compromise my independence with respect to the school board. This wasn't an insuperable problem, but it was a consideration.

Another concern was that I had been accepted to article with the Vancouver law firm of Ladner Downs. In the event that I was elected, my articles would be affected. After much consideration, I decided to run, for the experience. I arranged to take a leave of absence from the school board during the campaign. (It wasn't necessary to resign a municipal office to run provincially.) Campaigns last only twenty-eight days in British Columbia, so it didn't seem like a major disruption. When the premier finally dropped the writ, I discovered that the election campaign would coincide almost exactly with my law school exams. I wrote six exams during the campaign and did respectably, but it was a little nerve-racking.

The campaign taught me a great deal. It was my first experience at door-knocking and main-streeting, a form of campaigning that wasn't done in the city-wide civic elections. Heading off that first day, I remember my horror at being told I was expected to approach strangers on the street and ask for their vote. I soon discovered that most people wanted to meet the candidate, so that wasn't a problem. Campaigning with Philip Owen and his wife, Brita, who are two of the nicest people in Vancouver, was a lot of fun. Even the NDP incumbents, Emery Barnes and Gary Lauk, were quite friendly. They could afford to be; they trounced us. I called to congratulate them after the election and to commiserate with them, too. Although the two of them had succeeded in holding their seats, the Socreds were returned to government with a healthy majority, leaving them once again in opposition.

Among the positive outcomes of what I affectionately refer to as my kamikaze run in Vancouver Centre in 1983 was that I met some wonderful people. Diana Lam, who at that time had her own public relations company, Chilvers Lam, came to work on the campaign. Years later when I became a federal minister, she became my senior staffer in British Columbia. I consider myself very lucky to have had the personal and professional support of such a remarkable woman. To the 1983 campaign I also owe my friendship with Ginny Richards. Ginny, who is a political junkie and a doer, has been my interior designer and general life organizer as well as astute political adviser. Her husband, John, regards all her frenetic political activity with a certain amusement. They are among my closest friends and supporters.

Perhaps the most important lesson I learned from the campaign was that the danger in becoming a "star" is that it can lead you to get stars in your eyes. Any star quality I had at that time was of a modest sort; I had some political capital as a result of my work on the school board, and certainly my time as chairperson had raised my public profile considerably. This had made me a desirable commodity for a political party. Some years later, in a different context, Patrick Kinsella's wife, Brenda, who had run our campaign in Vancouver Centre, said to me, "Because of who you are and what you can do, many doors will open for you. You have to decide which ones you will go through." Wise words. I have repeated them to other "stars" even when it was my own party that was wooing them. Running for political office is a huge step. It is for many high-profile people the end of innocence, because they lose whatever special status they had with the public and become fair game for partisan attack.

The provincial election of May 1983 ushered in a period of political confrontation in British Columbia. Because of the size of the provincial deficit, a reflection of lower revenues in the recession, the government set out on a program of fiscal restraint. When the legislature reconvened in the fall of 1983, no fewer than twenty-six bills were introduced to implement the program. In hindsight, the fiscal direction was the correct one, but the measures were unnecessarily divisive. My final period on the school board was taken up with the question of restraint, and I discovered just how difficult this is. The officials you rely upon to help you find the areas for economies have their own views and interests to protect. It was an enormously frustrating exercise for elected trustees.

At the end of 1983 I stepped down as chairperson of the Vancouver School Board and became vice-chairperson. I didn't intend to seek re-election in 1984, and it made sense that someone who planned to stay should take over the chair. After being called to the British Columbia bar in May of 1984, I was invited to stay on as a litigator with Ladner Downs. At the end of the year my term as school trustee came to an end and so, to my mind, did my political career for the foreseeable future.

I made my first trip to Ottawa, to visit friends, in the spring of 1985. My law school classmate Paisley Woodward had been working since graduation as an assistant to NDP MP Ian Waddell. Paisley gave me the full tour of Parliament Hill. I had thought about coming to work in Ottawa as a staffer some day, but Paisley thought I should come as an MP. "This is where you belong," she said. Thinking of how far it was from Vancouver and looking at the snow on the ground in April, I wasn't convinced. Besides, I was determined to devote myself to the law.

Not everyone was persuaded by my new-found determination. In discussing my inability to resist the offer to run provincially in Vancouver Centre, Bruce Cohen, the senior partner who was my adviser at Ladner Downs, wondered if I could really give up politics. Comparing the lure of political life to the lure of the circus, he warned, "Some people can't get the smell of sawdust out of their blood, even after the tent has folded."

5

The Longest Shot

In the summer of 1985 I heard the siren call of politics again. I was attending the annual meeting of the Canadian Bar Association in Halifax when I received a telephone call from Bud Smith, who had taken over from Patrick Kinsella as principal secretary to Premier Bennett, inviting me to come to Victoria as executive director of the premier's office. As Bud described it, the position would involve policy and strategy. Because the premier had no one in his office from Vancouver, they thought my perspective would be useful. The position appealed to me for several reasons. I had concluded that much of what the government was doing was on the right track, but that the political handling of it could be better. Working in the premier's office would be an interesting way to participate in the political process, would make use of my legal training, and would give me the opportunity to assess whether I was interested in going back into politics at the provincial level and in what capacity. What I didn't in my wildest dreams think about, and would have dismissed as sheer fantasy if anyone had suggested it, was the possibility that within a year I would run for the leadership of the Social Credit party.

I wondered how my firm would react to the offer. Although I was enjoying the practice of law in some ways, I frequently felt restless. Ladner Downs is a large firm and, while the general litigation I was involved in could be engrossing, large firms aren't very flexible about integrating new lawyers. The first few years of practice are designed to develop not only competence in the law but also the necessary maturity of judgment. Occasionally I was given a task that challenged and stretched me, but as I was already older than most new lawyers at thirty-seven, I sometimes felt frustrated and underutilized. Perhaps I would have been better off in a smaller firm where there was more flexibility. In any event, I thought a stint in the premier's office might make it easier to define a career path in the law that would be more suited to my particular interests, and I was delighted to find that the firm felt the same way. Bruce Cohen thought it would increase my value to a law firm and said he could see me returning to become the partner in charge of government relations.

In the more than two years I had spent at Ladner Downs I had become friends with another political junkie, David Camp. David had grown up in the heart of the Conservative Party. He is the son of Dalton Camp and the nephew of Senator Norman Atkins. His father is best known as the party president who engineered the ouster of John Diefenbaker as leader in the late 1960s. For that reason alone, Dalton is a villain or a hero in the party, depending on your view of Dief. David, who had spent several years as a journalist, had come to Vancouver to make his career in the law and to escape from the shadow of his father. He was one of a number of friends from the firm that I would continue to count on for support and advice long after I left the practice of law. Although not a "political" firm as such, Ladner Downs had solid Tory connections. Its founder, Leon Ladner, had been a Conservative member of Parliament, and Howard Green, Diefenbaker's external affairs minister, had trained as Leon Ladner's law clerk before World War I. Tom Ladner, Leon's son, was always particularly kind to me.

I hadn't entirely abandoned my public life while practising law. In 1985 I was invited to join Stan Persky as one of the B.C. correspondents on Peter Gzowski's popular CBC Radio program *Morningside.* Stan and I had known each other since UBC days. We were far apart ideologically. Stan was hard-core NDP, anti–Vietnam war, and an activist for gay rights at a time when very few gays were public about their sexual orientation. I wasn't NDP, and though I had serious reservations about the Vietnam war, I didn't accept all the other positions that seemed to be required of those who were active in the anti-war movement. We were a good match — two people of different political perspectives who nonetheless liked and respected each other enough to spar with good humour and a little wit. We had great fun giving our often conflicting interpretations of events in the province.

Since the program was broadcast live to Halifax and our segment came on a few minutes after 11 a.m., we had to be at the CBC studios in Vancouver just before 7. I would get up, throw on some jeans and a sweater, go down to the studio (a five-minute drive from my house), do the show, return home to shower and change, and then go into the office.

When Peter Gzowski came to Vancouver and we could do our report with him in the same studio for the first time, I still remember the thrill of meeting the face behind the voice. Peter looked older than the picture I remembered of him on one of his book covers. With his grey hair and beard and casual sweater over a not-thin body, I said to myself, "This national treasure looks like a grizzled couch potato." But that voice — with its wonderfully intimate quality that sounds as if he is sharing a private joke with just you — was captivating. Alas, going back into the political world would spell the end of my radio relationship with the inimitable Gzowski, at least for a while.

After I accepted the executive director's job in late August, Bud Smith took me to meet Premier Bennett in his Vancouver office. I had met the premier during the 1983 campaign and been struck then with the contrast between his public image and his private demeanour. It wasn't so much that he acted differently in private, but, like most political figures, he had little opportunity to express the lighter side of his nature in public. Premier Bennett was an intensely private man, even shy, but very professional and disciplined. An astute judge of his colleagues, he could occasionally be wryly humorous in his observations of them, but I never heard him disparage them in front of staff.

When I arrived in Victoria in September, I was introduced to the rest of the team: Norman Spector, the premier's deputy minister; Ann Vice, his press secretary; and Ian McLaine, his executive assistant. These three, plus Bud and I, made up the premier's core staff and met with him regularly to discuss his schedule and current issues before the government. I also met the people who managed the premier's correspondence. As I would later come to appreciate, they are a key part of any ministerial team. It is impossible for a minister to deal personally with all correspondence. Having staff that understand how you think and express yourself is crucial. There was also a team of policy advisers led by a genial, fey thinker named George Gibault. His job was to digest enormous amounts of information on sensitive policy areas to help the premier map out the general directions in which the government should be going.

The Halifax Canadian Bar Association meeting where I had heard about the position in the premier's office was memorable for another reason. It was there that I first met Howard Eddy, who would become my second husband. Howard was a forty-five-year-old lawyer with the Department of the Attorney General in Victoria, and before the meeting I had talked to him on the phone about a possible joint action on behalf of clients who were suing the same person in Washington state. Since Howard was originally from Washington and had earned his first law degree there, the attorney general had asked him to manage the file. In Halifax, Howard was invited to our firm's reception, where we met briefly, just to shake hands and chat about our mutual file. On my return to Vancouver, I found a message from him suggesting that we should conclude the matter. I phoned him to say that yes, we must, because I was leaving the law to work in the premier's office. We met, hit it off, and began what quickly became a serious relationship.

Howard Eddy is tall (almost six foot three) and thin with an angular face and quiet, thoughtful manner that reminds people of Abraham Lincoln. People found us an unlikely couple because I was much more outgoing than the intensely private Howard. When we met, Howard had been divorced for several years. I was attracted to his wonderful mind and his general niceness. We liked many of the same things — music, nature, good food. In Washington state, Howard had clerked for an appellate court judge, and since the judgeship was an elected position, much of his work had consisted of travelling around the state with the judge, tending to his political constituency. So my political interests weren't foreign to Howard, although his position as a public servant imposed neutrality upon him.

Working in the premier's office, I learned a great deal about how a government is managed. I was asked to sit in on some of the cabinet committees, although I didn't attend meetings of full cabinet. It was interesting to see how the ministers related to one another. What was particularly fascinating was the relationship between ministers, members of the legislature, and the premier's staff. In any government, the time of the premier or prime minister is naturally limited. Because his support was necessary for major ministerial projects, members of Premier Bennett's staff were seen alternately as barriers to the premier or as possible channels of access to him. It seemed incongruous to me that cabinet ministers would treat me with kid gloves in the hope that I could be cajoled into taking up their cause with my boss. I was definitely in the second tier of such staffers; the principal secretary and the deputy minister were much closer to the premier than I was. There were some ministers — like Grace McCarthy, who had served in the government of Bill Bennett's father, W.A.C. Bennett — who objected strenuously to the power of non-elected people in the premier's office. Having been an elected person myself, I understood that objection and was careful to bear in mind that I was there because the premier had appointed me, but that the premier and his colleagues were there because the people had elected them.

In 1981 Premier Bennett had set out to modernize and update his party and government. He had brought in Patrick Kinsella, at that time executive director of the Ontario Progressive Conservative Party, to apply some of the methods that had made the Tories and their Big Blue Machine so successful in Ontario. Norman Spector was also an import from central Canada, in his case, the Ontario public service. This use of "imported talent" in the heart of the Social Credit government was viewed in some quarters with suspicion and, occasionally, downright hostility. In 1984 Patrick left government to form a consulting firm. He was replaced by Bud Smith, a lawyer from Kamloops who had had experience in numerous campaigns at both the provincial and federal levels.

I'm not sure what had led Bud to recommend me for the executive director's job. As the position was described to me by phone when I was in Halifax, it made sense. However, when I arrived in Victoria I discovered that what Bud had in mind for me was somewhat different. To begin with, he put me in charge of political appointments. For someone with very little in the way of party connections or political experience at the provincial level, it was odd casting. It was my first "hands-on" experience with patronage, and the terms of reference were mildly partisan but not overly so.

From time to time there were occasions when I felt that I really earned my keep. In 1985, as a result of their unwillingness to abide by provincial government budget guidelines, the Vancouver and Cowichan school boards had been fired and replaced by trustees. The government was on sound legal ground in its actions, but politically it was a risky strategy. The question in early 1986 was what to do in light of the upcoming school board budgetary process. In my opinion, it wasn't tenable to have a budget that could affect taxation levels decided by appointed and unaccountable trustees. By-elections would have to be held to replace the fired boards before the budget process was complete. There was a vigorous discussion at the premier's staff meeting. Norman pointed out that if we had elections, it was very likely they would be won by candidates hostile to the government. He thought the government could wait until the regular civic elections in the fall of 1986. My view was just the opposite. It might well be, I argued, that we would lose the by-elections, in the sense that anti-government candidates would win, but in fact, this was even more likely to happen if we waited until the fall. The most important thing was to do what was right, namely, making sure that the taxpayers had a say in who would set their tax levels, and, from a political perspective, getting the issue off the table for the fall elections. Ultimately the premier accepted my arguments and the by-elections were held. Anti-government COPE trustees did form a majority of the board in Vancouver, but as I had predicted, the COPE victory was short-lived. The voters returned an NPA board in the fall. The NPA, although not necessarily uncritical of the provincial government, was more sympathetic to its efforts to keep spending under control.

The only time I travelled with Premier Bennett was in April 1986, on a trip to Toronto and Quebec City. When the premier was in Toronto, he was entertained at the home of the newly elected Liberal premier of Ontario, David Peterson, who was riding a wave of popularity at that time. Peterson thought a great deal of

Bill Bennett and had quite purposefully made him the first political leader he entertained at his home.

Howard and I had agreed that when one of us was sent on a business trip east, the other would travel east so that we could rendezvous in Ottawa. It was during this trip that I first met Howard's two younger children, who lived with their mother across the river from Ottawa in Aylmer, Quebec. Howard's oldest son, Jonathan, was married and living in Kingston. Andrew, Howard's second son, was in his last year of high school in Quebec, and Abby, his daughter, was just getting ready to enter high school. Howard and I had surprised ourselves by how quickly our relationship had turned serious. I suppose we were both ready for commitment and we soon began to talk of marriage. We were thinking vaguely of a summer wedding, but didn't realize how hectic a time it would turn out to be.

What none of us knew was that the premier's trip east would be his last. At the end of May, Bill Bennett announced that he would be stepping down as leader of the B.C. Social Credit party. Like most people, I was dumbfounded. Premier Bennett had just presided over the opening of Expo 86, the wildly successful world's fair commemorating Vancouver's centenary. The Prince and Princess of Wales had been present and were but the first of a series of foreign dignitaries who would parade through the city that magical summer. A leadership convention was scheduled for July, which would permit Bennett's successor to officiate at the closing ceremonies.

Bennett's decision to resign suited his personal political agenda and political reality. The period since the 1983 election had not been a happy one. British Columbia's economy had been devastated by recession. Unlike Ontario, which had recovered its job losses by 1984, B.C. would not regain pre-recession levels of employment until 1987. Much of the province's subsequent fiscal strength was a result of painfully difficult decisions made at that time, but the government's "bedside manner" was non-existent. Bennett himself didn't come across as a sympathetic personality. I liked him, however, and I admired his total lack of pretension. It was fashionable for intellectuals to deride Bennett and his government as unsophisticated. To my mind, he struck a good balance between the populist politics that were his political legacy and a high-minded view of the country and what was needed to keep it together. It was customary in B.C. for governing parties to "run against Ottawa," an art that Bennett Senior had perfected. But his son never played fast and loose with the country for the sake of political gain.

The political battles of the restraint program had taken their toll. With a realism that was later to elude Brian Mulroney, Premier Bennett understood that his party's prospects in the next election would be improved if it could put some distance between itself and the fractious Bennett years, and he set about giving his successor the maximum opportunity to do just that. First of all, he made sure that his successor could ride the wave of Expo 86, which he rightly predicted would bring a new sense of confidence and worldliness to Vancouver and be an important stimulus to the economy of a beleaguered province. The timing of his resignation also gave his party and his successor time to remake the government agenda and articulate a new vision. The current mandate would not expire until the spring of 1988, so the new leader would have as much time as he or she needed to prepare for the next election.

Shortly after the premier announced his decision, it became known that Bud Smith, who had left the premier's office unexpectedly in March, had already begun organizing to contest the leadership. Surprised by the premier's announcement, some members of cabinet now began to see a plot. They assumed that Bud had known of Bennett's intentions and that his departure had been designed to give himself a leg up in the upcoming race. I have no idea who knew what and when. Nor do I have any idea whether Bennett had a preferred successor. He kept scrupulously neutral during the entire campaign as far as I could see, but some people remained convinced the whole thing was manipulated.

The 1986 Social Credit leadership campaign would mark the first time that someone other than a Bennett would lead the party. It was an opportunity to distance the party from some of the more negative aspects of its image and to reach out to a new constituency of women and young people. The idea came to me that if Bud Smith, who had never run for anything and was unknown to the public at large, could run for the leadership, why couldn't I? I discussed it with Howard, who felt that it would be an important opportunity to articulate a political vision with some independence. Neither of us thought for a moment that I could win, but I might stake out some territory on the political landscape and perhaps draw some new people from the political centre and centre-right to the party who might not otherwise be attracted to it. Among many city dwellers, the Social Credit party had negative connotations, dating from its small-town and rural beginnings. This was a good time to broaden its base in an increasingly urban British Columbia.

Working in the premier's office had taught me many things, not least of which was that I was not cut out for the back rooms of politics; I preferred to be in the thick of things. I had talked to Howard about my vague intentions of returning to politics some day, and I knew that if I ran unsuccessfully for the leadership I would still have to follow through and seek a nomination for the next election. Looking back, I am struck by my naiveté. I had never been involved in a leadership campaign before and knew next to nothing about it. One thing I didn't know, and few people realized, in those first days after Bennett's resignation was that the race was already over once Bill Vander Zalm decided to run. Vander Zalm had been a minister in Bill Bennett's cabinet from 1975 to 1983 but had declined to run again in 1983, after his "gutless" cabinet colleagues refused to accept his revised municipal land use regulations. As a minister, his most famous comment had been that those on welfare who wouldn't work would have to "pick up a shovel." Coming from the minister responsible for social services, this comment created a commotion. Not all of the response was negative, and Vander Zalm supporters proudly wore the little gold shovels he had made to commemorate the comment. At public events, he would auction off gold-painted shovels as a fundraiser.

I had met Bill Vander Zalm during my first term as a school trustee when he was minister of education. I had travelled to his Surrey constituency office with board chairperson Pauline Weinstein and her COPE colleague Wes Knapp. I remember thinking that Vander Zalm was very handsome in a cold sort of way. It would not be an overstatement to say that Pauline Weinstein and Bill Vander Zalm were on opposite ends of the political spectrum, yet he charmed her during our meeting. It was an extraordinary demonstration of his ability to size up his audience and say what they wanted to hear. People loved him because, by the oddest coincidence, he always thought just the way they did. Unfortunately, Vander Zalm was also known for this habit of holding the opinion of the last person who had spoken to him.

As a young man, Vander Zalm had sold tulip bulbs from the back of a truck, and eventually he became the owner of a successful chain of garden shops. In 1986, he had only recently bought the Boda Gardens, which he renamed Fantasy Garden World. It was this recent acquisition and the financial implications of taking himself away from his business that convinced many observers he would not stand as a candidate for the leadership. I have been told that among those who encouraged him to run was Grace McCarthy. A candidate herself, McCarthy believed that she could count on Vander Zalm's support in the later ballots of a convention. However, as Patrick Kinsella's polls of the party membership showed, if Vander Zalm were a candidate, no one could beat him. Patrick's friend Brian Smith, then attorney general, asked him to run his campaign. Patrick told Smith that, based on his polling results, the best he could do for him if Vander Zalm ran was to get him onto the final ballot. He was as good as his word.

"The Zalm" kept everyone guessing until the last moment. At the press conference where he was widely expected to announce that he would not run, he changed his mind on entering the conference room at his garden complex — not the last time he would use his public profile to market his new enterprise — and declared his candidacy. His absence from the political scene during the recent difficult times served him well. It is ludicrous to think that he would not have supported the government's budget-cutting agenda; if anything, he would have been among the hardest of hard-liners. But another problem plagued the Bennett government at that time. Three ministers had been involved in scandals. There were allegations that a minister had used an escort service, an activity offensive to many in the party. Another minister associated with these allegations, although later exonerated, had paid a heavy price in public embarrassment and would ultimately lose his seat. Yet another minister had had a violent confrontation with the husband of his mistress. Even party members somewhat tolerant of those who indulged in the temptations of the flesh found these scandals an embarrassment.

Bill Vander Zalm arrived on the scene as the embodiment of wholesome family values. His wife, Lillian, a striking woman, famous for the headbands she wore on her lovely prematurely white hair, had been his youthful sweetheart, and they had four attractive grown children. There is no denying the two were a charismatic couple. Vander Zalm, an enthusiastic Catholic who had played a key role in the visit of Pope John Paul II to Canada, played the morality card for all it was worth. He was rabidly anti-abortion. He would often say that if it was his choice he would not fund abortions under medicare, but that since the law relating to legal abortions was under federal jurisdiction, there was nothing he could do about it. Thus the anti-abortionists knew that he was on their side, and the pro-choice people were convinced that his anti-abortion rhetoric was ultimately harmless. Despite the fact that he had been in politics for twenty years, first as mayor of Surrey and then as an MLA and provincial minister, in 1986 Bill Vander Zalm seemed fresh and new.

Meanwhile, my own campaign got under way. Kathleen Kelly, who had been a year ahead of me at law school and was now a marketing consultant with a major accounting firm, became my campaign manager. How she coped is beyond me. We learned as we went. We didn't have the resources to influence delegate selection, so we had to concentrate on winning the support of already selected delegates. This involves telephone polling, an expensive business, and mine was not, to say the least, a well-funded campaign. Many people were generous. My friends Chris and Lele Mathisen donated the money that enabled me to rent an office. Other friends contributed because they agreed it was important to reach out to new constituencies. I travelled on a shoestring to meet and speak to small groups of delegates all around the province. That part of the campaign was great fun and a wonderful learning experience. Years later, when I was running for the federal Conservative leadership, many of those same people would become my delegates. Seventy per cent of the delegates at the Socred convention were members of the federal Conservative Party.

Not all of the lessons of the campaign were pleasant. There were twelve candidates in all, and the Vancouver *Sun* ran a series of profile interviews with the contenders. My interview with reporter Gillian Shaw was conducted in my home. Kathy was present; however, it never occurred to us to record the interview ourselves — a mistake I would learn from. Shaw appeared to approach the interview from the perspective that I was an intellectual who couldn't possibly have anything in common with members of the Social Credit party. I tried to explain that I liked all sorts of people and that if you couldn't communicate with ordinary people, not just the kind who spend all their time thinking about politics, you weren't likely to be very successful.

While I made no apologies for my "intellectual interests" such as music and literature, I had never described myself as an "intellectual," especially in relation to my approach to politics. Trying to make the point more clearly, I referred to Pierre Trudeau, our recently departed "intellectual" prime minister. In my view, I said, Trudeau had failed to communicate his vision to western Canada. If he was heartily detested, that was why. As far as I could see, Pierre Trudeau had dismissed those westerners who opposed bilingualism as rednecks. But people fear change, I told Shaw. If you don't take the trouble to try to communicate your vision in terms they can understand, they will react angrily. I felt that Pierre Trudeau had missed the opportunity to do this and the result was a deeply divided country. The great failure of governments and politicians is to communicate in the language that ordinary people speak.

When I look back, I realize that Shaw kept asking questions designed to confirm a preconceived notion of me. Later, two of my friends who had been interviewed (but not quoted) complained about Shaw's approach with them, too. Paisley Woodward was quite upset; she told me she felt that she was being manipulated into describing me as some sort of bitch. Another friend in Vancouver, Larry Pierce, said that his interview opened with the question, "People say that Kim Campbell is an elitist. What's your side of the story?" His reply — "No one who knows her would say that" — didn't appear in the article.

The resulting profile was negative, to put it mildly. I have long since learned the futility of complaining about one's treatment by the media, but two things struck me as unfair. First, the profile took statements made by me in a variety of different contexts and strung them together, without dots, as if they were all spoken in the same breath. The result was a distortion of what I had said. Second, when I asked the *Sun* to provide me with a transcript of the interview, they refused.

The profile came out the day I was to speak in Port Alberni on Vancouver Island, the town where I was born. Howard was travelling with me — thank goodness, because I was just devastated. Few people in Port Alberni had seen the article yet. I made some vague reference to it, and generally all went well. The next day, however, I was speaking down island and I knew that everyone would have seen it. I arrived at the hall and was met by a fair-sized media contingent, including Vaughn Palmer, the *Sun*'s provincial affairs columnist, who was disturbed by the article because we had often spoken at length and he knew what I had been trying to say. His intervention would ultimately result in a spoken (not written) apology from two members of the *Sun*'s editorial board, but he did me a more important favour that night. Seeing how upset I was, he asked me if I could laugh at it. He reminded me of how W.A.C. Bennett used to deflect jibes by turning them against the perpetrator. He was right. If I was going to stay in the political game, Gillian Shaw's article was far from the worst I could expect. I simply had to remember who I was and what I was about. When my turn came to speak, I addressed the interview head on, tried to answer it with humour, and was warmly received.

The Social Credit leadership convention of July 1986 was held at Whistler. This beautiful ski resort, an hour and a half's drive from Vancouver, had been rescued by the Bennett government during the recession of the early 1980s, surely one of the best of its investments since the village went on to prosper and has amply repaid its debt in taxes. Some people later claimed that the "surreal" outcome of the convention was directly related to the unreal atmosphere in which it took place. If the delegates had been required to go out on the streets of Vancouver between events, they said, they would have decided differently. Be that as it may, the convention took over the entire village and candidates set up their tents on a large green space not far from the convention centre. I couldn't afford to have an elaborate tent of my own so I shared one with Mel Couvelier, former mayor of Saanich and former candidate for the leadership of the provincial Liberals.

The first night of the convention was taken up with a tribute to Bill Bennett. Peter Lougheed, then premier of Alberta, gave the keynote speech. The next afternoon and evening would be devoted to the candidates' speeches, a long program since there were twelve in the running. By an extraordinary stroke of good luck, I drew number ten in the speaking order. Brian Smith drew number eleven and Bill Vander Zalm number twelve. Because I was to be followed immediately by two candidates who were seen as real contenders, my speech would be broadcast in prime time and I would have a large audience.

Speech night was Tuesday, and I had begun to write mine at 5 a.m. Sunday, sitting at my dining-room table in Vancouver. I polished and changed it, with help from Howard, right up until late Tuesday afternoon. Not having the resources to pay for an elaborate demonstration, I entered the hall that evening accompanied by a lone piper, Andrew Peck. I don't usually like speaking from a text, but time constraints demanded that I do so in order to avoid being cut off in midstream. Because I had written the speech myself, I was comfortable with the language and was able to deliver it well.

At the end, I spoke the line that would be remembered long after. "It is fashionable," I said, "to speak of political leaders in terms of their charisma. But charisma without substance is a dangerous thing." Those in the audience who had watched with dismay the advance of Bill Vander Zalm, largely on the basis of what was described as his charisma, went wild. The next line was not quoted as often but turned out to be prescient. "It [charisma] creates expectations that cannot be satisfied. Then come bitterness and disillusionment that destroy not only the leader but the party." Rumour has it that at these lines Lillian Vander Zalm turned to her husband and said, "She won't be in your cabinet." Her comment was also prescient.

My speech received a standing ovation, the only one of the night. It was brought on not just by the "charisma without substance" line but also by my vision of what the party should be. Many letters from around the province arrived after the convention from people praising my speech. My supporters were jubilant, but I warned them against thinking that the response to the speech would be reflected in the vote. No one thought I could win the convention, including me. I was simply happy that I had accomplished my goal: I had defined myself and put forward a vision of the Social Credit party that in the minds of many like-minded members gave the party credibility. A steady stream of delegates flowed through my tent that night, full of congratulations. I went to bed feeling euphoric — hoping that I would make a respectable showing on the first ballot but not really believing that my speech could overcome my deficit in resources and organization.

I was right. As we assembled the next day to hear the results of the first ballot, from last to first, the announcer's voice rang out, "Kim Campbell — fourteen." I have often had occasion to chuckle since then at the number of people who have assured me that they were among the fourteen. If all the people who say they voted for me had in fact done so, I'd have been on the second ballot. I was disappointed but philosophical. There was no time to mope; I had to get on with helping the candidate I hoped would win, Attorney General Brian Smith.

On the first two ballots Bud Smith did well, then shocked many of his supporters by going to Bill Vander Zalm, who he knew was going to win. Grace McCarthy, who had run an elaborate campaign, released her delegates after being knocked out on the third ballot. She would remain bitter for a long time about plots, real or imagined, that had denied her the prize. Although it might have been expected that I would give my support to the other woman candidate, I did not know Grace well. I admired and respected her, but felt more in tune philosophically with Brian Smith. In a choice between Vander Zalm and McCarthy, however, I'd have supported McCarthy hands down.

The final ballot was between Bill Vander Zalm and Brian Smith. The announcement of a Vander Zalm victory produced deep distress and tears in the Smith camp and jubilation on the Vander Zalm side. Many of the "Zalmoids," as they came to be called, saw his victory as a vindication of their belief that Bill Bennett had been too moderate and pragmatic.

Bill Bennett made a gracious speech in which he assured the delegates that the winner could listen to people and work together with them. At best his remarks were wishful thinking, at worst, the kind of poetic licence required on such occasions. He had worked for many years with Bill Vander Zalm. He must have known only too well what kind of ticking time bomb the party had just placed in the premier's office.

6

THE ZALM

BILL VANDER ZALM enjoyed an incredible honeymoon with the media in B.C., who no doubt found him a welcome change from the less quotable Bennett. In later years, when he found himself in the midst of scandal, he would blame all his troubles on people who didn't accept the result in 1986. That was neither fair nor true. Even those who, like me, had felt extremely uncomfortable with the new leader wanted him to succeed. He seemed to catch the public imagination and that, combined with the positive media coverage, led us to believe that perhaps the party could continue to enjoy political success. Part of the optimism was a result of Vander Zalm's propensity to tell people what they wanted to hear. This is why I had no idea what he was really thinking when, just three weeks after the convention, I went to beard the newly anointed lion in his den.

When I declared myself as a leadership candidate, I had said that I would seek a nomination to run in the next election. In other words, I wasn't running just to raise my profile but as part of a commitment to try to make change at the provincial level. The purpose of my August 1986 meeting with the premier was to mend fences and to ask if he knew whether Garde Gardom, one of two members for the riding of Vancouver–Point Grey, would be seeking re-election. I was ushered into the same Vancouver office where I had first met Premier Bennett a year earlier. Premier Vander Zalm showed no rancour or hostility towards me despite my convention speech. He was in great spirits, as were the people around him. It was a week before Howard and I were to be married, and we joked about the fact that the premier's Fantasy Gardens wouldn't be available for my wedding, as one of his own children was to be married there on the same date. In talking about his experiences since winning the convention, the premier raised the issue of abortion. We both knew that it was an issue on which we differed fundamentally. Now that he had become premier, Vander Zalm confided, the pro-life forces were pressuring him to do something about it. Of course, he repeated, since it was all controlled by the federal government, there was nothing he could do. He gave the clear impression he was not particularly interested in taking on the abortion issue and was quite content with the status quo. We parted amicably, although he was either unable or unwilling to answer my question about Gardom.

At that time discussions must have been ongoing about Gardom's future because it was widely rumoured he wanted to step down and be appointed B.C.'s agent general in London, England. The riding of Vancouver–Point Grey was held by Gardom and Dr. Patrick McGeer. Elected as Liberals, they had both crossed the floor in 1975 to sit as members of the Social Credit party and had been appointed ministers in Bennett's first government. Shortly after my meeting with the premier, it was announced that Gardom would be appointed to London, and I decided to seek the nomination for his seat. Dick Vogel, a lawyer who had been deputy attorney general in the early 1970s, would also be seeking the nomination.

The nomination battle began and McGeer announced that he was supporting Vogel. As the campaign heated up, I went to see McGeer at his home because I wanted to make sure that if I won the nomination there would be no ill feelings. We would have to campaign together and, if elected, serve together. He told me that he thought it was important for a person with Dick Vogel's experience to be in the Vander Zalm government. He implied that without that kind of heavy legal presence, all kinds of disasters might occur. I found his reasoning unobjectionable in theory, but there were other experienced lawyers standing for election, including the incumbent attorney general. Unlike Vogel, moreover, I had some political experience and a high public profile in the riding, an area where I had been strongly supported when I topped the poll for the school board in the 1982 civic elections, so I wasn't persuaded to step aside. McGeer didn't know me very well, and it seemed natural for him to prefer a candidate who was his long-time colleague's chosen successor. In the end, I won the nomination, helped in no small part by the support I had garnered through the leadership race.

Running on the slogan "A Fresh Start," Vander Zalm called an early election, capitalizing on the popularity he enjoyed right after the leadership campaign. Although Bill Bennett had left his successor ample time to govern before going to the polls, there was a general sense in the party that Vander Zalm's early popularity should be exploited sooner rather than later. Many of those who had had experience working with him feared that he could easily dissipate that initial goodwill.

The campaign, which began in September, turned into a tough fight in Vancouver–Point Grey. Pat McGeer was very confident and campaigned as if it were enough to know that "there are no socialists in Point Grey." But I took nothing for granted and campaigned flat out. I knew that the NDP's nomination of Darlene Marzari had to be taken as a serious threat. Her running mate, lawyer Dick Gathercole, lacked a public profile, but Marzari had been a very popular alderman in the 1970s. As the co-proprietor of Kaboodles, a well-known toy store in the heart of Point Grey, she also had respectable business credentials. Her public profile combined with her entrepreneurship threatened to be sufficient to overcome the reservations of the liberal-minded riding's "non-socialist" voters.

On election night, October 22, 1986, it was evident quite early on that I had topped the poll and would be elected. Although he was running just ahead of Darlene Marzari, Pat could see from the location of the polls yet to report that he wouldn't hold on to second place. As we drove down to the party's election-night headquarters at the Hotel Vancouver, he was philosophical about the loss of the seat he had held for so long. We were met by a tumultuous welcome from our supporters, who assumed we had both been elected. As we stood on stage, Pat raised my hand, introduced me as the new member of the legislative assembly for

Vancouver–Point Grey, and generously described me as "a new political star in B.C."

The Social Credit party was returned to government with forty-seven out of sixty-nine seats. In some ridings, Vancouver–Point Grey being one of them, it had been shown that Vander Zalm's charm had limited appeal. Had I not been able to define myself as an individual during the leadership race, I think I would have shared Pat McGeer's fate.

Howard and I had been married on August 23 in Vancouver. Abby and Andrew flew out for the wedding, and our honeymoon was a family trip to the Eddy family's summer home on Mayne Island in the Gulf Islands. Howard's father was an American doctor who was posted to the Pacific coast during World War II. After the war, he brought his family out to live on Mercer Island, near Seattle, and later purchased a large piece of land on the southern tip of Mayne Island, where Howard developed his passion for boating. Howard fulfilled his military service obligation between college and law school by serving two years in the navy, and when I met him he was an avid subscriber to *Wooden Boat* magazine and confessed to a lifelong dream of living on a boat.

After our marriage, Howard began to think about leaving the attorney general's office and going into private practice in Vancouver. But in the autumn of 1986, after I was elected, we knew we would need a place to live in Victoria, no matter what Howard might do, so we made a change in our lifestyle that was to bring us considerable pleasure for a number of years. One day I was looking at the marine advertisements in the Victoria *Times-Colonist* and came upon an ad for a forty-six-foot boat, "ex Forest Service, yellow cedar on oak, excellent liveaboard." When I pointed it out, Howard got very excited. The old Forest Service fleet of the B.C. government had been auctioned off in 1984 after its job was largely taken over by float planes, and some of the boats were legendary.

We drove out to Van Isle Marina in Sidney where the *Western Yew* was moored. She had been built in 1946 in North Vancouver as a pleasure boat, then in 1952 sold to the Forest Service, which replaced her small Buda engine with a 365-horsepower Jimmy diesel. With her classic lines and mahogany interior, the *Western Yew* was my idea of a boat; she possessed a quality that Howard called "shippy." You entered the pilot house, which also served as saloon. Forward, in the bow, there was a cabin with four bunks; in the stern were a large, comfortable galley and the after-cabin, with two bunks and a head with a shower opening off it. Hot and cold running water and an enormous Dickinson diesel stove in the galley made her cosy and comfortable. We fell in love. After a few tense weeks of getting her surveyed (she was very sound) and sorting out the finances, we took possession of the boat that would be our home on the water for several years.

Van Isle Marina, where we continued to moor the *Yew*, was just a five-minute drive from the B.C. Ferries landing at Sidney and a thirty-minute drive from Victoria. It was a convenient location, as one or both of us were often travelling between the Island and Vancouver, where our house and my constituency were. It is also one of the best points of departure for boating on the west coast. Within twenty minutes of heading out, you can be dropping anchor in some secluded bay for a meal.

We had many happy times as liveaboards. Returning home from the city, we would change out of our city clothes, and our city cares would vanish with them. Because we owned another home in Vancouver, we didn't have to cram all our worldly goods on board, so we were really comfortable in what I liked to call our "pied à mer." The *Western Yew* took a lot of work to maintain, but our efforts were amply rewarded by the admiring glances she would attract and the sheer joy we derived from "messing about in boats."

Once elected, I set about learning how to be an MLA. The first job was to build a relationship with the riding association. We were new to each other and new to the challenge of serving in a divided riding. (Two-seat ridings no longer exist in B.C., but at that time they were the rule rather than the exception in the urban areas.) I stayed on at the former constituency office on West Tenth Avenue, which my predecessors, both cabinet ministers having the use of cabinet offices downtown, had rarely visited. I hired as my constituency assistant Nancy Peck, a young woman I had met when she was a legislative intern during my time in the premier's office. It was her brother, Andrew, who had piped me in to the convention centre at Whistler.

Nancy was a find for a rookie MLA. Her time in Victoria and

her involvement in my leadership campaign had given her a good sense of the legislature and of the personalities in the new government. Along with my secretaries in Victoria, first Pam Waller and then Vivian Vosberg, she managed to organize my life. The small office budgets of MLAs and the higher cost of living in Vancouver, compared with other ridings, made it a challenge to set up a presentable office and hire capable staff. Nancy did a wonderful job of managing the office by herself.

It was no surprise to anyone when my name didn't appear on Premier Vander Zalm's list of new cabinet ministers. Vancouver hadn't been a hotbed of Vander Zalm support during the leadership campaign, and three of its MLAs elected in 1986 — Grace McCarthy, Stephen Rogers, and myself — had been candidates ourselves. As if to demonstrate his distaste for the city, the premier named only two ministers from Vancouver, McCarthy and Rogers. Russ Fraser, Rogers's seatmate in Vancouver South, who had served in Bill Bennett's last cabinet, was dropped and I, of course, wasn't even considered.

Not being a minister, I had time to devote to my constituency. However, although Vancouver was divided into five ridings, it was hard to draw boundaries for the activities of an MLA. This was particularly true in 1986 because the provincial riding of Vancouver Centre, which included so much of the business community and so many important cultural organizations, was held by the NDP. Thus, people in that riding who wanted to approach the government tended to ask Social Credit MLAs from other Vancouver constituencies for help. The time I spent working with numerous individuals and organizations from my own riding and elsewhere in the city was enormously educational.

People often speculate about why any sane person would want to hold public office in light of the low pay, long hours, and lack of appreciation. The truth is, the work can be absolutely fascinating. It provides an unparalleled opportunity to learn about your community and its issues. Notwithstanding the cynicism one frequently encounters, I think the majority of people in public life come to have a positive view of human nature. You meet so many men and women who are leading heroic lives, either as members of organizations performing public service or as individuals who need advice and help or who simply want to influence government policy. Sam Sullivan comes instantly to mind. A quadriplegic, he first came to see me about the needs of disabled hang-gliders. These weren't people who had been disabled *by* hang-gliding, but disabled people who *wanted* to hang-glide. Sam has devoted his life to opening up opportunities for disabled people in areas previously assumed to be closed to them. We continued to work together when I became an MP and it was his band, Spinal Chord, that played for a rally at B.C. Place welcoming me home as prime minister in June 1993. The experience of meeting and working with people like Sam changes the way you see the world. With all I have been through in my life, I have never experienced anything like the frustration of a body that wouldn't do what I wanted, or the pain of the many parents I have met trying to make life meaningful for children with physical and mental disabilities.

John Dixon, then president of the B.C. Civil Liberties Association (BCCLA), was another person I met at that time who would continue to be important to me after I moved on to other challenges. We met in 1987 to discuss some impending changes to the Health Act that were causing anxiety in the gay community. The provisions dealt with compulsory quarantine for people with a contagious illness who "recklessly" exposed others to the disease. The gay community was concerned that a combination of homophobia and ignorance about AIDS might lead to such provisions being used in a discriminatory way against gays. John suggested that a few simple changes to the wording of the provisions would allay their concerns without undermining the perfectly reasonable intent of the legislation. I was able to convince the health minister, Peter Dueck, to make the changes.

When the provisions were tabled in the House, I pointed out in my speech that AIDS is not a particularly contagious disease. Some years later, during the campaign for the leadership of the federal Conservative Party, these comments were put forward as evidence of my lack of knowledge or concern about AIDS. Quite the contrary. AIDS is definitely an infectious disease, but it is not highly contagious. In other words, it can be passed on, but not easily; it requires an exchange of body fluids. Tuberculosis, on the other hand, is highly contagious. Sitting in a bar next to a person with TB puts you at risk. It was TB, in fact, that had generated the legislative changes that would allow for compulsory quarantine.

Not long after the legislation passed, it was used for precisely that purpose when a TB carrier refused to take the appropriate precautions to protect the public from infection.

I enjoyed working with John Dixon. Although he looks like the stereotypical bearded academic philosopher, he is a keen outdoorsman with a broad experience of the realities of practical politics. After Peter Dueck agreed to introduce the changes to the legislation, he received a letter from the BCCLA expressing its support and appreciation for his actions. It was a delicious moment in the House when Peter was able to read this letter in response to attacks from the NDP.

I continued to meet from time to time with John to discuss issues of mutual interest, and as a result of this association and at the suggestion of Stan Persky, I became an honorary member of the board of the B.C. Civil Liberties Association. I supported the work of the association even though I didn't agree with all its positions. I thought it important for the BCCLA to be participants in the public dialogue.

In 1987, Bill Reid, the minister of tourism, asked me to chair a task force on heritage conservation, which came to be known as Project Pride. This was a tricky area, and a revision of the law was long overdue. The task force was to write a report that would help the government balance the interests of communities that wanted to save their physical heritage and the interests of owners of private property that would be affected by conservation activities. Among the other members of the task force, I developed a friendship with Chief Manny Jules of the Kamloops Indian band. Manny was behind the revision of federal policy towards taxation of Indian Lands, and our paths would continue to cross until I left government. As the task force toured the province, hearing from groups as diverse as archivists and underwater archaeologists, I was struck by how many communities were attempting to preserve their history. At just over one hundred years of age, B.C. was at a point in its development when its citizens were becoming aware that many of the old structures in their communities represented the last remnants of a time that could not be recreated. If steps weren't taken to preserve them, important links to history would be lost. Our report was presented to the minister in the spring of 1988 and formed the basis of a government White

Paper. A new Heritage Act was passed by the NDP government, based on much of the work of Project Pride.

In addition to the task force, I participated in the work of a number of legislative committees. I was named chairperson of the Standing Committee on Labour, Justice and Intergovernmental Relations and served on the Forestry Committee, which examined the relationship between the large forest companies and independent truck loggers. No strong tradition of independent committee work existed in the B.C. legislature. With the exception of the Public Accounts Committee, which was always chaired by a member of the opposition, the committees could consider only issues referred to them by the government. Two issues were referred to the standing committee that I chaired: the salary levels of provincial court judges and a revision of the Builders' Lien Act.

I chaired the examination of appropriate salary levels for provincial court judges, an exercise that would prove useful when I became Canada's justice minister, responsible for appointing the federal judges who sit on the superior and appeal courts of each province. Of the two levels of judges, the federally appointed bench is seen as more prestigious, although, in fact, provincially appointed judges deal with 90 per cent of criminal cases. Federally appointed judges are certainly paid more than provincially appointed judges, and this puts unwelcome pressure on the provincial governments when the matter of provincial court salaries rolls around. Our recommendations trod a careful line between the need to keep the provincial court bench competitive for recruitment and prevailing fiscal restraint. When I became minister of justice, I would face a similar problem when salary increases recommended for federally appointed judges by the triennial commission ran up against unsympathetic members of Parliament whose salaries had been cut several times since 1984 and were, at the time, frozen.

The process of reviewing the Builders' Lien Act was a good example of the kind of work backbenchers do in all legislatures that doesn't make the headlines but contributes to good policy-making. The Builders' Lien Act helps people in the construction trades to get payment for their services and helps contractors to deal with their creditors without costly and counterproductive work stoppages. We travelled the province listening to people from all parts of the industry.

At public hearings, where many of the participants are people who have never made a public presentation before and are often nervous, I have observed over the years that people are always articulate when they are speaking about something they know. That is why there is no substitute for listening to people who are directly involved in an issue and therefore directly affected by the public policy you are considering. Their personal experiences and perspectives can give you an insight that helps you avoid making stupid errors and produces much better legislation or policy. I loved these consultative processes because I learned so much. It was work that I knew was important if not terribly newsworthy.

In early 1988, however, I found myself in the middle of a controversy that propelled me unexpectedly onto the front pages. On January 28, 1988, the Supreme Court of Canada struck down Canada's abortion law in a decision known as *R. v. Morgentaler*. The provision of the Criminal Code providing for therapeutic abortion committees, which determined whether the procedure was necessary to protect the health of the woman, was held to be a threat to a woman's "security of the person" and, as such, unconstitutional. Because hospitals were not obliged to form such committees, many women had no access to abortions without breaking the law. In their decision, the majority of the justices upheld a woman's right to choose to have an abortion.

Premier Vander Zalm was on holiday in Hawaii when the decision was rendered. Immediately upon his return, he gave a press conference at the Vancouver Airport and announced that henceforth British Columbia would not provide public funding for abortions. I was dumbfounded. It was a decision that defied the spirit of the Supreme Court decision. I felt betrayed, since what the premier had told me in the summer of 1986 wasn't consistent with this unilateral declaration. But obviously the Supreme Court's decision had, in his mind, removed the impediment that had always been the rationale for his restraint. Because there was no longer provision in the Criminal Code for determining the legality of abortion, he saw no obligation to fund abortions as "medically necessary." There had been no meeting of cabinet or caucus to discuss this dramatic step. While Vander Zalm was in Hawaii, the pressure on him from pro-life forces — who had always seen funding as a second line of attack — had been growing. He had to put his money, or lack thereof, where his mouth had frequently been.

Shortly after the premier's return, a caucus meeting was held in the small coastal community of Powell River. I arrived ready to do battle on the abortion issue. There were only four women in our caucus: Rita Johnston, a Vander Zalm loyalist who was herself pro-choice, and Grace McCarthy, who liked to declare herself "both pro-choice and pro-life," were in the cabinet; Carol Gran and I were on the backbench. The night before the meeting Carol, who had become a good friend, was very uneasy about the prospect of a confrontation between the premier and me the next day. Brian Smith and some other colleagues were also concerned that I was often the only one to challenge the premier; they urged me to let other caucus members who disagreed with him carry the fight. I took their concerns to heart and decided that whatever happened, I would at least remain calm.

When we convened the next day, I could see that the abortion question was some way down the agenda. Towards the end of the meeting, we finally got to it. The premier made a few remarks about the policy, as did two or three of the ministers. The atmosphere in the room was extremely tense. A few backbenchers spoke weakly in favour of the premier's position. Those who opposed it were afraid to speak out on an issue about which they knew Vander Zalm was extremely committed. I didn't know what to do. I wasn't afraid to take him on, but this wasn't the forum to make the premier change his mind. Then I learned that cabinet had not yet met to confirm the policy. I couldn't believe the premier would act in the face of legal advice he would receive from government lawyers, so I decided to hold my fire and see if cooler heads in cabinet could persuade him to back off.

It's often hard for people outside the legislative process to understand the importance of caucus solidarity. Obviously, in a group of almost fifty people, there will be differences of opinion. Even among members of the same political party, these can be dramatic. Most people join a political party because they share beliefs about economic and social policy, the role of government, and other general matters. Issues like abortion cross party lines and in most parliamentary systems are seen as inappropriate subjects for the imposition of party discipline. But even in the areas where party members share similar perspectives, significant differences can arise over how to realize their objectives, and over priorities. To enable the policy-making process to go forward, members of a caucus commit themselves to working together to find common ground. They agree to support the result of this process, seeing it as the only way something even approaching the public interest can be found. My operating principle was that I would express my views forthrightly in caucus, but if I lost the argument, I would support the caucus position in public. If individuals are always free to insist on their own way or no way at all, the challenge of lawmaking in a diverse country like Canada or province like British Columbia would be impossible to meet.

Bill Vander Zalm wasn't alone among political leaders in equating criticism with disloyalty. But although I had often been critical, I had never been disloyal or indiscreet. Once, when caucus members were up in arms about the premier's plan to hold a formal caucus meeting at Fantasy Gardens, I wrote him a careful letter advising against such a move. The plan was, in fact, cancelled, but someone in the premier's office leaked the existence of my letter. This did me no particular harm, but it emphasized the dissent in the caucus and destroyed any expectation by MLAs that they could communicate in confidence with their leader. I hoped against hope that on the abortion issue I would be spared the need to do what I had never done — break ranks publicly.

I had reckoned without the media. On leaving the caucus meeting, I was beckoned by the caucus chairman, Doug Mowat. Doug uses a wheelchair and wasn't sufficiently mobile to avoid the print and TV reporters who rushed into the room as the MLAs and ministers were leaving. One television reporter called out a question to me on abortion. I wasn't ready to speak publicly about it, fearing that a statement by me at that time might lessen my ability to influence my colleagues in cabinet, so I walked away from the cameras. The footage of me trying to avoid the cameras led one Vancouver *Sun* columnist, Nicole Parton, to write the next day that, in not criticizing the government's policy, I had been a coward.

I called Nicole Parton the following morning and told her that I wasn't sure what the final policy was, and she admitted that she wasn't either. I said that I was waiting to see the minister of health to find out what cabinet had decided. Once I knew what the official policy would be, I explained, I would be more than happy to comment. Late that afternoon I met with Peter Dueck. Like many of the ministers, he had serious reservations about the course the premier was taking, although his Fraser Valley constituents were very much of the same school as the premier on the issue. My heart sank as Peter told me that cabinet had decided to go ahead and promulgate a regulation to end public funding of abortion in B.C. I went over all the reasons why the policy would probably be tossed out by the courts, since it was clearly motivated by a desire to prevent abortions, something only the federal government had the right to do. I said that it would be devastating to the party. He assured me that all those points had been raised and considered. There was no hope of changing the decision. "Well," I told him, "I'm afraid I can't support this policy."

We parted amicably but I was apprehensive. It would be the first time that I disagreed publicly with a decision of the government. It would not be pleasant, but I knew I couldn't remain silent. There was a mean-spiritedness about it all and an insensitivity to the effect of the decision that made me angry. I knew I had no persuasive power with the premier, but I had hoped that Brian Smith, who had retained his position as attorney general in the Vander Zalm government, would be able to change the premier's mind.

As I left Peter's office, I was confronted by a small group of media people who had seen me walking towards his office and were waiting for me. "It would be hypocritical of me to suggest I support the policy," I said. "My pro-choice views are well known." Interestingly, although my comments would give others the courage to express their disagreement over the next few days, I would be the only one of my colleagues to declare outright that I was pro-choice. After speaking to the media, I hurried to catch the last helijet to Vancouver. I returned home with that awful feeling of vertigo I get when I know I'm out on a limb in the centre of a major political issue. To my surprise and relief there were numerous messages on my answering machine, some from as far away as Fort St. John in the northeast corner of the province, supporting my position. Many of the callers expressed relief that someone in the Social Credit party had finally spoken out against the premier's decision.

I had no way of knowing what a cause célèbre the issue would become. British Columbians share with Quebeckers the distinction of being those Canadians most liberal on abortion. Many Socred party members were mortified at being associated with a policy that not only went against their own strong views but also seemed to thumb its nose at the Supreme Court decision. The clear intention of the premier to impose his own religious and moral views on the province, even though they were in conflict with the law, left them deeply troubled.

Abortion is a very difficult and divisive issue. I have respect for those who hold a different opinion from my own. Bill Vander Zalm's views on abortion were well known, but he was chosen by an electorate at a time when he was powerless to act on them. The BCCLA challenged the new regulation on the somewhat technical ground that there was no legislation authorizing such a move by cabinet. This position was accepted by the court, which struck down the regulation. Immediately after reviewing Chief Justice Allan McEachern's decision, Brian Smith announced that it could not be appealed. In fact, the government could have attempted to pass a law authorizing the regulation, but the political cost of this controversy was finally sinking in, even in the premier's office. Vander Zalm made no attempt to take the issue further. Meanwhile, it had torn the party apart.

I received an incredible amount of mail on the abortion issue, not all of it favourable. Many people wrote to praise me for my courage in standing up to the premier and standing up for choice. However, as John Kenneth Galbraith once remarked, often "simple integrity is taken for great courage." The premier having closed any door to reasoned discussion, it was hardly courageous on my part to be as forthright about my views as he was about his. Those who had counselled restraint on my part at Powell River had hoped that I would someday be invited into cabinet. I had no such concerns. I felt then and would come to feel increasingly that I would never be comfortable in Bill Vander Zalm's cabinet.

The implication for my future was one of the issues Nicole Parton raised with me. I replied, "I'm not prepared to sell my soul to get into cabinet." Our Whip, Angus Ree, took issue with me over this statement in caucus a few days later. He felt I was implying that others were prepared to sell their souls to become cabinet ministers. I was taken aback because it was certainly not my intention to criticize others or impugn their integrity. Ree's response underscores the delicacy of the caucus relationship. I took his remarks to heart and was more prudent in the future. Unfortunately, the strains on caucus solidarity originated with the premier, not with me. True to form, the premier himself lacked the fortitude to speak to me directly on the issue.

The Vander Zalm government accumulated even more troubles throughout 1988. It was revealed that the premier had personally intervened to try to alter the bidding process for the sale of the Expo lands to permit his friend Peter Toigo to bid after the official closing date. Toigo was also under a cloud as a result of efforts to get approval for a neighbourhood pub in which there appeared to be interference, at his request, from the premier's office. At one point in the spring, when the scandal was creating consternation in our party, the premier arrived in caucus just before we were to go into the House for Question Period. He provided a rambling explanation of the allegations with respect to Peter Toigo that didn't answer the questions at all.

In light of the silence that followed his remarks, I was dismayed that the premier was going to leave caucus with the impression that everyone had accepted his explanation. It is difficult to convey the tension in the room. Vander Zalm's body language spoke volumes — legs twisted around his chair, eyes darting around the room trying to gauge the impact of his remarks. It was almost time to go into the House. It was now or never. I stood up and said that I wanted the premier to know that I didn't find his explanation satisfactory and wasn't convinced that it was true. "Are you calling me a liar?" he immediately replied with a half smile. "No," I answered. "But I am not convinced that what you have said is true." I was not calling him a liar because I was unsure that he knew what the truth was. There are people who are capable of rewriting scenarios in their own minds, and the force of their explanations comes from the fact that they have convinced themselves what they are saying is true. For all I knew, Bill Vander Zalm really had persuaded himself that what he was saying was true, but I personally couldn't believe it.

It was time to leave for Question Period. My cheeks were burning and my heart pounding; I was too upset to go into the House so I went to my office. After Question Period I received a call from Vaughn Palmer at the *Sun*. "Is it true you called the premier a liar?" he asked. "No," I said wearily, "I did not. I just said that I didn't believe his explanation. I have no idea what he really thinks or believes." I didn't bother to ask him who had been so quick to breach the confidentiality of caucus.

Throughout that spring I became more and more uncomfortable with what was happening in the government. Everyone seemed to be paralyzed. In May I attended a meeting of the five Social Credit MLAs from Vancouver and some prominent businessmen who were strong supporters of the party. They were all gravely concerned that Vander Zalm was leading it towards certain defeat in the next election. Grace McCarthy had convened the meeting, but she didn't seem to have a clear idea of where we should go next. I said that if the party endorsed Vander Zalm's leadership at the upcoming convention in October, then in my view it was game over for the Social Credit party. It was extremely important that the party communicate to the public the deep concern within its ranks about those issues that were causing the public to move away from Social Credit. If the party convention did endorse the premier, I said, the only solution was to form a new party, and in the interim all of us should be keeping track of our correspondence from disgruntled Social Credit members. The businessmen were horrified at the prospect. "You can't split the free-enterprise vote," one of them burst out. "But it's already split," I replied. We were already losing the support of our traditional electorate. I had concluded that something dramatic was needed to win back voter confidence.

Meanwhile, I had been approached by members of the Vancouver Quadra Progressive Conservative Riding Association about seeking nomination for the federal election that would probably be called before the end of 1988. This was the seat held by Liberal leader John Turner. That spring I had been awarded a place in the European Community Visitors Program, which invited politicians, journalists, and other community leaders from non-European countries to visit and learn about the institutions and direction of the EC. Howard could accompany me if he paid his own fare, so we decided to make the trip together and conclude with a week-long tour of Burgundy with Howard's son Andrew, who was in school there. I told the people in Vancouver Quadra that I would seriously consider the question of running federally and get back to them when I returned.

Howard and I arrived back in B.C. in mid-July after a fascinating study trip that had taken us from Ireland to Denmark to France. Later in the summer we took Abby and a friend of hers on a cruise to the warm waters of Desolation Sound north of Vancouver. In Refuge Cove we called on John Dixon and talked about the state of the province over enormous helpings of fresh chinook salmon cooked Wickinninish style. I had decided not to run federally. We were going to have a life. We were going to have some dinner parties and revive the friendships that had become casualties of our frenetic life.

In late August I received a phone call from Lyall Knott, a key figure in the Conservative Party in Vancouver. Lyall was very close to Pat Carney, the MP for Vancouver Centre and president of the Treasury Board in the Mulroney government. He told me confidentially that Pat wasn't going to contest the next election for health reasons, and he wanted to know if I would consider being the Conservative candidate in Vancouver Centre. I was noncommittal, to say the least, having just gone through the process of weighing and then turning down the prospect of running in Quadra.

When I discussed Lyall's call with Howard, I was surprised to find that he didn't dismiss the idea. This, he thought, was a completely different scenario from Quadra. There I would have been running against a national party leader who would be on television every day. It was unlikely he would be defeated. Vancouver Centre, on the other hand, would be a fairer fight, and because the Tories had taken it in 1980 and again in 1984, there was a reasonable chance that it could be held. I agreed, but I was looking for reasons to say no. I didn't want to open up the question again, and going to Ottawa held no special magic for me. I had learned in 1983 not to get stars in my eyes. Just because a party wanted me to run, that didn't mean I was obliged to.

In September, I attended the annual meeting of the Union of B.C. Municipalities in Whistler. Liberal leader John Turner gave a passionate speech denouncing the Canada-U.S. Free Trade Agreement. I had followed the negotiations from my days in Premier Bennett's office, and I shared Bennett's view that the agreement would be good for B.C. Turner's characterization of the agreement and the issues seemed wrong to me. However, most of the audience, who appeared to be unfamiliar with the details of the agreement, were disturbed by his negative message, and this left me with an uneasy feeling. This was obviously a preview of the kind of speeches Turner would be making during the federal election. I made a mental note to find a way to help out on the issue during the campaign.

As we moved into fall, the atmosphere in our caucus and party was becoming more and more strained. Brian Smith had resigned from cabinet in June, and a month later, Grace McCarthy had declined to take a portfolio in the new shuffle. Both then resigned from caucus. A party convention was scheduled for the weekend of October 20 in Penticton. A resolution of support for the leader was a feature of every convention, and because of the cloud now hanging over Bill Vander Zalm in the minds of many, a move was afoot to make that vote a secret ballot. I came out publicly in favour of this. Although I didn't believe that the premier would lose the vote, a significant number of negative votes from disquieted party members would send a message to the public and, just as important, to the premier.

On October 1 Prime Minister Brian Mulroney called a federal election for November 21. After Pat Carney had announced publicly that she wouldn't be running again, there had been much speculation about who would succeed her as a candidate in Vancouver Centre. By the date of the election call, no candidate had been chosen, and I began to wonder if I had done the right thing in refusing to run. On October 8 I was having lunch in Vancouver with my secretary, Vivian Vosberg, and my constituency assistant, Violet Nelson. We were joined by Ginny Richards. I mused out loud about whether I should reconsider my decision and told them about Howard's surprisingly positive response. Vivian and Violet shook their heads adamantly. Ginny, on the other hand, said she would talk to a few people if I wanted her to.

I called Lyall Knott and arranged to meet with him the next day at his office. Patrick Kinsella was there as well, and we discussed the situation in Vancouver Centre. The major threat was the NDP candidate, Johanna den Hertog. She had run against Pat Carney in 1984 and had been campaigning in the riding ever since.

The Liberals had nominated Tex Enemark, former head of the Mining Association of B.C., whom I had known since university. Patrick was less than enthusiastic about my running federally because he had always seen a bright future for me in B.C. politics and was concerned about the risk. However, I was feeling more and more that I was at a dead end provincially. As far as I could see, the premier was leading the party over a cliff and considered anyone who pointed this out to him disloyal. Pat Carney had been very successful as a member of Parliament, first in opposition and then, after 1984, in the cabinet. Perhaps I could do more for B.C. in Ottawa than I could beating my head against a brick wall in Victoria. At the end of the meeting, I told Lyall and Patrick that if they did a poll in the riding that showed that I could win, I would be their candidate.

Two days later, Lyall phoned with the results of the quick poll. My recognition rate was much higher than Johanna den Hertog's, but the poll showed the Tories fourteen points behind the NDP. Feeling somewhat deflated, I phoned my friend Tim Charron, a labour lawyer at Ladner Downs. Tim had studied polling as an undergraduate at Dalhousie and had used those skills in a number of campaigns in Nova Scotia. His reaction was far from negative. "I wouldn't be discouraged by those numbers," he said. "The NDP vote tends to be firm. There won't be much movement there. The Conservative numbers are misleading because they have yet to nominate a candidate." Given my recognition factor and the generally positive response to me overall, Tim was convinced that if I became the official candidate, the Tory numbers would go up. In short, he thought I could win.

It was now the weekend and time to talk seriously to Howard about Vancouver Centre. Right from the start, he had been more positive about it than I had been. But it wasn't just my life that would be affected. On the positive side, Howard had been talking all year about going into private practice, and as a member of the Ontario bar, he could work in Ottawa. He had lived there during the 1970s when he had done work for the Law Reform Commission of Canada, and his two younger children still lived in the Ottawa area with his first wife. Moving to Ottawa would allow Howard to be closer to his children. On the negative side, our parents and siblings were on the west coast, mine in Vancouver and his in Seattle. After a long talk, I asked Howard what he thought we should do and his reply was, "Go for it!"

Before I announced publicly that I would be seeking the nomination, there were some courtesies to observe. The first was to advise the premier of my decision; the second was to tell my riding association executive in Vancouver–Point Grey. Howard and I were in Vancouver for the weekend when all this discussion took place. I woke up suddenly in the middle of the night before we left for Victoria. "I can't run federally," I cried. "I can't abandon my constituency because I haven't delivered on the Endowment Lands!" The University Endowment Lands, which were situated in my riding, were the last major green space in the city, and I had been working with other concerned Vancouverites to preserve them as parkland. "After Penticton," replied Howard, "you won't be able to deliver on anything." He was right. I was heading for a confrontation with the premier at Penticton, and the chances of my winning any battles for my constituents after that were very slim.

On Monday morning in my Victoria office, I called to arrange a meeting with the premier that afternoon. I told Vivian what I was planning and asked her to keep it confidential. Although she was employed by caucus and would continue to work there, she was unhappy with the decision and I was sorry to end our working relationship. The effects of political decisions on staffers and volunteers are always stressful. In particular, I worried about Violet, who had just begun to work as my constituency assistant in September after Nancy Peck went off to law school, and who would be out of a job. An old friend, she urged me to go ahead and run federally. She knew that she would continue to work for me if I won and was prepared to take the risk.

I also called several of my closest friends among the MLAs to advise them of my plans. Carol Gran was aghast.

"You're the only one who stands up to the premier," she said. "You're the one who always tells the truth."

"Well," I replied, "it's lonely out on the end of the limb."

I was tired of always being a critic after the fact instead of a constructive part of the decision-making processes. The premier's style of doing things precluded his caucus colleagues from playing a positive role. As a result, we were always in a reactive mode. Certainly I was disturbed about the scandals that were destroying public confidence in us, and I thought the ministers who knew more about what was going on than I did were unwilling, for whatever reason, to do anything about it. I also shared the feeling of many party members that I didn't want to be tarred with the same brush as the premier. However, my motivation in leaving to run federally was not based on these negative factors. Rather, here was a chance to work *for* something for a change. I believed the Free Trade Agreement could be a great boon for B.C. and that it depended upon a Conservative victory. It was risky; if I lost, I would be out of politics completely. But at least I would have gone down fighting for something I thought was important.

When I was ushered into the premier's office, Vander Zalm greeted me cordially. Although I doubt he would have shed a tear if I had been run over by a bus, he was always careful to mask his hostility and greeted me in his jovial salesman's manner. Indeed, he had reason to be happy because I was bringing him good news. I told him of my plan to seek the nomination in Vancouver Centre. He certainly didn't try to dissuade me. I made it clear that I had no intention of trashing either him or the government. On the contrary, I was not leaving in a huff, but taking on a challenge to work for B.C. in a cause he could well understand. Because my departure would necessitate a by-election in Vancouver–Point Grey, I told him I thought our party had a chance of winning only if we finally resolved the issue of the preservation of the University Endowment Lands. Before I left, I explained that I hadn't yet had the opportunity to advise my riding association and a few other close associates of my plans, so I asked him to keep our conversation confidential until I had had a chance to do this that evening in Vancouver. He agreed and we parted on good terms, neither of us feeling regret that our association was at an end.

My request to the premier to keep my confidence was clearly the triumph of hope over experience. Technically, Vander Zalm didn't call the press gallery himself, but no sooner was I out of his office than he was on the phone to Elwood Veitch, his deputy premier, to tell him the news. Elwood called the press gallery, who then scrummed the premier as he left his office. He confirmed that I would be leaving the government.

All this happened as I was on my way back to Vancouver by the thirty-five-minute helijet flight. I arrived home to dozens of media calls. A meeting was hastily arranged at the Vancouver Centre campaign office, where I announced officially that I would be seeking the nomination and asked for the support of Conservative Party members in the riding. In many ways the premier's action summed up the man. It did him no good; there was no reason not to let me make the announcement in my own way. It meant that people who were entitled to have advance notice were taken by surprise and unnecessarily hurt or embarrassed. He just couldn't seem to help himself.

The nominating meeting was set for the evening of October 18. Pat Carney, who would give the nominating speech, called me to express her pleasure at my decision. I told her that I didn't know much about Prime Minister Mulroney and asked her what he was like. "Well," she said, "he always comes down on the right side of an issue." She went on to say that he was an "Irish family man." Being of Irish descent herself, Pat regarded this as a considerable recommendation.

During its first mandate, the Mulroney government had had a number of scandals and some of his ministers had been required to resign. There seemed to have been a burgeoning of high-profile lobbying in those first years. In addition, although he had nailed John Turner on the patronage issue in the 1984 campaign, Mulroney did not differ from his Liberal predecessors in this regard. I knew that the Tories had been furious at Joe Clark for not making appointments during his nine months in government, and I assumed that Mulroney's patronage practices were by way of response to that anger. By 1988, the excesses of patronage had diminished, and the government had introduced legislation to regulate lobbyists. The controversies of the early years seemed to have had little lasting effect. However, some had eroded the foundation of the public's goodwill and its trust in the prime minister, in ways I was not aware of at the time.

I had never met the prime minister, but I had been impressed by the fact that the Conservatives had weathered some very difficult periods and still seemed to be a united force after four years in government, whereas Bill Vander Zalm couldn't keep his caucus, including his own supporters, happy six months after the election. I thought Brian Mulroney must have considerable leadership skills, and if Pat was comfortable about where he came down on issues, I was likely to be, too. Of even greater importance to me was the fact that I could recall no period in my life when B.C. and the west had enjoyed as much clout in Ottawa as they had since the election of the Conservatives in 1984. This was a situation worth fighting to maintain.

The nominating meeting went smoothly, as I was unopposed, and I spent the next few days in Victoria packing up my office. It was the weekend of the Social Credit party convention in Penticton. As I was putting my papers and books together, I listened to the convention on the radio. I was absolutely disgusted when I heard Don Phillips, a former cabinet minister in Bill Bennett's government turned government affairs consultant, or lobbyist, give an impassioned speech opposing the secret ballot. Later I was told that Phillips had arrived with a planeload of businessmen, including a number from the forest industry whose forest licences were at the discretion of the provincial government. They sat in the front row and indicated their support for the premier. It was a gesture of the utmost cynicism. The motion for a secret ballot was defeated; the vote on the leadership would be by a show of hands. The motion indicating support for Vander Zalm passed, but with a significant number of abstentions. As I filled the boxes in my office, I was convinced I had just heard the Social Credit party commit political suicide and was glad I wasn't there to see it.

The agony of the Social Credit party under Vander Zalm would continue for some time after my departure. By Christmas 1989 the main talk in Vancouver was of Vander Zalm's political problems. Speculation that he would step down as party leader was widespread when he scheduled a special TV broadcast for the evening of January 17, 1990. That night I had dinner in Ottawa with three political consultants who all thought I was crazy when I told them that Vander Zalm wouldn't resign. For all their time watching the political world, they had failed to take the measure of this particular man — he was incapable of admitting any wrongdoing, and nobody as yet was forcing his hand.

I went back to my office to watch the broadcast and wished I had bet money on it. Just as I predicted, the Zalm wasn't going anywhere. It was a masterful performance. When Jack Webster interviewed him afterwards and tried to force him to fess up,

Webster just came across as heavy-handed in the face of the master of denial. In the end it would take a formal finding of conflict of interest to force Bill Vander Zalm to step down, and he will go to his grave denying that he was anything other than the victim of a plot.

On October 22, 1988, I resigned my seat in the British Columbia legislature, two years to the day after I had been elected. I was now officially the candidate for the Progressive Conservative Party in Vancouver Centre. The campaign had already been under way for three weeks and we were fourteen points behind the NDP. It was going to be quite a struggle.

By the time I entered the campaign, the Free Trade Agreement had already become the dominant issue. I worked hard to master its details and headed out to speak wherever I could. Feelings ran high at all-candidates meetings, but nowhere more so than at the West End Community Centre, which was known for its fractious political atmosphere. I was the fifth candidate to speak at the meeting there. My supporters had listened politely to the other speakers, but when I stood up to speak, the anti-free-traders tried to shout me down. Although I was no stranger to hostile audiences, this was the first time I had actually been prevented from speaking. Finally I pointed to some of the loudest demonstrators and shouted, "What are you so afraid of?" The television clip of that outburst was shown throughout the campaign, including a few times on national television. I was mortified because I thought it was uncharacteristically shrill. Interestingly, many people who saw it loved it, and some thought it won me the election. The problem was that when I arrived in Ottawa, people expected a Tory version of Liberal "Rat Packer" Sheila Copps at her most outrageous, and the real me was rather a disappointment.

The prime minister attended a rally in Vancouver Centre for all of the Vancouver-area candidates. Because my riding was the host, I had the responsibility of introducing the prime minister. I first met him on the ride to the rally in his campaign bus. Mila was with him and our short conversation was pleasant, but they each had a slightly preoccupied air, no doubt because they were focussed on the rally. When we arrived at the Russian Hall on West 4th Avenue where the meeting was to take place, there were hundreds of anti-free-trade demonstrators outside and an impressive contingent of police. A local rugby team had volunteered to help maintain order and keep the demonstrators at bay. The prime minister was very impressed with this novel use of rugby players and for a long time afterwards spoke with real enthusiasm about the rally. I think he liked this kind of confrontation during an election. It seemed to get his adrenalin pumping.

When we entered the hall, I was surprised at the seating arrangements. Instead of the podium being on the stage, it had been put on the floor at one side, with people standing around in a semicircle as well as on the stage and in the balcony. Only later did I learn that the PM didn't like to speak from a raised podium. The crowd was enthusiastic and the prime minister spoke well. The national campaign committee later made a video of the speech available. Alas, my introduction wasn't included.

The campaign was hard slogging and the weather didn't add to the comfort level. November is often a rainy month in Vancouver and 1988 was no exception. We'd start early in the morning at bus stops around the riding, accosting damp constituents on their way to work. On the morning of the famous "rogue" poll, which showed the Liberals ahead with 43 per cent of voter support, David Camp was bus-stopping with me, and we had to make a real effort to overcome our gloom. There were a few other bad days after the prime minister, campaigning in the Okanagan, made a tasteless joke about the prospect of the openly gay NDP MP Svend Robinson becoming minister of national defence. Vancouver Centre had a large gay community, many of whom were Tory supporters. We expected that they would find the PM's remark insulting, as in fact they did. What we found interesting, however, was the negative reaction of people who were not particularly liberal on the issue. It was one of many occasions where I've observed the distinction people make between their own personal likes and dislikes and what they think is fair in the public arena.

I discovered after the election that campaign headquarters in Ottawa had written off Vancouver Centre. On election day, November 21, I made a tour of all the polling stations to thank the people who were serving as my scrutineers. That evening I took my family out to dinner at Bridges Restaurant, and then we returned to the house to watch the first reports of the results. I planned to go to my campaign headquarters once we had some sense of the outcome. The first phone call came from Lyall Knott, my campaign manager, saying that I was about five hundred votes behind. The problem with interim results is that they depend so much on which polls are reporting. If the areas where you are strong report first, the results can be misleadingly good. In this case, the opposite was true. As the evening wore on, the vote narrowed. We headed off to the Hotel Vancouver with the count showing us a hundred votes ahead of Johanna den Hertog. It was going to be a cliffhanger. When Howard and I left the hotel later that night, I thought it likely that I had lost but that there would almost certainly be a recount. It was about 1 a.m. when Howard and I went to bed. I was philosophical but mentally prepared for the worst. At about 4 we were awakened by a phone call from a reporter at the Vancouver *Sun*, who was surprised to find me asleep. The vote counting had just been completed and I was the winner by 279 votes. How did I feel?

We woke up Andrew, who had come out for the last week of the election and was staying with us. By now I was fully awake, "banjo-eyed," as one of my friends would say, but it was too early to call everyone and tell them the news. When the vote count was finally verified, my lead was reduced by ten, to 269. I thought about all those cold, wet mornings, all those hundreds of small events that had seemed of marginal use, and realized that every vote really had counted. It took some time to sink in. I was a member of Parliament.

7

Local Girl Makes Good

WINSTON CHURCHILL ONCE remarked that of all the many letters he had carried after his name, the ones of which he was most proud were "MP." Now that I could put those letters after my own name, I felt a powerful sense of history and connectedness to the parliamentary tradition.

A short session of Parliament had been scheduled for December 12 in order to pass the free trade legislation by the January 1, 1989, deadline. Arriving on Parliament Hill this time was obviously very different from my visit with Paisley in 1985. A series of small things brought home my change in status. I could now enter the Centre Block through the West Door, or Members' Door, rather than the Centre Doors. Instead of just peeking into the Parliamentary Dining Room, I could take a seat there at any time and be welcome. After being formally sworn in, I found the office of the sergeant-at-arms and picked up my identification pin. It was the open sesame to any of the places I wanted to go.

Before leaving for Ottawa I had addressed the question of staffing a constituency office. Pat Carney had employed two assistants, one of whom, Freda Betker, was willing to stay on. Violet had also agreed to stay and would have the benefit of Freda's experience. Pat mentioned that she had about six months left on the lease of her apartment in a development known as the Botanica. Although it wasn't close to the centre of Ottawa, Pat thought it was the nicest apartment she had found in her career there, and she offered to sublet it to us for those six months while we figured out exactly what the two of us would be doing and where we should live. It was a mutually beneficial offer and we were happy to take her up on it. Eventually we moved to an apartment overlooking the Ottawa River.

Because of my own inexperience, one of Pat's efforts to be helpful almost got me into trouble. She asked her former driver, André Deschamps, to meet me when I came to Ottawa. Ministerial drivers work for the government, so André was still on salary, waiting to be reassigned. I was grateful for his help because I didn't have a clue about where things were, and he was pleased because it gave him something to do. I simply assumed that if he was giving me the occasional lift, it must be okay. One day I received a call from Stephen Ash, the Speaker's chief of staff, advising me that it was not a good idea for me to be seen driving around in a ministerial car! My heart sank. Stupid me — I didn't even know that it was a ministerial car. No one had told me that the dark blue sedans hovering around the MPs' entrance to the Centre Block were official cars. From then on André confined his chauffeuring services to an occasional lift in his own car.

Shortly after my arrival, I received a call from Phil Evershed in the deputy prime minister's office. He told me that the prime minister wanted me to give the Address in Reply to the Speech from the Throne when the House opened. The single subject was to be free trade, since that would be the only item in the Throne Speech for this short session. It would be the first speech of the new session and my maiden speech. I realized that I was being recognized, but I wasn't sure why. Perhaps I was being asked because I had been such a strong defender of free trade in B.C. during the election campaign. Perhaps I was being vetted for future preferment. Mary Collins, who had been re-elected as MP for the B.C. riding of Capilano–Howe Sound, told me that she had once given the Address in Reply. But because she had not been in cabinet during the first Mulroney mandate, I then wondered if it might not be a form of consolation prize for those who, for whatever reason, wouldn't be given a portfolio. I had no idea and I certainly didn't worry about it. I was too excited.

It is a parliamentary tradition that members are not heckled during their maiden speeches. After that, it is a free-for-all. I was going to have the honour of giving my one unheckled speech to a full House. As I was working on the speech, it occurred to me that I should probably give part of it in French. I believed it was important to show that British Columbians could also speak our other official language. Phil said that if I picked out the appropriate parts, he would have them translated. I hadn't spoken French seriously for years, although my trip in the summer had given me a chance to brush up a bit. Nevertheless, I had always had a reasonable accent, so I thought I could do a respectable job.

Another new MP, Gilles Loiselle from Quebec City, was chosen to speak as the seconder of the Address in Reply. Later we often joked that our fates were intertwined from that day. We entered cabinet together, joined the Priorities and Planning Committee together, and generally seemed to proceed in lockstep. Not only were we first elected to Parliament at the same time, but neither of us had a history of any length in the Conservative Party. We got along famously. Gilles, a former journalist, had served as Quebec's agent general in London during the period when the Parti Québécois government of René Lévesque was fighting against the patriation of the Canadian Constitution. A friend from the LSE who was a regular guest of Gilles and Lorraine Loiselle in London has told me of the fine quality of the cuisine and conversation at the home of the Quebec agent general in those days. The genial Gilles was not able, however, to convince British parliamentarians to vote against patriation. Because of these diplomatic activities he was included among the group identified as Quebec nationalists who had been attracted to Ottawa by Brian Mulroney. But I always felt that Gilles's commitment to Canada was strong and not in conflict with his powerful attachment to Quebec.

Before the House reconvened, the new MPs had a taste of the regular meetings held by Conservative members to work out problems and build solidarity. Provincial caucuses met on Tuesday evenings, usually over dinner. On Wednesday mornings at 10 national caucus met as a group.

That first meeting of national caucus after the 1988 election was a boisterous affair. In those days the caucus met in a large oblong room called the Railway Committee Room, not far from the Chamber. Brian Mulroney attended national caucus meetings religiously. He would miss them only if it was absolutely necessary for him to be away. Usually his travel schedule was planned to ensure his presence.

The mood of that first caucus was very friendly as MPs took the opportunity to catch up with colleagues they hadn't seen since before the election. A few of the defeated MPs who were in Ottawa to clear out their offices attended that day to congratulate their victorious colleagues, who commiserated with them in return. When the meeting was called to order, I noticed that the prime minister wasn't present. I had yet to be exposed to the ritual of the prime-ministerial entrance. As the caucus chairman, Bob Layton, announced the arrival of Brian Mulroney, everyone immediately stood up and started cheering and shouting — a well-deserved welcome for a leader who had just led his party to a second majority mandate. But it turned out that this greeting was not just for special occasions: we would continue to give him a similar rousing reception at caucus for almost five years, including those times when we were at 9 per cent in the polls.

After his triumphal entry, the PM would take his place at the head table and the regular agenda of caucus would continue. The first item of business was always a health report from the oldest member, Stan Darling. Stan's reports would include any illness of a member or member's family as well as the death or illness of former colleagues and their families. Then came the Whip's report. Later, this included the "surprise" list — people who had been absent from votes without the Whip's permission. Between 1984 and 1988, the Conservative majority was so large that it was hard to keep discipline. However, our majority was much reduced now and it was important for the Whip to manage attendance in the House. The Whip's report was followed by the House leader's review of the legislative schedule and other House business.

The next item was the reports from provincial or regional caucuses, bringing forward items that had been discussed in the Tuesday-evening meetings. Discussions at provincial caucus meetings could get hot and heavy, but for the most part the format of national caucus tended to discourage overly contentious debates. Other agenda items would include reports from ministers on various initiatives, and issues that individual MPs wanted to raise.

The meeting concluded with the prime minister's remarks.

These were the legendary Mulroney performances, said by some to "mesmerize" caucus. That is perhaps a little strong, but they were carefully thought through. The PM would begin by responding to issues that had been raised during the meeting. Then he would often report on his travels or on events he, or he and Mila, had been involved in. A common feature of the speeches was the reading of excerpts from newspaper articles that made some point he wished to emphasize. When we were under attack and someone wrote in our defence, you could be sure that article would be shared with caucus. Later, when we were at record-low levels of public support, the prime minister liked to quote American essayist Charles Krauthammer's comment that at this time in world history, any leader who left office on a wave of popularity deserved to be shot. The implication was that such a leader had failed to take the difficult decisions demanded by the times. Mulroney took great personal (and possibly actuarial) comfort from this observation.

Perhaps the most skilful part of Brian Mulroney's presentations to caucus was the creation of the impression that nothing about our position in the polls or political situation was unanticipated or worrisome to our leader. Were we at 20 per cent in the polls? That's about where he expected we'd be at this point in the mandate. He communicated an attitude of unwavering confidence that he knew exactly what had to be done to put us in a position where we would win the next election. This whistling in the graveyard was extremely effective in maintaining caucus morale through difficult times. I never could figure out how much of it the PM actually believed himself, and how much was the quite natural and appropriate rhetoric of a coach to his team.

Although MPs might challenge ministers during caucus, no one ever took on the prime minister. This was a marked change from what I'd been told was the practice in earlier Conservative caucuses under Joe Clark or Robert Stanfield. The prime minister never missed an opportunity to remind caucus that he had led the Conservative Party to two consecutive majority governments. Winning is the ultimate power source of a party leader, and even when there was a lot of evidence to suggest Brian Mulroney had become a liability as a leader, his skill in convincing people that he knew better than anyone how to turn things around kept the caucus loyal. An equally important factor was the quite genuine respect that members had for him. In addition, the Tories had come to see the value of discipline and loyalty. One of Mulroney's greatest achievements was to make Conservatives think like a governing party and stop killing their leaders.

During that first national caucus meeting, criticism of the prime minister was the last thing on anyone's mind. Not surprisingly, the mood was jubilant. It had been an incredibly hard-fought campaign, making every victory sweet. No one had expected that the incredible 211-seat landslide of 1984 could be repeated, and frankly, it was just as well it wasn't. With a majority that is too big, it is hard to keep up morale: there is little prospect for preferment, and a member's attendance in the House seems irrelevant. We now had a comfortable majority, but not so great as to lead to a slackening of discipline or an abandonment of hope for interesting jobs to do. There was genuine regret over the loss of colleagues, but in general the atmosphere was euphoric.

I was as captivated as anyone by the prime minister's humorous and feisty speeches in caucus. In that first meeting I remember being aware that Brian Mulroney was a master at blowing his own horn without seeming to. This was part of how he communicated a sense of mastery of the situation. It served a deadly serious purpose: discouragement of any dissent against his leadership. This hardly seemed necessary at the time, but it would later become crucial. In explaining the election result, the PM kept coming back to the point that it all came down to leadership. In his explanation, Canadians had chosen Brian Mulroney over John Turner. Sometimes he would broaden the meaning of leadership to include "Brian Mulroney and his team" as compared with "John Turner and the Rat Pack." I remember thinking that while leadership had indeed been important, in the 1988 election the issues had been just as significant. Free trade, for example, represented a major philosophical divide. Still, I wasn't about to rain on the prime minister's parade, not even in my own mind. I thought he was terrific and if he couldn't show a little "swagger and strut" over his victory among his caucus colleagues — well, where could he?

On December 12, the House formally resumed. In the morning we listened to Governor General Jeanne Sauvé read the short

Throne Speech. That afternoon we convened to start the Throne Speech Debate. When I gave my speech, Howard was sitting in the Speaker's Gallery, which runs along both sides of the House. Visitors sit on the opposite side from that of the party they support so that they have a clear view of it. Howard was seated almost directly across from the prime minister and was joined there by my former colleague Bud Smith, who had replaced Brian Smith as attorney general in B.C. and was a long-time federal Conservative. Both Bud and Howard told me that when I switched languages, the prime minister looked over in astonishment, then turned with a big grin on his face to his seatmate, Don Mazankowski, and clearly said, "She speaks French!"

I had campaigned hard for free trade and was pleased to have the opportunity to put the case for the agreement before Parliament. It was a serious topic, but I tried to inject a lighter note here and there. In speaking of the capacity of Canadians to balance the impact of the United States with their own sense of who they are, I remarked that it was that sense of balance that had led one writer to describe a Canadian as "someone who can make love in a canoe." I was a bit surprised that the line got only a small chuckle, until about fifteen seconds later when the francophones reacted appreciatively. In the video of the speech, my startled reaction to the delayed laughter is quite amusing. It took me a few seconds to realize why people were laughing at a part of my speech that wasn't funny! It was a lesson on the need to go slow and wait for the reaction after translation. Incidentally, the writer I quoted was Pierre Berton. Phil Evershed had suggested that I not mention Berton by name because he wasn't greatly liked by some Conservative members. I went along with his advice but felt a little guilty — my academic training had taught me to credit my sources, and you can't exactly footnote a speech.

The short, intense session to pass the free trade legislation proved to be a good introduction to a new Parliament, especially for me. Because I had been nominated three weeks into the campaign, I had not attended the "campaign college" in Ottawa, where new candidates and incumbents receive training on campaign techniques and get to know one another. This short session necessitated some rare night sittings of Parliament and, as a result, the Parliamentary Dining Room was full for dinner and many of us had an opportunity to get acquainted. The Parliamentary Dining Room, on the top floor of the Centre Block, is charming. In the middle of the room are curved ceiling arches, which are reputed to permit people to hear conversations at other tables. I've never found the eavesdropping all that good, but new MPs are warned with great seriousness to watch what they say when sitting at certain tables. Along the sides of the room are alcoves, some with small tables and some with large ones. The first alcove on the left has three small tables, one of which is traditionally used by the prime minister.

Farther along the dining room are larger alcoves, each with a big table. These are assigned to the MPs and senators of the different parties. Because the Conservatives had such a large majority after the 1984 and 1988 elections, we had two alcoves for MPs, one designated for French conversation and one for English. Any Conservative member was welcome to join either table. It was nice to feel you could go in alone and find congenial company for lunch or dinner. In December 1988 I found it quite magical sitting around with some of the veterans, listening to their often hilarious stories about life in the House, many dating back to a time that has ceased to exist when members drank heavily and played poker till the wee hours when the House was in all-night session.

The finale of that first post-election session of Parliament was the prime minister's Christmas party. Brian and Mila Mulroney hosted a black-tie dinner in the Hall of Honour for MPs and their spouses every Christmas, an occasion enhanced by just the right combination of formality and familiarity. Against a backdrop of beautifully decorated tables and sparkling Christmas decorations, everybody looked wonderful and was in high spirits. A choir and a small ensemble favoured by the prime minister from his days at the Ritz-Carlton in Montreal took turns entertaining us. Some of my colleagues sang, and then the PM stood up to sing a couple of songs. I think I have only ever heard him sing "Paper Doll" and "When Irish Eyes are Smiling," and he sang both that night. The reception was enthusiastic and sincere. Brian Mulroney could do no wrong in that crowd. That evening the Mulroneys were surrounded by friends and admirers, and I was certainly one of them.

The House wasn't scheduled to reconvene until early April, to allow for the preparation of a new Speech from the Throne and a budget. Of course, there was also the question of the prime minister's new cabinet. No changes had been made after the election. The functions of ministers who had not been re-elected or had retired were temporarily taken over by other ministers. Like many of my colleagues, I had hopes of being considered for a cabinet post, but knew that such decisions were based on a process in which regional and demographic factors played as large a part as any merit one might have. Perhaps the strongest factor I had on my side was that I represented a key riding. We had lost ten seats in British Columbia in 1988 and two of the four B.C. ministers had not returned — Pat Carney because she had retired, Gerry St. Germain because he had been defeated. The other two B.C. ministers, Tom Siddon and Frank Oberle, had been re-elected. If B.C. retained four ministers, meaning that there would be two new appointments, then I might have a chance; otherwise, I thought it unlikely I would be appointed in this round.

Although I had no idea of the protocol of ministerial appointments, my heart skipped a beat when I returned to the constituency office on Friday, January 27, to be told by Violet that Stanley Hartt, the prime minister's chief of staff, was trying to reach me. It was about 3 p.m. Vancouver time when we finally spoke. "The prime minister would like to speak with you in Ottawa sometime after noon on Sunday," Stanley said in his slightly hoarse but lively voice. "You may want to have members of your family in Ottawa Monday morning, and you and your spouse are invited to a luncheon on Monday. I can't tell you anything more than that. You should not tell anyone other than your immediate family about this." Well, you didn't have to be a rocket scientist to figure out what was up, but I was afraid to make any assumptions. I immediately tried to call Howard in his office in Victoria. Unfortunately, he had left for the ferry and when he got home that night for a weekend he thought we would be spending with his mother in Seattle, he didn't have anything but casual clothes with him. Because he worked in Victoria, Howard kept his good clothes there. He would have to return to the boat to get a suit. The next morning he left early on this errand and, because of the time it would take, we decided to take the red-eye flight to Ottawa on Saturday night. Before we left, I called both my parents to tell them the news.

When we boarded in Vancouver, there was Mary Collins. No one in their right mind would take the red-eye on a Saturday night unless they had to be in Ottawa early on Sunday, so we both knew we had received the same call. We smiled at each other, but didn't say anything. When we changed planes in Toronto, Howard and I were joined by John McDermid, who had been Pat Carney's parliamentary secretary when she was minister of international trade, and who had gone into the cabinet just before the 1988 election. He gave us a lift home from the Ottawa airport and said he assumed we were in the capital for a reason. Again, we smiled conspiratorially, but I was paranoid about saying anything to anyone.

By the time we were settled in the apartment, it was after 11 a.m., and since Stanley Hartt had said that the PM wanted to speak to me sometime "after noon," I was afraid to fall asleep. I didn't want to be dozy for his call. The hours went by, and no call. I began to wonder if the PM had asked a few extras down in case someone said no. The wait was excruciating. At 4:30 the phone rang and I almost jumped out of my skin. It was my father; he was at the Ottawa airport. He had decided that whatever was happening, he didn't want to miss it. He arrived a little after 5 and, somewhat appropriately, we watched the television program *Question Period*. Just before 7, Rick Morgan, the prime minister's executive assistant, called. "The prime minister would like to see you at 24 Sussex Drive at 7:30. Will you be taking a taxi?"

I turned to Dad and Howard. "Honestly," I said, "this is real cloak and dagger. I have to be at 24 Sussex Drive at 7:30 in the morning." "We'd better book a taxi tonight, just to be sure," said Howard.

I couldn't stand the tension any longer. "I don't feel like cooking," I said. "Let's go out and get something to eat." When we arrived home after dinner at a little local restaurant, the phone was ringing. It was Stanley Hartt. "Where are you?" he asked. "The prime minister was expecting you at 7:30. He even called the commissioner of the RCMP."

My whole life flashed before my eyes. How could I have been so stupid! "You mean 7:30 tonight? I thought he meant 7:30 in the morning!" I explained in a trembling voice. "Well," replied Stanley, "the prime minister has gone back to Harrington Lake. He'll have to contact you by phone."

A few minutes later the phone rang and it was the unmistakable voice of Brian Mulroney. He couldn't have been nicer — I wanted to die of embarrassment. "Well, Kim," he said, "we should be having this conversation in person. I want to invite you to join the government as the minister of state for Indian affairs and northern development. You'll like your senior minister very much — all I can tell you now is that he's from eastern Canada. This will give you a chance to learn without being under attack from the media." "Yes, yes, oh thank you, thank you," I grovelled. As I hung up the phone, I felt like a reprieved prisoner. I told Howard and Dad what my position was to be and they were very excited. Howard then wondered if perhaps his own job as counsel to the B.C. government on Indian cases would create a problem. He wasn't involved in land claims but was often sent as legal support to Crown counsel in prosecutions of native people for violations of hunting or fishing laws. I called Stanley back to advise him of this. He didn't foresee a problem because Howard was planning to move to Ottawa. When he returned to Victoria, Howard immediately stopped working on those particular cases. There was some negative comment from native leaders, but it was short-lived.

The next morning, Monday, January 30, we arrived at Rideau Hall for the swearing-in ceremony. Howard's children Andrew and Abby joined Howard and Dad in the beautiful gilded ballroom with the other guests. Ministers and ministers-to-be gathered in the Tent Room, so called because it is decorated with striped fabric on the walls and ceiling to look like a tent, albeit a rather luxurious one. There was much comparing of notes and congratulations. I met my senior minister, Pierre Cadieux, who would be sworn in as the minister of Indian affairs and northern development. My title, minister of state, indicated that I was the junior minister. Pierre, whom I would describe as small, dark, and handsome, had been minister of labour prior to the election. As I congratulated Lucien Bouchard, the new minister of environment, I told him I thought his portfolio was going to be key to our reelection next time. He seemed a little taken aback by this. He would indeed be key to the results of the next election — but not in his capacity as environment minister.

When the time came to begin the ceremony, we marched into

the ballroom in order of precedence. This was determined by the date of our first election to Parliament as well as the date of appointment to cabinet. After we had taken our seats, I craned my neck to find my family contingent, who were sitting on the other side of the aisle looking very excited and proud. We all stood as the arrival of Governor General Jeanne Sauvé, her husband, and the prime minister was announced. Then, one by one, we were called up to be sworn in to our new positions. By the time my turn came, third from the end, I had a pretty good idea of what to do, but I was still nervous.

All the new ministers took the Privy Council oath, which is long and written in archaic language. As new members of Her Majesty's Privy Council for Canada, we swore to keep Her Majesty's confidences. Not all privy councillors are current or former ministers. New Democratic Party leader Audrey McLaughlin was made a privy councillor during the Gulf War so that she could be "privy" to military and intelligence secrets. The head of the Security Intelligence Review Committee is also sworn in to the Privy Council. And, occasionally, the position is given as an honour.

After the ceremony a formal portrait was taken of the new and reassigned ministers with the prime minister and the governor general. Then, after a reception in the Tent Room, during which the prime minister moved through the crowd and had his picture taken with ministers and their guests and families, the new cabinet members and their spouses went off to the ninth-floor dining room of the Lester B. Pearson Building, the headquarters of the Department of External Affairs, to join the rest of the cabinet for a luncheon. The new ministers were seated at the table with the PM. Mary Collins and I were on either side of him, looking like two blonde B.C. bookends. I felt very shy in the company of Brian Mulroney, a feeling I would never completely overcome. I had read that the Queen dealt with the many lunches and banquets that threatened her waistline by barely touching what she was served, and wondered idly if the PM did too. Aside from the fact that he didn't drink his wine, he ate his lunch just like anybody else!

A meeting of the full cabinet was scheduled for 3 o'clock. The cabinet room is located in the Centre Block of the House of Commons, one floor above the entrance to the House. Although I would spend a great deal of my life in that room over the next few years, I felt overwhelmed on entering it for the first time. I knew that it had been the cabinet room only since Trudeau's time, but the sense of what those walls with their beautiful carved panelling had seen and heard was still quite humbling. Name tags had been set around the enormous wooden table that almost filled the room, and I found my place almost directly across from the PM's chair. His place was in the middle of the table with his back to the windows, facing a large portrait of Sir John A. Macdonald on the opposite wall. The deputy prime minister, Don Mazankowski, was on his right, and Joe Clark, as a former prime minister, on his left. The ministers sat in order of precedence, alternating right and left, starting from the prime minister's chair. That was why the most junior of us wound up sitting opposite the PM. At the far end of the room stood two small desks. Paul Tellier, the clerk of the Privy Council and the most senior public servant, sat at the one closest to the window. He was rather like a deputy minister to the prime minister. Various officials worked at the other desk and at a desk directly below Sir John A.'s portrait. The chairs around the edge of the room were used by officials and senior ministerial staff. At this first meeting of cabinet, only the prime minister's chief of staff was present.

The cabinet table and desks were wired with microphones and earphones. The translators worked in soundproof booths behind windows at the end of the room closest to the entrance. They needed to be able to see what was going on in order not to miss someone speaking. The prime minister made a point of speaking both English and French in the course of his remarks. It was fascinating to watch lively conversations or debates carried on in two languages. The translators were sworn to secrecy, and ministers spoke candidly, generally forgetting that the translators were even there.

I was, quite naturally, in awe of all this at my first cabinet meeting. I was somewhat startled, then, to see the prime minister pull a Binaca breath freshener bottle from his pocket, open his mouth, and unselfconsciously spritz himself a couple of times. I would become accustomed to this odd habit in a man who was otherwise so fastidious about his image, but that first day I just stared in amazement. The prime minister read us the riot act about cabinet secrecy and the importance of taking great care in appointing ministerial staff. A book containing ministerial guidelines would be waiting for us in our offices and we were to read it thoroughly. We were reminded that many of our colleagues who were just as able would also have liked to be in cabinet. The clear implication was that if we screwed up, we would be out. It was a message I took very much to heart.

That evening Dad, Howard, and I went out to dinner at a favourite Chinese restaurant of Howard's. It had also been a favourite of Pierre and Margaret Trudeau, and there was a photo of them on the counter from those happier times. We relived the day over dinner, especially the Rideau Hall portion. Howard has a great love of history, so he particularly appreciated the significance and ancient language of the Privy Council oath. As a former American, he also took particular pleasure in the intimacy and accessibility of Canadian political institutions and ceremonies. Dignity without pomp pleased him. That we could participate in a ceremony in the formal surroundings of Rideau Hall in the morning and be tucking into steamed rice in an unpretentious Chinese restaurant in the evening appealed to his sense of occasion.

In all his life my father had never expected to be at Rideau Hall, chatting with the governor general and having his picture taken with the prime minister. He headed back to Vancouver the next morning bearing his precious treasure of photographs to share with the rest of the family. I was so happy he had decided to come. People who live in central Canada don't always appreciate the time and expense involved in travelling from the west coast. I've been part of some wonderful occasions in Ottawa and have always regretted that it was so difficult for my family and Vancouver friends — my greatest supporters — to share them with me.

The next challenge facing me was to find political staff for my office. All MPs have office staff in Ottawa whose job is to assist them in serving their constituents. I had great help in this from Stephen Ash in the Speaker's office. Not only was the Speaker, John Fraser, a fellow British Columbian, but we had also attended the same high school and practised with the same law firm, although not at the same times. Elevated by his election as Speaker to a realm above partisanship, John was nonetheless concerned to be as helpful as he could to a fellow Vancouverite. I was a rookie in Ottawa and was grateful when Stephen offered his advice.

Before I went into cabinet, he had helped me to find two staffers for my Parliament Hill office, Sheila Rafter and Heather Monette, both of whom had worked for B.C. MPs. (One had decided not to seek re-election, the other had been defeated in 1988.) The two of them set about organizing my life. As well as being very knowledgeable about the Hill, they were familiar with many of the B.C. issues. We had been assigned a small suite of offices in the Centre Block, but were moved when I became a cabinet minister. Jean Charest, who had been named deputy House leader, needed an office in the Centre Block to be close to the House, so I moved to Flora MacDonald's old offices in the West Block. I was tickled to have the offices that had been occupied by such a dynamic woman.

Now that I was a minister, I needed staff to help me in my ministerial responsibilities. I asked André Deschamps to be my driver and he happily accepted. I think most ministers would agree that in few other relationships with staff members is personal chemistry more important than in the one between a minister and his or her driver. Your driver sees you first thing in the morning and last thing at night. André became a member of my family. The full title of a ministerial driver is "chauffeur and personal assistant." He makes life possible. André was smart and competent and took on increasing responsibilities as I moved up in government. He worked for me until the day I left.

Pat Carney had also recommended her former secretary Wendy Waite to me, should I be named to cabinet. Wendy came to work for me and was my private secretary until I left government. I still miss the quiet, competent way she kept the myriad threads of my ministerial life untangled.

As a minister of state, or junior minister, I wasn't entitled to a chief of staff. Instead, my staff would be led by an executive assistant. I committed a terrible gaffe in my first effort at hiring an EA. I offered the job to the first person I interviewed, only to discover that the chemistry wasn't right. The only solution was to advise him that I couldn't confirm the appointment. It caused him some embarrassment and was my fault entirely. I felt very bad because he was a perfectly nice young man, just not the right one for the job.

Eager as I was to get my office up and running, I realized that I needed to proceed more slowly and carefully. Stephen Ash came to my rescue by offering to do some preliminary interviewing of candidates for the position. He called one day to say that he had Michael Ferrabee in his office and that I should talk to him. "Don't be concerned that he looks like a baby," he said, "he's very mature for his age." When the new applicant walked in, I couldn't help exclaiming, "You *are* a baby!" Michael was a young-looking twenty-six-year-old, but he had been on the Hill since 1984. His father is a journalist, James Ferrabee, and he had grown up in a household where political figures were regular features of the landscape. I offered Mike the job, but only after Senator Lowell Murray graciously agreed to let me steal him from his staff. Mike told me he could only promise to give me two years, as it was getting to be time for him to leave the Hill. In the end, he worked for me for two and a half years and proved to have those greatest of all virtues in a political staffer — integrity and judgment.

Once on board, Mike set about completing the staffing of my office. I told him there was room for only one rookie in my office, and I was it. I was and continued to be very lucky in the quality of the people around me. In Vancouver, Diana Lam, who had recently wound up her ten-year partnership in a public relations firm to seek new challenges, became my senior staffer in B.C. She and Mike got along famously and managed to survive all manner of crises with their senses of humour intact.

I discussed with Mike my goal as a minister. It was to earn a reputation for being sound. I realized that the key to having an impact on decisions was to be respected. This could come only from doing my homework and working hard. I wasn't interested in doing things to get my name in the paper. In Vancouver, I would have to keep up my profile so that my constituents would know what I was doing. But in Ottawa I wanted to concentrate on building relations of trust with my colleagues so that I could count on their help and support for the projects and policies I was there to champion.

The next step was to understand my ministerial responsibilities. There were two sets of these: those relating to the portfolio and those relating to my committee assignments. The Department of Indian Affairs and Northern Development, or DIAND, is enormous. In order to make the workload more manageable, Pierre Cadieux decided we should divide up the responsibilities. He would take responsibility for the North, as well as economic, educational, and constitutional issues. I was to take the lead in British Columbia as well as focus on issues such as housing and policing. Pierre was always very pleasant and supportive. It can be awkward to have two ministers in a department, but dividing responsibilities helps.

The deputy minister was Harry Swain, an old Ottawa pro who had earlier served a stint in the Privy Council Office. Once I was settled in, I began to meet with him on Monday mornings for an hour, the beginning of a day of meetings in Hull because the headquarters of Indian Affairs was there, as was my ministerial team. Harry and I would go over the issues, then, if there was time, I picked his brain about how things worked in Ottawa. When I arrived at his office, I used to ask his secretary if "Sir Humphrey" was ready for me. She always looked at me oddly. Perhaps she was unfamiliar with the *Yes, Minister* TV series.

When the prime minister had told me he wanted to appoint me to DIAND, I was delighted. I would be the first British Columbian to hold an Indian affairs portfolio since Liberal Art Laing in the 1960s. A lot had happened in the interim. A decision of the Supreme Court of Canada in 1973 had led the Trudeau government to change its view on the legitimacy of Indian land claims. Previously, Trudeau had rejected such claims, declaring that the government couldn't go back and rewrite history. However, in 1973 the Nisga'a land claim of British Columbia arrived in the Supreme Court of Canada. The B.C. Court of Appeal had ruled that there was no unextinguished aboriginal title in British Columbia, and had denied the claim. The effect of the Supreme Court's decision was to uphold the Court of Appeal. However, the fact that three judges out of seven held an opposing view, and a fourth decided the case on a technicality, sent a message to the government that the issue was arguable. Another case arriving in the court, to be heard by the full complement of nine judges and without any procedural barriers, might result in a different finding. Rather than go through the enormous cost of continuing to litigate such claims, the Trudeau government decided to try to settle out of court by negotiating.

The process set up to negotiate Indian land claims soon led to frustration and delays. Many people considered the rules by which a claim could qualify for negotiation unfairly narrow. Only six claims would be under active negotiation at any one time. As frustrations grew, many Indian bands became more and more assertive over the lands in their claims. This created resentment in non-native communities as well as uneasiness among the holders of rights to harvest timber or explore for minerals on disputed lands. The issue of comprehensive Indian land claims was particularly important in British Columbia because there were almost no treaties with Indians there. Of the twenty-four claims accepted for negotiation when I arrived at DIAND, eighteen were in British Columbia.

In early 1986, Bud Smith had asked me to do a review of the provincial policy on land claims. I had spent a great deal of time researching the issue and talking to the government lawyers concerned, who were encouraged that there was interest from the premier's office in an issue that required serious political support. But the premier's retirement meant that I never had the opportunity to present options for a new policy to him. One study I read in 1986 had shown that more than a billion dollars of investment was on hold in B.C. as a result of the uncertainty over aboriginal title. Although the provincial government had always taken the position that responsibility for negotiating and settling the claims belonged to the federal government, B.C. had requested that the federal government set out its views of what might be reasonably expected of the province, and it had never received a response. I was delighted to be in a position to push for a resolution to an issue that was threatening the economic well-being of my province and its native and non-native citizens.

When I began to moot the issue with DIAND officials in the spring of 1989, their response was cautious. I remember one meeting in my Hill office when an official remarked that the government of British Columbia was recalcitrant and that surely they should make the first move since the province would benefit disproportionately from the resolution of the claims. I got very angry. "The last time I looked," I retorted, "British Columbia was part of Canada! We do all sorts of things that benefit one part of the country more than another. The ball is in our court to tell British Columbia what it will take to get the process moving." The poor official was taken aback by my vehemence. He meant no harm, but his comment reflected an attitude I found all too common in Ottawa. Because B.C. was prosperous and a long way away, one didn't have to worry about it.

In documents that had been prepared previously for cabinet on the subject of B.C. claims, it was always pointed out that the benefits of resolving the claims would not extend outside B.C. For this reason, it was readily admitted, support for significant federal expenditure to resolve the claims would be hard to come by. When I think of some of the big-ticket items during my time in Ottawa, this makes me furious. Hibernia in Newfoundland, huge bailouts to prairie farmers, support programs for the east coast fisheries, the rescue of de Havilland in Ontario — I begrudged none of these, even though they didn't benefit British Columbia in any significant way. But we are all Canadians, and it seems to me we all have a stake in the prosperity of our fellow citizens. Because B.C. is one of only three provinces (the others being Alberta and Ontario) that are net contributors to equalization payments, its prosperity is especially vital. If important economic development was being stalled because of the uncertainty created by unresolved land claims, then surely it was a matter of national interest to solve the problem, especially since the responsibility for doing so was largely that of the federal government. My goal was to bring B.C. to the table, but nothing could happen without Ottawa.

To be fair, once the officials realized that I was prepared to pursue this, they threw themselves into the issue and were not unhappy to have a minister who came to the department with a priority of her own. We created a departmental coordinating committee under Rick Van Loon and set about examining what we needed to know to make a proposal to B.C. that would get the negotiating process moving.

There was one problem, however. In order to make progress, we had to have the goodwill of the government of B.C. Although I still had many friends among the B.C. ministers, Premier Vander Zalm and I were not exactly soulmates. I discussed the issue with Pierre Cadieux. He was enormously supportive and agreed that he would be the front man on the issue with the B.C. government. He was as good as his word and met with Premier Vander Zalm, with some success. I might add that Pierre's support was typical of Quebec ministers. I always found my Quebec colleagues helpful and supportive on B.C. projects.

At the end of July, we convened a meeting in Vancouver of all the regional directors of Indian Affairs in B.C. These were the men and women who worked closely with native communities around the province administering the department's policies. We asked them for their views on what would work in resolving claims. The feedback was excellent. They were a little surprised to be consulted directly in a think tank with a minister. They had strong opinions and valuable insights into the communities they served. There still remain, among some officials in Indian Affairs, vestiges of the attitudes of the old Indian agents. That lingering condescension and paternalism has been difficult to eradicate. But many others welcome the prospect of an eventual winding down of the department's responsibilities in favour of autonomy and self-reliance by native Canadians, even if it means the demise of their own positions.

I travelled widely around the province, especially during the summer, often using helicopters and small planes to reach remote communities. From Kitimat, I flew by helicopter with members of the Haisla band along the Kemano power line. At the power plant we walked literally inside the mountain to see the enormous generators that provide energy for the Alcan aluminum smelter in Kitimat. The Haisla were worried about the possible effect of an extension of the power project on the oolichan — a small, oil-rich fish — and on the salmon. Both are a fundamental part of native diets and culture in B.C. No scientific opinions to the contrary could convince them that the project would not be a disaster for their fishery. No amount of new jobs promised by the company was seen as adequate compensation for this feared loss.

Wherever I went, no matter what other problems were on the agenda, I turned the discussion to claims. What were their aims? How did they think we could best get the process going in a way that wouldn't take forever? I became more and more convinced that Indian frustration at the process was increasing the attraction of more socially disruptive means to draw attention to their concerns. But that was not the only reason my determination to succeed was growing. I had worked with native people before. The Musqueam in Vancouver had been my constituents when I was an MLA, and I admired Wendy Grant, their chief, enormously. Manny Jules, chief of the Kamloops band, had become a valued colleague and friend during Project Pride. But being the junior minister of Indian affairs was different. Native Canadians understood only too well the power of the department over their lives, and I was a representative of that power. Sitting around a table with perfectly intelligent and able people, I often felt painfully uncomfortable representing a power I thought I had no right to exercise. Normally I was quite comfortable meeting with constituents and various groups who were petitioning the government for some cause or other, but here I felt the federal government had too much to say about the lives of aboriginal people. I didn't want to be the Great White Mother. It was insulting and incongruous. If anything, the kindness, generosity, and respect shown to me when I visited native communities increased my sense of unease. In talking with native leaders across Canada, I was struck by the degree to which broken promises characterized their experience of government. This was reflected in a strange combination of hopefulness and resignation in their attitudes towards me. I made up my mind never to raise expectations or to make promises if I wasn't sure I could deliver.

I came to believe that the relationship between the government and Indians was the worst of all possible worlds. On the one hand, enormous sums of money were dispensed without proper mechanisms of accountability. But the accountability of government to native people was also lacking. We were groping towards greater autonomy on the part of bands, but the tiny size of so many native communities meant they simply weren't able to provide all the services they needed.

Being in Indian Affairs brought me face to face with one of the most profound dilemmas of Canada. How can we do justice to aboriginal peoples who claim a right to preserve their cultures and to be fairly compensated for the loss of what was theirs at the time of European contact, and, at the same time, avoid the negative aspects of political regimes where rights are defined by race? Integration without assimilation — should that be the goal for aboriginal peoples? Is it achievable? I didn't know then how deeply this question would preoccupy me, even after I left DIAND.

That this was a propitious time to try to revive the land claims process in B.C. was reflected in the increasing interest and concern expressed by the forestry and mining industries. There was a growing recognition that the issue was not going to go away, and that cooperation between industry, governments, and bands could help to create settlements that would benefit all parties. Industry was looking for certainty, bands were looking for recognition and economic opportunity. Common ground did exist.

Another encouraging sign was the declared willingness of Mike Harcourt's New Democratic Party in B.C., which had a good chance of forming the next government, to participate with the federal government in negotiating and settling claims. While emphasizing that the federal government should pay most of the cost of settling land claims, Mike Harcourt had begun to say that he didn't rule out a provincial contribution. He also emphasized the overall benefits to British Columbia of removing the economic uncertainty created by unresolved claims. By the end of 1989, Premier Vander Zalm was also making positive comments about land claims. Although he still stuck publicly to the position that the federal government would have to assume all the costs, his tone was positive.

On September 11, 1989, Pierre and I travelled to Greenville, B.C., to participate in the signing of the framework agreement of the Nisga'a land claim. This was the first claim to be accepted for negotiation under the new land claims policy, and it had taken thirteen years just to get to the point where a framework agreement could be signed. The ceremony was a happy one with great pageantry and colour. But it also underlined the protracted nature of the existing process and the desperate need to find something different. The B.C. government had attended the negotiations as an observer only, and was represented at the signing by the deputy minister for native affairs, Eric Denhoff. I had known Eric since my days in Premier Bennett's office, and he knew I understood the political constraints on the provincial government and that I would look for an approach that would enable them to join the land claims talks without committing political suicide.

The work continued and a draft memorandum to cabinet was prepared for review by Pierre and me in late October. We would not be able to place the issue before cabinet until the new year. Cabinet would be the most difficult hurdle. It would be a challenge to persuade a cash-strapped government to see the resolution of B.C. claims as a priority.

The limits imposed by lack of funds provided the context for virtually everything the government did when I was in Ottawa. After the 1988 election, Finance Minister Michael Wilson had renewed his efforts to bring the federal deficit under control. The principal reason for voters' defections from our party to the Reform Party in 1988 had been a failure to accomplish this during the first Conservative mandate.

I must confess that I have never understood the position of the political left on the deficit and the debt, although some of it may arise from a confusion between the two terms. There seems to be an obliviousness to the way rising debt costs erode a government's ability to finance programs. The argument that "we only owe it to ourselves" is the most misleading form of avoidance. Not only do we owe increasing sums to foreign lenders, but unless you are prepared to default on your debt, you have to pay interest — it doesn't matter to whom.

When the Conservatives came to power in 1984, three very scary figures in the 1984–85 national accounts faced them: a national debt of $210 billion, an annual budgetary deficit of $38 billion, and an annual program deficit of $16 billion. As a country we had to pay interest every year on the $210 billion, and we were continuing to add to that debt because our expenditures were $38 billion greater than our revenues. Not only were we paying the entire interest bill on the debt with ever-increasing amounts of borrowed money, but in that last Liberal budget, $16 billion of government programs were also being financed with borrowings: that is, we were taking in $16 billion *less* in taxes than we needed to pay for them. Put another way, fully 32 cents of every tax dollar received by the federal government was going to pay for interest, not programs, and this proportion of taxes going to interest would continue to rise.

Now, there is nothing wrong with debt. Most of us have some, usually in the form of a mortgage. However, to determine how big a mortgage we can afford to take out, we look at our income and expenses, and calculate how much of the cash flow is available to service debt. If we cannot pay the mortgage out of income and start borrowing to make those payments, eventually our debt costs will lead us to bankruptcy. What holds for our personal finances is no less true for a government, which must be able to service its debt from revenues while still paying for all the other necessities of life — in the case of government, the cost of programs.

There are only two ways to get out of such a financial hole: spend less money, or earn more. The approach of the government after 1984 was to do both. Many people who objected to cutting expenses by cutting programs argued that it wasn't social programs, for example, that had caused the problem, and they were right. To a considerable degree, the ten-fold growth of the national debt during the Trudeau years was a result of declining revenues, largely resulting from changes to the tax system brought in when John Turner was finance minister. But the new government couldn't simply jack up taxes to solve the problem. Just to break even, at the current level of expenditure, the government would have had to increase tax revenues by $38 billion annually. Raising taxes to that degree would have been counterproductive since it would have encouraged businesses to relocate south of the border. Mike Wilson did raise taxes (which annoyed a lot of Conservative voters) and closed many of the loopholes that reduced revenues to government. But the best way to raise revenues is through economic growth, and the government had to tread carefully not to kill the goose (the economy) that would lay the golden egg (tax revenues).

So to stop the growth of the debt, the government also had to lower expenditures. The sooner the government tackled this unpleasant task, the less of it would have to be done. By the time I came to Ottawa, the government had managed to turn the $16-billion operating deficit into a $13-billion operating surplus, meaning that the first $13 billion of interest payments were now being paid by revenues, not by borrowed money. But while the annual deficit had been stabilized, it had not been eliminated, and the debt was still growing. The sooner the budget could be balanced so that the government no longer needed to borrow money to meet its annual expenditures, the sooner interest costs could be stabilized and the increased revenues from economic growth could go to paying down debt, lowering taxes, or spending more on programs — whatever the priorities of Canadians were at any time. One thing was for certain, though: the longer it took to deal with the issue, the more at risk government programs would become. That the left, who are most devoted to spending by government, did not see this peril and were not out on the barricades demanding an end to this march to bankruptcy truly perplexed me.

The 1989 budget was at first overshadowed by the events surrounding its leak by Global Television reporter Doug Small. Wilson responded to the leak by releasing the budget the night before it was to be tabled in the House. The controversy surrounding the leak delayed a more substantive response to the document itself.

Much was expected of this first budget of a new mandate. The response from many Conservatives was disappointment. When the B.C. ministers held a conference call to discuss the budget with members of the party executive in the province, we heard almost uniform criticism that it didn't go far enough to restrain expenditures. In rereading the briefing papers put out by PC Caucus Services on the spending cuts, I am struck now by how apologetic they are, emphasizing how much we were spending, rather than how much we were saving to reduce the deficit. With all the cuts, overall government spending was still up over the year before. I shared the concern about whether we had done enough, but consoled myself with Mike Wilson's prediction of an end to the need to borrow by 1993–94.

What I remember best from this time, however, is the unrelenting attack from the opposition and various groups around the country about the cuts that *were* made. Reductions to VIA Rail's ridiculous subsidy became the rallying point for every critic of the government. Reducing VIA's annual subsidy of just over half a billion(!) dollars in 1989 was seen as the moral equivalent of exterminating the beaver. The controversy actually harmed VIA because it led to the erroneous impression in Canada and elsewhere that one could no longer travel across the country by rail. The VIA Rail controversy was an example of politics gone mad. Instead of a rational public debate about how much money Canadians should borrow to maintain passenger rail service in the face of increasing preference for travel by car, bus, and airplane, people argued for passenger rail as if there had been no developments in transportation since Confederation. The fact that railroads continue to be important carriers of freight was lost on those who determined that since Canada was built on the railway, passenger rail should be preserved no matter how much debt future generations would have to pay for it. An exhausting ideological battle over the national soul developed over a sensible proposal to help get our children out of debt. Several years later, when reports about the improvement in VIA Rail's operations as a result of its being put on a more self-sustaining commercial footing received minimal coverage, I felt really angry.

After the 1988 election, the regular policy committees of cabinet had been simplified and reduced in number. Any minister could attend any cabinet committee meeting (except Priorities and Planning, and Operations), and if an item that touched your portfolio came up in a committee of which you were not a member, of course you would be there. But otherwise there was a lot of material to wade through, so ministers tended to stick to their own assignments. I was appointed to the Human Resources Committee and to the Special Committee of Council, among others.

The Special Committee met regularly every Thursday morning (unlike policy committees, which met less often) and was chaired by the deputy prime minister, Don Mazankowski. "Maz" was the PM's right-hand man and well respected for his judgment and enormous capacity for work. This particular committee vetted all the regulations to be passed by cabinet and dealt with a wide variety of other issues, including grievances in the Canadian Forces and criminal pardons. The work was interesting but not usually earth-shaking. However, every once in a while something would come up that raised a red flag. Serving on Special Committee provided an overview of the business of government. For that reason, it was good training for new ministers and a good way for the deputy prime minister to see what kind of political judgment and common sense a minister had.

In addition to the permanent policy committees of cabinet, ad hoc committees were formed from time to time to deal with particular issues. In 1989, I served on the Ad Hoc Committee on Sales Tax Reform, which began meeting in February in long evening meetings about twice a month, chaired by Michael Wilson. The initial briefings explained the rationale for a multi-stage value-added tax, and I began to read as much as I could about tax policy. It is an extremely important subject for a legislator because in creating tax regimes, the "how" is as important as the "how much."

The Goods and Services Tax (GST) was not a new tax but the proposed replacement for the Manufacturers Sales Tax, also called the Federal Sales Tax (FST), implemented in 1924. The FST had come under increasing attack as economically counterproductive and unfair. Simple abolition without a replacement source of revenue was not an option, however, since the FST brought in $16 billion annually. Replacing the FST was not a partisan goal of the Conservatives. Numerous inquiries and royal commissions had recommended replacement. Mike Wilson's proposal to finally deal with the problem was in line with a study by the Liberal-dominated Senate, which had recommended replacing the FST with a multistage value-added tax, which is what the GST is.

The old FST was levied on our manufactured goods, but, because of the way it was applied, it was very difficult to trace. It was not supposed to apply to exports, but in fact, it was causing an estimated price increase in exports of about 1 per cent, a not insignificant penalty in a competitive export market. At the same time, since it could not be applied to imports, it was actually giving imports an advantage over domestic products. Over the years the FST regime had grown so complex that by 1989 there were no fewer than 22,000 special rules and exceptions to it. Courts were jammed with cases from companies challenging the applicability of the tax. And the FST was based on out-of-date assumptions. When it was put in place, manufacturing was the mainstay of the economy, and services were of lesser value. Now the proportions had reversed: manufacturing constituted only a third of Canadian economic activity and the FST-exempt service sector accounted for two-thirds. To put it succinctly, the FST was an eroding source of government revenue, it unfairly burdened the manufacturing third of the economy, it penalized our exports, and it was a silent killer of Canadian jobs. It had to go.

The GST is a tax on consumption. Although some people believe that consumption taxes are inherently regressive, experience in other countries has shown that, properly designed, such taxes can actually be more progressive than income taxes. Unlike income tax, the GST does not penalize savers (thus encouraging the growth of capital pools available for productive investment) and is difficult to evade or "shelter" from. It can be applied to imports, thus putting them on an equal footing with domestic products, and can be easily removed from exports. Its biggest downside is that it is complex to administer, although its complexity allows for fairness of application. The committee saw no trouble-free replacement for the FST; the GST was the best of the unappealing alternatives.

The rate of the GST would depend on what it applied to, and the extent of rebates to low-income people. Ideally, such a tax should be at a low rate and apply to everything. However, before the 1988 election, NDP leader Ed Broadbent had attacked the government for its proposal to "tax food," and the political decision was made to exempt food and other necessities. Although this exemption reduced the amount of political flak, it considerably complicated the design and application of the tax. The rate originally proposed was 9 per cent, but eventually the components were refitted to permit a rate of 7 per cent. The GST became one of the most unpopular initiatives of the Mulroney government, and the opposition parties played the political value of an unpopular tax for all it was worth. Although promising to abolish the GST during the 1993 election, the Liberals appear to have become reconciled to it, since they haven't unveiled any plans for changes beyond the possibility of a new name.

One of the chief tasks of the GST committee was to make the huge number of specific decisions and recommendations necessary to complete the design of the GST. We examined an array of expenditures in the grey area to determine whether they should be exempt from the tax. One important factor to consider was the basic cost of the item, in order to determine whether the GST would be such a significant addition to the price as to be a disincentive to purchase. One evening we considered whether the degree of necessity of personal hygiene products warranted making them tax-exempt. Among the items on this list was condoms. Lowell Murray remembers hearing my voice, the only female one present, inquire from the end of the table, "How much does a package of condoms cost?" There was a prolonged silence broken by the voice of Defence Minister Bill McKnight, "Well ... it's been so long ... I just don't remember."

When members of the public watch the proceedings of the House on television, they are often surprised by the sparse attendance. That is because much of the work of MPs is done in committees. Ministers spend less time in the House than other MPs, but since there must be at least two ministers in the House when it is sitting, each of us was assigned about two hours every week. If we couldn't make it, we had to arrange for a replacement from among our colleagues. The one time most ministers and MPs were in the House was for the daily Question Period, which begins most days at 2:15 and lasts for forty-five minutes.

Every day, ministers were briefed by their legislative assistants on the major issues that might form the subject of a question in the House. In addition, each minister had a briefing book with notes on both urgent and ongoing issues. As a junior minister, I took a question only if Pierre Cadieux was absent. I was briefed by Pierre's legislative assistant, Suzanne Goyette, either with Pierre, if he was there, or by myself. Ministers also met in the cabinet room at 1:30 for Question Period strategy, chaired by the deputy prime minister or the House leader, during which we would review issues to ensure that ministers were prepared and to clarify who would be dealing with them if they included more than one department's responsibilities. I attended QP strategy faithfully and sat in the House with my trusty binder every day, but there wasn't much happening of a controversial nature in DIAND, and when there was, Pierre took the questions. He was good at it, and besides, ministers like the practice. When you are peppered with questions, as I would later discover, you become quite comfortable answering them.

In the thirteen months I was minister of state for Indian affairs, I answered only two questions in the House, and neither was a DIAND question. The Canadian Aboriginal Economic Development Strategy, or CAEDS, was administered not by Indian Affairs but rather by the Department of Industry, under the supervision of Tom Hockin, the minister of state for small business. On two occasions, when Tom wasn't in the House, questions were asked that the minister replacing him didn't realize were his. Everyone looked at me to answer them because Pierre wasn't in the House either.

On the first occasion, looking up absently to the Speaker's gallery, I saw a delegation of aboriginal people. They could have been from anywhere; introductions of guests weren't made until after Question Period. If I had known that they were a delegation from the government of the Northwest Territories, I might have been more alert. Because Pierre had taken responsibility for the North, I had had no opportunity to travel there or meet members of the territorial governments, so I didn't recognize anyone. Members of the opposition often asked questions for the benefit of visiting delegations. In this case Jack Anawak, Liberal MP for Nunatsiaq, had asked the CAEDS question. My colleagues started looking at me, urging me to reply.

I didn't have a clue about the answer, but remembered seeing something in my QP book about a recent meeting of provincial and territorial leaders in Edmonton, where it had been stated that the North had the highest rate of economic growth in Canada. Shaking like a leaf, I stood up and, barely controlling my voice, answered by repeating this declaration of confidence in the northern economy. As I looked up at the now attentive faces in the Speaker's Gallery, I heard the word "Canada" come out of my mouth as "cannibal." I quickly corrected myself and sat down, red-faced, to the applause and shouts of my colleagues. I couldn't tell if they had heard my mistake or were just giving me the usual good-natured response that accompanies the first question answered in the House. I was in torment until the "blues" arrived at my office later that afternoon. The blues, so called because they are printed on blue paper, are the unofficial transcript of remarks made in the House. Members can correct their comments, if necessary, before the official Hansard is produced. I was relieved to see that the Hansard reporter had corrected my slip, but the experience was a blow to my dreams of being a silver-tongued orator in Parliament.

I am often asked about my experience as a woman on the Hill. Forty-one women were elected to Parliament in 1988, twenty-six of them Progressive Conservatives. Sitting in the House, I thought of what it must have been like for women like Agnes Macphail, Ellen Fairclough, and Flora MacDonald, all of whom were, in their time, lone women MPs. When Pat Carney went to Ottawa in 1980 and began challenging the rule that would have paid the travel costs of a "spousal equivalent" but would not allow her as a single parent to use that allowance for a child, she was told she should be grateful that women MPs were now paid the same as men! By 1988, the House was much less the boys' club it had been, although it still had a way to go. The presence of forty-one women made the sound of a woman's voice nothing out of the ordinary. There were now convenient washrooms for women MPs and a daycare centre on the Hill. The more regular hours instituted by the previous Parliament were a boon to the family life of all MPs. The biggest challenge for women MPs was to bring the reality of women's lives into policy-making.

One of the downsides of going into cabinet right away was that I didn't often have an opportunity to interact with the women in the opposition. Private members meet regularly across party lines in the work of parliamentary committees. I didn't sit on these committees, and my schedule as a minister limited my time for casual socializing. Still, I was determined to be an advocate for women when I could. I believe that if we are to create understanding between women and men, women have to be able to speak in their own voices, to articulate what life as a woman is like. An opportunity to do this arose during a cabinet discussion in 1989 about the abortion legislation that had been proposed to replace the law struck down the previous year by the Supreme Court. One of my male colleagues, who was anti-choice, suggested that we should be emphasizing the importance of birth control as part of any legislative package to show our commitment to reducing the demand for abortion. I replied that, while I obviously had no objection to making information about contraception more widely available, I was concerned that we not create the impression that only women who were careless about contraception found themselves with unwanted pregnancies. I reminded my colleagues that many unplanned pregnancies were taken to term by women who had access to abortion. Many families refer lovingly to the last child as "our little surprise" or "our happy accident." I could see Pierre Cadieux looking at me with an interested expression and nodding; everyone, in fact, seemed to be listening.

I then went on to speak more personally. "There is," I said, "no universally safe and effective method of contraception." I explained that I was a married woman of child-bearing age, but I was too old to use birth control pills safely, and even they have a ratio of failure. An intrauterine device had led to scarring of one of my Fallopian tubes and I wasn't keen to go that route again. As I was susceptible to urinary tract infections, diaphragms weren't practical for me because they compress the urethra and have to be left in place for several hours after intercourse, thus increasing the risk of infection. To be effective, they must be fitted properly and used with spermicide, and not be in the drawer at the crucial moment. Condoms, when they don't break, are reasonably effective, but many men don't like to use them and they are no good if you don't have one handy. "And of course," I added, "we all know that old joke: What do you call people who use the rhythm method? Parents!" The point was, I argued, that like most women, I had taken responsibility for my fertility for most of my life. Although I couldn't conceive when I wanted to, no doctor had ever been able to tell me that I could never conceive, and so birth control was still a concern for me. I concluded by saying that contraception was much more complicated than it might seem, and that we should not assume that unwanted pregnancies occur only when women fail to use it.

There was a moment of stunned silence; then the prime minister thanked me and we moved on. Barbara McDougall, who was the senior woman in cabinet as minister of employment and immigration and minister responsible for the status of women, passed me a note with a heart on it. As we left the meeting, Charlie Mayer, the minister for grains and oilseeds, shyly passed me a note expressing his appreciation for my candour and saying he had learned a great deal from my comments. A few others said the same thing to me directly. What did the others think? I have no idea. Perhaps they thought nothing of it or were horrified. But I said to myself, I didn't come here not to be who I am. I respected my colleagues and wanted them to understand how the whole question of birth control seems to a woman. It helped that there were six women around the table, not just one or two.

Every member of Parliament is faced with the challenge of keeping in touch with people at home in the riding. At our first meeting of cabinet, the prime minister had warned us about the importance of not being complacent about this just because we were in cabinet. All MPs have a budget for creating and mailing regular "householders" to constituents. I also used to try to do interviews live with radio stations in Vancouver and telephone interviews with the print media. But the half-hour per month of cable-TV time made available to every member proved one of my most effective communications tools. I found that if I could come up with programs with good production values, the Vancouver cable station would replay them several times a month. We discovered that for very little money we could hire a camera crew from the cable station in Vancouver or Ottawa to film in interesting locations, and we used video clips from the House of Commons. For my first "Ottawa Notebook" we took the camera into the chamber to give viewers a close-up look at the House as it looks to MPs. Many people in Vancouver have never travelled to Ottawa, so I tried to make Parliament and the city come alive for them.

It was fun trying to think of imaginative ways to convey information. When the Meech Lake Accord began to heat up, I did a special program filmed at the Meech Lake conference centre. On Remembrance Day, 1989, my father and I both laid wreaths at the cenotaph ceremony in Vancouver. Dad was national president of the Army, Navy and Air Force Veterans of Canada that year, and I was the senior federal politician in Vancouver and so laid the wreath for the Government of Canada. Before the ceremony, I filmed an interview with my father in front of the war memorial on Cordova Street. That interview and the footage of Dad and me laying our wreaths, combined with footage from the Peace Tower in Ottawa and an interview with Mike Ferrabee about his summer as a tour guide at the Vimy Ridge memorial in France, made a Remembrance Day program that received many favourable comments. We reran it for several years around November 11.

When I look at my schedules from 1989, I am struck by how much travelling I did — back and forth between Ottawa and Vancouver, and around the country on ministerial business and speaking engagements. One of the reasons was that Michael and I had identified two major priorities for that year, land claims and Meech Lake. The rumblings that would eventually lead to the failure of the Meech Lake Accord to be ratified had begun in earnest in 1989. Senator Lowell Murray, who as minister for federal-provincial relations was responsible for the Meech Lake file, told Michael that he was comfortable with the well-received speeches I had been giving on the subject and urged me to speak often on the subject. Meech Lake now began to eat up more of my time.

The Meech Lake Accord had been negotiated in 1987 while I was still an MLA in B.C. The Vander Zalm government had been one of the signatories, and I was supportive of the accord personally. The patriation of the Canadian Constitution and the adoption of the Charter of Rights and Freedoms had taken place in 1982, while I was in law school. One of the troubling outcomes of that process that I began to notice throughout the 1980s was what I called the "fetish for codification." From a country that had relied largely on an uncodified, common-law approach to rights, we were becoming a society where not only were people more litigious in support of their rights, not necessarily a bad thing, but people seemed to see some magic in the reduction of those rights to black and white in a constitution, at the expense of the social, legislative, and attitudinal ways of assuring them. Having taught about American government, I knew well that constitutional formulations were no guarantee of particular outcomes. Constitutionalism is no substitute for the social and legislative commitments that express and preserve values.

The purpose of the Meech Lake Accord was to address Quebec's concerns about the patriation of 1982. For the first time in Canadian history, the Constitution could be amended in Canada, and this necessitated that an amending formula be codified within it. It had been a tradition in Canada that no significant amendment would be sought over the objection of Quebec. Although that right of veto did not exist in law, the patriated document contained an amending formula in which Quebec's practical veto was confined to issues requiring the unanimous consent of the provinces. Furthermore, the Charter had serious implications for the exercise of provincial powers and was imposed over Quebec's objections. From Quebec's perspective, patriation had resulted in a change in Quebec's traditional relationship to the federation.

It was not just Quebec that objected to the implications of the new regime; other provinces, including British Columbia, were concerned that the Charter might restrict their ability to legislate in the area of social policy, their primary and most expensive area of jurisdiction. The "notwithstanding" clause, allowing provinces to exempt legislation from certain provisions of the Charter for five-year periods, was the compromise reached to allay the concerns of those provinces and win their acceptance of the patriation package. Although Trudeau would later declare the clause that made patriation politically possible "an abomination," the truth is that it did not lead to widespread evasion of the norms of the Charter. The constraints on governments were not legal, but social and political.

In 1981, in the first provincial election after the intent of Trudeau's patriation process was known, Quebeckers indicated their opposition by re-electing what had been thought to be the mortally wounded separatist government of René Lévesque. Quebeckers had rejected "sovereignty-association" in the referendum of 1980 because Trudeau had promised them "renewed federalism," but the patriation package was not what they had had in mind. In the first federal election following patriation, 1984, the Liberals were routed from their traditional Quebec stronghold by the Conservatives, despite the departure of Trudeau.

The Meech Lake Accord was designed to reassure Quebec that the new constitutional order in Canada did not weaken its ability to preserve the French language and culture within the province. Chiefly this was to be done by recognizing, as an interpretive principle in the Constitution, that Quebec constituted a "distinct society" within Canada. In my view this added very little substantively to the Constitution, since Quebec's distinctiveness had been recognized by the courts since Confederation. But in this new era of the fetish for codification, and in light of the dramatic new powers conferred on the courts by the Charter, Quebeckers wanted it "in black and white." It was a symbol of enormous importance to them.

The value of Meech Lake, as I saw it, was that it bought time to allow the Quiet Revolution, the social transformation that had begun in Quebec in 1960, to be completed. People commonly assume, erroneously, that the period in which they happen to be living represents the final phase or conclusion of a historical epoch. So dramatic have been the changes in Quebec since 1960 — the secularization of society, the precipitous drop in the birth rate, the transformation of education, and the rise of a francophone business class, among other factors — that it is easy to believe that the major changes are over. I think not.

The consciousness-raising of the linguistic majority in Quebec in the 1960s, like the political movements among women and racial minorities in those years, resulted in an initial reaction of rage towards and distancing from the identified "oppressor." This sharing of the metaphor of liberation could be seen in the works of such Quebeckers as Pierre Vallières, whose book *White Niggers of America* borrowed explicitly from the imagery of the American civil rights movement. How that initial anger plays out varies from person to person. Whether one becomes a "separatist," holding out no hope for co-existence with the oppressor, or simply a more determined seeker after equality depends on a whole range of circumstances.

In Quebec, this playing out of initial anger was complicated by the fact that while it was easiest to identify the oppressor as the "anglo," the reality was more complex. To a considerable degree Quebeckers had been held back by their own elites, as well as by the ultramontane wing of the Catholic church. Many of the intellectuals in the vanguard of the Quiet Revolution were also professors at Catholic universities (there being no secular francophone educational institutions at that time) and so, while the path being mapped for the future was a modern, secular, and even anti-clerical one, the version of history that had supported the *ancien régime* by demonizing the anglos remained largely in place. That anti-anglo view lies at the core of the ideology of Quebec separatism and, unfortunately, is still reflected in the way history is taught in Quebec schools. As Quebeckers come to experience Canada outside Quebec, however, either directly or through the media, the hold of that perspective on their imaginations is gradually weakened. Without this change of perspective, the future of Quebec in Canada is doubtful. I supported Meech because I thought that if we could buy another twenty years to complete the opening up of Quebec, the result would be a strong, united, vibrant Canada.

This happy ending would not come naturally. It would require serious effort and open-mindedness outside Quebec as well. I believed that Pierre Trudeau had been the unwitting architect of division in the country. He had attempted to address the cultural concerns of Quebeckers by giving them what they hadn't asked for — power in Ottawa — in a way that increasingly alienated the west: hence the arrival in Ottawa of Preston Manning and Lucien Bouchard as the leaders of both disaffected constituencies in 1993. I strongly supported the policy of bilingualism, but not only for its stated rationale of ensuring that francophone

Canadians would have full service from their national government. I also believed that the creation of even a small French-speaking population in the other provinces and territories was essential to enable the reality of "the rest of Canada" to permeate Quebec, and to enable anglophones outside Quebec to understand the distinct culture there. I also agreed entirely with Trudeau's hostility to the nationalist ideology that underlies Quebec separatism. Despite the efforts of Lucien Bouchard and Jacques Parizeau to put a fig-leaf of respectability over it by insisting that it is not an "ethnic" but a "territorial" nationalism, statements by Parizeau, Bouchard, and the temporarily muzzled Pierre Bourgault in the 1995 referendum demonstrated the utter falsity of that assertion. That ideology rests on the myth of the "humiliation" of Quebeckers. Unfortunately, as Robert Stanfield pointed out in 1982, with the abandonment of the conventional Quebec veto on serious constitutional change, "Canada had given the separatists a stick to beat it with."

Meech Lake was not perfect, but it was a bridge, and I thought it was enormously important to Canada that it be ratified. One of the provinces showing signs of reluctance to ratify was Manitoba. On October 21, I was the guest speaker before an audience of 1,500 in Winnipeg at a fundraising dinner for Premier Gary Filmon's Tories. It was two days before the legislative committee was due to report on the Meech Lake Accord, and the situation was delicate. I wanted to avoid any suggestion of federal government interference in the provincial process, so I spoke strongly about the country without mentioning the "M" word. One person described my speech as "Meech Lake without Meech Lake." When the prime minister and the premiers met in Ottawa on November 10, I was on call as camera fodder for the closing afternoon session. At the time, with the first ministers' meeting ending on an upbeat note, I felt encouraged and believed that a constitutional crisis would be averted. Nonetheless, I accepted as many of the growing number of invitations to speak on Meech Lake as I could. It soon became clear that the unity of the November premiers' meeting would be short-lived.

Howard and I flew to Vancouver for Christmas, and in early January 1990 we took a French immersion course in Quebec City. Budget day was to be Tuesday, February 20, and Michael and I had decided that I should be in Vancouver that week so that I could speak at a conference of the Young Presidents' Association in Whistler and then do direct, live media on the budget.

At about 8:30 Monday morning, I picked up the phone in Vancouver to hear the familiar voice of Stanley Hartt.

"The prime minister wants all the ministers in their seats in the House during the budget speech," he said.

"But I've arranged a whole week of budget-related speaking and media here," I protested. "How do you expect us to get re-elected out here if we're never around for the serious issues?" I knew that it wasn't a matter of an empty seat on the cabinet benches because other MPs always moved forward to sit in the seats of ministers who weren't in the House. My seat was nowhere near Michael Wilson's, so I wouldn't be visible on the television screen anyway.

In the same calm voice, Stanley went on, "No, the prime minister wants all the ministers in the House for the budget on Tuesday. He'd also like to have a little chat with you on Thursday afternoon."

"Can I get the six o'clock flight out of Ottawa on Thursday?" I asked. "I'm speaking to the Victoria Chamber of Commerce on Friday about Meech."

"You won't be able to make your Friday speaking engagement," he replied. Then he added, "And what's more, you will be so happy, rocks will melt in your mouth."

The penny dropped.

"My bottom will be in my seat tomorrow," I replied.

As soon as we hung up, I called Michael.

"I have to come back to Ottawa. Stanley Hartt just called. The PM wants us all back for the budget and he wants to talk to me on Thursday afternoon. There's going to be a shuffle."

"Shit!" replied Michael. We decided that I would take the red-eye that night so that I wouldn't have to cancel any of the day's events. I arrived in Ottawa early the next morning and went home to sleep since I wasn't needed until QP strategy at 1:30. There was a full cabinet meeting after Question Period, followed by the budget speech in the House at 4:30. My staff couldn't see why I was so philosophical about being called back after all the arrangements we'd made for Vancouver and Victoria.

Michael and I tried to figure out where I might be going. A few weeks earlier, Harry Swain had said that he'd heard solicitor general mentioned as a possibility for me. Mike decided to go to the parliamentary library to pick up a clipping file on SolGen so that we could see what the issues were. In order to cover his tracks, he copied the clipping files on the Justice Department, too, then threw them away since we were certain that Doug Lewis wouldn't be going anywhere. On Thursday, Michael and I had lunch together and fretted a bit more. The suspense was terrible. At 3:30 Pierre Cadieux and I had a briefing with officials. Shortly after we began, he was called away while we all pretended we didn't know what was up. At 4:30 a call came for me from the PM's assistant, asking me to be at 24 Sussex Drive at 5:15. This time I knew he didn't mean the next day.

As before, the process of shuffling the cabinet was surrounded by great secrecy. However, as a minister I now had that greatest of all intelligence sources, my driver. As we drove into the driveway at 24 Sussex, André said, "There's Mr. Siddon's car, and there's Mr. Andre's car." With these tidbits I could narrow down the possibilities, but not much. I was ushered into the sunroom at the back of the house and offered a glass of mineral water, which I declined out of nervousness. I could hear people moving about in the hall but couldn't identify any voices. Then I was asked to come and sit in the living room. I was so jumpy, I sat on the sofa as if I were trying not to wrinkle the upholstery. At 5:40 the prime minister came rushing in. "I'm sorry, Kim," he said breathlessly, "there's a vote at six and we've got to go to the House. We'll have to talk in the car."

I followed the PM and joined him in his car. Unlike my simple sedan, the prime minister's car was a limousine with a partition between the passenger section and the driver so that he could have private conversations. "Well, look, Kim," he began, "I'm having a bit of a shuffle tomorrow ..." I can't remember all he said. We were being escorted through Ottawa by police cars with their lights flashing, and it was all a bit disconcerting. I do remember he told me that I was to go onto Priorities and Planning, that I would be the political minister for British Columbia, and that I was to be sworn in as minister of justice and attorney general of Canada. I wanted to throw my arms into the air and shout "Yahoo!" but was afraid of injuring the prime-ministerial mandible.

I was brought down to earth by what the prime minister said next. He was concerned that when the media saw that I was to be political minister for B.C., they would start to say that I was now the most powerful woman in cabinet. He was afraid that Barbara McDougall would be hurt by that sort of speculation. She had been going through a terrible time because of the illness and death of her younger sister. For that reason, the PM was going to accede to Barbara's long-standing request and relieve her of the responsibility for status of women. She would continue as minister of employment and immigration, a very powerful and important position that, along with her cabinet committee assignments, was certainly not eclipsed by my promotion. The prime minister's concern about Barbara's feelings was a reflection of his insight and thoughtfulness. (Fortunately, he was wrong about the media. They were so struck by my becoming the first woman minister of justice, and especially after such a short time in Ottawa, that they didn't notice the political minister part of the announcement and never, to my knowledge, made comparisons between Barbara and me on the matter of clout.)

When we arrived at the Parliament Buildings, I went in ahead of the prime minister so that no one would notice that we had arrived together. Michael was waiting for me in the lobby, but I could only smile at him because I had to go in for the vote. When I came out, we made our way to the elevator that connects the Centre Block to the West Block tunnel. We were alone in the elevator, so I quickly said, "P&P, political minister for B.C., minister of justice and attorney general." We hugged each other and jumped up and down. Then, as the elevator stopped, we regained our composure and walked out towards my office as if nothing had happened.

Howard was waiting for me in my office. Like me, he was stunned but pleased. When we called Diana Lam, she said she wasn't going to miss this and decided to take the red-eye to Ottawa so she could be there for the swearing-in. I called my parents and my sister and they, too, were thrilled. To avoid leaks, Mike and I decided that we would not advise the rest of the office but would have a staff meeting first thing in the morning. As I told my team the next day that I was on my way to Rideau Hall to become the first woman to be sworn in as minister of justice, there were a few tears.

Since this swearing-in involved fewer positions than the year before, it took place in a small reception room at Rideau Hall. Pierre Cadieux became solicitor general, and Tom Siddon and Shirley Martin replaced us at Indian Affairs. Doug Lewis, who was moving from Justice to Transport, had thoughtfully invited his deputy minister, John Tait, to meet me. When I came out of Rideau Hall after the ceremony, there was a slight sprinkle of snow. I walked over to the microphone to answer a few questions from the media. In a picture published in the *Ottawa Citizen*, the snow gave a luminous quality to the scene, and the expression on my face captured exactly my feeling of honour and joy. As a welcoming gift, the Justice officials gave me a framed copy of that picture, which I hung in my office to remind me, when things got rough, how happy and full of wonder I was on that first day.

8

BEING MINISTER OF JUSTICE

"SO HOW DO YOU be minister of justice?" I asked John Tait, the afternoon of the swearing-in. I had very little idea of what the minister of justice did. John would later recall that question with amusement.

To my surprise, it took me very little time to figure out what I wanted to do as justice minister. My appointment was a major turning point for me: the period of apprenticeship was over, and I was now in charge of my own department. I had to decide whether I was going to be a proactive minister, or just concentrate on minding the store. As I read through the briefings that laid out the scope of the department's work, ideas began to form rapidly in my mind. It was as if all that I had learned, thought, and felt until then was crystallizing into a sense of what needed to be done and how.

With my move to Justice, two new people came into my life who quickly won my admiration, respect, and friendship: John Tait, a tall, balding man with a warm but reserved manner, and Myles Kirvan, an outgoing fellow with a wicked smile. John and I soon found that we think very much alike. Because neither of us wanted to do the other's job, ours became a great working partnership. I inherited Myles as chief of staff from Doug Lewis and was grateful when he agreed to stay on for another six months or so to give Michael Ferrabee, who continued as executive assistant for the time being, a chance to learn the ropes.

All the judges loved Myles, and I soon came to see why. He is one of those people who don't know how to be anything but a straight arrow. John thought he walked on water. Myles and I developed a real friendship based on trust, and I appreciated his many qualities, not least of which was his wry way of seeing into the heart of an issue.

A couple of weeks after taking office, I met with Mike Ferrabee and John one Saturday morning to try to define the main themes I wanted to pursue as minister. I had been mulling over how best to describe my three priorities. As the minister responsible for crafting the criminal law, I wanted to articulate my commitment to "the protection of society." "Fairness in the relationship between citizens and the government" captured a second theme. This involved equalizing the relationship between individuals and a powerful state, and giving citizens ways to keep government accountable. The third theme, in many ways the most important to me, seemed more difficult to put into words. "I want the justice system to serve all Canadians," I said. "I want each Canadian to see himself or herself reflected in it. I don't want people like women or aboriginal people to be pressing their noses against the glass, separated from the system by invisible but very real barriers." I used the term "inclusive justice" but wasn't sure that was the best way of expressing what I meant. We finally decided to talk of "inclusive justice" until we could think of a better term. We never did. The words proved to be more than adequate in describing a vision of the Canadian justice system and are still used by those who share it.

I have always welcomed experiences that force me to grow. Personal philosophies develop not in a vacuum but only when we bounce our sensibilities off real life and ideas. It's one of the reasons I love the theatre so much. The best plays or movies engage the mind and feelings, and leave you deeply touched and moved — not always in the sense of being emotionally moved, as we usually think of it, but moved to a different vantage point on your life, a different perspective, so that you discover insights you haven't consciously articulated before. Being minister of justice and attorney general of Canada was a non-stop experience of growth and self-discovery. It was one of the best periods of my life, and if I entered it somewhat uncertain, still groping to define my vision of governance, I left it feeling strong, formed, and full of passionate conviction.

Not only did I have a whole new set of portfolio responsibilities, but as the minister responsible for giving legal advice to the government, I would find myself at the centre of a number of important issues in areas very far from the policy areas of the department itself. My first year in Justice also brought me face to face with the unpredictability of government. By the end of the year, I would be a veteran of crises I couldn't have predicted in my wildest dreams on that snowy February morning.

There was a certain magical feeling about being minister of justice, which I never entirely lost. Justice is a special portfolio because, with rare exceptions, the minister is a lawyer and so shares a professional connection with most of the people who work in the department. That sense of collegiality is unique to Justice.

Among my earliest meetings was one with the Right Honourable Brian Dickson, chief justice of Canada. Myles, who at that time was judicial affairs adviser as well as chief of staff, accompanied me to the Supreme Court of Canada. I was a great admirer of Chief Justice Dickson. When I was in law school, I had written a paper on the law of libel and slander and, in particular, the defence of fair comment. The law in that area had been established in a case called *Cherneskey v. Armadale*. In my view, the 1979 ruling of the Supreme Court of Canada in the case had been wrong. My hero, Mr. Justice Dickson, as he then was, had dissented and I had been a fan since that time. It seemed incredible to be sitting in his corner office in the Supreme Court building discussing issues with him as minister of justice. Chief Justice Dickson was scheduled to retire in June of 1990, and I remember telling him how much I regretted that we would have such a short time to work together. In the months that followed, he was wonderful to me.

When I became justice minister, I worried that, just seven years out of law school, six years at the bar, I wasn't senior enough in the law to command respect in the job. But I soon felt comfortable working with the departmental lawyers. My job wasn't to give legal advice, it was to ask the right questions, and I sensed that I was doing all right in that department. One advantage I had was that I was the first minister of justice to have attended law school in the era of the Charter of Rights and Freedoms.

It didn't bolster my ego during those first weeks after my appointment to read an article by Ottawa journalist Claire Hoy attacking my legal credentials. Although not a lawyer himself, Hoy had strong opinions of my abilities, or lack thereof. An ardent foe of abortion, he was also furious that a self-proclaimed pro-choicer had now become the minister responsible for the abortion legislation. It struck me as a particularly vicious and mean-spirited article. Myles came into my office and sat quietly while I fretted. "Why do I need this?" I complained. "Why should I or anyone have to take this?" I can't remember my exact words, but I am sure they conveyed a surfeit of self-pity.

"Well," Myles began in his thoughtful tone of voice, "I suppose you're right. You could resign. No one should have to put up with this sort of trash. But, of course, then you just let jerks like the Claire Hoys of this world decide who holds public office."

"You're right!" I said, horrified at the prospect. "The hell with him!"

Any time I was tempted to let a journalist's opinion discourage me, I would think of Myles's words.

The first occasion on which I gowned up as minister of justice was a ceremony in the Supreme Court to mark Chief Justice Dickson's retirement. I had to scramble to retrieve my barrister's robes from a law school friend who had borrowed them. I remember that the president of the Canadian Bar Association was dismayed to find the minister of justice wearing the plain robes of a simple barrister, rather than the silk ones of a Queen's Counsel. It's customary for the minister of justice to be named a QC. Normally this appointment would be made by the federal cabinet, but shortly after my appointment, Myles received a call from B.C. attorney general Bud Smith. He asked if I would be willing to accept a QC from the government of British Columbia. I was very touched. People at home were proud that the first woman attorney general of Canada was from B.C. I said I would be delighted and honoured to "take silk," as the British say, from my own province. However, shortly after making this offer, Bud resigned as attorney general, so there was a delay, and until the formalities were concluded, I wasn't entitled to wear the silk gown of a QC.

When I did receive the appointment, I turned to Matz Wozny Tailors in Vancouver, who had gowned all the Campbell lawyers. I had just picked up the new robes on the day in August that a young photographer, Barbara Woodley, met me at my house to take my photograph. She suggested taking my picture with my cello. I demurred because it had already been done, and I am not a professional cellist. "What about wearing my new robes?" I asked. "No, I did Beverley McLachlin in her robes," came the reply. "Perhaps you could hold them in front of you," she mused. We both realized that holding the robes while I was fully dressed would look silly, but we had no idea at the time that her photo of me, bare-shouldered and holding the robes on a hanger, would become so notorious two years later. In 1994, at an event to launch the National Archives' presentation on Canadian prime ministers, I wasn't surprised to see the famous portrait included in the display. When Pierre Trudeau paused to look at it, I attempted to explain its origins.

"I had just picked up my QC robes," I began.

"Ah," came that familiar nasal voice, "and what were you doing *before* you picked them up?"

The move to Justice dramatically affected the way I was viewed by my colleagues. My promotion was a clear "laying on of hands" by the prime minister and therefore an indication that I was someone to watch. It also meant that there were now two senior women ministers in the cabinet. Before the shuffle, all the women in cabinet, with the exception of Barbara McDougall, had been junior ministers. Of all the women in caucus, Barbara was touted as the most likely to have a shot at becoming leader of the party if the prime minister retired. Even before I went into Justice, some people thought that I might be a contender for leader as well, but that speculation, which seemed highly premature to me, grew considerably after I became justice minister.

As justice minister I found I sometimes had considerable impact on the political lives of my colleagues. The issues I would be dealing with were controversial. As conservatives, we might all have similar views on the role of government in the economy (although I would not want to overstate even this), but we were profoundly divided on issues like abortion, gun control, and gay rights. In all of these areas I had initiatives to shepherd through caucus and Parliament.

As political minister for British Columbia, I was responsible for all appointments in the province. This changed my relationship with the other B.C. MPs, who watched carefully over the first few months to see whether I would try to keep all the appointments for myself, or invite other members to nominate candidates. Benno Friesen, MP for Surrey–White Rock, approached me one day after I had invited the Fraser Valley members to nominate candidates for a position in that area. He wanted to know if I was serious, or if I was just going through the motions. In the previous mandate, he said he had never been invited to make such a nomination, but it seemed to me to be the only democratic way to ensure that competent people were nominated for cabinet approval.

When it came to judicial appointments, there were a few battles, not all of which I won. Coming from British Columbia, I was amused to learn that in parts of Atlantic Canada, a mixed marriage is considered to be one between a Liberal and a Conservative! I soon came to see that this was not a joke and the views of some of my colleagues on the subject of appointments were, to put it mildly, a revelation to me. Fortunately, there was an independent process for vetting candidates for judicial office, which considerably reduced the partisan nature of appointments.

Either in my capacity as justice minister or as senior minister from B.C., or both, I found my presence required at almost all cabinet committees dealing with crisis management. This brought me into much closer contact with my cabinet colleagues. One of my favourite people was Shirley Martin, who had moved into the minister of state's position in Indian Affairs from minister of state for transport in the February shuffle. We had become friends during the previous year while serving on Special Committee of Council but seldom saw each other outside of work. On one rare occasion when we were able to arrange a quiet dinner together, we had a long conversation about how hard it is to form friendships with colleagues. Many parliamentary friendships are between people who knew each other before they became ministers or during periods in opposition. The demands on a minister's time are so great that it's difficult to find time for socializing with a colleague, particularly when your riding is far from Ottawa. In each of my years as an MP, I was in Vancouver more than a hundred days a year. Perhaps because I became so visible as justice minister in Ottawa, people at home had the impression I was in B.C. much less than I was.

In that conversation about ministerial life, Shirley and I agreed that we felt guilty about abandoning our spouses so frequently. Free evenings were first and foremost for family. We both loved our work, which increased the guilt when it took us away from our husbands. My promotion to Justice could not have come at a worse time from the perspective of my marriage, although I didn't realize it at the time.

Howard is an enormously talented lawyer. When I went into cabinet, he discovered that conflict-of-interest rules governing cabinet ministers and their spouses would make it impossible for him to practise at a firm that did government work. This obviously posed a problem in a place like Ottawa. In early 1989, Howard had accepted a job as counsel to the Immigration and Refugee Board, an independent agency. The following year the board decided to send him for French-language training. So at about the same time that I began in Justice, Howard started the one-year public service language-training program. It is an exhausting course and a big departure from the life of a practising professional. It's a bit like going back to high school. Finishing at 4:30 in the afternoon, tired, but without any particular demands on his evening time, Howard found himself alone many weeknights. I tried to set aside long weekends for us to be alone together, and arranged trips to Whistler and the Shaw Festival, and two weeks in Paris at Christmas. But Howard's frustration and loneliness were matched by my growing resentment at what I saw at his lack of initiative in the relationship and his dependence on me to make things happen. As the year progressed, I kept thinking that things would improve once Howard finished his course and returned to work.

The friendships I made in Parliament tended to be with like-minded colleagues, and were forged during hours of deliberation around the cabinet table, and occasionally in each other's ridings. In the summer of 1990, Howard and I visited Benoît Bouchard's riding of Roberval. Like Gilles Loiselle, Benoît was a Quebec colleague whom I came to know well. I was the first anglophone minister he had ever invited to his riding. The occasion was his annual fundraising golf tournament. I don't play golf, so my job was to ride around the course to say hello to the various players. This was a completely francophone group — no English. On the boat ride over from Roberval to Dolbeau, where the golf course was, Benoît talked about the great number of regional expressions in that part of Quebec. For example, he said, when you want to describe someone as very wise and worthy of respect, you describe him as "dadon."

Benoît Bouchard was a unilingual francophone when he arrived in Ottawa in 1984, where he became minister of state to, and best friends with, the unilingual anglophone transport minister, Don Mazankowski. Benoît's progress in English was truly remarkable; his errors were few and, more often than not, amusing. He once complained that there weren't enough "sluts" in the Toronto airport (he meant "slots" for airplanes). It was fun to share his amazement and delight in discovering words such as "nincompoop." Although he came from the most nationalist part of Quebec, he opened his heart to Canada and Canadians from all regions. He fell in love with British Columbia, and British Columbians returned the affection. Later, when he was the health minister and dealing with AIDS strategy, we toured the palliative care ward at St. Paul's Hospital in Vancouver, one of the leading centres for the treatment of AIDS. His compassion was so genuine. We stopped to talk to a patient who asked Benoît if he could help him with anything. Benoît was deeply moved by the fact that this dying man was asking if there was anything he could do for *him*. When I was asked to speak after the golf tournament dinner, I told the people of his constituency how much their MP was admired in my home province, where, I said, people found him "un homme dadon." It brought the house down!

However difficult it may be to form friendships, good relations with caucus colleagues are essential to the achievement of a minister's goals. Caucus solidarity is fundamental to a government's ability to govern. In 1990 I saw very clearly that it is not enough for a party to win an electoral majority to govern the way it wants to. Two factors can limit a majority government's room to manoeuvre — strong public opposition and dissension within caucus. Members of Parliament will not lightly threaten the defeat of their own governing party. But sometimes, if they feel a political realignment is taking place, they may consider abandoning their party to join whatever force emerges from the ashes. This was a scenario that began to unfold for the Conservatives in 1990 as the Reform Party made gains in the west and the Bloc Québécois eroded our support in Quebec. It significantly influenced my ability to pursue my Justice agenda and affected how I set about doing it.

In early April 1990, I drove to Montreal to visit the École Polytechnique, where, on December 6, 1989, Marc Lépine had shot and killed fourteen young women, mostly engineering students. At one point during his murderous rampage he had shouted, "You're all feminists." The killings had horrified the entire country and had led to calls for tighter gun control legislation and for a serious response to the problem of violence against women. I felt very sad as I met the student representatives, who presented me with a petition containing more than 500,000 signatures, calling for tighter gun control.

My predecessor, Doug Lewis, had begun a review of the firearms provisions of the Criminal Code the previous summer, but the Lépine killings had raised the profile and sensitivity of the issue dramatically. Any gun control initiatives on my part would have to be carried forward not only in the emotional climate of the events at the college but also in a caucus facing more than the usual number of strains on its goodwill and solidarity. Myles told me that at some point in the 1970s a document had circulated in the Department of Justice claiming that gun control was the most contentious justice issue in Canada, more divisive even than abortion. I found myself in the unenviable position of being able to make a direct comparison. But as I took over responsibility for the abortion bill, C-43, which had already passed second reading in the House, and for gun control, which was still in the legislative drafting stage, I began to wonder if it was not all academic and if I might not turn out to be the shortest-serving justice minister in Canadian history. The reason was the unravelling of the Meech Lake Accord.

The accord had started to come apart with the election of Frank McKenna in New Brunswick in 1987. Although his predecessor, Richard Hatfield, had been a signatory to the accord, he had not put the required ratifying resolution through the New Brunswick legislature before the election. McKenna, who won every seat, had run on a platform of opposition to the accord. This encouraged Clyde Wells in Newfoundland to rescind his province's ratifying resolution, while Gary Filmon's minority government in Manitoba delayed ratification under the pressure of anti-Meech Liberal leader Sharon Carstairs and NDP leader Gary Doer.

I was a member of the Cabinet Committee on Federal-Provincial Relations, chaired by Senator Lowell Murray. Our job was to consider positions the government could take to enable Meech Lake to be ratified. As we got closer to June 23, the deadline for all the provinces to pass ratifying resolutions, tension grew and some of our Quebec colleagues had difficulty understanding that they were part of the federal government, not the government of Quebec.

Among the criticisms of the accord, particularly among westerners, was that it didn't make specific provision for the reform of the Senate, but simply committed governments to a further set of constitutional meetings on the issue. A belief began to grow that once Quebec got what it wanted — recognition as a "distinct society" — it would stymie reform of the Senate. The accord called for the prime minister to appoint senators from lists provided by the provinces. That provision guaranteed that the federal government would support Senate reform, because the loss of its appointing powers would make the persistence of an appointed body, equal in powers to the House of Commons but over whose membership the government had no control, unacceptable. Both the prime minister and Lowell Murray had given speeches indicating federal government support of an elected Senate.

At an early-morning cabinet committee meeting on April 10, Lucien Bouchard, the political minister for Quebec, arrived with all his Quebec ministerial colleagues. Their mood was far from mellow; they had obviously just been conferring. Marcel Masse, among the most nationalist of the group, seemed particularly truculent, although, in Lowell's words, they were all "loaded for bear." When we began to examine the issue of an elected Senate, Lucien hit the roof. "Why are we discussing this?" he demanded. "Because," replied Lowell calmly, "our leader has committed us to an elected Senate."

Within six weeks, Lucien Bouchard was gone. During the third week of May, he flew to Paris. Once there, he sent a public telegram of congratulations to a meeting of the separatist Parti

Québécois, honouring their founder René Lévesque. Holed up in the city where in happier times he had served as Canada's ambassador to France, he refused to take calls from anyone in the government, including Jean Charest, who had with Lucien's full support chaired a parliamentary committee to consider ways of salvaging the accord and whose report Lucien would blame for his departure.

When he heard about Lucien's telegram, Brian Mulroney exploded. Lowell returned to Ottawa on the May 21 holiday Monday to learn that Lucien was at 24 Sussex Drive with the prime minister. Unwilling to agree to the prime minister's insistence that he apologize for the telegram, Lucien Bouchard resigned. Mulroney would later claim that it was all orchestrated in advance, that Lucien had been plotting his departure for some time and had simply seized the convenient pretext.

Five members of our Quebec caucus and two Liberals joined with Lucien Bouchard to form the Bloc Québécois. It was a stressful time for the remaining Quebec caucus members. Lucien had been the political minister for Quebec and was respected for his intellect and political commitment. His departure was truly shocking because he had been very close to the prime minister. It is not an exaggeration to say that Brian Mulroney created Lucien Bouchard as a politician. Some people in the party were convinced that the PM was grooming Lucien to be his successor. If other ministers had anything negative to say about Lucien, it was that he wouldn't accept the results of cabinet committee processes. If he couldn't get his way, he went directly to the top. The perception was that he usually got what he wanted.

Although I served with Lucien on the cabinet committee that reviewed his early proposals for the Green Plan, I never knew him very well. We spent some time together in 1989 when he came to Vancouver to investigate an oil spill. After we had toured a facility in Stanley Park where birds were being cleaned, we walked along the Stanley Park seawall.

"Is this your constituency?" he asked with some wonderment as we looked at the beautiful vista.

"Yes," I replied proudly. I made some comment about my hope that Quebeckers would see my part of the country as part of their heritage too. But Lucien wasn't really interested in the rest of

Canada. He didn't really understand what Canada outside Quebec was all about.

Lucien's departure was a personal blow to the prime minister. Brian Mulroney has been criticized for bringing so many Quebec nationalists into the Conservative Party and the government. But to be a nationalist in Quebec is not necessarily to be a separatist, and there is no question that Mulroney's goal was to keep Quebec in Canada. The Conservatives had done well outside Quebec, but without access to that 25 per cent of the seats in the House of Commons held by Quebeckers, a majority government was impossible, although Joe Clark had come close in 1979. After the patriation of the Constitution in 1982 without Quebec's agreement, many Quebeckers felt betrayed by Pierre Trudeau. Mulroney's commitment to find a way to bring Quebec into the Constitution "with honour" was attractive to those nationalist Quebeckers who hadn't completely given up on Canada and were looking for a political home.

The extent to which Brian Mulroney was able to evince a sympathy with and understanding of francophone Quebec was brought home to me in a bizarre conversation I once had with Marcel Masse. He explained to me that the reason Mulroney was so much more understanding of French culture in Quebec than Trudeau was that culture is transmitted by the mother, and of course, Trudeau's mother was an anglophone. The implication was that Mrs. Mulroney was French.

"But, Marcel," I said, "as far as I know, Brian Mulroney's mother doesn't speak a word of French."

"Really?" he asked. "Are you sure?"

"Quite sure," I replied. As a young man the prime minister had gone out on his own to learn French and even at Laval law school, he had taken his exams in English. Marcel seemed dumbfounded by this, and I thought it extraordinary that this was news to him, because he'd been a member of Mulroney's government since 1984.

Some legitimate criticisms can be made of Brian Mulroney's position on the constitutional issue. In 1982, he had supported the patriation of the Constitution and had urged Joe Clark to give Trudeau his support. His adoption of the nationalist interpretation of the events of 1982 as a betrayal of Quebec was a complete switch. His use of the expression "bring Quebec back into the Constitution" was also misleading because Quebec was and is bound by the Constitution like every other province.

What cannot be denied, however, is that federal-provincial relations were seriously impeded as a result of Quebec's refusal to participate in federal-provincial meetings from 1982 onwards. Those who support the actions of Trudeau in 1982 point out that his Liberals won seventy-four out of seventy-five Quebec seats in the 1980 federal election, thus making the notion of Quebec's "exclusion" untenable. But there is also a legitimate argument that the patriation of the Constitution in the face of the all-party opposition of the Quebec National Assembly was a repudiation of a long-standing practice of Confederation.

When Robert Bourassa's provincial Liberals defeated the Parti Québécois in 1985, the door opened to a solution to the "Quebec problem." At their annual meeting in Edmonton in 1986, the premiers agreed to consider the position that Bourassa had been circulating, and the negotiations that resulted in the Meech Lake Accord began. The premiers called this the Quebec round. The idea was to get Quebec back to the federal-provincial discussion table.

When Meech began to unravel in the spring of 1990, a companion accord was negotiated that firmed up the commitment to and timetable for dealing with Senate reform and aboriginal self-government. This last-gasp effort, in which Frank McKenna was now one of those pushing hardest for acceptance, was unsuccessful. As the eleventh hour approached, it became clear that the Manitoba legislature wouldn't be able to overcome its procedural problems and vote before the deadline. Clyde Wells, not wanting to leave Manitoba out on a limb, decided he would not have his own legislative assembly vote on the accord a second time. Even had Manitoba's ratification come late, I believe the accord could have been approved if Quebec had been willing to ratify again. But it was not to be. We were a gloomy group of ministers as we sat in disbelief before a television set in the cabinet room, watching the Newfoundland House of Assembly decide not to vote on the accord. As we walked out, I wondered if our government could possibly survive this defeat.

Brian Mulroney felt betrayed by Clyde Wells, who had invited him to address the House of Assembly and had promised him that he would allow the vote to go ahead. Mulroney would repeat again and again what he had said to the Newfoundland legislators: another Quebec referendum was inevitable now that Jacques Parizeau, a hard-line separatist, was leading the Parti Québécois. If that referendum succeeded, as the PM knew very well it was likely to do, what would we say to our children when they asked, "You mean all this could have been avoided if Meech Lake had been ratified?"

Nothing attests better to Brian Mulroney's capacity to inspire loyalty than the subsequent solidarity of the Quebec caucus. Fortunately, the House was about to rise, so there would be no test of confidence in the government in the short term. But if our Quebec colleagues, or even a fair number of them, had given up in disgust, we would have lost our parliamentary majority.

A wave of criticism swept over Brian Mulroney in the aftermath of Meech Lake. Critics disliked the fact that it had been negotiated "behind closed doors" by the first ministers. Although this was exactly the way the agreement to patriate the Constitution had been negotiated, the process was attacked as suspect. Mulroney was depicted as a consummate "deal-maker" whose goal was to get an agreement at any cost. Shortly before the deadline for ratification, the PM had given an interview to the *Globe and Mail* in which he said that at a certain point in the negotiations he had decided to "roll the dice" and commit to a position. Although he probably meant to echo Julius Caesar's comment "The die is cast" at the Roman general's crossing of the Rubicon, many people took it as an expression of Mulroney's willingness to gamble with Canada's future in order to reach a deal. As was so often the case, the reaction said much more about people's attitude towards him than about his actual words. By now distrust of the prime minister was widespread and coloured the public reaction to everything he did.

At a time when he must have felt most weakened on the national front, Mulroney was, paradoxically, at his strongest in his own party and caucus. Everyone knew it was only the personal loyalty of our Quebec members to their leader that was keeping us in government. The failure of Meech Lake was a major turning point because it guaranteed that the Constitution and unity considerations would hang over everything else we did until the referendum on the Charlottetown Accord at the end of 1992, by which time everyone, me included, was heartily sick of the Constitution.

As far as the solidarity of the Quebec caucus was concerned, gun control wasn't a difficult issue because about 75 per cent of Quebeckers supported it. Our Alberta caucus was another story, since their constituents were among the strongest opponents of gun control. In 1990, the Alberta Tory MPs were also taking an enormous beating in their ridings on the subject of the GST, a problem made worse by the PM's appointment of eight additional senators when the Liberal majority in the Senate threatened to defeat the GST legislation. Our Alberta colleagues' solidarity was sorely tested as they watched the Reform Party eat away at Conservative support.

In this happy context I attempted to move the gun control agenda forward. My goal in the winter had been to table legislation in the House (the first reading of the bill) in the spring, then refer it immediately to a parliamentary committee for public input over the summer. This would have allowed MPs to voice their opinion of the bill before the second reading debate and vote. Although amendments can be made after second reading, the basic concept of the bill is by then determined. In such a contentious issue, it seemed unwise to force members to put themselves on the line before they had had a chance to get their constituents' reactions and perhaps suggest changes.

Getting permission from cabinet and caucus to table the legislation was like pulling teeth. In innumerable cabinet committee meetings in which I tried to earn my colleagues' support, I listened patiently to the litany of political problems I was causing.

The legislation was finally tabled as Bill C-80 on June 6, 1990, but by that time it was too late to set up the parliamentary committee before the summer break. I had gained considerable respect for the many ways my colleagues could make life difficult for me without challenging me head-on, and I knew the battle was far from over. On the other hand, given the widespread public support for gun control measures, it was better to have the legislation tabled than to have to live on promises over the summer.

Since the majority of Canadians favoured tighter restrictions on firearms, I was astonished at the public and media reaction to the events that began to unfold in July at Oka, Quebec. The Oka situation was one of the most appalling examples of a double standard in media coverage I have ever seen. While there were a few voices of reason and balance, the overall shallowness of the coverage and the ethics of some of the media people were frightening. The confrontation arose when the town of Oka decided to expand its local golf course on land that had been the subject of a land claim by the local Kanesatake Mohawks. The response of the Mohawks to the decision was to put up barricades on the road to the disputed land. In sympathy, a group called the Mohawk Warriors put up a barricade at the Mercier bridge, thereby blocking one of the important access routes to Montreal from the south shore of the St. Lawrence. When the Mohawks refused to obey a court injunction to take down their barricade in Oka, the town council called the Sûreté de Québec. The police attempted to storm the barricade and in the ensuing confrontation, a policeman, Corporal Marcel Lemay, was killed by gunfire. The government of Quebec then attempted to negotiate a resolution of the standoff.

According to the press, the federal government could easily have prevented the confrontation: the actions of the Mohawks were the understandable result of years of frustration at the failure of Ottawa to resolve their land claim. The presence of masked Warriors in battle fatigues carrying firearms, some of which may have been unlawful in Canada, was treated as a perfectly normal and defensible reaction to the perfidy of the federal government. Ottawa was urged to respond to the Mohawk claims and send in a negotiator.

What the media failed to report was that all the steps they were recommending as surefire ways to have avoided the problem had in fact been taken a year earlier. The Mohawk claim had been rejected by the courts in 1989. However, the federal government had appointed Yves Desilets, the most senior Indian Affairs official in Quebec, to try to negotiate a satisfactory resolution to the question of additional lands for the Mohawks. Negotiations between the provincial government, the band council, and the municipality had begun on August 8, 1989, and by September, a framework agreement had been agreed to by all parties, including commitments to extend the Kanesatake lands to meet the community's needs, to create processes for resolving disputes between the Mohawks and the local non-native community, and to make

My mother, Phyllis Cook, at age eighteen in her naval uniform. Her war service was a powerful influence on my expectations of what I should do with my life.

1953. Alix and I attended Dad's graduation from UBC Law School, from which we would both obtain law degrees, Alix in 1979 and I in 1983.

My first public performance — age four — singing "Little Boy Blue" in a local church's Mother Goose *pageant.*

June 1964, in a dress I made myself. My graduation from high school, whose supportive environment I would miss in the next few difficult years.

August 1972. With Nathan Divinsky, dressed for the opera at Glyndebourne, England, a month before our wedding.

April 1972, Samarkand. The only photo I thought to have someone take of me during my three months in the U.S.S.R. These Uzbek girls wanted my photo — they found me quite exotic!

April 1983. Main-streeting with Premier Bill Bennett during my "kamikaze" provincial run in Vancouver Centre.

October 18, 1988. Three weeks into the federal election campaign, outgoing MP Pat Carney raised my hand in victory after I was nominated as the Conservative candidate in Vancouver Centre.

Howard at the hatch of the Western Yew, *our beautiful forty-six-foot liveaboard, as she cruised in Desolation Sound in the summer of 1988.*

Election 1988. Although campaign headquarters in Ottawa would write off Vancouver Centre, Deputy Prime Minister Don Mazankowski came out to main-street with me and Lyall Knott, my campaign chairman.

January 31, 1989. Celebrating over Chinese food at the Shanghai Restaurant in Ottawa with Howard and Dad the evening of my swearing-in as minister of state for Indian affairs and northern development.

Autumn 1989. On a visit to Ottawa, my constituency assistants Freda Betker (second from left) and Violet Nelson (right) are thrilled to have their picture taken with Barbara McDougall, minister of employment and immigration.

1989. With Pierre Cadieux and Nisga'a chiefs at the signing of the Nisga'a framework agreement.

(Photo: Barbara Woodley)

When Barbara Woodley's bare-shouldered photo was published in Ottawa in November 1992 — two years after being displayed in Vancouver — one MP accused me of wanting to be "the Madonna of Canada."

June 1990. In my simple barrister's robes at a ceremony honouring my law school idol, Chief Justice Brian Dickson, on his retirement from the Supreme Court of Canada.

March 1993, at a party conference in Prince George, B.C., after the PM's announcement but before my own. My three B.C. cabinet colleagues had now declared their support. Left to right: Tom Siddon, myself, Frank Oberle, Mary Collins.

"Don't mess with me, I've got tanks!" CFB Lahr, Germany, March 1993.

(Photo: Lisette Lafontaine)

February 28, 1990. On my way to my first briefings as minister of justice with (left to right) John Tait, deputy minister; Myles Kirvan, chief of staff; and a bearded Michael Ferrabee, executive assistant.

July 1990, with Benoît Bouchard in his constituency of Roberval. Behind us is MP Jean-Pierre Blackburn.

1991, Iqaluit, Baffin Island. With Mike Wilson (left) and Joe Clark in a bus during our cross-country tour with what we informally called the "unity committee" of cabinet.

(Photo: Ken Ginn. Courtesy Rt. Hon. Brian Mulroney)

Getting my dog fix from Clover during a courtesy call to Prime Minister Mulroney on March 23, 1993, to advise him of the upcoming announcement of my candidacy for the leadership. Beside the PM are the notes from which he read to me. This is the same room at 24 Sussex Drive where I later met with the PM to discuss the transition.

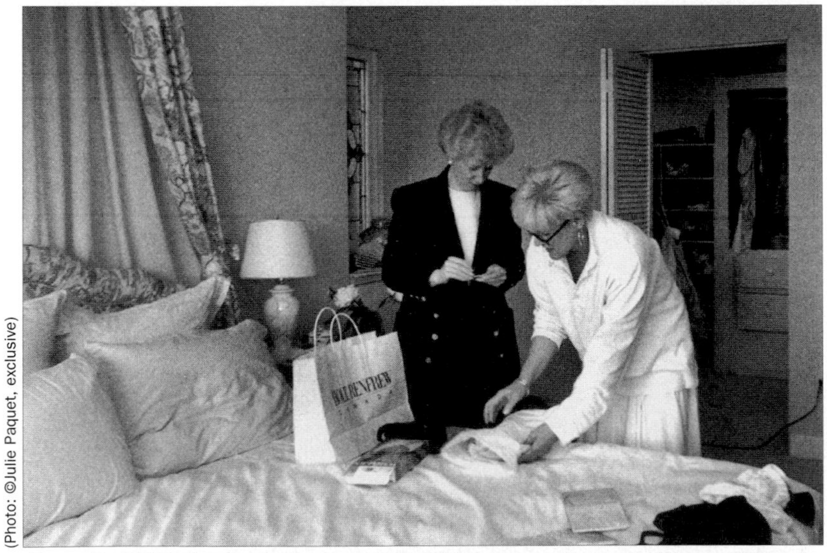

(Photo: ©Julie Paquet, exclusive)

June 5, 1993, in the bedroom of my Vancouver house with my friend Ginny Richards, who had picked up some items of clothing for me. She was one of the few people around me who fully appreciated the problem of trying to take care of such details during a campaign.

(Photo: Norm Betts, *Toronto Sun*)

Named for the close physical formation in rugby, press scrums can be incredibly claustrophobic, as my expression during this one at the leadership convention illustrates. At my right shoulder is Denis Boucher, taping the scrum for our own records.

My family threw themselves into the spirit of the leadership convention. My father, here with my stepmother, Marguerite, is wearing one of the famous pink hats.

Mum and Alix in the convention hall. Despite her shyness, Mum described the convention as the most exciting time of her life.

(Photo: ©Julie Paquet, exclusive)

Speech night at the leadership convention. Joking around to relieve the tension before my speech with Shirley Martin (left) and the delightful Ellen Fairclough, Canada's first woman cabinet minister.

compatible by-laws in the two communities. The Kanesatake band council undertook to obtain approval from band members by March 1990.

In January 1990, the clan mothers of Kanesatake appointed a new band chief and council, which requested an indefinite suspension of negotiations. Shortly afterwards, the municipality lifted its moratorium on golf-course expansion and the barricade was erected. The minister of Indian Affairs, Tom Siddon, and Yves Desilets tried to bring the parties back together, but their efforts were overtaken by the arrival of the Sûreté.

I don't wish to suggest that only the Mohawks acted in bad faith or foolishly during this crisis. But I was struck by the tolerance for the Warriors, who were not the elected leadership of the community and who were well known for their illegal activities. The silence in the coverage regarding the firearms that the Warriors brandished extended to the intimidation and violence that they perpetrated against other Mohawks. The Warriors decided which journalists would be allowed behind the barricades, and few in the media seemed to question the ethics of taking sides in the confrontation. The constitutional relationship between the federal and provincial government concerning law enforcement was conveniently ignored while the spotlight was turned on Ottawa. Poor Tom Siddon was vilified for saying that he refused to negotiate with armed people!

John Tait met regularly with other senior officials on this issue, and there was growing interest in having me play a role in communicating the government's position. At first, the theme of law and order seemed to be what they wanted me to push. John knew that I wouldn't be comfortable with that sort of line, but that a message emphasizing the rule of law would be one I could deliver with conviction. We worked on the statement, and on August 23 I delivered it in both official languages from Vancouver. The message stated emphatically that the Criminal Code applies to all persons in Canada, without exception, and pointed out the need to resolve the issue in a way that would enable the parties to live together in the long run. I also spoke at some length about our many initiatives in the area of aboriginal justice. Shortly after I gave the statement, Bernard Roy, the federal government's negotiator, ended talks because the Mohawk negotiators refused to accept Canadian sovereignty and the application of Canadian law, including the Criminal Code, to all participants.

It is always easier and simpler to take decisive action in a crisis than to show patience. This was very much the case with Oka. There was no quick and simple way to resolve the issue. "Decisive" action, such as that attempted by the Sûreté, had led to bloodshed. If we were going to avoid more death and injury, we would have to be patient. When Quebec asked for the army to be sent in, that removed the tension that the Sûreté's presence had created. The soldiers were trained to ignore provocation, and their restraint in contrast with the belligerence of the Warriors sent a powerful message. In the end, patience won out. So did important principles. The rule of law was upheld and the Government of Canada was not seen negotiating at gunpoint.

I learned a lot from Oka and was proud of my colleagues for resisting the temptation to give in to the demands for action of a sort that would have betrayed Canadian democracy. A few voices in the media saw beyond the hype. Doug Fisher of the *Ottawa Sun* kept a sceptical and independent eye on events and pointed out the hypocrisy of the subscribers to a large advertisement in the *Globe and Mail* containing an open letter to Brian Mulroney. Below the large-type title "A Solution at the End of a Rifle Is No Solution at All," the letter urged the prime minister to end the Oka crisis peacefully. Fisher asked, "Who from the beginning had unlawful automatic machine-pistols and anti-tank rifles? Who insisted on keeping their firepower unless the authorities accepted their solution to the confrontation?" But it was Lysiane Gagnon in *La Presse* who caught the full flavour of the irony. In her column, she identified parties who she felt had lost credibility in the affair: "The Toronto intelligentsia and a part of our trendy left. What an extraordinary sight to see the 'ecolos' of Greenpeace, the professional feminists, New Democrat pacifists, in short, all the people who want to prohibit toy guns and ban *Playboy* in the cause of violence, succumb to the charms of our virile Warriors, armed with machine guns and paid by the casino industry! Have you read *Radical Chic*, by Tom Wolfe? Replace the Black Panthers with the Warriors, and you have it exactly!"

Our insistence on the rule of law did eventually have an effect. When Assembly of First Nations leader Georges Erasmus gave a press conference on September 14, he was asked some tough questions regarding his earlier comments about “bringing Canada to its knees.” Erasmus was forced to admit that taking up arms could hurt the Indian cause and pledged that the AFN would not favour violence. It was a far cry from the rhetoric of the summer and a welcome return to reason.

Sadly, not much has changed in Kanesatake since the summer of 1990. There has been little media interest in following up the fate of the community. However, on March 25, 1995, the Montreal *Gazette* carried a front-page article entitled “Oka: The Guns Point Inward: 5 Years after the Crisis, Kanesatake Remains an Armed Camp.” It is the story of a dispirited community held hostage by a small group of thugs in alliance with the band council. The Sûreté de Québec have been warned that “force will be met with force.” The federal government has spent millions of dollars to buy up land for the band and gave it $1.5 million from July 1990 to July 1994 to finance the research for claims. An additional $400,000 was paid for 1995. No negotiations have taken place since December 1992. It is hard to believe that resolving the land claim will change the situation in this benighted community, where the threat of violence is still wielded as a political weapon.

When MPs returned to Ottawa in September 1990, the mood in caucus was tense. The prime minister had managed to rally the Quebec caucus, but there were definite rumblings of discontent from other parts of the country, including B.C. As difficult as Oka and the GST had been, the issue that seemed to evoke the most anger was the PM’s appointment of John Buchanan to the Senate, which was seen as the last straw by beleaguered MPs. At that time the former Nova Scotia premier was under attack for alleged improprieties when he was in office. Nothing had been proven (nor ever would be), but MPs weren’t keen to revisit the scandals of the first mandate. The prime minister defused the issue with a strong defence of Buchanan, portraying him as the “man with the shiniest suit” at first ministers’ meetings, a man of unimpeachable honesty.

With the resumption of Parliament, the Senate struggle over the GST continued. Conservative senators were confronted with an unprecedented array of disruptive tactics by their Liberal counterparts, ranging from a refusal of Liberal senators to attend in the Chamber to a virtual filibuster. There were two issues at stake: first, whether the legislation would be passed at all, and second, whether it would be passed in time to let the tax come into force, as planned, on January 1, 1991. A great deal rode on this timing. Businesses had been planning on the basis of a January 1 implementation date, and the Department of Finance needed some lead time to make final arrangements. As the Liberal senators continued to delay the business of the upper house, Finance Minister Michael Wilson became more and more anxious. Every day there were tense meetings in the deputy prime minister's office just outside the House of Commons.

It might seem as if this was an impossible time to push forward with gun control, but public pressure for stricter laws was as strong in some parts of the country as resistance to changing the laws was in others. So I continued with a process that I hoped would defuse the issue somewhat and focus the discussion on what was actually being proposed and what problems there might be. I started a series of intense meetings with members of caucus. In order to make it clear that I was sensitive to the political pressures on them, I told them, "I don't get to be minister of justice unless you get elected." I believed it crucial to reassure people on all sides of the issue that the process would be fair. There was an enormous amount of paranoia on both sides.

The first thing I wanted to do was to create a public process of consultation. The Standing Committee on Justice and Solicitor General wasn't keen to take on the issue, so the House formed a special committee in November under the chairmanship of John Reimer, Tory MP for Kitchener. Government MPs often find that their role on legislative committees is to protect the government's bill, rather than amend it. I was determined not to lose the basic features of the bill, but I also wanted MPs' input before asking them to go on record in support of it in second reading. The special committee was the perfect vehicle. It was also important that the many Canadians who would be affected by this legislation understood it and had a chance to advise us of any unforeseen consequences.

In the same month we set up the Canadian Advisory Council on Firearms to give me advice on specific issues. I wanted to send a clear signal that I was not the captive of any one position on the issue. My goal was to improve public safety in Canada with legislation that would be effective and fair. Creating the advisory council was one of those great Canadian exercises. The fifteen or so people on the council needed to be balanced in terms of point of view, expertise, regional origin, and gender. My policy assistant, Deborah McCorkell-Hoy, had the task of trying to achieve this. We asked MPs for nominees, and many of their suggestions were accepted. In the end, the council included members of the medical and legal professions, urban safety experts, experts on the technical aspects of firearms, competitive shooters, hunters, representatives of law enforcement agencies, and aboriginal people. I asked Jacques Flynn, who had just retired from the Senate and had been minister of justice in the Clark government, to be chairperson. Senator Flynn turned out to be the perfect choice, a man of great charm and tact, with the stature of a former minister. To support him, we had two vice-chairs: Linda Thom, Olympic gold medallist in the pistol shoot, and Vern New, retired chief of police of Regina.

As I was launching the gun control process again there was a further significant diversion. I began to be invited to meetings of the ad hoc committee of cabinet on the Gulf crisis. Iraq had invaded Kuwait, and the international community, led by the United States, was considering its response. It was the first crisis of the post–Cold War period, and the major players of the Cold War each thought they had a stake in it. Of all the ad hoc committees I was involved in, this was the only one that was chaired by the prime minister himself. Watching how the PM brought together the military and political sides of the government to consider Canada's position and hearing about his communications with the leaders of other countries provided a fascinating glimpse of the world of the prime minister in times of international tension. Clearly, the personal leader-to-leader contact was very important. It was an example of how the relationships forged in summitry are crucial in time of crisis.

During this period, the powers that be decided that the members of the cabinet committee should all be assigned security details. Ministers were usually provided with security only when there were actual threats or perceived danger. For example, Otto Jelinek as minister of revenue was guarded when his department, which was responsible for customs and excise, cleared Salman Rushdie's book *The Satanic Verses* for entry into Canada. The sudden new demand on resources during the Gulf crisis stretched the RCMP to the limit, and many Ottawa officers were pulled from desk jobs. The Mounties stood guard outside our apartment door in Ottawa, much to the pleasure of our neighbours. I remember one day going up in the elevator with two of the constables.

"I'm glad I'm not having an illicit affair," I joked.

"Oh," one of them replied very seriously, "we're very discreet." A friend whose dinner with me in Vancouver involved being picked up by Mounties, who then sat at a nearby table in the restaurant, still laughs about "Kim's chaperones."

The meetings of the ad hoc committee during the Gulf War were a bit surreal. There was an undeniable whiff of testosterone in the room. This was my second exposure to General John de Chastelain, the charismatic chief of the defence staff (CDS). I had met him during the Oka crisis, when he was much admired for the clarity and calmness of his briefings to the press. A very polished operator, he used to lead the brass in to give us briefings on the situation in the Gulf. The PM seemed to love the camaraderie with the military types. He always referred to the CDS familiarly as "John." There is a fundamentally masculine quality about the military, and he appeared to be very much at home with it. I read somewhere of a government leader who had claimed that you don't really count as a world leader unless you have the ability to declare war. I think Brian Mulroney felt that the Gulf War put him — and us — into the big time. To be fair, however, he was among those who urged George Bush not to act unilaterally, but to go through the UN.

There was an odd sense of remoteness about this war. For one thing, there was political opposition over our involvement. The newly elected leader of the opposition, Jean Chrétien, took the extraordinary position that we should send our troops to the Gulf but bring them back as soon as they were shot at.

I made no pretence of being an expert, but my background in international politics and strategic studies meant that I didn't feel at a disadvantage. One senior official who attended these meetings described me later as having asked "all those tough questions." Some of the ambivalence about our involvement reflected the lack of a clear understanding of Canada's interest in the post–Cold War world. This confusion was not confined to Canada. How to deal with aggression is still an issue that vexes the international community. In World War II my parents knew exactly why they were in uniform. It is easy to forget that that certainty of threat and the willingness to confront it took some time to crystallize.

When the war was over, we had a final meeting of the committee on a Sunday evening, followed by an informal supper hosted by the PM at 24 Sussex Drive. It was the first time I had been invited to a social occasion at the prime minister's residence. A buffet supper was set out on a table in the bay window of the dining room and we all sat around a long table. There was no sign of any other members of the Mulroney family. I remember reflecting on what an unusual experience it had been for any minister to participate in decisions involving military deployment for combat at that time in our history. This "last supper" was perhaps the PM's way of acknowledging the unusual nature of the work we had been doing. As I chatted with senior officials from External Affairs and Defence, I knew that I had made the passage from rookie or junior minister relatively unscathed and was now without question a senior minister of the government.

I was approaching the first anniversary of my appointment as justice minister. After a year, the department was now used to my working directly with the lawyers and advisers who were doing the real work on a file, rather than having everything filtered through senior officials and the deputy. Fortunately, John Tait supported this approach. I liked to sit around a table with the front-line people and a few of my staff. Meetings were intense and collegial because only people directly involved with the issue at hand attended. Because of the way we worked, I now knew a considerable number of the department's lawyers and policy analysts. I admired the quality of their work, which was aided in no small way by their first-hand knowledge of what I wanted or needed from them.

John shared my commitment to the advancement of women in Justice. The first speech I had given in the department had been on March 8, 1990, International Women's Day. The occasion was a luncheon of our Equal Opportunities Committee, and I spoke about my commitment to fair opportunity for women. Two of the three associate deputy ministers were women, Mary Dawson for public law and Anne Marie Trahan for civil law. Working with the hands-on lawyers on a file gave me more exposure to the junior women in the department and, at the same time, enabled the senior officials to see them at work.

In January 1991, John Dixon came to Ottawa to work in Justice. One of his first tasks was to help me institute a bimonthly minister's seminar for the senior members of the department. We invited eminent people to speak to us on important issues related to our work. I had said when I became minister that I thought the Department of Justice should be one of the major creative centres of the government, because the issues of justice are so fundamental to the relationship between the citizen and the state. The need to be reactive is part of the inescapable reality of any government, but it is important not to be so captured by events that you cannot step back and think broadly. What the seminars underlined was the need to be ahead of the issues if we were to serve well not just the government but the people of Canada.

Unfortunately, much of the past year had been taken up in totally unpredictable crises, two of which, Meech Lake and the GST, had threatened the very survival of the government. I had a new appreciation of the fragility of power and the impossibility of prediction in government. The lessons I drew were that if I wanted to accomplish things in government, I couldn't assume that I would have a full parliamentary mandate in which to act, and that I should at all times be prepared for the unexpected.

It wasn't just in government that I had to confront impermanence. My personal life was also showing the strains of the previous year. Although our security details had been cancelled after a few weeks, it was a taste of what life is like for the prime minister, and I think Howard was horrified by it. He was aware of the speculation that was already mounting about my possible candidacy if Brian Mulroney should decide to retire. Howard also knew that I was intrigued by the possibility, even though I was in no hurry for the PM to step down. The longer he stayed, the better it was from my point of view.

At Christmas we flew to Paris for two weeks. Andrew was studying there, so it was a chance to relax, practise our French, and visit with him. There was an undeniable tension between us that even two weeks in Paris couldn't dispel. When we returned to Ottawa, Howard prepared for the last stretch of his French course, which would end in early March. In February, he spent three weeks in Quebec City, and I had to leave for Vancouver before he returned home. When my birthday passed on March 10 without even a phone call, I knew something was seriously wrong. Howard was to take his exam the following day, and when I didn't hear from him that day either, I called early on Tuesday morning. He told me he had passed and would be awarded the highest level of qualification, the "C" certificate. He mumbled something about sorting out his head.

I felt uneasy through the rest of the week as I carried out my constituency obligations in Vancouver. When I arrived back in Ottawa the following Sunday, Howard met me in the apartment. He had moved all his things out and wanted a separation. I was surprised but not surprised. I was surprised because he had never said anything to me about his feelings. On the other hand, I knew things weren't right between us. When Michael Ferrabee asked me the next day how I felt about it, I heard myself say, "Relieved." The tension of the previous few weeks had been awful.

I don't want to give the impression that I was indifferent to the end of my marriage. I was devastated. It seemed to me that Howard and I had always been friends, and I was deeply hurt to find he hadn't felt able to confide in me. As he left the apartment that Sunday, he handed me a note in which he said he didn't want to be a political spouse. The next morning, I was scheduled to make an early-morning presentation to the Operations Committee of cabinet about a strategic issue relating to my firearms initiative. Distraught and edgy from lack of sleep, I snapped at House leader Harvie Andre when he began to give me some difficulty. Surprised, Lowell Murray tried to ease the tension with the remark, "Well, the best that can be said is that you're not a morning person." It wasn't until the next morning, sitting next to Lowell at P&P, that I could explain my uncustomary outburst.

Later that spring, a woman friend who also had a high-profile career suggested that Howard had done me a favour. "It was probably unthinkable for him," she said, "to ask you to stop doing what he knew you loved to do and what he felt you did so well." I think there was a lot of truth in that. After our separation, Howard told Michael that I was exactly the person who should be doing what I was doing. He had always been very supportive of my political career.

Before we were married, Howard told Alix that he resembled Ferdinand the Bull, the Walt Disney character who liked to sit under a tree and smell the flowers. My sister thought at the time, "You're marrying the wrong woman." However painful the nature of our parting, I think it was the only way. Love had created the illusion that we could harmonize our lives. Reality had shown that we couldn't. In the words of Rita MacNeil's song, I was once again "flying on my own."

9

INCLUSIVE JUSTICE

ON AUGUST 22, 1991, the Supreme Court of Canada struck down the rape shield provisions in the Criminal Code, in a decision that came to be known as *Seaboyer*. "Rape shield" is a term describing rules of evidence that prevented the prior sexual conduct of a complainant in a sexual assault trial from being discussed unless the defence could establish its direct relevance to the case at hand. The Supreme Court said these limits were too broad as drafted and could deny an accused person the chance to make a full and fair defence, a decision that created considerable anxiety among women who feared that we might return to the bad old days when a sexual assault trial was as much a trial of the victim as of the accused. For many years, the chief purpose of a rape trial had seemed to be to determine if the victim was chaste enough to deserve the protection of the law.

When the judgment in *Seaboyer* came down, I decided that, although the court had suggested that a new regime could be developed by the courts in dealing with specific cases, we should draft new legislation as soon as possible. Bearing in mind the Supreme Court's discussion of the old law, we would try to create a legal framework for sexual assault trials that would be fair for both the accused and the complainant and, as a result, for society. We set out to make consultation on the bill a benchmark of openness.

On November 27 I went to an unusual meeting on the subject at an Ottawa hotel — unusual because I excused my staff and officials, with the exception of John Dixon, who knew and was trusted by many of the participants. We met with the front-line groups, as we called them, including representatives of poor women, women of colour, disabled women, lesbians, and prostitutes. We were ready to print our draft legislation, and I wanted to get the views of these women on some key proposals, in particular, a definition of consent and the wording of the preamble to the bill. As they began to pour out to me their experiences with sexual assault and the justice system, I knew that this was what "inclusive justice" was all about. I shared their fear of sexual assault and a resentment of the myths and assumptions about female sexuality that were reflected in the law. But these women encountered many more prejudices than I as a white, middle-class, university-educated woman, would ever know. "If *you* are sexually assaulted, the police will treat you with respect and take you seriously," they told me. They could not count on the same treatment for themselves.

Telling their stories was not easy for these women. The conditions they related were disturbing, whether it was the indifference of law enforcement officers who assumed the "naturalness" of sexual assault in certain racial or cultural communities, or the vulnerability of the physically and mentally disabled to those charged with caring for them. For whatever reason a woman consents to sex — love, lust, or money — that consent is for her alone to give. During the time I was justice minister, an Australian judge ruled that because a prostitute "is incapable of feeling shame," she cannot in law be "raped." That extraordinary point of view was expressed in a case where the victim, a prostitute, had been raped at knifepoint and left for dead. Whatever one thinks of prostitution, the notion that prostitutes cannot look to the law to protect their safety is unacceptable. Although the world these women were describing was foreign to my own experience, I knew it was a reality that had to be reflected in any approach we took to the law on sexual assault.

By now I had come to define inclusive justice as a process of four steps. The first step is to acknowledge that the justice system doesn't work equally well for all people. This is a difficult premise for legal professionals to accept. They tend to see justice in terms of universal principles that are meant to apply to everyone. Recognizing that there may be a problem is the first and biggest challenge. The second step is to invite those who feel excluded to articulate their own reality. It requires a willingness to listen, and not just by sitting politely while someone else talks, but a willingness to engage in what is being said, to hear not just the words but the meaning and the newness of the ideas. The third step towards inclusive justice is to invite those whose problems you are addressing to join in the search for solutions. This requires you to give up any "I'm from the government and I'm here to help you" mentality. The final step is the implementation of the solutions through legislation, policy, or other changes. All in all, inclusive justice required a profound change in the way we thought about justice.

As my officials listened carefully to my report on the women's presentations and proposals later that day in Ottawa, some were uncomfortable with this unconventional approach. These were not the people they were used to looking to for ideas about how to reform the law. But in the days that followed, the women's suggestions as well as many others we received would be carefully considered as the bill was being revised. Because the consultation process had been uncharacteristically open, critics of the bill would later accuse us of letting women's groups write it. That was quite untrue. The basic features of the bill had already been presented to cabinet before we began the consultative process, because I was determined to table the legislation before Christmas. The genesis of our thinking had been in an earlier exercise in listening, six months before in Vancouver.

Obviously I knew that being the first woman minister of justice was a significant milestone. But it had become even more apparent in the days following my swearing-in. In Vancouver, when people stopped me on the street to congratulate me, there was a special quality in the congratulations of women. Irrespective of their politics, they felt validated by the fact that such an important portfolio was now occupied by a woman. The significance of my appointment was emphasized that same month when Madam Justice Bertha Wilson, the first woman appointed to the Supreme Court of Canada, gave a speech in which she identified serious gender bias in certain areas of the law. Her speech offended some people who thought a judge of the Supreme Court should not be making such "provocative" comments. However, for many people who knew the legal system, her remarks were a welcome public acknowledgment that a problem did exist. The first reaction of B.C.'s chief justice, Allan McEachern, was that Wilson's remarks were exaggerated. However, a dinner in Ottawa with his old friend Madam Justice Beverley McLachlin of the Supreme Court of Canada convinced him otherwise. On his return to B.C., he began to invite senior women at the bar to give him their views. When they confirmed what Justices Wilson and McLachlin had been saying, he began to consider ways of identifying and dealing with the problems in the courts and the law. Others in the justice system were coming to the same conclusion. As minister of justice, I was in a position to do something.

What sort of problems are we talking about? They can be summed up in comments made by three different judges in three different courtrooms over the last twenty years. A judge in New Brunswick turned to a woman lawyer who was there with her clients and said, "Well, little girl, and what do you have to say?" A judge in British Columbia commented in the late 1970s, "Women don't get much brains before they're thirty." And a Quebec judge declared in 1987, "Rules, like women, are meant to be violated." Women regularly encountered barriers to their participation in the legal profession. Their credibility as witnesses or complainants in court was often questioned. Some law enforcement authorities turned a blind eye to domestic violence, and in many cases women were held responsible for violence and sexual assaults perpetrated against them. Poverty and racism denied many women the protection of the law. As the number of women in the legal profession had grown, these concerns had been voiced more frequently. When the women on the Supreme Court of Canada started speaking out, they could no longer be dismissed.

My approach to feminism is based on my view of democracy. Since women constitute more than half the population, it is only reasonable that their lives be taken into account when public policy is being made. In many ways, women experience the world differently than men, and this gives them very different perspectives on issues like sexual assault. There is nothing radical or subversive about the idea that women's different realities are just as worthy of consideration as those of men.

The concept of inclusive justice was not just about women. Other groups also felt excluded or not understood by the justice system. I identified two groups for special attention: women and aboriginal people. In 1991 I hosted two national meetings designed to push the agenda ahead in these two areas. At the federal-provincial meeting of ministers responsible for justice in June 1990, Jim Lockyer, attorney general of New Brunswick, had proposed the creation of a federal-provincial working group on gender equality in the justice system. I offered to host a national conference to provide input, and a year later, in June 1991, the National Symposium on Women, Law and the Administration of Justice was held in Vancouver. At the same federal-provincial meeting, Margaret Joe, minister of justice of the Yukon, had proposed a national conference on aboriginal justice issues to be held in Whitehorse in September 1991. Because the Yukon's resources were limited, I co-hosted that meeting with her.

When I was named minister of justice and made no secret of the fact that I regarded myself as a feminist, some people in my party thought this was a risky thing to do. Many Canadians thought feminists were radical, left-wing activists like Judy Rebick, at that time the president of the National Action Committee on the Status of Women. But feminism is a broad belief that encompasses many different approaches with a common commitment to the equality of women. As justice minister, I was prepared and eager to be proactive in working for women's equality. I discovered, however, that the politics of feminism could impede my ability to make progress. In the eyes of some feminists, I was suspect. The main issue that divided us was abortion.

Of all the issues with which I have been involved, perhaps none has created stronger feelings or, in my view, more serious misunderstandings than abortion. During the summer of 1988, two cases gained notoriety as a result of attempts by men to prevent their partners from obtaining abortions. Barbara Dodd in Manitoba and Chantal Daigle in Quebec found themselves in court battles to obtain what was otherwise a legal medical procedure. In Daigle's case, her predicament was compounded by the fact that she was getting to the stage in her pregnancy when she would be unable to obtain an abortion. In Quebec, as elsewhere in Canada, doctors would not generally perform abortions after the twentieth week of pregnancy. Finally, Daigle travelled to the United States for the abortion to avoid the restraining order that her boyfriend had obtained. Her position was ultimately vindicated by the Supreme Court of Canada, which ruled that her boyfriend had had no right to interfere with her decision.

All of this convinced Brian Mulroney that new abortion legislation was needed. At that time I had taken the position that I was not uncomfortable with the absence of a law. However — and this is important — I had also said I would not object to a law that simply confirmed the status quo, which was that the decision was one for a woman and her doctor to make. I was uneasy about talk of a new law, but there was a general expectation that the old law would be replaced with something different; after the Supreme Court judgment in *Morgentaler*, it seemed unlikely that any government would come forward with something more restrictive than the old law.

In January 1989, a committee of ministers was formed to try to draft a new law. Barbara McDougall, the senior woman in cabinet and still the minister responsible for the status of women, joined the small group of men, but after a number of meetings, they were unable to come up with a formula they could all accept. The next step was a committee of caucus. It worked under the close guidance of the prime minister's chief of staff, Stanley Hartt, and, surprisingly, was able to come up with a bill.

The morning of the national caucus meeting when the proposed legislation was to be presented, I was apprehensive. Before I left home I told Howard how much I feared that something would be put forward that I couldn't accept and that I would have to resign from cabinet. Here we go again, I thought. I remember sitting next to Alberta MP Ken Hughes, also on the pro-choice side of the issue, and watching with amazement as the overhead projectors put the proposed wording on the screen. I had said I could support legislation that confirmed the status quo, and this was it.

Because the statute was a provision of the Criminal Code, it was worded as a prohibition, but the area of prohibited conduct was extremely narrow. Abortion was to be prohibited unless performed by or under the direction of a doctor who had formed the opinion that failure to induce the abortion would threaten the life or health of the woman. For greater clarity, "health" was defined as mental, physical or psychological health. What was primarily rendered illegal by this bill was abortions performed by someone who was either not a doctor or not acting under the direction of a doctor. The inclusion of the word "psychological" responded to one of the pro-choice criticisms of the definition of health in the old law, that "mental and physical" was not broad enough to make certain that a woman's own subjective evaluation of what was best for her was part of the definition. The judgment of Chief Justice Dickson in *Morgentaler* had spoken of "a woman's own goals and aspirations" as an important part of the considerations determining the legitimacy of abortion.

Ken and I were both astonished and relieved. We had feared the worst, but here was a formula we could actually defend. The proposed bill provided no basis for looking behind the physician's opinion. Abortion was to be a private matter between a woman and her doctor. Out in Vancouver, John Dixon, still president of the B.C. Civil Liberties Association and strongly pro-choice, immediately expressed his amazement at the positive step the legislation represented. His greatest surprise, he said, was that such an enlightened proposal had come from a Conservative caucus.

This spirit of generosity and understanding would turn out to be far from widespread as the debate unfolded. Whatever my joy and relief at a proposal I could support in good conscience, many of my colleagues were crestfallen. Like all other party caucuses (including that of the NDP, despite its official pro-choice stance), we had members who were strongly opposed to abortion. Some came to accept that this proposal was as far as the law could go without running afoul of the Charter. Others believed it was just a validation of "abortion on demand" and could not accept it.

One day in cabinet, the justice minister, Doug Lewis, brought his officials to discuss the various legal and Charter aspects of the proposed bill. Among the complaints of pro-choice advocates was that any new law that replaced the struck-down provisions of the Criminal Code would have the effect of "recriminalizing" abortion. It was an emotive expression and conjured up all sorts of negative images. I had always understood that the Criminal Code was the only vehicle available to the federal government to legislate in this area because the provinces had constitutional jurisdiction over health care.

Another approach, which I had heard argued, was that the "peace, order and good government" powers of the federal government could be used. These powers give the federal government authority to act in emergencies in areas that are not part of its constitutional jurisdiction. It occurred to me that the kind of controversy created by the Barbara Dodd and Chantal Daigle cases and the emotionalism and social divisiveness created by abortion might justify using these powers. This would circumvent the "recriminalization" issue because the new law would not be in the Criminal Code. I raised the possibility in cabinet, but was told it was not feasible. The feeling was that the courts would not recognize its legitimacy.

Public opinion research shows that attitudes towards abortion in Canada have remained relatively constant over the past twenty years or so. About 25 per cent of Canadians believe that abortion should be a matter entirely between a woman and her doctor, about 15 per cent think abortion should be illegal, and the remaining 60 per cent think there should be some limits on the practice. From my perspective, the only compromise the pro-choice side was being asked to make was to agree to a reflection in the criminal law that abortion was not just another issue, but something that was taken very seriously by most Canadians.

What was often missed in discussion was that this bill also treated abortion seriously from a medical point of view. Women seeking abortion were entitled to the same medical care as women seeking any other medical procedure. Recriminalization became the epithet thrown, often angrily, by pro-choice activists at this remarkably respectful piece of legislation. But the Criminal Code deals with all sorts of actions that are perfectly legal and acceptable, even desirable, under certain circumstances. Laws against "sexual touching" do not imply that sex is a bad thing, only that under certain circumstances it may incur criminal penalties.

Recalling my experience in B.C., I felt this bill put abortion firmly back into the mainstream of medical practice for the purposes of funding. Like the old legislation, this bill would make it difficult for provinces to treat abortion as a non-essential procedure, and give them a rationale for resisting pressure to limit access to abortion. An existing federal law can be very helpful to the courts in weighing the validity of a provincial law that may stray over the line into federal jurisdiction. This is what I meant when I said that I thought the new bill, which became Bill C-43, was preferable to no law at all. I had, after all, first-hand experience of a provincial government intent on using its health care jurisdiction to limit access to abortion.

In September 1995, the government of Alberta announced it would cut off funding for abortions that were not "medically necessary." The ostensible rationale was budgetary. The Alberta proposals were exactly what I feared and why I supported having a law. A provision of the Criminal Code establishing that every abortion performed is "necessary to protect the life and health of the woman" would make it very difficult for a province to justify cutting off funding. Although the Alberta government backed off when doctors refused to assist in a definition of "medically necessary," other provincial governments may be more willing to pursue a limit on funding. I cannot think of a circumstance in which I would less want to be in a position to say, "I told you so."

On November 21, 1989, I spoke in the House during the second-reading debate. I said that all wanted pregnancies are alike, but each unwanted pregnancy is unwanted in its own way. The only just way of dealing with the issue was to acknowledge that each woman had to make that balance of judgments about abortion herself, supported by a physician who was obligated to ensure that the decision was as fully considered as a decision about any other medical procedure. I spoke after my cabinet colleague Jake Epp, who made a case for the bill from the opposite pole of the issue. In particular, Jake argued that it was important that the law not be silent on this issue. Jake is a Mennonite from Steinbach, Manitoba, whose constituents were strongly anti-abortion. His support for Bill C-43 created a rift that was never resolved and contributed to his decision not to seek re-election. Brian Mulroney had decided that MPs would have a free vote but that, as it was a government bill, cabinet ministers had to support it. I often wondered at the pro-choice side's apparent disregard of the discomfort of the anti-abortion supporters of the bill.

When I became justice minister in February 1990 I inherited Bill C-43. It had passed second reading and was now in committee stage. It passed to third reading unamended and was ready for final passage. The vote would be close because the opposition parties had no reason to support a controversial piece of legislation, irrespective of its merits. Why take a position on abortion if you could avoid it? For opponents of abortion, it was easy to vote no. For pro-choice members, opposition to recriminalization provided an easy out. Only two Liberals voted for it: Peter Milliken from Kingston and John Turner, who came from Toronto especially to support the bill that was, in his words, "the best we could do under the Charter." Turner, a former justice minister as well as prime minister, is a devout Catholic who has written on theological issues. I walked across the floor to thank him for coming to vote in favour of the bill.

The House was very quiet while the vote was being tallied. When passage by a margin of seven votes was announced, there was a disturbance in the public galleries with pro-choice opponents of the bill shouting, "No new law, we're never going back!" To those for whom "no law" was the only acceptable pro-choice position, my support for Bill C-43 meant that I was a traitor. Some of the women who attacked me publicly were more reasonable in private. They knew I was pro-choice and unabashedly so.

The abortion bill was defeated by a tie vote in the Senate later in 1990. For some reason, Pat Carney, who was now in the Senate, decided to make a secret of her return to Ottawa to vote against the bill after having advised the Senate Whip that she would be absent. Pat had not attended any of my meetings with senators to discuss the bill, and it was only with the greatest difficulty that I persuaded her secretary to put my call through to her on the morning of the vote. She was not interested in anything I had to say.

Because I had previously said that I was not uncomfortable with "no law," some people suggested I hadn't tried hard enough to get the bill passed. Others claimed I held a grudge against those senators who voted against it. Neither statement is true. The vote was a free vote, but I went to great lengths to discuss it with the senators and respond to their concerns. My complaint against Pat was that she did not do me the courtesy of letting me do my job. The bill had been drafted with great agonizing by our caucus. As the sponsoring minister, I felt obligated to respond carefully to all the concerns raised by MPs and senators, out of respect for the enormous effort and soul-searching our colleagues had put into drafting the bill. Many of us who, like Pat, were pro-choice, including her good friend Barbara McDougall, had voted for the bill in the House. I remained on good terms with the other opponents of the bill, but my relationship with Pat became strained after what I considered her breach of caucus collegiality.

Preparations for the June 1991 National Symposium on Women, Law and the Administration of Justice were completed in record time. Usually two to three years are required to arrange a national conference of this sort; we did it in one. In order to decide what might be appropriate issues to discuss, a departmental team travelled across Canada speaking with a wide variety of interested groups and individuals. The consensus was that the meeting should focus on two major factors in women's relationship to the justice system: poverty and violence. In the spring, we chose the logo we would use for the symposium. Following my suggestion that we combine the international symbol for a woman, the circle with the cross on the bottom, with the scales of justice, we finally chose to have the crossbar on the woman symbol slightly tilted, with the scales of justice suspended from it. The slight tilt symbolized our desire to rectify gender inequalities and our goal of putting the scales of justice in balance.

The three main organizers from Justice, Susan Campbell, Susan Christie, and Bea Cleary, met with me to discuss the sensitive issues that had emerged in planning the conference. I soon learned that there were groups and people who felt very proprietary where women's issues were concerned. My goal was to be inclusive and to invite representatives of national organizations concerned with issues relating to women and the law. Did that include R.E.A.L. Women? This group was anti-feminist, and other groups were threatening not to attend if R.E.A.L. Women were represented. However, one of the things that interested me was why these women felt so alienated from the women's movement. Surely the removal of gender bias from the operation of the justice system was a benefit to all women? If some women didn't think so, what were their objections? Their exclusion from the conference would lead only to further alienation. Besides, this was a publicly funded symposium and the members of R.E.A.L. Women also paid taxes.

In the end, no one boycotted the meeting and the symposium was unprecedented in its range of participants (including R.E.A.L. Women). It brought together judges from all levels of courts, officials from all the provincial government departments responsible for justice, academics, and representatives of more than sixty national organizations concerned with issues of gender and justice. There was a sense of anticipation as we concluded the opening ceremonies and this amazing array of delegates prepared to get down to work.

It would be an understatement to say that there was no love lost between the Conservative government and the National Action Committee on the Status of Women. NAC is an umbrella organization whose job is to lobby governments on issues relating to women's equality. Although their financial support from government had doubled under the Conservatives and Brian Mulroney had appointed record numbers of women to cabinet posts, senior government positions, and ambassadorships, NAC was hostile. For one thing, NAC president Judy Rebick was a declared NDP supporter and sometimes seemed unable to separate her personal partisanship from her role as president of a national organization.

Some years before I came to Ottawa, NAC had devised an annual "lobby day." This consisted of a public meeting, where the participants gathered to attack the government and its policies. Some Conservative ministers attended NAC lobby days when I was in government, but I never did. I was publicly accountable every day in the House of Commons and almost never gave a public speech that was not followed by public questions. But NAC's lobby day was completely devoid of the civility and mutual respect essential to the kind of deliberation that leads to good public policy. It was interest-group politics at its worst and made Question Period seem positively genteel. I was always happy to receive a delegation from NAC in my office, and most years they came and made their points to me in a calm way.

It seemed NAC was not about to allow a Conservative justice minister to organize a genuinely open and consultative process that would provide an opportunity for the voices of Canadian women to be heard by decision-makers of all kinds. Shelagh Day, the NAC representative in Vancouver, began by putting together a caucus of what she blithely described as "equality-seeking groups."

Well, you may ask, wasn't everybody there seeking equality? Not according to NAC. As far as I could make out, the only offensive presence in their view was that of Gwen Landolt, a lawyer and president of R.E.A.L. Women. Now, Landolt's views are rarely my own, but she represented a fair number of women. More important, she represented women who rejected the views of many of the other women present. It was highly unlikely that Gwen Landolt would succeed in singlehandedly subverting a symposium of 250 participants, most of whom were hardly shrinking violets.

The caucus of "equality-seeking groups" set out to undermine the symposium, but with little success. For many of the delegates, it was their first opportunity to speak directly to a judge, or, if they were judges, to hear directly from someone with a devastating critique of the courts. No delegate was going to throw away the opportunity to participate in these exchanges just in order to satisfy NAC's sense of its own self-importance. Despite my instructions to the organizers to be cooperative with the equality-seeking groups and offer them whatever they needed for their meetings, they were able to attract twenty or thirty people at most to their gatherings.

At the final morning plenary, I was astonished by the comments of a young aboriginal woman. She had come with her baby, and our organizers had gone to great pains to look after the child while the mother was participating in the conference. At the microphone, she suddenly began to berate me for ignoring her at the reception following the keynote address on the first evening by Rosalie Abella, chair of the Ontario Labour Relations Board. Since there had been no formal receiving line at the gathering and people had just come up to me freely to say hello, I was flabbergasted at the idea that I could have "snubbed" this woman. Her comments and the crankiness of the equality-seeking groups were part of an understandable phenomenon. As Susan Christie put it, "We disarmed a great many people by opening the door." Some people are so accustomed to banging on a closed door that they are at a loss when the door is opened. Their whole mode of communicating has been developed to be heard through a closed door. Building trust takes time, and however much it may be painful for people in government to accept, the distrust of government is real and not infrequently well founded.

This national symposium was a landmark event in the mainstreaming of women's justice issues. It was particularly gratifying for me because, as I said at the closing meeting, it has always been my belief that when people come together and can appreciate each other's humanity, they can move beyond the distrust that abstraction and distance create and begin to listen to and understand one another. A number of the judges told me that while they had thought they were fairly liberal on the main topics of the symposium before they came, they realized after being there that they had a great deal to learn. A few days later Chief Judge Albert Gobeil informed me excitedly at a Quebec City luncheon that he had returned from the Vancouver conference with wonderful ideas and had already started a program on gender bias in his court. Susan Campbell reported an encounter with a "crusty old eastern judge" after the meeting who said, "I've never spent two more horrible days," then, just as Susan was trying to think of some mollifying comment, added, "and I've never learned more."

The symposium's mainstreaming of many sensitive issues created a better climate in which I could speak candidly to judges as minister of justice about the problems of gender bias. I also made serious efforts to increase the number of women judges, a task that will become easier as the proportion of women in the eligible group of lawyers increases. After a speech I gave at a conference of Canadian judges in Strasbourg in 1992, several of the women judges came to meet me. One said, "Because you are there, it gives us the courage to speak out."

The purpose of increasing the proportion of women judges is not only to make the courtroom more representative but also to change the judicial culture itself. I did not approach the problem as one of males versus females. Rather, it was a question of fairness and the full enfranchisement of women. If women weren't there to contribute their perspective, how could the system not make errors of exclusion? Of course my efforts were not welcomed by everyone. John Crosbie once complained to me that to be appointed a judge in Newfoundland, a candidate he favoured would be well advised to have a sex-change operation. It was easy to view my rejection of a judicial candidate, for any of a number of good reasons, as a reflection of reverse discrimination. Interesting how the shoe pinches when it is on the other foot!

My concept of inclusiveness with respect to justice was fundamental to my view of aboriginal justice issues, but also a source of controversy. During the Oka crisis I had said, "The justice needs of aboriginal peoples must be met through a national system of justice that is flexible and able to include alternatives that meet community needs, not through separate systems." The question of "separate systems" was at the heart of aboriginal justice issues. Practically, separate justice systems for aboriginal communities were just not feasible. But my objection went deeper. As far as I was concerned, the Canadian justice system should serve all Canadians; the separate systems approach was a cop-out by the larger community.

While some aboriginal leaders argued that the Charter should not apply to their communities, others believed adamantly that it should. It seems to me that many of the goals of making the administration of justice for aboriginal communities more responsive to and reflective of their cultural values can easily be accommodated. Aboriginal people are mobile. They should expect to interact with a culturally literate justice system wherever they go in Canada. A form of justice-apartheid just doesn't make sense to me.

The goal of the Aboriginal Justice Conference in September 1991 was to begin the dialogue and plan the strategy for opening up the department's thinking to the potential of full justice for aboriginal peoples. On September 3 and 4, the annual federal-provincial meeting of justice ministers was held in Yellowknife, and from there we all flew to the conference in Whitehorse. Fifty per cent of the participants were aboriginal people. Aboriginal people would be articulating their own realities, but how to bridge the cultural abyss? The conference was organized so that every day started with a piece of theatre. The ministers arrived for the last day and a half only, so we saw only one performance. It was a play called *Toronto at Black Rock*, performed by an Indian theatre company from Manitoulin Island. The use of theatre was a remarkably successful way of transcending cultural differences, and each non-native member of the audience gained a better understanding of the strangeness of mainstream society to aboriginal people. I remember thinking that if a picture is worth a thousand words, a play is worth a thousand speeches.

The Vancouver symposium and the Whitehorse conference

were both launching pads for broader policy initiatives and approaches. In the Department of Justice we set about putting the recommendations of the conferences together and following up a wide range of ideas.

At the time of the Vancouver meeting, the *Seaboyer* case had yet to be decided by the Supreme Court of Canada, and we wanted to be ready in the event that the court struck down the rape shield law. We looked at the provisions relating to sexual assault in the Criminal Code and began to think of approaches that would reflect some of the concerns we had heard in Vancouver. This is not to say that everything we had heard at the symposium was appealing to us. When one speaker suggested that we consider doing away with the presumption of innocence in sexual assault cases, my hair curled.

Although the *Seaboyer* decision eventually struck down the rape shield provisions, the Supreme Court nevertheless supported their philosophy and purpose. The challenge was to redraft the law in such a way that the concerns raised about the accused's ability to make a full and fair defence could be met. At the federal-provincial meeting in Yellowknife I received support for my intention to pursue sexual assault legislation immediately. Two weeks later, consultation began with provincial and territorial officials. Our department gave them an issues paper that included options for a revised rape shield provision, a legal definition of consent in cases of sexual assault, and restrictions on the defence of honest belief in consent. The last two items weren't included in a second version of the issues paper presented by department officials to a September 20 meeting of women's legal groups, because the changes we wanted to make in the law of sexual assault were very broad and we didn't want to say too much publicly about them until I had had an opportunity to gauge the likelihood of acceptance by cabinet. The September 20 meeting wasn't productive because, despite assurances to the contrary, the women's groups insisted that we were proposing a minor tinkering with the law and wanted no part of it. With the exception of Gwen Landolt of R.E.A.L. Women, they were opposed to our desire to move quickly to fill the legislative void created by *Seaboyer*. Meanwhile, the department was moving full steam ahead to prepare a submission to cabinet on the broader agenda.

A second consultation with these women's groups on October 23 was also disappointing. The participants didn't want to address the issues and accused us of proceeding too quickly with legislation. In fact, representatives of the Legal Education and Action Fund (LEAF) threatened to challenge any legislation that was passed. The only explanation was that we were facing a deliberate strategy of delay. I couldn't understand this, because leaving the courts to work out a new approach to the admissibility of evidence in cases of sexual assault would turn victims into jurisprudential guinea pigs and discourage the reporting of sexual offences.

On November 7, 1991, cabinet gave me authority to draft amendments to the Criminal Code, including a new rape shield regime, a definition of consent, restrictions on the defence of honest belief in consent, and a preamble. It is unusual for criminal statutes to have a preamble, but since the courts cannot consider the parliamentary debates in interpreting legislation, this was a way of ensuring that the social circumstances in which the bill was drafted would be considered by a court in the event that its constitutionality was challenged.

After the fruitless October 23 meeting, my officials suggested that I meet personally with the women's legal groups. Because the legislation had not been tabled in Parliament, only I could make the judgment call of how much to reveal about what was in it. We met on November 20 in the Justice boardroom. Seated around the table were John Tait and senior officials as well as Sheila McIntyre and Anne Derrick of LEAF, Judy Rebick of NAC, Sherry Wiebe of the Canadian Nurses Association, Lee Lakeman of the Canadian Association of Sexual Assault Centres, Roz Currie of the National Association of Women and the Law, and Renate Mohr of the Church Council on Justice and Corrections. They wanted to begin the discussion, so I sat quietly and began to listen to their views.

"Perhaps you should just hear some of the things we have in mind for the legislation," I said, interrupting after about five minutes. Their presentation showed clearly that they had no idea of how far our thinking had gone. I picked up my confidential briefing notes and read carefully, indicating the extent of our thinking without breaking the protocol of describing actual legislative wording before Parliament had seen it. I made it very clear that we were not just interested in codifying *Seaboyer* or tinkering with the sexual assault legislation, as these women had feared, but were proposing a systematic modernization of that area of the Criminal Code. Around the table, jaws dropped. They were astonished at the range and breadth of concerns we had addressed. We had done our homework. To my delight, Judy Rebick and Lee Lakeman instantly understood what they had heard and offered their help on the spot. Anne Derrick too was "very encouraged" by the proposed changes and my willingness to engage in dialogue. The mood of the meeting changed quickly. A number of the women present were experienced constitutional litigators. Their help was particularly important in drafting a preamble that would serve as a legislative record for the bill and strengthen it against constitutional challenge. We invited the women's groups to meet again in a week with Justice officials.

Although certain cabinet and parliamentary protocols prevented us from laying all our cards on the table, the initial unwillingness of these women to engage in a discussion with our officials delayed our getting their views and, as a result, delayed the tabling of the bill by several weeks. It was a fascinating example of how slowly attitudes change. Notwithstanding the level of the discussions at the symposium, these activists in the area of women and the law couldn't believe that those discussions would actually affect anything in government.

The new rape shield law, called Bill C-49, reflected the input from the legal and front-line groups and other organizations. It received first reading in the House of Commons on December 12, 1991. The bill included a preamble setting out the rationale for the amendments, and a reaffirmation of the principle that evidence of a complainant's prior sexual activity is admissible only when it is specific and relevant to an issue to be proved in a trial, and where its value is not outweighed by the danger of unfair prejudice. Procedures for assessing the admissibility of such evidence were included in the bill, as were a definition of consent for the purpose of sexual assault offences and limitations on the defence of "mistaken but honest belief in consent." The law was clear that consent could not be obtained from a third party nor inferred on the basis of the complainant's prior engagement in sexual activity. I was determined to table a bill before Christmas so that the parliamentary recess could be used by any individuals or groups that wished to appear before the legislative committee to prepare their responses.

The debate around rape shield raised the profile of sexual assault as an issue. For some, it represented a threat to men, because they feared that women would now be able to use charges of sexual assault against men more easily for illegitimate purposes. This accusation angered supporters of the bill. In their view, the problem was not false charges of sexual assault but an underreporting of the offence because of victims' fears of being further victimized by the legal system. This bill was the first legislation that actually tried to reflect the perspective of women on this issue, but it was also faithful to the notion of a fair trial. It couldn't have survived otherwise. When the bill was tabled, the two opposition justice critics, Liberal Russell MacLellan and the NDP's Ian Waddell, rose and spoke in favour of the bill. Their sensitivity to the problem of sexual assault would probably have been unthinkable for male members of Parliament ten years earlier. Even if they had thought that way, they would have been reluctant to speak so glowingly in favour of such a bill in the House.

The draft bill was considered again in a consultation in January with a broad range of women's groups including the front-line groups. They made proposals for changes or additions to our draft. A few amendments were made to the bill, including a recommendation by the Canadian Bar Association that strengthened protection for the accused in a sexual assault trial. There was the predictable criticism from the criminal defence bar, who have a bias against anything that constrains the conduct of a criminal defence. But because we had held true to the principle of the right of an accused to a full and fair defence, I was sure the bill could withstand their attacks.

There were other criticisms from those who felt that the participation of the various women's groups in the drafting of the bill was illegitimate. This proved my point about inclusivity. Why was their participation any less legitimate than that of the Canadian Bar Association? These women had important things to say about the reality of sexual assault. They knew that laws designed to protect women would fail to do so if they accommodated prejudice about women's sexuality and false assumptions about the behaviour and competence of disabled women, prostitutes, lesbians, women of colour, and others. In the end, what came to be known as the "No means no" law passed comfortably. I felt we had received the highest compliment for our proposals when some of the early sceptics were eager to claim authorship of them. It is said that success has many fathers but failure is an orphan. In this case, success had a surprising number of mothers!

Consultation means having your say, not necessarily having your way. We didn't accept every suggestion made by the women we consulted. Nevertheless, they supported the legislation because they knew that not only had they been listened to, they had been heard. The public process for Bill C-49 has become the standard against which others are still judged. Even today, I'm told, groups seeking input into Justice policy ask for "a C-49 consultation." Because the work of the department had been so advanced, the substantive changes made as a result of the consultation were not major, although the drafting of the preamble gained a great deal from the consultative process. But the process was certainly open to such changes if we had missed something. That openness made the breadth of political support for the legislation possible. For the first time, many women could look at the justice system and feel what I hoped some day all Canadians would feel about it, that it was truly theirs.

10

Doing the Right Thing

On April 17, 1992, David Milgaard walked out of Stony Mountain Penitentiary, where he had been incarcerated since his 1970 conviction for the murder of Gail Miller. On April 15, as minister of justice, I had ordered that he be given a new trial, but on April 16, the attorney general of Saskatchewan had entered a stay of proceedings against Milgaard: after twenty-three years, the evidence relating to the 1969 murder was too stale. There would be no new trial; David Milgaard was a free man.

In my almost three years as justice minister, I had to exercise a quasi-judicial authority, or act "like a judge," in a number of different contexts. The Milgaard case was the most difficult of all. After I left government following the 1993 election, I received a letter from a former senior official in Justice who had worked with me on the case. He wrote of his appreciation for my desire to "do what was right, not what was politically expedient." The Milgaard case had shown me how incredibly difficult it can be to determine what the right thing is, and how politics can get in the way of doing it.

In May 1990, I was in Winnipeg to address a business luncheon on the Meech Lake Accord. As I was getting ready to leave my hotel room to go down to the meeting, one of my staffers ran up to tell me breathlessly, "Mrs. Milgaard is downstairs with a whole load of TV cameras!" Although David Milgaard's application had not yet arrived on my desk, I already knew who Joyce Milgaard was. Her son David had applied for a review of his conviction under section 690 of the Criminal Code, which allows convicted people who have exhausted all other legal avenues to ask the justice minister to determine whether their conviction constituted a miscarriage of justice. I thought it was completely inappropriate to be lobbied in this way by the mother of an applicant. I also knew that a televised confrontation with this very determined woman would be a no-win situation.

As a decision-maker in a legal process, my role in this instance was akin to that of a judge. Unfortunately, people who would never have dreamed of approaching a judge thought it perfectly acceptable to approach me — after all, politicians are supposed to be accessible. However, it was fundamentally important that anyone who applied for a remedy under section 690 should know that they would receive a fair review, irrespective of whether they were telegenic, or had a persuasive mother, or had public support. The task before me was to provide a fair and unbiased review of the application based on the evidence and the law.

In what became an oft-repeated video clip, I said to Mrs. Milgaard as she bore down on me with a phalanx of blinding television lights, "Madam, if you wish to have your son's case dealt with fairly, please do not approach me." I then went through the first door I could find. My reaction was characterized by many as heartless. I was torn between my normal instinct to reach out and listen to someone in distress, and my deep sense that it was entirely inappropriate to personalize my function in this matter. If I had had more time to think, or perhaps had more experience, I could have figured out a better way to deal with this situation. Joyce Milgaard subsequently admitted that she shouldn't have approached me the way she did. But this was just the first incident of a public relations campaign that would attempt to turn David Milgaard's application into "trial by television."

In Canada, the right of the executive branch of government (the cabinet) to address miscarriages of justice derives from the royal prerogative of mercy. It is to this power that people have recourse when they have exhausted all legal remedies. It is a cliché of our legal tradition that it is better for ten guilty men to go free than for one innocent man to be convicted. The Department of Justice receives about thirty applications for review of alleged wrongful convictions every year.

Canadians are reasonably confident in their justice system, but they are also prepared to accept that it makes mistakes. This has been particularly so since the case of Donald Marshall Jr., whose conviction for murder in 1971 in Nova Scotia was subsequently described by a royal commission as reflecting a "total failure" of the justice system. The conviction resulted from incompetence, racism, or error at virtually every level, from the way the investigation was conducted to the actions of the prosecution, defence counsel, and the trial judge. Eventually, the minister of justice, using the provisions of section 690, referred the matter to the Nova Scotia Court of Appeal, where the conviction was quashed and a verdict of acquittal entered.

The process for dealing with a section 690 application is straightforward. It is reviewed by lawyers in the Department of Justice and a recommendation is made to the minister. The final decision is that of the minister alone. Very often, a section 690 application will trigger a considerable amount of investigative activity. The RCMP may be called in to assist, forensic evidence may be reviewed by specialists retained by the government, and interviews may be carried out with witnesses, under oath. The test on which the recommendation for action is based is: "Is there a reasonable basis on which to conclude that there has likely been a miscarriage of justice?"

My interest in miscarriages of justice predated my arrival in the Department of Justice. When I was a teenager, I used to enjoy reading the books my father brought home about the law — not law texts but biographies, memoirs, and accounts of trials. One that made an impression on me was *The Trial of Steven Truscott*, by Isabel Lebourdais.

Steven Truscott was convicted in 1959 of murdering Lynn Harper. The evidence against Truscott was almost entirely circumstantial, and Lebourdais set out to show that he was innocent. She made a strong case and the book had a powerful impact on many Canadians. The Ontario Court of Appeal had dismissed Truscott's appeal, but his death penalty was commuted to life imprisonment by the federal cabinet. Partly as a result of the public interest created by the book, the minister of justice asked the

Supreme Court of Canada, which had rejected Truscott's application for appeal, to render an opinion as to what the result would have been had they agreed to hear the appeal. Eight of the judges upheld the conviction. The dissenting judge, Mr. Justice Emmett Hall, would have ordered a new trial, because he found serious errors in the way the trial had been conducted. The minister of justice at the time accepted the majority opinion and didn't order a new trial.

Now, many years later, as minister of justice and attorney general of Canada, I found myself dealing with cases just as perplexing as the Truscott case. In the matter of David Milgaard, I too would seek an opinion from the Supreme Court of Canada. Chatting about all this with Dad one day, I recalled the Lebourdais book. Like me, he had been shocked by the Supreme Court's decision. We had both been strongly influenced by *The Trial of Steven Truscott*, and Hall's critique seemed to us to be a clear rationale for a new trial. After my experience with the Milgaard case, I'm less certain of what I know about Truscott.

Almost as soon as I became minister of justice in February 1990, I came under considerable pressure about the section 690 application of David Milgaard. The file had not yet been given to me because there were ongoing submissions by Milgaard's lawyers and discussions between them and Justice officials. Nonetheless, I was bombarded with questions from the media and during Question Period. At my first appearance before the Commons Standing Committee on Justice and Solicitor General, John Harvard, the Liberal MP who represented the Winnipeg constituency where Joyce Milgaard lived, insisted that I was in possession of a forensic report that established with certainty the innocence of David Milgaard! Part of the media strategy of Milgaard's counsel was to accuse me and the department of delay in dealing with the file. In fact, it was they who created the delay throughout 1990 by continuing to add to their submissions. I couldn't deal with the application until it was complete.

In mid-January 1991, I finally received the file. The materials covered a third of the large conference table that stood along one wall of my office. Looking at them, I decided to set aside the weekend of January 26 to review them. The past few weeks had been incredibly hectic and the upcoming weeks didn't show any signs of being less so. The Senate was getting ready to vote on the abortion bill, so I was in frequent meetings with individual senators and small groups, in addition to appearing before Senate committees. The prime minister had just formed a new ad hoc cabinet committee on national unity, and pre-budget meetings of the Expenditure Review Committee of cabinet also appeared with regularity on my schedule. The Canadian Advisory Council on Firearms was up and running, and preparations for the symposium on women and the law were in high gear. Oh yes, and the Gulf War was on. I wanted two clear days to immerse myself in this file; it was January 26 and 27 or never.

I enjoyed working in my Justice office on the weekend because hardly anyone was around. The office had a small kitchen where I could make coffee and put my lunch in the fridge. It was a comfortable environment in which to hunker down and focus on serious matters. Peter Lugli, my senior policy adviser, met me there on Saturday morning with Eugene Williams, the highly professional departmental lawyer in charge of the Milgaard file. Eugene's competence and encyclopedic knowledge of the section 690 files always impressed me.

One of Michael Ferrabee's more inspired hiring decisions had been the appointment of Peter, a young lawyer from Thunder Bay, Ontario. With just the right mix of legal judgment and political acumen, Peter steered a variety of difficult and complex problems through my office. His job was to supplement the legal advice of the department with strategic advice on the management of issues. Remarkably productive, Peter not only created hundreds of memoranda for me but also managed to marry and have two children before we left Justice, and a third shortly after.

I told Peter and Eugene not to stick around. As long as I could reach them by phone for urgent questions, I preferred to go through the materials all at once on my own. Later, Peter and Eugene came in to discuss what I had read up to that point, and we met until about 10:30 that evening.

The entire weekend was spent becoming thoroughly familiar with the issues. It was all there — the crime scene, the statements, the trial and appeal records. I found myself deeply affected by the sadness of the crime itself, the senseless and brutal murder of Gail Miller, and by the implications of whatever decision I would make for a man who had been in jail since he was seventeen years old. I went through it all, carefully making notes about the points I wished to pursue further.

My sense after that weekend was that there just wasn't enough there to grant the application. However, this was a very serious matter, so I wanted to take some time to reflect. There was another reason for delaying my decision. During the department's evaluation of the application, Milgaard's lawyers had publicly called into question the impartiality of Eugene and other government lawyers. Although I had seen no evidence of bias, in order to ensure confidence in the integrity of the process, I decided it would be a good idea to retain "eminent counsel" — someone of unimpeachable credentials and from outside the government — to provide me with a second, independent opinion. We had retained the Honourable William McIntyre, a recently retired justice of the Supreme Court of Canada and one of the country's leading criminal law experts, and I was waiting to receive his opinion. I had the benefit of his advice throughout the process.

A concerted effort was made by Milgaard's advocates to convince the public that the Justice Department would be biased in favour of "the system." But while the federal government makes the criminal law, it is the provinces that administer it. Thus, we weren't evaluating ourselves. Throughout the time of Milgaard's application, his lawyers, his mother, and other supporters waged an unremitting press campaign implying bad faith on the part of me and the government, as a way of explaining any adverse ruling. But the section 690 process is not an adversarial one — at least, not in the sense that a trial is. The only clear "bias," if one can call it that, is on the part of the applicant. The adversary is not the minister of justice or her department. What the applicant has to fight against is the weight of the evidence that convicted him or her in the first place. My job was to understand the basis for that conviction as well as I could, in order to evaluate how well the arguments of the applicant called it into question. I had no interest beyond assuring that the process was fair.

After a series of meetings with my departmental officials, whom I cross-examined, posing questions and testing their arguments, I wrote to Milgaard's senior counsel, Hersh Wolch, to advise him that I had concluded that a remedy (a new trial or appeal) for

David Milgaard under section 690 was not appropriate in the circumstances.

What was the basis of this conclusion? There were a number of key considerations. I hope what follows will show how difficult it can be to make such judgment calls and illustrate some of the legal and political dilemmas involved. First, a review of the essential facts of the case, based on the trial evidence, most of which was either accepted by the defence or corroborated by other evidence.

On January 31, 1969, David Milgaard, aged sixteen, Ronald Wilson, aged seventeen, and a young woman named Nichol John, aged sixteen, set off from Regina between 12:30 and 1 a.m. in a car owned by Wilson. They were heading to Saskatoon, where they planned to pick up Milgaard's friend Albert Cadrain for a trip to Edmonton or Vancouver.

They arrived in Saskatoon around 6 or 6:30 in the morning and began to search for Cadrain's home. They saw a woman wearing a dark coat walking on the sidewalk in the same direction. Wilson, the driver, stopped the car; Milgaard asked her for directions. She was apparently unable to give any and they continued on their way. Wilson gave evidence that he heard Milgaard say "The stupid bitch" as they departed. The car became stuck in the entrance to an alley. This occurred at 6:30 a.m. or very shortly thereafter.

Wilson and Milgaard left the car and tried to free it by pushing. Not succeeding, they separated to seek help. Wilson carried on down the street, and Milgaard went back in the other direction, towards where they had encountered the woman. Wilson walked some distance from the car but found no help. He arrived back at the car to find Nichol John in what he described as a hysterical or upset state. According to Wilson, Milgaard had been out of the presence of his companions and away from the car for fifteen minutes. On his return, said Wilson, Milgaard said, "I fixed her," or something to that effect. Wilson testified that he then said to Milgaard, "You what?" but there was no reply. In Wilson's words, "Nicki kind of came over to my side of the car getting away from David," and "David was awfully cold and breathing heavy."

In due course they got the car moving and arrived at the Cadrain house. They all went into the house and almost at once, and in the presence of Albert Cadrain, Milgaard and Wilson changed their clothes, including their trousers and shirts. The soiled clothes were put into Milgaard's suitcase. Both Wilson and Cadrain noticed blood on Milgaard's clothing. It was also noted that his trousers were torn in the rear and in the crotch area. Milgaard then drove away in Wilson's car with the suitcase. Milgaard's soiled clothes were not seen again. He came back in about fifteen minutes, reporting that the transmission of the car was damaged.

The car was repaired and the three, with Cadrain as an additional passenger, drove off at about 4:30 p.m. Leaving Saskatoon, they mistakenly took the road for Calgary and continued to that city, with Milgaard driving. Nichol John, who was sitting in the front seat, opened the glove compartment and took out a woman's cosmetic case, containing various cosmetics. She asked whose it was. Milgaard took it from her and, without a word, threw it out the window of the speeding car. Wilson testified that the cosmetic case was not his and that it was not in the car at the time the three friends left Regina. He also swore that in the Calgary bus depot, when Cadrain and John were not present, Milgaard told him that he had "hit a girl" or "got a girl" in Saskatoon and had put her purse in a trash can.

Meanwhile, at 8:30 a.m. on the same day, a child on her way to school had found the body of Gail Miller in an alley. Miller was wearing a black fabric coat. She had been the victim of a savage attack and rape. A knife blade was found under the body and a maroon knife handle in the back yard of one of the houses backing onto the lane. According to RCMP testimony, they had originally been part of the same knife. Items from Miller's purse were also found in various parts of the lane, and her purse was found in a garbage can in another lane nearby. Her wallet was later found in the vicinity of the Cadrain house.

Four months later, in May 1969, Milgaard took a room at the Park Lane Motel in Regina, where a group of young people gathered for a party at which drugs were present. At the trial two Crown witnesses, Craig Melnyk and George Lapchuk, testified that they were there; so were two young women and another young man, in addition to Milgaard. Neither Melnyk nor Lapchuk had been drinking or using drugs. The group watched a TV news broadcast that referred to the investigation into the killing of Gail Miller in

Saskatoon. Melnyk said that when the news item was over, someone, he couldn't remember who, asked Milgaard if he had done it. Milgaard got up on his knees on the bed, put a pillow between his legs, and began hitting the pillow as if stabbing someone. According to Melnyk, he said either, "I killed her" or "I stabbed her ... fourteen times," and then he said, "I fixed her."

Lapchuk, in describing the incident, testified that he said to Milgaard after the news broadcast was finished, "Why don't you admit it? You know you did it." He then said that Milgaard got a funny look on his face, jumped off the bed, and straddled the pillow, and said, "Where is my paring knife?" He went through the motions of stabbing the pillow and then said, "Yes, I stabbed her. I killed her. I stabbed her fourteen times and then she died." Lapchuk said that, having completed his performance, Milgaard just looked at him, shrugged his shoulders, smiled, gave a little laugh, and sat down.

Five issues, or submissions, were raised in Milgaard's first section 690 application:

- that evidence from the two women who were in the room at the Park Lane Motel but who were not called at trial would contradict the evidence of the Crown witnesses Melnyk and Lapchuk;
- that the forensic evidence relating to a lump of frozen semen found at the scene of the murder was not properly handled at trial and, if understood properly by the jury, would have had the effect of exculpating (proving the innocence of) David Milgaard;
- that a statement was made by Wilson in June 1990, recanting some of his previous testimony;
- that one Larry Fisher may have committed the crime and that knowledge of his other crimes might have had an impact on the jury;
- that David Milgaard could not have killed Gail Miller because she was not killed where the body was found, or, in the alternative, if she was killed there, he had insufficient time to commit the crime or was not near the scene of the crime at the time it was committed.

It isn't difficult to see why the analysis of this application took a considerable amount of time and effort. In the end, it was my view that there wasn't enough evidence supporting these submissions to call the legitimacy of the verdict into question.

With respect to the first submission, I pointed out in my letter to Hersh Wolch that one of the girls at the party, Ute Frank, had been available to testify at trial. Milgaard's counsel decided not to call her as a witness. Her statement to the police appeared neither to refer to nor to refute the conversation between Lapchuk and Milgaard. As for Deborah Hall, who also wasn't called at trial, her statement differed from the testimony of Lapchuk and Melnyk only in the interpretation of Milgaard's words. She confirmed the testimony of the Crown witnesses as to what was said, but said that in her opinion Milgaard was making a "sick" remark and wasn't serious. Hall quoted Milgaard as saying that he had sexual relations with the victim after he stabbed her ("and then I fucked her brains out!"). Neither Melnyk nor Lapchuk had mentioned this in their evidence.

The frozen semen referred to in the second submission had been found at the scene of the crime four days after the discovery of the body. The crime scene had been considerably disturbed by this time, putting the integrity of the semen sample in doubt. Analysis showed the presence of A antigens in the sample. Approximately 15 per cent of people have type A blood. Of those, 85 per cent secrete A antigens into other bodily fluids such as saliva and semen. The remaining 15 per cent have A antigens only in their blood. David Milgaard has type A blood, but a test of his saliva performed after his arrest indicated that he was not a secretor, and thus would not have A antigens in his semen. At the trial, it was made clear that because of possible contamination of the sample with other substances, such as leather or leaf mould, which would have given what appeared to be a positive indication of A antigens, nothing should ride on that evidence. The jury was properly instructed on this. Counsel for the defence made no objection because, as the evidence stood, any consideration of it by the jury, in spite of their instruction to disregard it, would have worked in David Milgaard's favour.

A forensic report prepared for Milgaard's application appeared to suggest that the evidence ruled out Milgaard as the source of the sample, and thus, as the perpetrator of the crime. However, in an interview with the Justice Department, Dr. Rex Ferris, the author of the report, took the position that given the likelihood of contamination of the samples, the evidence neither inculpated nor exculpated Milgaard. Forensic experts also agreed that the method of testing for secretor status used at the time was unreliable. Milgaard was not re-tested for Dr. Ferris's report.

The third submission called into question the reliability of the evidence given at trial by Ronald Wilson. It claimed that Wilson, after being coerced and manipulated by the Saskatoon police, lied at the preliminary inquiry and at trial. Wilson made statements dated March 2, 1969, May 23–24, 1969, June 4, 1990, and July 20, 1990. In his June 4, 1990, statement, Wilson denied portions of his May 23, 1969, statement. Nonetheless, the May 23 statement and his comments during his July interview place Milgaard in contact with a woman wearing a dark coat, near the scene of the murder, at or near the time it occurred. Although Wilson denied seeing a knife in Milgaard's possession in June 1990, he admitted in July that he saw a bone-handled hunting knife in Milgaard's possession during their trip from Regina to Saskatoon.

In June 1990, Wilson also stated that he began to implicate Milgaard after lengthy interviews by police in Saskatoon. However, in July 1990, he acknowledged that he had forgotten that he had implicated Milgaard in conversations with police in Regina before he arrived in Saskatoon, where he was again interviewed by police. I considered this oversight by Wilson to be very important in assessing the allegations of police coercion and manipulation that he advanced to explain his incriminating statement of May 1969 and his trial testimony. In my letter to Hersh Wolch, I said, "Mr. Wilson now states that he has no recollection of Nichol John's hysteria when he returned to the car, nor of the incident involving a ladies cosmetic case. Although twenty years have elapsed since this event, others who witnessed it vividly recall the cosmetic case incident. Mr. Cadrain and Ms. John also confirm events, which were the subject of Mr. Wilson's trial testimony, that Mr. Wilson no longer recalls."

With respect to a lie-detector test in Saskatoon that Wilson described at one point as a "sweat session," I wrote: "Mr. Wilson has acknowledged that the questioning was polite and courteous and that the tone of the interview was pleasant. Further, he noted that he was neither threatened nor induced by promises to provide the statement. He confirmed this at the preliminary inquiry, at trial and during his July 1990 interview." On the matter of Wilson's testimony I concluded, "The current retraction by Mr. Wilson of much of his trial evidence is unconvincing."

The fourth submission was the allegation that there was another possible and even likely perpetrator of the crime in the area, Larry Fisher. Fisher, who by the strangest of coincidences actually lived in an apartment in the basement of Albert Cadrain's home, was subsequently convicted of a number of attacks on women. The attacks bore some resemblance to the attack on Gail Miller. At the time of the first application, however, information was incomplete, and there was not then or later any evidence whatsoever directly linking Fisher to the Miller murder. I wrote, "The observation of Linda Fisher, his former wife, that her paring knife was missing at the time of the murder was fully investigated, in addition to other assertions. Neither Ms. Fisher's suspicions, which were conveyed to the police in 1980, nor other well-publicized assertions by her, provide any evidence to link Larry Fisher to Gail Miller's death. Ms. Fisher noted that the photo of a knife similar to the murder weapon indicated a different handle type, colour and blade from her missing knife. However serious Mr. Fisher's criminal record may be, the entire record at trial and in this application reveals no evidence to connect him with the killing of Gail Miller."

The fifth submission, suggesting that David Milgaard could not have killed Gail Miller on logistical grounds, added no new evidence to that consideration and basically asked me to substitute my view for that of the jury. To this I responded, "It is important to remember that the jury heard all this evidence at trial. The jury heard the witnesses, counsels' addresses, and a proper charge on this aspect of the case before they reached their conclusion. Indeed, this was one of the primary defences raised at trial. There is no new evidence to suggest that their conclusion was probably wrong."

Since the remedies under section 690 of the Criminal Code are extraordinary remedies, it has always been recognized that, in evaluating an application, the justice minister is not bound by the rules of evidence. That is, the minister may take into account information that may not be admissible in a court. Such a piece of information was before me in considering the Milgaard case. You may have detected a gap in the trial evidence of Nichol John, who remained at the car when Milgaard and Wilson went for help. Wilson describes her "hysterical behaviour" on his return and her recoiling from Milgaard, but there is no clear explanation from her of why that was so. Here is what John was able to say before the trial about the events of that morning.

On May 24, 1969, John made a statement to the police in which she described the trip the three had made from Regina to Saskatoon. She told of seeing a knife in Milgaard's possession. She described it as a kitchen knife, "used to peel potatoes and things like that," with a maroon handle. She described the arrival in Saskatoon, the encounter with the young woman when directions were sought, and how the vehicle became stuck. She said they ended up in an alley behind the funeral home. She then described how Wilson and Milgaard got out of the vehicle and went in opposite directions to seek help. "The next thing I recall is seeing Dave in the alley on the right side of the car. He had a hold of the same girl we spoke to a minute before. I saw him grab her purse. I saw her grab for her purse again. Dave reached into one of his pockets and pulled out the knife. I don't know which pocket he got the knife from. The knife was in his right hand, I don't know if Dave had a hold of the girl or not at the time. All I recall seeing is him stabbing with the knife." Then Milgaard took the girl around the corner of the alley, she said. She thought she then ran in the direction Wilson had gone but couldn't recall seeing anyone. The next thing she remembered was sitting in the car. She seemed to recall Milgaard putting a purse into a garbage can. She said Milgaard came back to the car and she moved away from him because she didn't want to be near him.

At the preliminary hearing, John told essentially the same story as Wilson, and in addition described the events she had seen in the alley. At the trial, however, she said that she couldn't remember the events involving Milgaard in the lane and his encounter with the girl. She was cross-examined on her statement before the jury, and the jury was properly directed that her statements at the preliminary hearing, which incriminated Milgaard, would constitute no evidence against him unless she adopted them and swore they were true.

Nichol John was interviewed by Department of Justice lawyers during the investigation into the Milgaard application. She still claimed she couldn't remember some of the vital details. It was clear from her statement, however, that she saw something on that early morning in Saskatoon that affected her seriously and that left her tormented by dreams that involve a violent attack and killing. During the interview, she drew a sketch of the position of the vehicle and the T-shaped intersection of the two adjoining alleys. It is an accurate picture of the crime scene and illustrates at least part of her earlier testimony at the preliminary hearing as well as the accurate location of Gail Miller's body.

When I made my decision on the first application, my twelve pages of reasons were communicated to David Milgaard through his counsel, and once his counsel made them public, I made copies available to anyone on request. However, in the press commentary that followed there was very little reference to those reasons. The focus was on the hostile reaction of Milgaard's supporters and counsel to my decision.

Interviews with Milgaard, his family, and his lawyers charged either that I got bad advice and didn't exercise due diligence, or that I was an active co-conspirator in this alleged injustice. These were serious charges and cast aspersions not only on my own integrity but on that of all my advisers, including a retired justice of the Supreme Court of Canada. One of Milgaard's lawyers, David Asper, accused the government of using McIntyre "to legitimize its process by playing on his reputation and expertise in criminal law." Well, it was perfectly true that I sought McIntyre's advice to increase public confidence in the process. Asper went on to charge that I would not release McIntyre's opinion because it would reflect how tainted and slanted the evidence presented to him was. Suggesting that someone of McIntyre's integrity would ever consent to provide an opinion unless he had all the evidence available to the government or that the Justice Department would deceive him was outrageous. It was, ironically, McIntyre himself who cautioned me against allowing my anger at those offensive attacks to lead me to take the serious step of waiving solicitor-client privilege, when doing so would not put an end to the accusations of bad faith.

A second application was made by Milgaard on August 16, 1991.

It was based primarily on the possibility that if the jury had known about the criminal career and proximity of Larry Fisher, they would have acquitted Milgaard. This application generated renewed public interest and pressure. I continued to seek the advice of William McIntyre, but it became clear to me that the case needed a public airing.

The problem I faced was that in the course of the Justice Department investigation, I had learned certain things that I couldn't discuss publicly. I had no difficulty taking the heat for an unpopular decision that I thought was right, but that had ceased to be the issue. The challenge facing me was to find some way to put the specific facts of the case before the public in a way that would restore its confidence in the section 690 process. I was also genuinely perplexed as to how to deal with the presence of Larry Fisher, on the one hand, and what I knew about Nichol John on the other.

Since there was no direct evidence connecting Fisher to the Miller murder, it was unlikely that evidence of his similar offences would be admissible in court if he were to be charged with the murder of Gail Miller. On the other hand, knowledge of such events might have affected the views of a jury trying Milgaard. But the question before me was, Can it be said that a miscarriage of justice has likely occurred because the jury did not have this knowledge and, in fact, some of the Fisher assaults had not even occurred at the date of the Milgaard conviction? To say that a miscarriage has occurred requires one to overlook the evidence that was against Milgaard and that satisfied a jury of his guilt.

On the other hand, what was one to make of Nichol John's accurate knowledge of aspects of the crime and her ability to describe them when first questioned? I asked Eugene to inquire into the possibility that John was suffering from post-traumatic-shock memory loss, which is a recognized phenomenon in the psychiatric literature. Efforts to unlock John's memories weren't successful. Were we just to dismiss her comments, not in the context of admissible evidence at a trial, but in the context of determining whether there was a miscarriage of justice? With the exception of her testimony at the preliminary hearing regarding the events in the lane, testimony that she did not disavow but simply could not remember, all her other testimony was corroborated by other witnesses at the trial, and her own testimony withstood cross-examination.

At this point, I felt I needed to have these dilemmas considered by a court and that I should seek a legal opinion before going further. I didn't want to order a new trial. Realistically, a new trial wouldn't provide a public ventilation of the issues because it was highly unlikely that, twenty-two years after the fact, a fair presentation of the evidence could be made. The case was just too stale. So the result would be that Saskatchewan would probably have no recourse but to stay the charges. This would have the effect of freeing David Milgaard but without the public's knowing whether that was fair and without giving Milgaard any chance to establish his innocence. I didn't think the Saskatchewan Court of Appeal was the proper venue to seek such an opinion. Milgaard's former lawyer Calvin Tallis was now a judge of that court, as was the former attorney general of Saskatchewan. While I was sure that the Court of Appeal could deal fairly and impartially with the matter, my experience with Milgaard's lawyers led me to assume that they would waste no time in attacking the integrity of the court if Milgaard didn't win. I didn't want to recommend a process that had any potential for accusations of "cover-up." It became clear to me that we had to have a public process.

The credibility of this review process was an ongoing preoccupation with me. I had been annoyed at the attacks made on Eugene and the other Justice lawyers by Milgaard's counsel. Eugene had been accused of a pro-prosecution bias, which was certainly not evident to me, nor logical given his previous career as a defence lawyer. I had also been completely puzzled by suggestions by people who were not above gaining a little political mileage from the case that I was "playing politics" with the issue. Surely the most politically expedient thing for me, given the media hype about David Milgaard's "innocence," would have been to grant his application. But political expediency had reared its head from an unexpected corner.

In September, after a particularly exhausting morning at the aboriginal justice conference in Whitehorse, I had been sitting having lunch with John Tait and several of my staff. Partway through lunch, Peter Lugli was called away from the table to pick up an urgent fax from Ottawa. The newswire he returned with landed on our little group like a bombshell. It concerned an encounter the prime minister had had with Joyce Milgaard on a Winnipeg street. The PM had gone out of his way, according to the report, to salute her courage and determination and to show his concern for her son's health.

We were all floored. We just couldn't understand it. The PM had blindsided me on one of my most difficult issues. In the eyes of the media, the meeting signalled that the PM was involved. Norman Spector, the PM's chief of staff, called to assure me, somewhat sheepishly, that Mulroney had said nothing to Mrs. Milgaard about the section 690 application but had only agreed to look into her concerns about her son's living conditions in prison. Several months later, we began to understand the thinking behind this inappropriate intervention. In a chat with the B.C. caucus, Hugh Segal, who replaced Spector in early 1992, talked about the upcoming election and efforts to improve the PM's image. He then turned to the Joyce Milgaard incident in Winnipeg and said something like, "That's the kind of thing he should be doing more of. It was brilliant and portrayed a side of him that the people haven't seen before."

As I told the press, Brian Mulroney was much too good a lawyer to intervene improperly in this matter. He never breathed a word to me about Milgaard, nor did anyone in his office ever attempt to influence my handling of the case. However, Joyce Milgaard is convinced he did, and the media accepted this view. This sort of thing made it very difficult to establish that the only motivation guiding me and my officials was a desire to make the right decision.

The cabinet has the power to refer questions to the Supreme Court, as it did in the Truscott case. I chose this means of getting answers to the crucial questions: Was Milgaard's conviction a miscarriage of justice, and if so, what should be done?

The court held fifteen days of public hearings between January 16 and April 6, 1992, before a panel of five justices. This was not a trial, and a broad range of information that would probably not have been heard in a trial setting was available to the court — and to the public. For instance, David Milgaard was required to testify, something he had not done before. And the court required that both Milgaard and Larry Fisher give samples for lab testing. Since it turned out that both men had the same relevant biological characteristics, these tests neither implicated Fisher nor exonerated Milgaard.

The media were captivated by the extraordinary parade of witnesses into the august Supreme Court, which was jam-packed every day. People waited in line to get a seat. Several journalists were following reasonably closely, and for some, their view of what the right outcome should be changed from day to day.

Unfortunately, the media didn't pick up on some of the most important and disturbing aspects of the Supreme Court hearing. One day the media reports concentrated on the testimony of Lana Edwards, the former wife of one of the partygoers at the Regina motel. Her testimony started a chain of accusation and counter-accusation that ended up discrediting her and bringing the court no closer to the truth. What the press missed on the same day that Edwards testified was the testimony of Milgaard's counsel at his trial, Calvin Tallis, who contradicted his own former client on several points. Tallis also said that Milgaard told him he had looked at the woman pedestrian with a view to possibly robbing her, and that Milgaard had confirmed to him the incident with the cosmetic case. This was not reported.

When counsel for the Province of Saskatchewan attempted to question David Milgaard about his psychiatric history, the court refused to allow him to do so. At the same time, the court permitted Milgaard's lawyer Hersh Wolch to cross-examine Larry Fisher on his psychiatric record. Thus the court did not have before it crucial evidence about Milgaard's history of serious psychiatric problems going back to his childhood. It was only after his release that Milgaard's lawyers acknowledged that their client had a troubled psychiatric history and complained that he had been set free without support for his psychological condition. Milgaard did concede during the hearing that he takes lithium for a depressive condition. He then went on to compare his condition to that of Winston Churchill, with the indulgence of the court.

Milgaard's psychiatric history was highly relevant. Since one possible remedy for the court was to recommend a release of Milgaard by means of a conditional pardon, his continued presence in prison long after attaining eligibility for parole should have flagged this issue. Milgaard became eligible for parole in 1980 after serving ten years of his sentence. His counsel implied he was denied parole because he refused to admit his guilt, but this is not a requirement for parole. The myth that his assertion of innocence denied Milgaard parole was part of the campaign to malign the justice system. Eventually, Joyce Milgaard admitted on CBC's *The Journal*, "We've never said that he could have just walked out that way, by saying he was guilty. David was not a good prisoner."

Milgaard's conflicts with the law predated his arrest for the Miller murder. I think the Supreme Court had an obligation to look at that history. Again, this wasn't a trial. A man who by the court's own judgment had been convicted of murder in a fair process was claiming innocence. The burden of proof was quite rightly on David Milgaard.

In the end, the court gave me its opinion without providing a detailed analysis of the evidence. The court stated clearly that David Milgaard had had a fair trial in 1970 and that there had been ample evidence before the jury to convict him. It could find no fault with the investigation or the conduct of the trial or appeal.

The court then went on to say, "However, fresh evidence has been presented to us. Ronald Wilson, a key witness at the trial, has recanted part of his testimony. Additional evidence has been presented with respect to the alleged motel room confession. More importantly, there was evidence led as to sexual assaults committed by Larry Fisher which came to light in October 1970, when Fisher made a confession [to them].

"In our view, this evidence, together with other evidence we have heard, constitutes credible evidence that could reasonably be expected to have affected the verdict of the jury considering the guilt or innocence of David Milgaard. Our conclusion in this respect is not to be taken as a finding of guilt against Fisher, nor indeed that the evidence would justify charging him with the murder of Gail Miller."

The judges were not satisfied, even on balance, that Milgaard was innocent. The court concluded: "While there is some evidence which implicates Milgaard in the murder of Gail Miller, the fresh evidence presented to us, particularly as to the locations and the patterns of the sexual assaults committed by Fisher, could well affect a jury's assessment of the guilt or innocence of Milgaard. The continued conviction of Milgaard would amount to a miscarriage of justice if an opportunity was not provided for a jury to consider the fresh evidence."

The court advised me to quash the conviction and order a new trial, and I did. As was to be expected, the government of Saskatchewan chose not to go ahead with a new trial given the difficulty of doing so after so many years, and entered a stay.

The Supreme Court had come under considerable criticism during the hearings. Some thought television cameras should have been allowed into the review. At one point, the chief justice asked Ronald Wilson if he would submit to a lie-detector test, despite the fact that the Supreme Court had ruled in 1987 that such tests were inadmissible as evidence. The court's opinion to me was labelled by media as "at best tortuous" and "politically expedient." It seemed clear to me that the court had found the case as difficult as I had. Certainly they had been unconvinced of Milgaard's innocence.

Since the result of the Supreme Court process was the release of Milgaard, I came under criticism for not taking that decision myself earlier. Aside from my own doubts about the merits of the application, the Supreme Court process turned out to be, as I had predicted, the only public forum in which the Milgaard case would be ventilated. It provided the only mechanism for David Milgaard to at least try to convince a court that he had been wrongfully convicted.

I confess that I was perplexed at the opinion of the Supreme Court of Canada. The question I had asked them was whether the continued conviction of David Milgaard constituted a miscarriage of justice. "Reasonable doubt" is the standard of proof during the trial process, which is governed by a presumption of innocence. These concepts should not have been applied in this instance, where a conviction had been upheld on appeal and where the court agreed there was no fault to be found with the trial. It is well established that a person seeking an extraordinary remedy under the royal prerogative of mercy comes not with a presumption of innocence but with a presumption of *guilt*. To dislodge that presumption requires evidence that calls into question the whole weight of evidence that convicted, evidence that has withstood appeal. In Canada, we have phrased this test as whether evidence shows there has *likely* been a miscarriage of justice, or a wrongful conviction. The American law and practice regarding wrongful conviction also derives from the royal prerogative of mercy.

In a recent case before the Supreme Court of the United States, *Herrerra*, the court unanimously upheld a very high standard of proof to establish wrongful conviction, emphasizing that a person who comes to court with a conviction based on an apparently fair trial whose verdict has been upheld by a full appellate process comes with a presumption of guilt. In the U.S. Supreme Court decision, Justice Harry Blackmun said, "If a prisoner can show that he is *probably actually innocent* [emphasis added], in light of all the evidence, then he has made a 'truly persuasive demonstration.' " I quote the American language because it comes closest to the words used by the Supreme Court of Canada judges when they said clearly that they did not believe that Milgaard had established that he is innocent "on a preponderance of the evidence."

The Milgaard case shows, I think, a need to clarify the tests to be applied in evaluating section 690 applications. In its explanation of its opinion, the Supreme Court did not add to our understanding of this issue. In the Supreme Court's summary of the evidence linking David Milgaard to the murder of Gail Miller, the court used the term "ample" to describe the evidence that was before the jury when Milgaard was convicted but used the term "some evidence" later in their opinion. I'm unable to determine the basis for this change in terminology. In this matter the court gave credence to the recantation of Ronald Wilson, even though the chief justice threatened to cite him for contempt of court for giving contradictory answers within the space of a few minutes during the hearing! In its own jurisprudence, the Supreme Court of Canada has described the testimony of recanting witnesses as highly unreliable on principle, yet here the justices credited the recantations of a witness whose original testimony was corroborated by other witnesses and who was shown during the hearing to be patently unreliable. I was left scratching my head.

The Supreme Court seems to have set the evidentiary threshold in this case at the same level as for a new trial. Given that this was not a regular appeal, but an extraordinary remedy, the lack of weight that the court put on the decisions of the trial and appeal courts is surprising. The importance that the court attached to the Larry Fisher evidence ("speculation" might be a better term) constitutes a remarkably low threshold for challenging convictions past the appellate process.

What was the result of all this? Well, a great many Canadians, perhaps a majority, think that David Milgaard was found innocent by the Supreme Court of Canada. When Larry Fisher was released from jail in 1994, he was described by the media as the man "linked to the murder of Gail Miller," for which Milgaard served twenty-two years in prison. Now, Fisher is no candidate for the Order of Canada, but he has never been linked in any way that counts to the murder of Gail Miller. He has been found guilty by the media in the absence of any evidence. Milgaard is in a kind of limbo because his innocence hasn't been established in law and probably never can be. He's free, but it isn't clear that he was wrongly convicted. The attorney general of Saskatchewan at the time of his release, Robert Mitchell, said publicly that in his view, Milgaard was properly convicted.

Although the justices of the Supreme Court tried very hard to get to understand Milgaard's conviction, they were limited in their ability to assess the truth of what they had been told. In 1992, Joyce Milgaard provided RCMP investigators with a tape recording she had made of a conversation with Ronald Wilson in 1981 or 1982. The RCMP's 1994 report declared that in this conversation Wilson did not express any concerns about his treatment by the police or indicate that his 1969 trial testimony implicating Milgaard was fabricated. The recorded interview does, however, contain an exchange between Wilson and Joyce Milgaard regarding a $10,000 reward for anyone who could prove Milgaard's innocence. In his testimony before the Supreme Court, Wilson denied any knowledge of the reward before that very day.

David Milgaard was released without any formal supervision. Conditional release is an important vehicle for enabling prisoners to readjust to life on the outside. Since his release there have been several reports of Milgaard's brushes with the law. Unfortunately, he is under no obligation to accept any sort of supervision or guidance from the state unless he is convicted of another offence. Under the circumstances, given that the court was not convinced of his innocence, consideration ought to have been given by the court to what would follow the implementation of its recommendations.

After the Milgaard case, I initiated a review of the section 690 process in the Department of Justice. The recommendations stemming from that review, I'm told, are now making their way to the office of the current minister, Allan Rock. In advance of any major reform, Rock has made two departures from prior practice in dealing with the application of Colin Thatcher, a former cabinet minister in the government of Saskatchewan, who was convicted of the murder of his wife. First, he provided the department's investigation brief (a summary of the information gathered during the investigation of the application) to the applicant and his counsel for their response and comment before he considered it. That makes sense to me, although it could sometimes create problems of confidentiality. Second, his seventy-five pages of reasons for rejecting the application were immediately published in a form suitable for distribution. I'm also told that the Department of Justice is now more aggressive in responding to inaccuracies or attacks in the press relating to ongoing section 690 applications.

The unresolved issues in the Donald Marshall case led the government of Nova Scotia to convene a royal commission, which eventually recommended the creation of an independent body to review claims of wrongful conviction. These recommendations were raised with the provincial attorneys general as well as the Department of Justice in 1991 but didn't find much support. The most common concern was that the creation of such a body would become yet another level of court. The move from the courts to the executive responds to the need for some finality in the process.

The British have just concluded their royal commission into the workings of their justice system. The powers comparable to those granted under section 690 are exercised in Britain by the home secretary. The British situation differs from the Canadian in that Britain is not a federal state, and the home secretary, unlike the Canadian minister of justice, is in charge of the prosecutorial arm of government and thus not at arm's length from the review process. This royal commission has recommended the creation of an independent body to review applications for relief from wrongful conviction, or miscarriage of justice. To the extent that such an approach could reduce the politics surrounding these applications, it would be desirable, but I doubt that can really be achieved. I wouldn't want to do away with public interest or even public pressure, where it might lead to the discovery of evidence or witnesses capable of establishing a wrongful conviction. It is important to remember the desirability of erring on the side of innocence. The capacity for publicly expressed outrage at injustice is a hallmark of a free and democratic society. It is an important safeguard of justice, however uncomfortable it may occasionally be for those on the receiving end.

Did David Milgaard kill Gail Miller? Perhaps none of us will ever know for certain. I had some tough questions about the Milgaard case, but I don't for a moment begrudge Milgaard his freedom. The issue was never a personal one with me. Whatever my own views, there came a point when I had to let it go. Dealing with this and other cases has made me quite modest about my own ability to know the absolute truth. That is why we must find methods of post-conviction review that make possible a fair and open-minded approach to the possibility of error in our courts. But I hope I can be forgiven for saying that "wrongful conviction" can be as unjust when it occurs in the court of public opinion as when it happens in a court of law.

11

A Sense of Accomplishment

As a government we were now more than three years into our mandate, so in early 1992 my colleagues and I found ourselves thinking more and more about the election that would have to be called by the fall of 1993.

The national unity question had become a constant backdrop for everything we did. In order to provide some outlet for the frustrations of Canadians after the failure of Meech, and to find out if there was any consensus on the issues that would arise in any renewal of constitutional discussions, the prime minister had decided in the fall of 1990 to launch the Citizens' Forum on National Unity. If Canadians felt they hadn't been listened to in the process of negotiating Meech, this would be their chance. Keith Spicer, chairman of the Canadian Radio-television and Telecommunications Commission, was persuaded to take a leave from the CRTC to chair the public consultation process, which came to be known as the Spicer commission.

Unfortunately, what the Spicer commission found was very little consensus on the key issues of national unity and an enormous well of anger against government. Keith Spicer's introduction to the commission's report spoke, in particular, of the anger of Canadians towards Brian Mulroney. This, to put it gently, did not go down well with the prime minister. As Spicer himself makes clear, the PM made no attempt to influence his report. Nonetheless, he expressed very clearly among ministers his anger at what he considered Spicer's betrayal. Brian Mulroney could never accept that people he had appointed did not feel obliged to become his defenders. Perhaps anger was the only response open to a proud man who had been told that his fellow citizens detested him.

In April 1991, Joe Clark was named minister for constitutional affairs, replacing Senator Lowell Murray as the minister responsible for the unity file. Lowell's failure to ensure the ratification of Meech dictated his departure, and Brian Mulroney did not himself have the public credibility to lead another effort, although he could never bring himself to admit it. Joe wasn't ecstatic about leaving the Department of External Affairs, where he had been the minister since the 1984 election. I was a member of the Cabinet Committee on Canadian Unity and Constitutional Affairs (formerly Federal-Provincial Relations), which Joe now chaired, and he set out an agenda of meetings that took us around Canada during the spring and summer of 1991, bringing the unity discussions to the regions. Our mandate was to prepare proposals for constitutional change on behalf of the federal government. The resulting document, *Shaping Canada's Future Together: Proposals*, was published on September 28, 1991. The proposals were wide-ranging but dealt only with issues that could be amended on the 7/50 rule — that is, by the Parliament of Canada and the legislatures of seven provinces whose populations added up to at least 50 per cent of the national total. It was the inclusion of some provisions requiring unanimous approval that had scuppered Meech.

A House-Senate committee had been established, led by Senator Gerald Beaudoin and Winnipeg MP Dorothy Dobbie, to which our federal proposals were referred for consideration. To facilitate the public consideration of the proposals in time to meet Beaudoin-Dobbie's reporting deadline of February 28, 1992, five three-day national conferences were planned for early 1992. These forums were shaping up to be the same sort of "elite" exercises that had been criticized roundly in the final days of Meech Lake, only this time, instead of politicians, the participants were to be academics and representatives of organizations and interest groups. At one meeting of our cabinet committee I suggested that a number of ordinary Canadians be invited to attend, selected by a lottery. People could write in expressing their interest in participating and then a certain number would be chosen by lot. These RSPs (randomly selected persons) gave the meetings credibility and made contributions that weren't reflections of organized interests.

Once the consultation on our discussion document had been completed in February 1992, the unity committee's role was superseded by Joe Clark's activities in negotiating with the provinces and representatives of aboriginal organizations. Throughout the spring of 1992, I felt increasingly uneasy about this process. The only other federal minister involved in the negotiations was Benoît Bouchard, the political minister for Quebec since Lucien Bouchard's departure. Joe was trying both to chair the meetings and to represent the federal government's point of view. I told Hugh Segal, the prime minister's new chief of staff, about my frustration at not being at the table. I don't know if it was the prime minister's call or Joe's, but I wasn't invited. As justice minister, I thought my role there was obvious.

I was concerned about two things. First, Joe doesn't like lawyers and tends to discount legal advice. Although my deputy, John Tait, was asked to be close by to advise the federal team, John was never asked to brief Joe directly. I thought Joe might listen to me if I was at the table, supporting him. John's devotion to resolving our constitutional problems went beyond his concerns as a public servant. After the failure of Meech, he reminded me of the personal anguish that would follow a break-up of the country. John's wife, Sonia Plourde, is a Québécoise, "pure laine." John is an anglo-Montrealer. Since 27 per cent of anglophone Quebeckers are married to francophones, John's is but one of thousands of families who would be torn by conflicting loyalties if Quebec were to separate. The architects of division were playing not with abstractions but with flesh-and-blood human beings.

The legal implications of the concepts Joe and his provincial colleagues were bandying about were profound. In particular, I became concerned when the federal government was suddenly on record as supporting the addition of the recognition of an "inherent" right to self-government for aboriginal peoples without any sense of what this would mean. When I expressed my reservations about this at one of our now infrequent cabinet unity committee meetings, Joe's reaction was to get very angry.

The second reason I wanted to be at the meetings was simply

tactical. The federal government needed a "bad cop" at the table. As a Quebecker, Benoît couldn't easily play this role, but my portfolio made it a natural role for me. Since the dynamic of much of the discussion had the federal government on one side and nine provinces (Quebec wasn't participating) and four aboriginal organizations on the other, it was enormously difficult for the federal position to withstand that sort of concerted pressure. For the first time since I had arrived in Ottawa, the constitutional file was at arm's length from the prime minister. Joe Clark was flying solo. My impression was that he wanted to show that he, too, was a capable negotiator and could perhaps succeed in getting a workable constitutional agreement where Brian Mulroney had failed. When the announcement came that an agreement had been reached on July 7, I was surprised and apprehensive, but no more so, I'm told, than the prime minister, who was in Europe at the time.

The agreement included the inherent right to aboriginal self-government, the recognition of Quebec as a distinct society, a Canada clause to serve as a preamble to the Constitution, a reformed Senate, provincial vetoes over changes to federal institutions, and more. It was referred to as the Pearson agreement, after the building in which the final negotiations had been concluded. After private discussions with Premier Robert Bourassa indicated that Quebec would accept these proposals, the whole road show then moved to Charlottetown with the PM for the negotation and signing of the final agreement in order to reconfederate Canada in the same place where it had been confederated in the first place.

I remember receiving a telephone briefing from John Tait on the form of the final agreement and feeling my heart sink. The good news was a recognition of B.C.'s growing population by allocation of more House of Commons seats. The bad news was a guarantee of 25 per cent of the House of Commons seats to Quebec, even if its population dropped below that percentage of the total population of the country. I thought this was a non-starter. While it was supposed to be a trade-off for Quebec's agreement to equal provincial representation in the Senate, it was completely unrelated to Quebec's traditional position, which called for more autonomy as a province, rather than greater political weight in Ottawa. I knew it would be unpopular in the west.

Back in the fall of 1991, the cabinet unity committee had discussed a possible referendum on constitutional proposals. The Speech from the Throne in May 1991 had promised legislation "to provide for greater participation of Canadian men and women in constitutional change." I was wary because I feared that a national referendum could divide the country in the same way the 1917 and 1942 referendums on conscription had done. When the question came up in cabinet about drafting referendum legislation "just in case," I argued strongly that once we had it, we would have no choice but to use it. However, once Joe began negotiating with the provinces and aboriginal organizations in March 1992 and once Quebec had determined to hold a referendum vote on any constitutional proposals from the rest of Canada, a national referendum seemed unavoidable. Legislation providing for referendums was tabled in May and passed by the House in June, shortly before the Pearson agreement was reached. In view of the breadth of the agreement reached at Charlottetown and the new climate of participation, Canadians would demand a direct say. Unfortunately, that very breadth and the short time for consideration of the complex proposals — short because Quebec had already set a referendum date of October 26 — didn't bode well for such an exercise. I give Joe full credit for getting his agreement, but there were red flags sticking out all over it.

Not being a part of the constitutional negotiations in the spring of 1992 gave me time to turn my attention to the things I still wanted to accomplish in Justice. The gun control legislation had passed by a margin of 189 to 13 in November 1991. Liberal justice critic Warren Allmand declared that when it was implemented, Canada would have the best gun control legislation in the world, a claim that even I didn't make for it, proud as I was of our efforts. Critics of the bill turned their attention to the regulations yet to be passed. It was certainly true that some of the force of the legislation would rest in the specific features of the regulations, but the act itself was powerful even without them. The gun control bill had provided for Parliament to have thirty sitting days to examine regulations and make suggestions for change. I wanted the regulations finished as soon as possible, and on March 10, 1992, they were tabled in the House.

My staff had worked incredibly hard to help push the gun

control legislation through caucus. In September 1991, Ray Castelli had replaced Michael Ferrabee as my chief of staff. Michael had stayed longer than the two years he had promised me in 1989 and was determined that his successor would be a British Columbian. Ray was originally from Prince Rupert and had been a Conservative Party field organizer in B.C. during the 1988 election. Soon after, he joined the staff of Fisheries Minister Tom Siddon as executive assistant. To put it bluntly, Ray and I didn't like each other much at first.

Our mutual antipathy dated from 1989. When Brian Mulroney appointed his new cabinet that year, he didn't designate new political ministers. Pat Carney had been the political minister for British Columbia, and her retirement had left the position vacant. The political minister is responsible for coordinating the political strategy in the province, reporting to the prime minister on issues that affect the province, and supervising appointments. He or she has a small additional allocation for staff. Although he wasn't formally designated political minister in 1989, Tom Siddon was given the allocation for staffing. Marjory LeBreton, the PM's deputy chief of staff, insisted that Tom wasn't the political minister, so naturally the other B.C. ministers thought they should have some say in how this money was spent. Tom, however, was being encouraged by Peter White, the PM's principal secretary, to go ahead as *de facto* political minister. When Tom appointed Ray Castelli to oversee the Ministers' Regional Office in Vancouver, this created some resentment among the other ministerial staffers there. The situation could easily have been clarified if the PM, or his chief of staff, had made it clear what Tom's role was to be. Instead, the situation festered and created unnecessary bad blood for more than a year, until the next shuffle, in which I got the nod.

For several months before he was scheduled to depart, Michael tried to convince me of the merits of Ray as his replacement. I knew that Ray, who had become Tom's chief of staff in 1990, had done an excellent job for him, but because of the resentments of 1989, I just couldn't see how we could get along. Finally, I agreed to have dinner with Ray. As we began to talk that evening, we both realized that we had completely false impressions of each other. The more we talked, the more I liked Ray, and by the end of dinner, I had offered him the job. Ray agreed and Tom Siddon was gracious about his joining my staff.

My new chief of staff and I got along famously. He was not in the least interested in policy, except in the broadest sense, but he was very astute politically and a superb manager of people. Realizing that I needed a full-time scheduler, Ray hired Jane Hamilton, who did wonders for my efficiency and comfort and whose friendliness won her many admirers. Another of the new additions was the delightful Marianne Campbell, a young lawyer who came to work on my policy and issues staff. Aside from being very bright and having a talent for working closely with MPs and responding to their concerns, Marianne fit right in because of her off-the-wall sense of humour. She quickly discovered how much she needed it! The youthful but politically sophisticated Frédéric Loiselle became my legislative assistant.

When it came to pushing my legislative proposals through caucus, my approach had always been to be honest about my own view but to try to find ways of reducing the political peril for those who were opposed to the initiatives being represented. A key part of this strategy was not to shut out caucus members who opposed us, but to make sure that they had a full and fair hearing. More important, we wanted to let Canadians who shared the views of the opponents know that their points of view were being argued. This process not only created a climate of fairness and respect, it also enabled us to develop better legislation.

When John Dixon joined our staff, he brought with him a very special knowledge of the gun control issue. John was a hunter with a keen interest in preserving the right of Canadians to enjoy shooting sports. He supported good gun control and could talk knowledgeably about our proposals. He also helped us to keep our attention on the technical feasibility of what we were trying to do by telling us how firearms owners would be affected. This required a significant shift in the attitude of the Justice officials managing this file, who seemed to have no idea of how hunters and sports shooters actually used and handled their firearms. John and Marianne became a formidable team in working with members of Parliament and the public.

My staff kept in constant contact with MPs to hear their concerns and provide them with answers to a myriad of questions from their constituents. The opponents of gun control were active in promoting false information about the effects of our proposals. My staff helped arrange well-informed speakers for public meetings and answered phone calls carefully. Everything was done to avoid the paranoia that results from rumour.

Gun control advocates often assume that the proximity of "shooters" to the policy process means it will be undermined. The reality was quite the opposite. When gun owners realized that I was being advised by people who knew something about firearms, their paranoia level dropped and they could focus on what we were actually proposing, which was "All guns out of the wrong hands, and the wrong guns out of all hands." Alas, John Dixon's phrase tended to make people's eyes glaze over. The basic philosophy was, however, firmly grounded on the available research as to what forms of gun control do reduce firearms deaths and what forms do not. Our intent, while continuing to respect the interests of law-abiding firearms owners, was to make sure that people who ought not to have guns didn't have them, and that certain types of firearms with no legitimate hunting or sporting purpose were taken out of circulation altogether.

To that end the Firearms Acquisition Certificate (FAC) became harder to obtain. Strict storage and handling requirements were introduced for all firearms to reduce accidental death and injury and to make theft of firearms more difficult and less rewarding. What this meant was a legal requirement for *every* firearm in Canada to be stored under lock and key. Many previously unrestricted types of firearms joined handguns on the list of restricted weapons that must be registered and are subject to especially stringent rules on storage, use, and transport. Other types of high-power semi-automatic firearms were prohibited outright. The size of cartridge magazines permitted for centrefire semi-automatic firearms was limited. Maximum penalties for firearms-related offences were extended, as were the lengths of orders prohibiting possession of firearms. Police were authorized to seize FACs as well as firearms. Courts were required to consider firearms prohibition orders in every application for bail or a restraining order, a boon in cases of domestic violence. While we increased dramatically the number of guns that had to be registered, we rejected the idea of universal registration as too costly in view of its marginal effect on public safety. Implementing this sweeping legislation was going to be expensive and time-consuming, and that became our next priority.

Our concern for proper implementation led to close work with the provinces and the mailing of a tabloid-sized brochure to every Canadian household, describing the main provisions of the new law and explaining how to obtain more detailed information. Our focus was on the "field and stream" gun owners.

The final stage of the lengthy gun control process was the review by MPs of the regulations in the spring of 1992. The Standing Committee on Justice and Solicitor General chaired by MP Bob Horner took on the task. The day that I received its report, I felt jubilant. The recommendations were sensible and readily acceptable. They could be put into effect right away. I called Bob to thank him for his committee's excellent work and for confirming my faith in a more open and inclusive legislative process.

With the struggle for gun control now over, I could turn my attention to the Canadian Human Rights Act. When I was setting out my agenda in 1990, I had told my officials that I could take only one divisive issue through caucus at a time. Abortion was already on our plate, and firearms control would have to be next.

Some of the proposed amendments to the act were only mildly controversial, such as those dealing with the requirement for "reasonable accommodation" of persons with disabilities. Although there were some rumblings from the direction of Treasury Board, where there was concern about the cost implications for the federal government, pressure from caucus members like Dr. Bruce Halliday, a strong advocate for disabled people, would prove very helpful in pushing this file forward. The tough issue was my proposal to include sexual orientation among the prohibited grounds of discrimination in the act.

This issue had surfaced in the first Mulroney mandate. In 1985, a parliamentary committee had issued a report called *Equality for All* that recommended sexual orientation be included among the forbidden grounds for discrimination in all federal law. The justice minister of the time, John Crosbie, had responded with a document, *Toward Equality*, that committed the government to doing this. There had then been a huge battle in the Conservative caucus. Those who opposed the change went to the prime minister and got a commitment not to act until after the next election.

Following a 1989 Supreme Court of Canada decision called *Andrews v. Law Society of British Columbia*, the federal government decided that sexual orientation should be treated as a prohibited ground of discrimination under the Charter. However, the Charter binds the actions only of governments, not private citizens or companies, whereas the Canadian Human Rights Act binds the federally regulated private sector, such as banks, railways, and airlines. The bottom line for me was that the government was on record as being committed to making this change. I felt we had to act before another election. If we weren't going to fulfil our promise, we had better say so.

The human rights community acts with a fair amount of unanimity in lobbying the government. Groups that would benefit from the less controversial proposed amendments insisted that all the amendments be dealt with as a package. This helped to keep the sexual orientation issue from being isolated. Many people in our caucus strongly supported the sexual orientation amendment; as with abortion, however, there was no consensus. The religious right was very unhappy. My goal was to find enough common ground to enable the opponents at least to acquiesce in allowing the legislation to go forward.

On October 23, 1991, my efforts to table the CHRA amendments received a setback from Defence Minister Marcel Masse. The policy of the Canadian Forces was that homosexuals could not serve. Although the government had accepted that sexual orientation was a prohibited ground of discrimination under the Charter, the military argued that its policy should be seen as a reasonable limit on that protection. This policy was being challenged in several pending court cases. The cases involved people whose sexual orientation had not come to the Forces' attention through any questionable behaviour. One man had left his duffle bag behind in a gym. In attempting to identify the owner, someone read a letter in the bag that revealed that the owner was conducting a homosexual relationship. A woman who had received outstanding evaluations of her work was subjected to aggressive interrogation that eventually elicited the information that she was homosexual. As these cases worked their way through the system, it was our view that the military was on pretty thin ground.

In addition, the treatment of the people involved was outrageous and wouldn't reflect well on the Forces in a public court hearing. Justice advised that the policy regarding homosexuals be changed.

Long discussions took place with the senior command of the Canadian Forces. Eventually, the chief of the defence staff, General de Chastelain, agreed to change the policy. As the military was about to announce the change, the defence minister decided that perhaps he should inform caucus. Marcel had done no preparatory work whatsoever for the meeting. He stood at the podium and simply said some changes to military policy were to be announced later that day, and that Mary Collins, as associate minister responsible for personnel policy in the Forces, would explain them. To my astonishment he added, "And then Kim will explain the reasons why Justice says we have to do this." With that he stepped off the podium, went out the door and caught a plane to Rome! Mary had received no warning that she would be called on, but she did her best to set out the policy changes relating to gays in the military. Her announcement was greeted with consternation by some members. I then took the floor to set out the legal framework. I would come to discover that the anti-gay element in our caucus harboured a deep suspicion of the Department of Justice on this issue, and my legal analysis of the cases working their way through the courts was greeted with outright hostility by a vocal few. My impromptu presentation wasn't as considered as it should have been in such touchy circumstances, and, following a ruckus from the opponents of the change, the announcement was hastily cancelled.

During this period I was less shocked by the homophobia of MPs who I knew espoused fundamentalist religious doctrines than by the almost casual disdain in jokes and comments from people I had considered to be of moderate views. Perhaps I was more sensitive because it reminded me of the sexist humour that had once been considered acceptable in polite conversation. At a meeting of P&P, as the chief of the defence staff and some other officers entered to brief ministers on the issue, there was some banter and Brian Mulroney joked, "Well, at least they aren't holding hands." This was greeted with great guffaws around the table, but I thought the comment was insensitive. Who was to know who, around the table, might be gay and be hurt by these remarks? At another meeting with ministers on the same issue, the discussion focussed on whether gays could be military leaders. I found the mindless stereotyping annoying, and since I had been reading Mary Renault's historical novels about Alexander the Great the previous summer, I decided to vent my irritation. I passed a note to John Tait, who was sitting beside me. It said, "Alexander the Great was a homosexual, for heaven's sake. His troops didn't mind as long as he was carrying on with his childhood friend Hephaestion. They did begin to grumble when, after the conquest of Persia, he took up with a young Persian eunuch. This was because the Persians were considered utterly effete. They wore trousers, unlike the manly Macedonians, who wore skirts!" John's eyes widened; then he carefully folded the note and put it in his pocket.

In the end the policy was changed, but the process had been damaging. Since a copy of the military's prepared announcement had become public at the same time caucus was first learning of the proposed changes, it was evident that the delay between proposal and implementation had been caused by caucus opposition. This suggested that the opponents were a more significant force in caucus than they were. The credibility of the government suffered from what appeared to be an inability to manage its own agenda. Such problems could have been avoided by giving MPs an opportunity to understand the origins of the change and the reasons the military had finally accepted it. The approach we had taken in dealing with gun control was the only way such issues could be dealt with without tearing caucus apart.

Working closely with MPs and listening to their concerns was the way we also set out to move the Human Rights Act amendments forward. In the fall of 1991 I met with a small group of the most adamant caucus opponents to hear them out on their objections. This also gave me a chance to remind them of the government's commitment in 1986 and to try to point out that the sooner we dealt with the issue of sexual orientation, the sooner it would "fall off the table." When similar changes had been made to provincial human rights statutes, most recently by a conservative government in Nova Scotia, the controversy had tended to disappear soon after the issue was resolved.

My main contacts with the religious opposition in caucus were John Reimer, who had chaired the special committee on Bill C-80, the first version of the gun control bill, and Benno Friesen, both well respected among their ideological confrères in caucus. Neither John nor Benno supported the idea that gays should be discriminated against, but they were both deeply committed to the view that homosexuality was wrong and were unwilling to support any initiative that would communicate approbation for it. In meetings with them from the fall of 1991 through the spring of 1992, members of my staff proposed ways that would enable the two men to support the proposed amendments and still stay true to the beliefs of the constituencies they represented. We would make progress, only to have agreements fall apart when they returned to Ottawa from visits to their ridings.

The approach I finally proposed in April 1992 was to model our legislation on the Ontario Human Rights Code, in which sexual orientation was a prohibited ground of discrimination but a definition section put some limits on the interpretation. The term "spouse" was defined as someone of the opposite sex. "Marital status" referred to the state of being single, engaged, widowed, divorced, separated, married, or living in a conjugal relationship with a person of the opposite sex for more than a year. This second definition neither denied nor conferred any benefit; it simply reflected the legal status quo, namely that people of the opposite sex who live in a conjugal relationship for more than a year are recognized as married at common law and have legal claims against each other on that basis. The definition of "spouse" did not prevent the recognition of same-sex spouses for certain purposes, but it did not grant it as a matter of law. The presence of these definitions in our bill reassured the opponents of the measure that we were not making a radical change. Since we were putting the federal statute on the same basis as Ontario's provincial law, I felt we were on pretty safe ground. I was beginning to feel optimistic because many of my caucus colleagues who had been adamantly opposed were won over by our approach, which enabled them to argue for traditional family values while making a change they knew would have to come sometime.

As with gun control, we carefully briefed associations that were opposed to us. On this issue we met with various church groups. Many church people complimented us on achieving the laudable goal of protecting people against discrimination, while at the same time making it possible for those whose beliefs did not accept homosexuality to support the legislation. These personal conversations were almost always followed up with faxes indicating that, unfortunately, the government would not be able to count on these sentiments being expressed publicly by the religious organization. Whereas in private, representatives of these congregations seemed quite capable of recognizing the difference between public policy and religious belief, and between protection against discrimination and the advocacy of a belief or practice, in public they often appeared more sensitive to the politics of their own membership than to those of the broader society. I was dismayed by their lack of courage.

I urged caucus to let me table the legislation before the summer. There were cases making their way through the courts related to the rights of same-sex couples, and I warned my colleagues that if Parliament didn't say something on the issue, the courts would be making the law. Some opponents of the legislation argued that we should let the courts force us to make the change. I pointed out that this was a total abdication of our responsibility as legislators, as well as a dangerous path to take. The courts might well make a law, but it might not be one they liked. At one caucus meeting a long list of MPs spoke on the issue, many very supportive, others opposed, either because they were against gay rights or because they were afraid it was too close to an election. In the end, I couldn't get the go-ahead to table before the summer.

My frustration at the unwillingness of my colleagues to take the responsibility of legislating in an important area of human rights was particularly acute because I had been giving a great deal of thought to the role of Parliament versus the role of the courts. I used this theme in a number of speeches that spring marking the tenth anniversary of the Charter of Rights and Freedoms. In one I emphasized that the Charter was only one mechanism for achieving just government in Canada; it only worked if the other institutions of government fulfilled their responsibilities. I pointed out that the courts do not have the resources available to legislatures in the making of public policy. To the irritation of those who support a broader role for the courts, I said that I was opposed to the doctrine of "extension," the American practice where courts not only judge whether a law is constitutional but also prescribe how it must be written rather than leaving it to the legislatures, or in some cases even mandate specific actions that must be taken by government.

My hostility to the doctrine of extension was matched by my hostility to the tendency of legislators to abdicate their responsibilities to the courts. Over the past two years, I had been struck by how often some of my caucus colleagues would urge me, as attorney general, to *push* the Charter (in other words, be aggressive in defending the prerogatives of Parliament against Charter challenges in court) but would then run for cover rather than take on the task of legislating in precisely those controversial areas where the Supreme Court of Canada had said repeatedly that Parliament should be setting the rules.

As Parliament adjourned for the summer, two questions dominated conversations on the Hill. Would Brian Mulroney step down as leader of the Conservatives, and would the Charlottetown Accord be approved by Canadians? When the position of secretary general of the United Nations was being filled in late 1991, the PM was touted as a possible candidate. People who claim to be in the know have told me that the position was his if he wanted it. It would have made a great exit from public life in the middle of a mandate. For one thing, going to the UN would have placed him a notch higher in prestige than his rival Pierre Trudeau, whose candidacy had been speculated about years before. But with the failure of Meech Lake, Brian Mulroney couldn't go anywhere. His departure would have led to the exit of much of the Quebec caucus. What was to have been a high note to depart on, Meech Lake, had turned out to be a humiliating defeat that needed to be vindicated. The question was, Would Charlottetown do the trick? All three national political parties supported it, as did all the provincial premiers and the major aboriginal organizations, so it hardly seemed possible that it wouldn't succeed. But then, people had thought the same thing about Meech.

Throughout 1992, Ray Castelli had been receiving regular calls from party members offering support if I should decide to contest the leadership. Since my appointment to cabinet in 1989, my profile in the country had risen considerably. The justice portfolio was controversial and, as a result, tended to transform the occupant into a national figure. My profile in the party had also grown.

I was a frequent guest speaker, and by the time the leadership campaign began, I had visited more than a hundred Tory ridings. In January 1991, I was the guest speaker at the annual Sir John A. Macdonald Society dinner in Toronto. At this event, the Toronto Tory establishment gathers in the Albany Club to listen to a speaker who is always a heavy hitter in the party. Luminaries like the not-yet vice-regal Hal Jackman puffed away on their Havanas as I spoke, and I left with my clothes reeking of cigar smoke. Back in 1990, John Bassett, a long-time Conservative, had seen me speak at the swearing-in of Charles Dubin as chief justice of Ontario. Describing himself as "captivated," he decided then and there, without having met me, that I was going to be the next leader. John was a loyal supporter of the PM but made it clear that if Brian Mulroney decided to go, he would be backing me.

In Ray's view, the last possible date the prime minister could step down (if he chose to) and still leave time for a successor to put a new stamp on the government was November 1992. At the beginning of the summer recess, Ray presented me with a binder containing a long memo on leadership campaigns. In it, he had put together everything he knew about what was involved and what kind of support would be needed. He asked me to read the memo and think about it over the summer. "If you're going to do this, you'd better know what you're getting into."

That summer I tried to wrestle with the question of whether I really wanted to be prime minister or just liked the idea of people thinking that I *could* be prime minister. I was worried about what such a commitment would mean for my life. Did I want to make the sacrifices in privacy and time that would come with being leader? I loved my work as a minister. It was hard to have a life, but at least I had some privacy. After Howard and I separated, I had little interest in a social life, at least insofar as dating was concerned. I enjoyed being with friends but hadn't been tempted to look for a serious relationship. In July, while in England on business, I was able to attend a country weekend in celebration of a friend's fiftieth birthday. It was a fabulous party and for the first time in over a year I devoted an entire weekend just to having fun. In my mind, it was my "coming-out" party after the divorce. Afterwards, I began to wonder if I wanted to subject myself to the loneliness that would come from being in the prime-ministerial spotlight. Weekend parties would be few and far between.

I spent hours discussing the leadership with friends and family. For some friends, it was a chance to fulfil the vision they shared with me about a different way of doing politics. We tried to figure out where my support would come from. Was there time to revive Tory fortunes? The Conservatives were at historically low levels for a governing party. Patrick Kinsella, whose MarkTrend polling company kept tabs on the political pulse in B.C., claimed that if an election were to be held that summer, no Conservatives would be elected in the province.

I did have many supporters in Vancouver, including a wonderful group of business women who were eager to get involved in a leadership campaign for a candidate who they felt would offer something new and different. It was this group who put together something very "new and different" for me in the way of a fundraiser in early September. Diana Lam and I had often talked about organizing a fundraiser that would be an evening of comedy. We thought entertaining supporters would be a better way of saying thank you than just charging them to listen to a speech. Eventually the group came up with the idea of holding the event at Punchlines, a Vancouver comedy club we would take over for an evening. The club's improv group would entertain after dinner, and then I would do a stand-up comedy routine based on my experiences in Ottawa. And so "A Night at the Kimprov" was born. The organizers designed a T-shirt given to everyone who bought a ticket that featured a caricature of me sitting on a stool in a spotlight and holding a microphone with the caption, "No one ever does me Justice." As plans began to firm up, I asked Jay Jacobson, a young man on my staff who did comedy as a sideline, to help me with my routine.

The week of the event, Joe Clark was in Vancouver and came into the Ministers' Regional Office. I told him about our unconventional fundraiser and gave him a T-shirt. "Stand-up comedy?" he said, raising his eyebrows. "Pretty risky, if you ask me." The night of the event, almost all of the guests wore their T-shirts, some under tuxedos, others over other clothes, which helped create a great mood. After dinner the improv team came on stage and, taking ideas from the audience, improvised some hilarious skits. Just as they were finishing, some of the Punchlines people approached me and said they wanted to wire me for sound so that I could do a skit with the cast. This was a complete surprise to me. "You'll just play yourself," they said, and introduced me backstage to one of the team, who would play interviewer Jack Webster, and another young man who would play my assistant. As I came on the stage, the audience was asked to suggest something that could be outlawed in Ottawa, and someone shouted out "photocopying." So I was the minister of justice explaining why I was bringing in legislation to outlaw photocopying.

I'm quite used to performing my own comedy routines with a straight face, but this was something different and I couldn't stop laughing. I remembered the news stories of years ago when photocopiers first appeared in offices and people were fired for photocopying their bare bottoms. So I started by saying that we had to outlaw photocopying because it was pornographic. The skit continued for about ten minutes to general hilarity, then it was my turn to go solo. Jay had helped me work out a routine that poked fun at government and my work as minister. At one point I said that what the opponents of my gun control legislation really objected to was that I had taken all the romance out of owning a firearm. I asked, "Can you imagine Mae West saying, 'Is that a prohibited weapon with a barrel length of less than eighteen inches, possession of which is grandfathered if registered before October 1, in your pocket, or are you just glad to see me?'" Everyone laughed and I thought no more of it until, reading the press coverage of the 1993 election, I saw it quoted in an article, without the Mae West reference, as something I had said to a member of an audience to whom I was giving a speech on gun control! Joe Clark was right — stand-up comedy *is* risky.

That summer, I decided that being a leadership candidate was only worth doing if I could be myself. I think that's why I was so keen to do the "Kimprov." If there was anything about me that was going to kill my chances, I wanted it out there. The thing I feared most was having to be something I was not.

I didn't know that summer how long it would be before I would enjoy Vancouver that way again. I loved my little house with its wonderful view over False Creek, the city, and the mountains. Vancouver was where people had known me all my life and where my political supporters understood where I was coming from, in more ways than one. But it was so far from Ottawa. I thought of the difference between a Brian Mulroney, whose Montreal friends were only two hours' drive from the capital, and me, whose family and friends were, at best, a five-hour plane ride away. I had seen how little Mulroney socialized with his colleagues. Of necessity, the PM has to maintain a certain distance. Old friends who "knew you when" become more valued than ever in a world where everyone wants a piece of you.

As the summer ended, so did the luxury of such reflections. A national referendum on the Charlottetown Accord was scheduled to take place on October 26, 1992 (subsuming the referendum required by legislation in Quebec), and I was asked to take on a number of national media appearances. Three debates on the accord were set up between me and Deborah Coyne, former adviser to Newfoundland premier Clyde Wells and an opponent of Meech Lake. Until that time, I had had no formal media training because I feared it would try to make me into someone I wasn't. Ray overcame my scepticism and I met with Ottawa consultant Barry McLoughlin. His first comment was that he wasn't interested in changing me, he just wanted to help me build on my strengths and be aware of my weaknesses. He said that there is a temptation during an interview to feel you are talking to your interviewer when, in fact, you should be talking to the television audience. Remembering that can help you avoid language that is overly technical or, just as important, avoid letting the interviewer get under your skin. This advice is even more relevant in a debate, where your opponent is trying to get a rise out of you. Barry asked me to imagine my audience, and I said it was a couple sitting on a couch in their living room in Kelowna, B.C. As I practised dealing with the various issues in the accord, my imaginary audience was that couple. During the debate itself, I appreciated the coaching. Deborah Coyne has a very aggressive debating style and likes to interrupt. In the past, this might have rattled me, but I was able to keep my cool and not let myself get talked over.

Another television debate proved the adage that politics makes strange bedfellows. I found myself on the same side of the table as Liberal MP Sheila Copps in a debate against Manitoba's Liberal leader, Sharon Carstairs, and political scientist Robert Jackson.

I found Sharon totally unsympathetic in debate, but pleasant as a person. Since Sheila Copps, unlike Sharon, had supported the Meech Lake Accord, there was more tension between these two Liberal women than between either of them and me. Interestingly, in a private conversation after the debate, Sharon cautioned me against becoming my party's "sacrificial lamb" if the prime minister resigned.

Politics tends to distort people. I had never much liked Sheila Copps, knowing her only from her House of Commons "Rat Pack" persona. Those political adversaries I had a chance to get to know personally, I often liked very much. There are some MPs who can put aside their partisan identifications when they are out of the House. My Justice critics, Ian Waddell for the NDP and Liberal Russell MacLellan, come immediately to mind. Ian was always cordial when we met outside the House, and Russ was visibly uncomfortable asking a question that he knew was just to make political points. John Turner once described Question Period as "bullshit theatre," an apt if not altogether polite description. I had seen Sheila Copps only in that context and found her manner offensive. However, I've met her since I left government and found her quite friendly. Perhaps now that the frustration of being in opposition is gone, she has become more mellow. We were able to work well together on the televised debate.

As the referendum campaign moved towards its conclusion, I became very concerned about the result. Reform Party leader Preston Manning had devised the No side's tactic of referring to the Charlottetown Accord as "the Mulroney deal." This was ironic given the PM's minimal involvement in the development of the agreement, but it played to the widespread public distrust of Mulroney. My approach in speaking about the accord was to try to explain as carefully as possible how it would work and to answer the criticisms lobbed at it. At many of the public meetings, I would wind up staying on for hours after the formal meeting ended, answering questions. As I became more and more exhausted, I became more and more fatalistic. I decided that the result would be self-justifying. If the referendum passed, then the provisions could work because there would be enough good will to make them work. If there wasn't the will to make them work, then it didn't matter how intrinsically good the agreement was.

On the night of the vote, when it became clear that the accord had been roundly defeated, I appeared on a national panel for the CBC. I was worried by the reaction of native leaders. Ovide Mercredi, president of the Assembly of First Nations, was angrily interpreting the defeat as a rejection of aboriginal aspirations for self-government. The implications were ominous. By the next day, however, it had become clear that native communities had rejected the accord as decisively as the rest of Canada. My fears that the referendum would divide the country were, happily, not realized. If a decisive Yes vote was my preferred result, the decisive No was number two. However, the issues remained, and only the self-deluded could believe that a crisis had been anything but postponed.

In November I tried to make sense of the overwhelming rejection of the accord to an audience at Harvard. There had been little time for serious post-mortems, but *Maclean's* magazine had published the results of a poll it had conducted on the referendum vote. There was a direct correlation between level of education and likelihood of voting Yes. Rather than suggesting a link between comprehension and support, I said this pattern reflected the views of some critics of the accord that it was an "elite" document. Educated people are more likely to feel what the social scientists call a sense of civic competence, a sense that they can make the system work for them. It has nothing to do with competence *per se*, but rather with a sense of empowerment. For me, the defeat of the accord reflected a feeling of powerlessness among many Canadians. Voting against the elite consensus that was Charlottetown was a powerful act of redress. I also believed that the rejection of the accord by a majority of aboriginal people meant I wasn't alone in my uneasiness over the "inherent right" to self-government. Members of native communities weren't ready to enhance the power of their own elites in undefined ways.

In the aftermath of two failed attempts to change the Constitution, I concluded that our priority as a society should be to focus on using the available legislative resources to respond to the aspirations that had been embodied in the Charlottetown Accord. My scepticism about constitutional formulations as the guarantors of truth, beauty, and justice had been confirmed by the referendum campaign, in which staking out constitutional territory had become an exercise in division. I believed strongly in a democratic, deliberative, legislative process that used the room within the Constitution — the permission that is extended to political communities to use their imaginations and good will in areas that are not codified — to respond to the issues left unresolved by the failed proposals for constitutional amendment. For example, some aboriginal self-government arrangements had been negotiated without any specific constitutional mandate. Although aboriginal peoples may want ultimately to have such "rights" written into the Constitution, there is nothing stopping them and the rest of the country from continuing the process that has already, in B.C. and Quebec, resulted in self-governing arrangements highly satisfactory to the communities involved. Similarly, a respectful federalism is a matter of political will as much as any rewriting of the division of powers. After all, the growing power of the federal government in areas of provincial jurisdiction, which belies the claims that our federation is among the most decentralized in the world, took place without such formal change.

We have survived as a country with differing explanations of what we represent. For some, we are a country with two founding nations. This model describes the reality that the unitary state favoured by our founding prime minister, Sir John A. Macdonald, was unworkable, as he recognized. The "distinctiveness" of Quebec was reflected in a federal structure that gave the provinces jurisdiction in those areas where language, culture, and religion were most salient. As the country grew, the notion of equal provinces became a compelling model. In this approach, anything resembling special status for Quebec is unacceptable. Both expressions, "two founding nations" and "ten equal provinces," are exaggerations of the realities they claim to describe, but they have come to represent profoundly different ways of looking at Canada. What the patriation of the Constitution did was to give much more constitutional weight to the theory of ten equal provinces and to minimize the importance of Quebec's role in protecting French language and culture in Canada by expanding the role of the federal government in that area. Where the Constitution had been silent, allowing for the use of two alternative models for Confederation depending upon the context, it now spoke in a way that made clear the superiority of one over the other, to the great dissatisfaction of the adherents of the losing view. The result was the constitutional conflict that has been brewing in the country since 1982.

The constitutional battles also resulted in a debasing of the political process. I became convinced that unless we returned to the parliamentary arena to solve problems and, in the absence of new constitutional provisions, exploited fully the ample room that remained in the existing constitutional framework for legislating to achieve our social goals, we would face a political fracturing of the country. Reconnecting Canadians to the political process in a way that enhanced and validated their roles as citizens became for me the first political priority. Without facing that challenge, I did not see how the country could survive.

When I returned to my regular ministerial schedule after the referendum, everything seemed out of sync. Things in Justice were in disarray because John Tait was in the hospital. At the end of the summer, Joe Clark had asked him to come to Edmonton for a meeting with aboriginal leaders. Although he had a touch of the phlebitis that occasionally bothered him, he had eventually decided to go. By the time he arrived back, he had to be hospitalized for the phlebitis. Then an unexpected reaction to one of the medications brought John close to death. In the department we were all numb with worry. I phoned the hospital one day to speak to his wife, Sonia, and was shocked by the distress in her voice. She later told me that I had called on the worst day of John's crisis, when she wasn't sure he would live. Happily, he began to improve, but a return to the full pressure of the deputy's job was out of the question for the fall. Our associate deputy minister for civil law, Anne Marie Trahan, filled in very capably. Still, there was a sense of unease as we tried to focus on what was to be done for the return of Parliament.

With everything else going on it was a great shock to my staff when I announced that I was determined to get the Human Rights Act amendments tabled before Christmas. "Is she crazy?" I could see them thinking. I was feeling bullish about the issue because a number of events had occurred in the summer that had fulfilled in spades my warnings about the dangers of losing control of the issue.

The Ontario Court of Appeal had upheld a lower court's decision in a case called *Haig*. The plaintiff had argued that if sexual orientation is deemed a prohibited ground of discrimination under the Charter, then it is a denial of equal protection under the law to exclude that protection from the Canadian Human Rights Act. By its decision, the Court of Appeal was reading the CHRA as though our amendments had already passed. I thought the decision wrong in law, but I wasn't prepared to appeal it. In the absence of any action by Parliament, I couldn't assume that the Supreme Court of Canada would agree with me rather than with the Ontario court. By not appealing *Haig*, the government was accepting the ruling and, in effect, letting the courts expand the protections of the CHRA without Parliament's input. Although the case technically applied only to Ontario, I made it clear that, from the government's perspective, complaints of discrimination based on sexual orientation could now be brought to federal human rights tribunals. My decision not to appeal *Haig* was a victory for those who supported the policy of the amendments, but I still felt Parliament had to recapture the initiative by legislating.

But what legislation could we introduce? The political goalposts had changed so that legislation acceptable before the summer was no longer feasible. A provincial human rights tribunal in Ontario had declared that the definitions of "spouse" and "marital status" in the Ontario Human Rights Code were too strict and contrary to the Charter. Although this declaration had no weight in law, it had great political significance — and these were the very definitions we had intended to duplicate. To our amazement, we found that the religious communities that had been so unhelpful in the spring were now eager for us to legislate. The failure of Parliament to establish its views had left the door open for the courts and tribunals, and opponents of gay rights were afraid of what would happen next.

I wasn't prepared to accept the tribunal's ruling with respect to the definition of "marital status." Aside from the fact that the tribunal was legally in error, the definition was of little import for gay priorities as I understood them. I had seen no indication from the gay community at that time that legalization of gay marriages (as opposed to recognition of spousal relationships for the purposes of benefits) was a high priority. There was certainly no move to have same-sex cohabitations of more than one year acquire the same legal significance and obligations as common-law marriages. In order to enable the anti-gay-rights members to support the bill, I *was* prepared to go back to caucus with one definition, that of marital status as in the Ontario act. The definition of "spouse" as someone of the opposite sex had to go.

The tabling of the Canadian Human Rights Act amendments was one of the riskiest moments of my legislative career. Because of the short period of time remaining before the House rose for Christmas on December 11, I could hope to table the amendments only in the last week of the session. Tabling of legislation requires that forty-eight hours' notice be given on the order paper. The scenario I had worked out with my staff was: approval by Priorities and Planning on Tuesday, approval by caucus Wednesday morning, notice on the order paper Wednesday afternoon, and tabling on Friday. On Tuesday, I received permission from P&P to table the amendments, subject to caucus approval. However, after P&P I was met outside by Marianne Campbell, who advised me that the House leader had been in discussion with the opposition about the possibility of ending the sitting of the House on Thursday. If that happened, I wouldn't be able to table the legislation on Friday.

After some earnest discussion with Marianne, I decided to gamble. I went to Harvie Andre, the government House leader, to request that he give notice of the CHRA amendments that afternoon in the House. This was risky because if I didn't get caucus approval the next day, I would be out on a limb and have no option but to resign. Harvie was worried for me and asked, "Are you sure you know what you're doing?" I replied that I was, and he agreed reluctantly. Back in my office, everyone was very tense. On Tuesday afternoon Ray had to urge the Prime Minister's Office to put the CHRA amendments on the caucus agenda. Ray told me that a number of my caucus colleagues who supported the amendments were also prepared to walk if caucus didn't take this last opportunity to give its approval.

There was a certain quality of finality to my farewells to staff Wednesday morning, Ray remembers, as I prepared to leave for the showdown. I wasn't feeling particularly nervous, just very determined. Before caucus convened, Ray and Frédéric waited anxiously in the anteroom as Newfoundland MP Ross Reid, who was among my supporters, paced nervously. Southam News justice reporter Stephen Bindman was lurking outside caucus. He had seen the notice on the order paper and was sure caucus wouldn't approve the tabling of the amendments.

My presentation to caucus was bolstered by some public opinion research we had done. As we were now even closer to an election, I needed to reassure my colleagues that they wouldn't be committing political suicide by supporting the inclusion of sexual orientation in the CHRA. For those who feared the reaction of the Reform Party, I had at hand a clip of Preston Manning saying he didn't think people should be discriminated against because of their sexual orientation. In our public opinion research we had not fudged the question but had put it directly: "Do you agree or disagree with the following statement: The Canadian Human Rights Act should be amended to ensure that homosexuals are not discriminated against by their employers because of their sexual orientation."

I described the reassuring response to my colleagues. Seventy-two per cent of Canadians agreed; there were regional variations but majority support across the country. Sixty-seven per cent of PCs who had voted in the last election — our winning coalition — were in favour, with 29 per cent against. The numbers were the same for Liberal and NDP supporters, and across income and educational lines. This issue was simply not a vote driver, one way or the other.

I don't think many of my colleagues understood what was at stake for me as I stood before them that morning. I laid out my arguments, including a review of how the ground had shifted since the spring. As in the previous session, there were opinions strongly in favour and some opposed. One of the most touching contributions came from an MP who confided that one of his sons had died of AIDS. Explaining how he had once told this son to go his own way, because he couldn't support his gay lifestyle, he went on to say that it was his other children who had convinced him that he was wrong. There was a palpable shift in the mood of the room. His story had reminded us that we were dealing with real people, not abstractions. As the discussion drew to a close, I knew I was going to be able to table the bill.

Up until that meeting, the prime minister had said nothing about the issue at caucus. This time, when he stood up to make his customary remarks at the end of the meeting, he referred to my presentation and asked, "Who are these people, after all? They're our children, or somebody's children. They're our neighbours." That was about it, but it sent a signal that the prime minister was prepared to see the legislation go ahead. Later that afternoon, we received a call from some PMO people, suggesting they had been tricked! No one could imagine what they meant. I assumed the "anti's" had expressed their opposition to the PM after caucus, and there was now some timidity in his office. However, it was too late.

The PM never alluded to any personal interest in the issue. For me, his comments were simply an interesting example of his way of leading by following. Always ambiguous about his personal views on contentious issues, he would wait until the caucus battle had been won before giving his support to a controversial initiative. I always thought this was perfectly appropriate because it preserved the PM's political capital for very difficult issues and forced ministers to fight for their own legislation. I remember as the gun control issue was nearing resolution, the prime minister made an emotional declaration during caucus: "We're not going to face the families of those young women murdered in Montreal without doing something." When reporters heard about this, they suggested to me that it was the PM and not me who had succeeded in pushing the issue through caucus. I'm sure his comments didn't hurt; they sent an important message to our Whip, Jim Hawkes, who had been in the process of assembling a legislative committee made up of opponents to the bill. The PM's remarks turned him 180 degrees. However, the PM would not have been supportive if we had not prepared the ground carefully. So I felt a bit like Jack Benny in the skit in which the famous comedian is trying to take a shopping cart at the supermarket. He pulls and he pulls and he can't get the cart free. Then a woman comes up and pulls the cart out easily. Benny looks at her with disgust and says, "Sure, after I loosened it!"

At the end of the caucus meeting I went into the anteroom to reassure Ray and Frédéric, who had been waiting anxiously. Ross Reid gave me a big warm hug. On our way out we were able to advise a surprised Stephen Bindman that the CHRA amendments would indeed be tabled on Thursday when, in fact, the session did end. Later, after the adrenalin had worn off, I realized just how much I had put on the line and felt a bit queasy. Much later Ray said to me, "I saw you do a lot of gutsy things in government, but that was the gutsiest." Thank goodness we won in caucus, or in light of what followed, he might have called it not gutsy but stupid.

On December 10 the amendments to the Canadian Human Rights Act were at long last tabled in Parliament. I wish I could say that the gay community appreciated my efforts. They objected to the inclusion of a traditional definition of marital status in which only conjugal relationships between persons of the opposite sex were recognized as common-law marriages, because they erroneously believed that it would prevent them from receiving spousal benefits. However, the amendments were silent on the question of who was a "spouse." That was a question to be determined on a case-by-case basis. I was frustrated that the gay community didn't recognize what a political victory the tabling of the amendments was. A few did. In the Vancouver *Sun*, Stan Persky advised the gay community to learn when to declare victory. As he pointed out, gay men and women had been pushing for protection in the Human Rights Act for years, and had been thinking about legalized gay marriages "for about five minutes."

Since there was no jurisdiction I was aware of that recognized gay marriages, I thought it was incredibly unrealistic for the gay community to have expected my amendments to take a step in that direction. But, more important, if gay marriages are ever recognized in Canada, it will not be through the Canadian Human Rights Act, which is not the law that determines who may or may not legally marry. All of our laws relating to marriage and the dissolution of marriage reflect the reality of the differences between men and women. Women get pregnant and have children; women on average earn less than men. These and other realities have led, for example, to the protection of women in common-law relationships. Surely we should be carefully examining the ways marriage is recognized in the law before deciding that it is an appropriate legal framework for same-sex partnerships.

When the amendments were tabled, Stephen Bindman bet me a dinner that the legislation wouldn't be passed. I was certain it would be, because I knew that the biggest political battle was behind me, but unfortunately I had to buy the young reporter dinner. What I didn't know was that I would be shuffled out of Justice before the House reconvened and that the bill's opponents would take advantage of a new minister who wasn't privy to all the negotiations with MPs that had preceded tabling. The criticism by the gay community destroyed the chance for passage in the spring session, which was short and had a crowded agenda. Without a sense that there was any political gain from pushing this legislation through, other more popular issues were given the scarce parliamentary time. When the House rose in June, that ended the prospect of the CHRA amendments' being enacted into law. As I write this, the Liberal government has yet to table similar legislation.

As we approached Christmas, speculation about the prime minister's future grew more intense. He had told caucus earlier in the fall that he would stay on to fight the next election, and at the time I had believed him. But when I told this to Ray, he just rolled his eyes. Ray was convinced that the PM would go and prepared a second memo for me on what would need to be done if he was right and I decided to contest the leadership.

As time went on, I found my actions being interpreted more frequently through the prism of my possible candidacy. My bare-shouldered portrait by Barbara Woodley, which had been exhibited in Vancouver without comment in November of 1990, caused a sensation when shown in Ottawa two years later. By this time, Barbara's book *Portraits*, which featured all the excellent portraits she had taken of Canadian women, was in print. Returning to Ottawa from Vancouver one day in November, I noticed that my schedule included an optional stop at the National Arts Centre for the opening of an exhibition of the portraits. I thought it would be nice to support Barbara, so I asked André to drop me off at the NAC. Barbara presented me with a signed copy of her book, and I thought nothing more about it until the next day, when the *Ottawa Citizen* featured a review of the exhibition on the front page under a reproduction of my portrait. The caption was, "Doing justice to art." The uproar began. The fat was in the fire when Lynn Hunter, NDP MP for Saanich–Gulf Islands, compared me to the uninhibited American singer Madonna. The British press picked this up and began to feature the picture with the caption "The Madonna of Canada." In the Italian press it was reported that I had posed with nude men! This apparently arose from a mistranslation of "bare shoulders."

I hadn't planned to say anything about the ruckus, but my staff convinced me that perhaps I should. I tried to defuse the issue by pointing out to the press that the difference between me and Madonna was the difference "between a strapless evening gown and a gownless evening strap." Barbara Woodley wasn't happy about the unauthorized reproductions of her photo, although the attention did wonders for the sales of her book. I just thought the whole thing was ridiculous. I was actually accused of deliberately raising my profile with the picture, a tribute to my capacity for strategic thinking that is quite undeserved.

A similar overreaction occurred in November when I spoke to a conference of women in the media in Ottawa. The audience of about 450 journalists was mostly female. I was part of a panel with NDP leader Audrey McLaughlin and Liberal MP Mary Clancy, chaired by the writer Christina McCall. We were to discuss our observations of the media treatment of women politicians and the lives of women in politics. At one point, I spoke of my life in Ottawa as sometimes being "unspeakably lonely." I wasn't suggesting that I was the only one who felt that way — many MPs live such lives — but the phrase caught the attention of some journalists and there was much discussion of my candid observations on the life of a woman politician in Ottawa. My contribution was well received by the women in the audience, a fact I would reflect on with some irony during the 1993 election. My explanation of the problems faced by women in redefining roles that have traditionally been seen as male seemed to strike a chord of recognition in the women in the hall, but it was an insight that would be entirely lost by the next year. What is more, when the press discovered, after the 1993 election, that I had recently begun a romantic relationship, there was the suggestion that this somehow made my "unspeakably lonely" comment of November 1992 dishonest!

By December I was beginning to wonder if the PM would, in fact, stay on. Ray had quietly set about putting together a design for a leadership campaign. He worked very discreetly on it because we both believed that the decision to retire or not was one the PM should make on his own. Ray was a loyal Mulroney supporter. Neither of us wanted to contribute to an atmosphere that would make it difficult for the PM to stay if that was what he decided to do. On the other hand, as the mandate moved into its fifth and final year, it was clear that a campaign, if it came, would not have the luxury of time, and so we wanted to be prepared for all eventualities. In 1991 the prime minister had started to talk about the time remaining in the mandate as if we would go right to the end. No one in caucus thought we could really go to the end of the fifth year, and I had always assumed his comments were just hyperbole to give MPs a sense that there was time to turn our political fortunes around. Surely the prime minister couldn't be working on a schedule that presumed a fall 1993 election.

The expressions of support I was receiving quietly from colleagues and party members helped me to decide that I would like to be a candidate if the PM resigned. There seemed to be a growing consensus among caucus and in the media that I would be a serious candidate. Whether I could win would depend on who else ran, but the response of party members was encouraging.

My experience as justice minister had enabled me to put into practice many of my ideas about how politics could be done in a less fractious way. I was disturbed at the level of hatred people expressed towards government in general and the PM in particular. The political battles of the last few years had been exhausting for all MPs. Although many of our supporters criticized us for not doing enough to reduce or eliminate the deficit, the political cost of each step we tried to take was enormous. There had to be a better way of dealing with these issues. One approach I believed in was to re-establish the role of MPs in policy-making. I had tried to do that in dealing with gun control and the Human Rights Act, and I wouldn't have succeeded on those issues if I hadn't. But I had tried to let MPs play a more central role in other ways as well.

During my time in Justice, we passed a record amount of criminal legislation. Much of it originated in proposals by MPs. For example, when a number of my colleagues complained in 1990 that Charles Ng, wanted by the police in California for a series of grisly murders, had been in Canada for six years without being extradited, I took their complaints to heart. A massive review of our extradition legislation was under way, but I moved quickly to amend and speed up the process of extradition appeals. Another example: it was octogenarian Stan Darling, an energetic servant of his Muskoka, Ontario, riding, who had convinced Brian Mulroney of the importance of acid rain as an issue in the first mandate. He had been trying for years to get a response from the minister of justice to his concerns about the lack of enforcement of federal water safety regulations on the lakes of his riding. At his urging we brought forward the Contraventions Act, which introduced an efficient ticketing system, rather like traffic tickets, for breaches of federal regulations. When the bill was introduced, it became known as the Stan Darling Bill, and I ensured that he got the front-and-centre attention he deserved.

After almost three years in the Justice portfolio, I felt I had begun to change the way the department operated. Slowly, the officials had come to understand that they could take some risks. I respected them and admired their work on policy, but that didn't mean we had nothing to learn from others. When the officials realized that changes to their proposals didn't constitute a criticism of their ideas, they began to enter into the process of consultation with more enthusiasm. Some, not all, began to see that the challenge was to start with your best ideas, based on what you knew, and then create the best, most complete process of consultation possible.

A gratifying example of a change in attitude occurred during the final days of the rape shield issue. A senior official in the criminal law policy section in Justice had been defensive of the work of his team and uncertain about where all this outreach was leading us. As the rape shield bill was making its way through Parliament, I was a bit disconcerted to read the criticisms of Gwen Landolt, president of R.E.A.L. Women. She had attended the initial consultative meeting and, alone of the representatives there, had supported our intent to legislate. At a meeting in my office, I asked the official about it.

"It's our fault, Minister," he replied. "We dropped the ball. We forgot to invite Mrs. Landolt to the subsequent meetings because we thought she was already on side with what we were doing. We should have kept her informed."

"Wow," I thought, "he really gets it!"

In many areas of policy reform, the federal Justice Department was now in the lead in the country. In the early days, during the meetings on Milgaard, for example, when I'd pressed officials and tested their arguments, they had been uncertain how to interpret this. In December 1992, as I looked back on all we had accomplished, it seemed to me that Justice officials now knew that my testing of them was based on my belief that they could do work of the highest standard. I wasn't trying to show anyone up, I was encouraging people to shine.

Just before the Christmas break, I hosted my third annual carol-singing party in the department. The first Christmas I was minister, I had held the party in my office for the senior officials. I played an electric piano and a crowd of about thirty sang. It was great fun, but I thought that it was perhaps a bit too exclusive, especially for a minister who was always talking about inclusive justice! The next year, I asked my staff how we could invite more people, and they figured out a way to invite the entire department. They set up the piano in the lobby of the third floor and big speakers were hooked up to it. My staff had ingeniously figured out a way to provide the words to the carols to everyone: they put them on transparencies that were projected onto a wall. Invitations were sent to the entire department, but the times were staggered so that the several hundred employees wouldn't arrive at the same time. From time to time during the festivities, I would sit down and play and we would have a good sing. Carols were sung in both English and French, and sometimes a solo would be performed by a particularly talented singer.

Christmas 1992 was to be my last Christmas as justice minister, and most of my staff realized this. Even without a shuffle, there would be an election before the next Christmas, and who knew what changes it would bring? So there was a sense of poignancy about our party. John Tait, looking so frail, came for a while although he was not yet back at work. He cared a great deal about the morale of all the people who worked at Justice. Despite his apparent shyness and reserve, John has a fair streak of the ham in him. In other years, he had always been in the forefront of the singing and assigning of parts. This time, he barely sang at all and left before the party ended.

At the department's annual Christmas dinner-dance, John and I gave our usual little speeches, but our remarks were particularly heartfelt, his because of his recent brush with death and mine because I knew this would be my last such occasion. I had missed the year-end retrospective that John and I had twice engaged in, meeting in my office for a quiet chat to savour the successes of the past year and imagining what might lie ahead. The gossips who were so sure that our friendship was really an affair would be disappointed to know that a quick hug as we wished each other all the best for the holidays was about as demonstrative as we ever got. As Ray Castelli once said, John and I were soulmates, and it was the absence of a more personal agenda that had enabled us to work so well and so happily together. I would never again in government know a working relationship of such absolute trust.

Christmas was always chaotic for me when I was in Parliament because I got home to Vancouver so late. After a last-minute scramble to shop for gifts and find a decent tree, festivities started with a Christmas Eve carol party for the family at my house and went non-stop until Boxing Day dinner at my father's. Usually, I could start to relax on December 27, but in 1992 I decided to have a party. Not surprisingly, the conversations with my friends always came around to a possible leadership campaign. The media focus on me throughout the fall had been intense. In the *Globe and Mail* of December 12, Graham Fraser's long profile on me began with the comment, "Everyone is watching Kim Campbell." Similar articles appeared elsewhere. In a long conversation with my friends Ginny and John Richards, the question again arose as to whether a new leader would be a sacrificial lamb. I was torn between my growing sense that this was a job I would really like to do, if I had the opportunity, and the strong feeling that the date when the PM could resign and give a new leader the time to refashion the party and the government had passed.

The day after the party, as I was preparing to do some serious relaxing, I received a call from Marjory LeBreton, the PM's deputy chief of staff, asking me to meet with the prime minister on the afternoon of Sunday, January 3. I had been through enough shuffles to recognize the signs, and Marjory wasn't particularly secretive. She said that the PM wanted to give me a chance to get some experience in an "economic" portfolio. I was puzzled. Surely Mike Wilson and Maz weren't going anywhere. What was left?

On New Year's Eve, the Richardses had a wonderful, elegant dinner party. The men were in black tie and the women in their evening finest. At the end of dinner, we were asked to make predictions about where we would all be next New Year's Eve. Although I had a feeling that 1993 was going to be an extraordinary year for me, I couldn't quite bring myself to say that in a year's time I would be prime minister. Looking back, I don't know whether I was being modest, or clairvoyant.

12

Will He or Won't He?

A BRILLIANT POLITICAL ORGANIZER, Ray Castelli was a terrible mind reader where Brian Mulroney was concerned. In the memos he had begun writing to me about leadership in the summer of 1992, he consistently misread the PM's intentions. He was clearly expecting Mulroney to step down on or before the unprecedented joint meeting of the National Campaign Committee, the National Executive, and the National Platform Committee scheduled for November 23. As he wrote: "The meeting is supposed to be the kickoff of the 6-month pre-writ campaign. I would find it very surprising that the PM would give the entire Party marching orders for an election if he planned to leave in January. Too many decisions about polling, advertising, and policy platforms have to be made by January if we are looking at a Spring option. As well, leaving in January creates problems for a successor. That would mean a convention in late April, leaving less than 6 months till the end of the mandate."

The November 23 date came and went without an announcement. The next Castelli memo, dated December 31, said: "There has been a great deal of activity out in the field over the past month, but almost none of it by us." Michael Wilson, for example, had had an organization in place for some time. Before Christmas, the PM issued an angry warning in P&P one day against ministers who were organizing leadership campaigns and threatened to destroy their chances if they persisted. Mike looked very uncomfortable at the rebuke. After the Charlottetown referendum campaign, rumours had started that I was organizing a campaign. Since we were not active, I was surprised to hear of them and even more surprised to discover that they had originated with Mike Wilson's people. With a little detective work, we discovered why. As political minister for B.C., I had made thank-you calls to ministerial colleagues who had travelled to B.C. to speak during the referendum campaign. One of these was to Mike, who had interpreted my call as a leadership-related manoeuvre.

Ray's memo continued: "If the PM is going to leave soon, the logical time to make the announcement is when he meets with Caucus at the end of January. Clearly he can't go in there saying he'll stay and quit a few weeks later. As well, I doubt he would announce his intention without informing the Caucus first. Therefore, I would conclude that January 29th is the logical day for an announcement if one is coming." Needless to say, the January 29th date also came and went. While not very good at predicting Brian Mulroney's future, Ray was extremely prescient about the political implications of his continuing delay in making his intentions known.

Looking back, I am astonished at the lengths to which the prime minister went to keep us all off balance. I was particularly susceptible to this manipulation because I really believed it was now too late for him to go. After the referendum, when the PM had announced in cabinet that he would stay, my reaction was described correctly by Graham Fraser of the *Globe and Mail* as one of "unfeigned relief." I was reassured when Mila Mulroney turned up as the mystery guest speaker at the annual Gatineau Hills Gentlemen's Club Dinner on February 13 and joked, "I don't know about him, but I'm staying!" What was one to make of this cat-and-mouse game? Did Mulroney himself know what he was going to do? And what was the significance of his recent cabinet shuffle, which had surprised no one more than me?

I had flown to Ottawa as requested on January 3. As always, Mulroney was very successful at keeping his impending shuffle a secret. The usual pre-shuffle meetings with ministers and potential ministers were again held at 24 Sussex Drive, where I was ushered into the PM's study and took my seat on a sofa below a large portrait of Mila. Marjory LeBreton's puzzling statement about a portfolio that would give me some economic experience was uppermost in my mind as I waited nervously.

I have always been amused by the suggestion that ministers ask for certain portfolios. I once read that I had asked not to be shuffled out of Justice in the February 1991 cabinet shuffle. Aside from the fact that I had had no inkling of a shuffle, I would never have dreamed of making such a request. I suppose some very senior ministers may have bargained over their positions, but if they did, I never heard of it — with one exception. I was told on a number of occasions that Barbara McDougall had asked not to be shuffled out of Employment and Immigration for a period of time. I believe this may have been because she was going through the very difficult period of her sister's terminal illness. True or not, that kind of personal consideration would be perfectly appropriate to raise. You could, in theory, simply refuse to serve at all if you didn't like what you were offered, but that would be a serious challenge to the prime minister. No, cabinet-making is the most important of the prime-ministerial prerogatives, and neither Mulroney nor his cabinet had any question about that.

I can't remember every detail of my conversation with the prime minister, only that I was dumbfounded when he told me he was going to name me minister of national defence and minister of veterans' affairs. The "economic" aspect of Defence was directly related to the size of the deparment's budget. I was told to pay attention to my colleagues' concerns in their ridings; because the defence infrastructure was so extensive, decisions relating to it would have a significant impact on certain communities and, hence, on the political fortunes of colleagues who represented those communities. After discussing my two new portfolios, the PM said that he was also naming me to the powerful Operations Committee of cabinet. In the press coverage of the shuffle, this change was not much noted, although it was a significant promotion to the committee that sets the political agenda of the government.

As I left 24 Sussex Drive I was in a state of shock. I had prepared myself for leaving Justice, but Defence was such a surprise that I didn't know what to make of it. I had an interest in defence issues and had taught some strategic studies in the 1970s. The end of the Cold War meant that this would be an exciting time for those involved in defence and foreign policy issues. What was clear to me, however, was that, given the short time that remained before we had to call an election, it would be difficult for me to do much in the way of a defence policy review. What didn't hit me until later in the day was that the PM had just given me a workload that up to then had been performed by three ministers. Marcel Masse had been supported as defence minister by Mary Collins as associate minister, but Mary was moving to Western Economic Diversification and the PM had said he wasn't planning to name an associate minister for me. In addition, Veterans' Affairs had been ably conducted by Gerry Merrithew.

I realized that the veterans' community wouldn't be happy about sharing a minister and that I would have to be careful to give that side of my responsibilities the attention it required. I think I was the first veterans' affairs minister not to have any military background, and I was the first woman in either portfolio, although Mary Collins had broken that barrier in Defence already as associate minister. Both my parents were war veterans and my father had served as national president of the Army, Navy and Air Force Veterans of Canada. During his term I had spoken to their national convention in Ottawa as minister of justice. I could only hope this would make it somewhat easier for veterans to accept me.

When I arrived back in the Justice Department, Ray was waiting for me. He was as surprised as I was. There would be a lot of speculation as to whether this shuffle was a promotion or a demotion. The PM's attitude suggested that he regarded it as a positive career move, although I don't know if he would have said otherwise. It certainly fleshed out my cabinet experience, but in view of events to come, it also added a considerable burden. I now had to plunge into learning two completely different portfolios. The combination of Defence and Veterans' Affairs may seem natural, but in fact, they have little in common. Veterans' Affairs deals with social policy and historical commemoration, whereas Defence is responsible for administering and equipping our armed forces while developing policy, in the context of our foreign policy, for just how that should be done. What the two did have in common was large budgets that were favoured targets for expenditure reductions.

Ever the good manager, Ray set about considering the challenges facing us in putting together ministerial staffs to run two different departments. I left Ray to his musings and called John Tait, not something to which I looked forward. Poor John: after his long illness, January 4 was to be his first full day back in the office. What he didn't need to hear was that he would be facing the additional work of briefing a new minister. He was disappointed but philosophical. I didn't know at that time who my replacement would be, so I invited John to the swearing-in ceremony to meet my successor, repeating the courtesy that Doug Lewis had shown when I was sworn in.

As the shuffle was not a large one, the swearing-in the next morning was a small affair. Pierre Blais was ecstatic at being named the new minister of justice, and I was happy for him. Justice is a prestigious portfolio in Quebec, possibly the most prestigious after the prime ministership. Sheila Rafter, my assistant, and Wendy Waite, my personal secretary, were thrilled to accompany me to Rideau Hall. It was a small way to recognize them for their help over the years. After the formalities, I took my turn in the foyer to meet the press. They were clearly uncertain how to interpret my change of duties. When questioned about what I might do in Defence in light of the new world situation, I commented that I thought it was "highly premature to beat our swords into ploughshares." The press puzzled over what my move meant in the light of recurrent rumours that the PM would step down. Later, when I was asked what the change might mean if there were a leadership campaign, I joked that I didn't need a campaign, I could just stage a coup d'état, adding, "Don't mess with me, I've got tanks!"

There was some foolish speculation that the PM had moved me because I was too prominent in Justice. The suggestion that Brian Mulroney would be jealous of the high profile of a minister was unfair. Although I'm sure he wouldn't have welcomed being upstaged on the same platform, he was an experienced enough leader to understand that when his ministers looked good, he looked good. Notwithstanding his considerable ego, I never saw him display that sort of pettiness. I did hear a suggestion, much later, that he was trying to "level the playing field" by moving me into Defence. "Level with whom and for what?" I wondered. It didn't make sense.

Returning to my office to get ready for the move, I phoned the heads of the major veterans' organizations to introduce myself and to tell them I was looking forward to working with them. What surprised me was how quickly I had stopped thinking of myself as justice minister and was anticipating the new issues I would be dealing with.

The next morning began with briefings at the Department of National Defence. The modern George Pearkes Building that houses DND is much bigger than the gothic Justice building and, with its serious security and numerous uniformed personnel, has a very different atmosphere. I quickly learned that Defence was like no other department, split as it was between two bureaucracies. The deputy minister, Bob Fowler, was responsible for the management of the civilian side, while the chief of the defence staff, General John de Chastelain, was in charge of the uniformed side. Instead of a one-to-one relationship between the minister and the deputy at the top, there is an awkward *ménage à trois* in which the deputy and the CDS have more to lose from alienating each other than from keeping the minister in the dark. I was acquainted with some of the senior military from the time I served on the cabinet committee for the Gulf War. Because General de Chastelain and I had both been present at many military briefings, we had a sense of each other and I was quite comfortable with him. Within a month, however, he would be named as our ambassador in Washington, and Admiral John Anderson would become the new CDS.

I had lunch that day with my predecessor, Marcel Masse. Marcel was one of five ministers who had resigned from cabinet because they weren't planning to seek re-election. They no doubt hoped to be named to other positions by the prime minister. Two were successful: Benoît Bouchard was named ambassador to France, and Robert de Cotret went to the World Bank. The other three — Jake Epp, Gerry Merrithew, and Marcel — didn't receive appointments. Marcel, however, confided to me over lunch that he expected to be named ambassador to UNESCO sometime in April, and he later appeared increasingly distressed when the appointment was not forthcoming.

Marcel and I had a good chat about the Defence Department, and we talked about some senior appointments in the offing. As was almost always the case when ministers met now, we also talked about whether the PM would be staying. Marcel seemed to think the PM's departure was likely and surprised me by offering to help me if there should be a leadership contest. Although we had always been friendly and he knew I had made an effort to get to know Quebec and Quebeckers, we weren't close. I was touched and pleased, but also uneasy about the whole topic. At the end of lunch we laughed as Marcel let me reach for the cheque. After all, he was just an ordinary MP now.

That afternoon I headed off with my political staff to the modest offices of the Department of Veterans' Affairs in Ottawa. The headquarters of this department is in Charlottetown, which leads to a rather cumbersome division, with some of the staff located in Ottawa and occasionally travelling to P.E.I., and the rest located in P.E.I. and occasionally travelling to Ottawa. The main concern of the DVA briefing was how the department was going to meet its budget targets. In the long run, one could expect a decline in the level of benefits paid to veterans, but in the short run, the World War II vets were getting to the age where they needed more help rather than less. In examining the various programs and the criteria for benefits, we got into a discussion of the benefits paid to certain rather youthful Greek immigrants who qualified because they had been resistance fighters in Europe during World War II. When I asked why we were paying benefits to people who had been babies during the war, one of the officials replied with great seriousness, "But, Minister, some of these people were carrying secret messages in their diapers." There was a pause. "Well," I replied, "we know they were carrying *something* in their diapers — messages of disdain for their oppressors, perhaps."

On Wednesday of that week, the Justice Department gathered to say farewell at a reception that filled the third-floor lobby in the Justice building. I felt like a guest on *This Is Your Life*, since each of the major issues I had worked on was represented by a lawyer here or a staff member there. There were a lot of dewy eyes, mine included. As I made a few remarks of thanks to everyone, it was all I could do not to break down in tears. My years as minister of justice were among the happiest and most rewarding of my entire life, and I felt a real sense of accomplishment. Lisette Lafontaine, who had snapped my photo with John, Myles, and Michael on my very first day in the department, gave me a present on behalf of the department. It was a beautiful brooch in three shades of gold to represent the three themes I had pursued as justice minister — the protection of society, fairness in the relationship between citizens and government, and inclusive justice. I still wear it often.

The next day was my last in my Justice office. I was scheduled to fly out to Vancouver that evening for a two-week stay. Walking past the packing boxes and bare walls in our offices with Peter Lugli, who was going to be my chief of staff at Veterans' Affairs, I had tears in my eyes again. Knowing what I was feeling, Peter sighed and said, "Bricks and mortar ..." We were both leaving a bit of ourselves within those walls.

The two weeks in B.C. were a mix of constituency and ministerial events. I realized that in Defence I was going to have to travel a great deal to bases, and I began by visiting CFB Chilliwack, the naval base at Esquimalt, and Royal Roads Military College.

I flew back to Ottawa on January 19 to prepare for five days of French-language training at the military college at Saint-Jean-sur-Richelieu, near Montreal, where the House of Commons had its French-language school. Because I spoke English over the Christmas holidays at home, I had made it a practice to do some French immersion each January before the House came back so that I would be at ease in French during Question Period and when talking to the media. This visit to Saint-Jean would be different, however, because I was arriving as minister of national defence. I was greeted by an honour guard of cadets, which I inspected with due solemnity, as I had already been taught to do.

The last week before Parliament resumed was very hectic. The days were taken up with meetings of cabinet committees preparing for the return to parliamentary business. My political staff had arranged a two-day retreat to become comfortable with the change in portfolios and issues. I attended the dinner for my combined staff and was struck not only by how our numbers had grown, but also by the great spirit of collegiality they had developed. The last weekend in January I attended two days of regional and national caucus meetings. Ray and I were at a loss to explain the meaning of the PM's assurance at caucus that he wasn't going anywhere. If anything, the vehemence of his declaration seemed to make people more uncertain than ever. As always,

Mulroney spoke as though he had everything figured out and had a clear strategy that would lead us to victory in an election.

The three weeks following the return of the House were surreal. I was scrambling to master my two new portfolios and squeezing political events in where possible. I was to attend a major defence conference, the Wehrkunde, in Munich from February 5 to 7, and planned to go on with the deputy and the CDS to visit our troops in the former Yugoslavia and then Somalia. For reasons that were never explained, the Prime Minister's Office wouldn't give the necessary approval for the Yugoslavia/Somalia leg of my trip, and so the deputy and the CDS continued on without me.

The Wehrkunde was my introduction to the Western defence and foreign policy elite. German Chancellor Helmut Kohl led the discussion the first morning. The day I arrived in Munich, the German government had announced the cancellation of all its defence capital projects, for budgetary reasons. Kohl used an expression I would come to understand well when he said that in most governments, "the budget of the defence department is a quarry in which all the other departments like to mine." I had meetings with Manfred Woerner, secretary general of NATO, and a number of ministers of defence including Les Aspin, only recently confirmed as President Clinton's first secretary of defence. An intense man who always seemed to be in motion, Aspin expressed interest in one subject only: how we had dealt in Canada with the issue of gays in the military. President Clinton's casual campaign remark that the barriers should be removed had mushroomed into a confrontation between the White House and the joint chiefs of staff.

The Wehrkunde conference was taking place at a time of growing frustration on the part of the Western powers over what to do in the former Yugoslavia. One speaker from Turkey claimed that the reluctance of the West to intervene forcefully on the part of the Bosnian Muslims was a reflection of religious prejudice — that had these people been Christians, the reaction of the Western countries would have been different. As the defence minister of the country with the third-largest contingent in the former Yugoslavia, I disagreed with that, but I was struck by how difficult it was going to be to create a framework for action to deter aggression that didn't create more problems than it solved. When my turn came to speak I raised this issue of how we were going to create rules of engagement that avoided the perception of a double standard or cultural hegemony on the part of the countries who might participate in such operations or the organizations that sanctioned them.

On my way back to Canada, I stopped overnight at the Canadian base at Lahr. We were in the process of withdrawing from Germany, and from the enormous airstrips and many buildings on the base I could see that our presence there had been substantial. No wonder the Germans were less than thrilled at the economic loss. The next morning I was taken on a tour of the base by the commandant. As we were driving alongside some large sheds, I spotted an old tank. "Stop!" I shouted. "I have to get a picture!" Remembering "Don't mess with me, I've got tanks," I didn't want to miss a chance of having my picture taken with the proof.

After two days in Ottawa, I was off again, this time to Charlottetown to visit the DVA headquarters. I was still squeezing political events in when I could, and that night I spoke to a fundraising dinner for Pat Mella's provincial Conservatives. The next morning, putting on my Defence hat, I flew on an Aurora reconnaissance plane to Shearwater, Nova Scotia, home of Maritime Command. While touring HMCS *Toronto*, one of our new state-of-the-art frigates, I had a look at the enormous bays on the top deck where the shipborne helicopters are stowed. Helicopters are the eyes and ears of these ships, vastly increasing their surveillance range. The forty-year-old Sea-Kings we were using had already been refurbished once, and the new EH-101s, which would be ready in 1998, had been chosen to replace them because of their great range, speed, and ability to fly in icing conditions.

I toured the IMP Aerospace plant nearby where much of the refurbishing of DND aircraft takes place. Seeing helicopters and planes stripped down to their frames and watching the painstaking process of examining each electrical and hydraulic function, I understood why refurbishing is so expensive. And of course, at the end, you are still left with the original technology, rather like bringing an old black-and-white television back to mint condition.

Everywhere I went, party members were on tenterhooks over

rumours of the PM's imminent departure. That evening I dined with some members of the Halifax Conservative Women's Caucus, who had for some time been very supportive of me and interested in my efforts on behalf of women. I found it awkward to respond to their questions, since unless the PM announced he was going, I had to assume he was staying. But although it was the middle of February, long past the date by which Ray and I thought the PM would have to depart if he wanted to, there were now signs that he was in fact going to resign. One was the build-up of political appointments given to people with links to Brian Mulroney. Although this could perhaps have been explained by an imminent election, there was a definite sense that the PM was making the appointments that were personally important to him.

Winnipeg is the headquarters of Air Command of the Canadian Forces and was my next stop for briefings. Afterwards the senior officers of Air Command accompanied me to the Paramax plant, one of the locations where components of the EH-101 helicopter were being developed and built. The work we observed was not on the Canadian order but on helicopters ordered by the British government. After the tour, I held a press conference with the officers to explain and answer questions about the EH-101 helicopter contract. The purchase of the helicopters was becoming controversial, but I believed that people would support the program once they heard that the money not only was designated for necessary equipment but was being spent largely in Canada, in industries that had enormous growth and export potential. Since Canada had joined the EH-101 project at the developmental stage of the aircraft, 50 per cent of each helicopter purchased by Canada would be made here. With Canada having acquired the world product rights to part of the technology, 10 per cent of every EH-101 built in the world would also be made in Canada. As a result of the economic benefits negotiated, a sum greater than the purchase price of the Canadian helicopters would be spent in Canada.

I flew to Vancouver for what would be my last reasonably tranquil weekend for many months. Friday afternoon, combining business with pleasure, I represented the new minister of justice at the swearing-in of Bob Edwards, a former B.C. deputy attorney general, as a justice of the B.C. Supreme Court. During the speeches of welcome, the representative of the Canadian Bar

Association kept congratulating Bob on becoming "chief justice," much to everyone's amusement. A noted wit, Bob capitalized on the error in his own remarks and at the same time caught accurately the mood of speculation about the Conservative leadership when he quipped, "I know the minister of national defence will understand when I say that I do not aspire to any position in which there is no vacancy."

But a vacancy there would, indeed, be. Back in Ottawa, on the evening of February 23, 1993, an excited Ray Castelli rang to tell me that CTV was reporting that the PM was having a dinner party at 24 Sussex for his closest friends that night and was evidently telling them he would be announcing his retirement the next day. The next morning, Wednesday, would be national caucus.

The atmosphere in caucus the morning of February 24 was electric. The room was abuzz with rumours of the PM's "farewell" dinner. Brian Mulroney entered to an incredible ovation of applause and shouts. Deputy PM Don Mazankowski was in tears. When he took the podium, the PM began to review his almost ten years as leader of the party. The main theme of his speech was that, having led us to two consecutive majority governments, he had one more task to accomplish as leader and that was to pass the party on to a leader who could win another election. To that end, he portrayed himself as a master strategist who had determined just how to do this. Brushed aside were any considerations of the fact that we were at 18 per cent in the polls, had been at historically low levels of support for two years, and were already well into the fifth year of our mandate. His remarks were punctuated by a number of standing ovations. It seemed churlish not to grant the PM the recognition he deserved for giving the Conservative Party the longest period of power it had enjoyed since the days of Sir John A. Macdonald. Besides, it was great to relive the triumphs of the past nine years.

MPs were moved, but few argued with the prime minister's decision. Those who did believed he should lead us into the next election. I thought it was a Hobson's choice by this time. Still, I was grateful to Brian Mulroney for giving me the chance to enjoy some of the happiest and most rewarding years of my career. Whatever else you could say about him, he had turned the Conservatives into a governing party.

I could see from the glances towards me that many of my colleagues were aware of what the PM's announcement meant for me. My feelings were mixed: relief that the suspense was now over, but also trepidation. That old sense of vertigo that comes when I am launched on a risky course from which there is no turning back began to wash over me. Only if the support that had been quietly communicated to me over the past months dissipated would I be able to avoid running for our party's leadership. However much I wanted to do the job, the timing was awful! I left caucus through the back entrance, hoping to slip past the crowd of media. But the press caught up with me in the lobby outside the House of Commons. I wouldn't speculate on what the future would bring. I told them, "This is Brian Mulroney's day."

13

Getting There Is Half the Fun

THE OTHER SHOE HAD finally dropped! It was time to see whether I really had enough support to run. All the groundwork for a campaign had been done over the past year by Ray Castelli and a few trusted supporters. Now I was free to solicit support directly. Ray's greatest fear was that I wouldn't be able to conquer my shyness and actually reach out myself. In his first memo to me he had written, "You are one of the most inclusive, open people I have ever met. Yet, as you know, until I came to work for you I did not have that impression. I felt you were surrounded by a clique of Vancouver Centre friends who were trying to keep you to themselves. Many others have held this impression, although I think you've taken tremendous strides to overcome this. I know much of it stems from shyness, but you are going to have to overcome it to win over these 500 key delegates."

It is hard for some people to understand how a person who is comfortable in the public eye can also be shy. I have no difficulty standing in front of a class or an audience, but I am often painfully shy in private encounters with people I don't know. Maybe performing is a deliberate strategy to get past this. I've tried to explain it sometimes as the difference between having a clearly defined role to play, a reason for "holding the floor," and a less defined role in purely social encounters.

My shyness is compounded by the difficulty I find in asking

people for help. As an adolescent, after my mother left, I acquired the habit of doing things myself. Long after I had learned to delegate at work, I still felt awkward asking for personal support, and my diffidence was often interpreted as standoffishness. It wasn't helped by the fact that I'm not overly fond of the telephone. In that first memo, remarking on the need to enable people to feel close to the candidate and the campaign, Ray said, "This will mean that you will have to network by phone like you never have before. If you are not prepared to do this, you will hurt your chances greatly." (I'm told Joe Clark suffered from the same problem, leading one frustrated campaign worker in the 1983 leadership campaign to resort to imitating his distinctive voice in a call to a delegate when he couldn't persuade his candidate to make the call himself.)

I can't remember any single "moment of decision" when I decided to run, but by now the momentum was sweeping me along. John Dixon told me about a conversation he had had before the PM's announcement with John Cruickshank of the *Globe and Mail*'s editorial board. In speculating about a leadership campaign and my possible role, John Dixon told him, "She may not do it." He was astonished to hear his friend reply, "That would be an abdication of her responsibility to Canadian society." I doubt that John Cruickshank meant that I was all that stood between Canadian society and disaster; rather, he thought it was unthinkable that anyone with the public support that I apparently had would refuse to be a candidate. It was as if that support obligated me to put aside any concerns I might have about the difficulties of turning things around at this late date, or any distaste I might feel for being a sacrificial lamb. In the end, though, given that I had done everything I could to make clear to my colleagues who and what I was, it would be the support of the caucus that determined whether I ran.

The PM announced his departure on Wednesday, February 24. On Friday the House rose for a week's break and I flew to Vancouver. Of the three other B.C. ministers, Frank Oberle had long ago said he would support me for leader, but Mary Collins and Tom Siddon were unknown quantities. I had brunch with Mary on Saturday, but she wasn't yet ready to make a commitment. In the afternoon I attended the funeral of the provocative, maverick, and original North Vancouver Tory MP Chuck Cook. Not surprisingly, the funeral was a gathering of Tories, and although it was an inappropriate venue for campaigning, there were many subtle comments and questions from the other mourners.

Later on Saturday I started calling caucus colleagues to solicit their support. The calls were set up by Steven Greenaway, who had been executive assistant to Brian Smith when he was attorney general, and who would travel across the country with me during the campaign as my executive assistant. I was very fond of Steven, a young man of real solidity combined with a great sense of humour. Both Steve and Ray were relieved, and not a little surprised, that I took to the phone calls with enthusiasm. In many cases, I started the conversation by simply indicating that I was considering seeking the leadership and asking for advice. Once I had figured out what I wanted to say, I found I wasn't shy about asking for support. Ray claims that I made two hundred calls in three days! I think the almost universal expectation that I would be a candidate, combined with the friendliness of my colleagues, even those who weren't ready to commit to me, made it seem less personal and more collegial. The responses were more favourable than I had hoped. Gilles Loiselle had already remarked to the press that he had "always had a soft spot for Madame Campbell." He told me that, out shopping on the weekend in his Quebec City riding, he had been overwhelmed by people congratulating him for supporting me. Doug Lewis claimed a similar response on the streets of Orillia, Ontario. I was very encouraged.

On Monday evening, I had a heart-to-heart talk over dinner with Tom Siddon. Tom had worked very hard to help make Brian Mulroney party leader. He was the first caucus member to declare for Mulroney in 1983, a very important psychological event in the campaign of someone who had never been elected to public office. Moreover, Tom had out-organized everyone to deliver the lion's share of B.C. delegates to his candidate. As prime minister, Mulroney had recognized Tom's support by putting him in cabinet, but I sensed that Tom felt hurt by what appeared to be offhand treatment by the PM. Mulroney's habit of using diminutive names seemed like a form of false camaraderie — a way of suggesting intimacy where there was none. I could see that for this reason, his habit of calling Tom "Tommy" in cabinet rankled. (Tom wasn't alone in this regard. The PM's well-known pattern of schmoozing and mollifying caucus members was not universal in its application; I knew many MPs who had never received a call from him. On the other hand, there was no denying his solicitude when colleagues had problems. On hearing that Howard and I had separated, the PM called me to see how things were. "Would you like me to phone him?" he inquired. For one fleeting moment, I had the wicked urge to respond, "Yes.") It was hard for Tom to watch Mulroney get all pally with people in Vancouver who had not supported him for leader, but who were happy to tell him now what he wanted to hear and reap the rewards of the prime-ministerial intimacy. I understood his frustration myself.

I grew to like Tom very much, and I had come to appreciate his loyalty. On one occasion, at a weekly B.C. caucus meeting, my colleagues were giving me a rough time over one or another of my contentious pieces of legislation, I can't remember which. It was the end of a very long day, and finally, I'd had enough and left the meeting, followed by a concerned and comforting Tom Siddon. After some kind words that cheered me up, he went back and gave the others a blast.

Aside from the strategic importance of being supported by the ministers from my own province, I hoped that Tom would join my campaign because I respected him. I had been among the sceptics when Tom had been appointed Indian affairs minister in 1990. But he performed well in that portfolio and pushed the B.C. claims process to a successful conclusion — a treaty commission and an agreement on funding — against difficult odds. I wanted the benefit of his advice and integrity, and was very pleased when he agreed to co-chair my campaign in B.C. with Marie Mervyn, a senior and well-respected party member from the Interior of the province.

Throughout the first week of March, I spent hours on the phone each day talking to colleagues. The same process continued when we returned to Ottawa the following week. In my conversations with the other potential candidates — Barbara McDougall, Michael Wilson, Perrin Beatty, Jim Edwards, Tom Hockin and Bernard Valcourt — I simply told them that I was considering running and that if they decided to run, I wished them well, but that if they decided not to run, I would be honoured to have their support. Barbara said she had made no firm decision about running. Mike, however, had moved quickly to consolidate his support. Some of my advisers were sure he couldn't go anywhere because, as finance minister, he had been too closely associated with the more unpopular policies of the Mulroney government. Perhaps it was just my fear of over-confidence, but I wasn't so certain. "He's got much more charm than you may be giving him credit for," I warned. After all, this was a man who partied with Mick Jagger! His stature in the party had grown since 1983 when he had contested the leadership unsuccessfully. I thought that once he was out of the shadow of the PM, he would be a very attractive candidate.

Some of my support was expected, but I was surprised at some of the heads who began turning up on my political pillow! I realized that it was the prospect of our remaining in power that brought some of them there. However, other colleagues had different reasons. Ross Belsher represented a riding in the Bible belt of British Columbia. He told me that he didn't always agree with me, but could be a "conscience" in my government. He respected the way I had worked with caucus on gun control. Don Blenkarn from Mississauga, Ontario, called to tell me that when I was ready to run, he would be there. I was astonished because "Blenkie" had been one of the tougher nuts to crack on gun control and the CHRA amendments. In a comment that would be quoted in my campaign literature, Don told the Montreal *Gazette*: "She's handled some very tough legislation. She carried the ball for us on abortion, gun control and on the human-rights bill. She's tough, no question about it."

Naturally many of my colleagues were loyal to ministers they had worked with for some time. They wanted to hold back to see if Barbara, Maz, Michael, or a regional candidate would run. I appreciated my colleagues' honesty. I also found myself enjoying the views of non-cabinet colleagues as to the challenges facing us. There was a general consensus that we had to offer the voters a new vision, and there were numerous opinions as to the most effective way of doing this. Many mentioned that they were finding considerable support for me in their ridings. In general, MPs seemed to think that a woman candidate could do well and would represent change. At the end of the week, I was delighted when Mary Collins, after grilling me about how I planned to involve my colleagues in the decisions of government if I won, agreed to support me and to head up the campaign's outreach to women. By now it was clear that I was going to have substantial support from caucus, and I was thrilled. There had been only one major setback.

Brian Mulroney angry is not a comforting sight. I had rarely seen him in such a rage as he displayed in P&P on March 9 over the idea that a minister might resign in order to become a leadership candidate. He didn't name names, but my cheeks burned because I knew he must have known I'd been discussing stepping down with a number of people. I was absolutely stunned when he insisted furiously that he would regard such a move as a sign of disloyalty. The point of my resigning from cabinet would have been to avoid controversy, not to create it. Ray worried that if I had to carry on cabinet duties as a candidate, particularly in a travel-intensive portfolio like Defence, I would be susceptible to charges that my ministerial travel was unfairly subsidizing my campaign. It would be an exacting task to separate campaign expenses from legitimate ministerial expenses, and we thought the whole issue could be avoided if I resigned. In addition, the shuffle had dramatically increased my workload. Had I remained in Justice, I could have coasted a bit over the four months of the campaign because I knew the portfolio so well. Defence and Veterans were a different matter, and not just because they figured large in discussions of the budget or because they required a minister to travel.

The end of the Cold War meant the end of the framework of Canada's defence policy since World War II. Although the time remaining in our mandate would be insufficient to do a complete policy review, certain processes needed to be begun in order to prepare for one in the future. But even more important, the demands on our forces for peacekeeping were at an all-time high. Canadian forces were in fifteen locations around the world, and our resources were stretched to the limit. Canada had never said no to a UN request for help, but we were now faced with precisely this possibility if further requests were made to us. The situation required constant monitoring.

Canada had also committed troops to the humanitarian mission in Somalia. As the spring unfolded, a number of disturbing events came to light involving the killing of Somalis by Canadian forces. These ranged from an accidental death from gunfire in a crowd to the torture and murder of Shidane Arone, an atrocity pure and simple. My position as a strong candidate made it irresistible for opposition members and members of the media to suggest that I wasn't paying enough attention to these events or was trying to downplay them, even cover them up, to avoid controversy that might affect my campaign. Even though I didn't yet know what I would be up against regarding the incidents in Somalia, I obviously knew that I couldn't just ignore my ministerial responsibilities during a campaign.

When I returned to my office and told Ray about the PM's outburst, he was dismayed. It was easy to rationalize staying on, and I had certainly not made up my mind to step down, but I felt angry at being told I couldn't make that decision myself. It was as if a bubble had burst with respect to my feelings about Brian Mulroney. I began to see more clearly just how determined he was to manipulate the entire leadership process and to ensure that no one criticized him or stepped too far from the government line as I would be freer to do if I left cabinet. Those close to Mulroney argue that he wanted to avoid attacks on our record by candidates in order to minimize divisions in the party after the leadership race, but as the plans began to unfold for a convention in June 1993 to coincide exactly with the tenth anniversary of his election as leader, it began to seem more and more as if the promotion of the PM's image was a higher priority than leaving the party in good shape. As the PM and Mila launched on an elaborate farewell tour around the world and the pace of appointments picked up, that impression was strengthened.

Although I wasn't uncritical of Brian Mulroney, I had never been anything but loyal since I arrived in Ottawa. I was certainly aware of the visceral distaste Mulroney inspired in some people. Some of it I attributed to his own personality and style, which were offputting to many people. There was a studied quality to Brian Mulroney, especially in public, a sense that he was *playing* himself rather than *being* himself. That impression of not quite "touching bottom" when you observed him generated enormous mistrust. Some of the hostility was obviously a residue of distrust from the scandals of the first mandate; and the remainder I thought was a natural result of being associated with contentious policies.

By the time I met Mulroney, he was already an experienced

leader, and as one of his ministers, I had no complaints. He left me alone to run my own departments and supported my work on behalf of women. I fought my own battles, never feeling the need to run to him to pull my irons out of the fire. In short, ours was a relationship of mutual respect, or so I thought. The point is that I accepted the need to be loyal to my leader and knew that any criticism of him or his government by me would be taken by the media and used as a weapon against both of us.

As the plans for the leadership campaign unfolded, I began to feel that we were trying to run a campaign without acknowledging why it was happening in the first place. Mulroney was resigning because he couldn't win another election. He hadn't stepped down after the referendum because it was unthinkable for him to resign in seeming defeat. The only chance I would have to win an election if I became leader would be if I were perceived to represent change.

I made many mistakes in the campaigns and other events of 1993, but I think the greatest one may have been not to call the PM's bluff and resign from cabinet. If I had resigned, I might well have lost the leadership. The PM might have followed through on his threat to punish anyone who left cabinet. I don't know what he would have done, but certainly he could have ensured that people he influenced did not support me. But I think in the long run, it might have been better to lose under those circumstances. And had I won anyway, it would have established my independence early on and given me the best possible chance to win the election.

In Ray Castelli's view, we were so fast getting out of the gate after the PM's announcement that we simply pre-empted all the other campaigns. Caucus support had started to fall into place to a degree that dispelled media speculation that I would be denied it because of the controversial issues I had championed. But other forms of party support were equally important. Perhaps the key event of those early days was the decision by party organizer Glen Wright of Ontario to join my campaign. No one doubted that I would gain considerable support in B.C. and the other western provinces; the real question was whether I could win delegates in Ontario and Quebec. Ontario delegates wouldn't want to commit to me if I couldn't gain ground in Quebec. Similarly, Quebeckers wouldn't join my cause if I didn't have access to the decisive votes of Ontario. Glen was key to this strategy. When Ray and I met with him over breakfast at the Westin Hotel in Ottawa in March, I was delighted to find him a truly thoughtful person with ideas about reviving the party that matched my own. A member of the National Executive for six years, Glen was "Mr. Grassroots" in the Ontario Conservative Party. There were twenty-two ridings around Quebec City waiting to see what would happen in Ontario. When Glen declared his support for me, Marc Dorion, who spoke for those ridings, and the influential Doug Lewis in Ontario did likewise.

My leadership campaign had been conceived as one where I would be running as an "outsider" in a strong field. But, to our astonishment, the heavy hitters began to drop out in mid-March. The first to announce that he wouldn't be a candidate was Michael Wilson, now the minister for industry. Michael had asked Glen Wright to head up his leadership campaign. When Glen declined, Michael knew he couldn't mount a winning campaign. With the departure of her chief Toronto rival, Barbara McDougall seemed like a certain candidate, but her testing of the waters was discouraging. Announcing her decision not to enter the race to her disappointed staff and supporters, I am told, Barbara said she had awoken in the middle of the night asking herself whether she really wanted to be prime minister, or more likely, leader of the opposition. Realizing that she didn't, she decided not to run. Barbara McDougall had no illusions about the challenge awaiting Brian Mulroney's successor.

The biggest surprise was Perrin Beatty. After his twenty-one years in Parliament, everyone assumed that this was the moment he had been waiting for. However, Perrin was unable to attract sufficient support from Quebec. He announced he wouldn't run in the face of what he called an "unprecedented consensus" in favour of my candidacy. I think that Wilson, McDougall, and Beatty were genuinely disappointed at their inability to draw the support they needed to run. They were all realists about our prospects, but it was then or never for Mike and Barbara, and even for the youthful Perrin if the party chose a young leader. The winner would become the prime minister. Whatever the long-term prognosis, it was hard to accept that this was a prize not worth winning.

As I became the clear frontrunner, the entire dynamic changed in a way I don't think my team and I fully understood or appreciated. At first, we were naturally delighted with the growing declarations of support. Before long, however, we began to see how difficult a position this was from which to run a campaign for a candidate like me. I had a strong idea of how I would approach policy if I were prime minister, but I wanted to give some thought to any specific positions I would take so that I wouldn't have to disavow them if I were elected. I thought that my general approach to the issues of governing was already understood from my years as justice minister. I was mistaken. The media people who began to cover me for the first time in 1993 seemed to have no idea of what I had been about in Justice, and furthermore, they weren't interested in what the Justice beat reporters could tell them, regarding them as hopelessly "captive."

As our campaign progressed, it suffered from having too many supporters. This may seem an odd observation, but as the other serious candidates dropped out, many of their supporters joined our campaign with the expectation of playing significant roles. There were simply not enough important jobs to go around after Pierre Blais and Shirley Martin were appointed co-chairs of the campaign and Ross Reid was named campaign manager. The campaign began to suffer from the weight of its own success and the inevitable sniping began. Dalton Camp wrote an article criticizing the campaign as being run by "children." Since his own son, David, was a key player on the strategy committee, there was a certain Freudian overtone to this criticism. Ray was particularly annoyed at this charge, because while it was true that many of my key workers were young, they were also extremely talented and in many cases highly experienced. To try to soothe the hurt feelings, David arranged a lunch between Ray and his father. Ray was astonished to discover that Dalton didn't have a clue who Glen Wright was. No wonder the names on our organization chart didn't mean anything to him! He was clearly out of touch and simply didn't know who some of the most significant forty-something organizers in the party were. Still, there was some truth to his comment since, in order to represent change, we felt we needed new faces in the campaign.

From my experience in 1986, I had a limited idea of how a leadership campaign is conducted. The first few weeks are usually taken up with the party's organization of the campaign — deciding on the rules and times for debates, for example — as well as with testing of the waters by potential candidates. During this stage, the crucial organizational task for a candidate is to sell party memberships before the deadline so that your own supporters can be selected as convention delegates. Ray Castelli estimates that we sold approximately 100,000 party memberships. Any speeches given at that time are to audiences of party members, who may seek delegate status themselves or will be voting to select delegates.

During the process of delegate selection, the second stage of the campaign, finding supporters and getting them out to delegate selection meetings is crucial. Delegate selection gives a first real sense of levels of support because most, though not all, delegates are elected on slates supporting a particular candidate. Our remarkably accurate system for tracking delegate preference and the strength of that preference was created by John Mykytyshyn. It enabled the campaign team to plan my campaign visits and telephone calls strategically and later, during the convention, maximized the value of the short time available for meeting with delegates.

During the third stage of the campaign, I began travelling to many small communities, often to meet with half a dozen or a dozen delegates who were as yet uncommitted. These people were key to winning. The final stage of the campaign would be the convention itself, which would be held in Ottawa the weekend of June 11–13 at the Civic Centre.

Right from the start, because most known support was going to me, the implications of being out in front directed the campaign. Instead of starting slowly to build support, it suddenly became an urgent priority for me to travel around the country before I had even announced my candidacy, to consolidate my support. Organizers and potential delegates were very conscious of their importance, and their initial declarations of support had to be acknowledged so that they would not feel unappreciated and therefore be susceptible to being wooed away. Events were organized in mid-March in Toronto, Montreal, and Quebec City, where I met with potential delegates and key organizers.

A major campaign requires proper photographs and an appropriate wardrobe for the candidate. Libby Burnham, whose

Conservative roots were in the New Brunswick of the Hatfield era, was now practising law in Toronto. She was one of the people Mike Ferrabee had urged me to get to know, and I came to share his enthusiasm for her. Intelligent, honest, and very down-to-earth, Libby used the entertainment-world associations she had developed as a member of the CBC board of directors to find people who could help me project an image that was true to myself. Toronto photographer Denise Grant took excellent campaign portraits and designer Lee Kinoshita-Bevington addressed the question of clothes. Known to his clients as "Lee K-B," Lee understood perfectly my desire to have clothes that I could wear comfortably and that wouldn't wear me. On several occasions when we were pressed for time, Lee, who was based in Toronto, flew into Ottawa to conduct fittings in the washroom of my office.

In Toronto in early March, Libby introduced me to Alan Schwartz, who had worked closely with Larry Grossman in his campaign to become leader of the Ontario Conservatives. Alan agreed to become my chief fundraiser. He did a wonderful job, but as he and other fundraisers would find, my position as front-runner didn't always assist their efforts. There was a tendency for people to assume that we didn't need money if I was heading towards a win. The party had set a limit of $900,000 for campaign expenses, but this excluded some major expenses such as travel. It would take two to three times that amount to wage a winning campaign.

My Quebec and Montreal meetings in March included meetings with Senator Mario Beaulieu, former senator Jean Bazin, and several other members of Brian Mulroney's circle. The Quebec team decided that our publicity and advertising there would be done by the firm Publicité Martin. (I found them pleasant and competent; it wasn't until after I had left government that I learned of the close link between the president, Yvon Martin, and Mulroney.) What was I to make of this embrace by the Mulroney old guard? Clearly, at that stage they viewed me as the best hope for keeping the Conservatives in power. The connection of these supporters to Mulroney was not the political liability in Quebec that it was in other parts of the country. It was not only in Quebec that I found myself being supported by members of the party establishment whose motives I couldn't ascertain. On a personal level, I found them all charming and helpful. On another level, though, I was uneasy about being politically indebted to people I didn't know well.

I have always taken the position that what I owe to those who support me politically is good government and a heartfelt thank-you. I realized, however, that being a candidate for the prize of the prime ministership meant I was now moving in an entirely new milieu, where the spoils of power are considerable. I consoled myself that, given that we were looking for a miracle worker to stop the Tories' slide into oblivion, any leader who could actually lead the party to victory would have enormous personal credibility and independence of action.

Although the earlier plan had been for me to declare my candidacy in early March, the need to accommodate the unexpected rush of volunteers and to consider the implications of the withdrawals of Michael Wilson, Barbara McDougall, Perrin Beatty, and Bernard Valcourt delayed my announcement until March 25, one month after Brian Mulroney's resignation. In the meantime, Jean Charest, who was environment minister, formally declared his candidacy on March 16. Once the delegates were selected, our tracking showed that I had about 40 per cent of the committed delegates and Charest had about 23 per cent. In light of the initial support for me, Jean had been reluctant to enter the race and did so only after serious arm-twisting by Mulroney. At only thirty-four, Jean was perhaps the only minister who could lose the race with no political detriment. However, Jean was not interested in "running for next time." After his announcement speech, he went on open-line radio in Montreal demanding to know "one thing that Ms. Campbell stands for!" Since I had been wearing my philosophical heart on my sleeve for some time, I found this rather hard to take. On the other hand, I accepted the fact that I was now the target — the one the other candidates would be running against.

I wanted to launch my campaign in Vancouver, but my organizers thought I should also announce it formally in Quebec. The idea was that I would begin my campaign in Vancouver, then fly to Montreal, where I would make a second declaration the next day. I would return to Ottawa to launch the youth campaign that evening and prepare to leave for NATO meetings in Brussels on the 27th after a campaign kickoff in Toronto. With the formal launch of my campaign, there were major changes in my office. Ray resigned to be a director of operations of the campaign, and Richard Clair, who had first come to work for me in Justice as my legislative assistant and had moved up to become second-in-command to Ray, took over as chief of staff.

Before going to Vancouver, I paid a courtesy call on the PM to advise him of my plans. At that time he read to me from what he said were intermittent notes he kept. It was an entry made after my appointment as defence minister in which he described me, as I recall, as "smart, disciplined, and hard-working." I wasn't sure at the time if I was to take this as a veiled indication of support or just a vote of confidence in my performance as a minister.

In Vancouver the night before the announcement, Steve Greenaway and Cindy Boucher came over to my house to settle a few final details. Cindy had become my press secretary in February, and she and Steven would accompany me on the road during the leadership campaign. The daughter of noted journalist Charles Lynch, Cindy had a strong professional background in communications both in government and out, and a sense of humour that made her a delightful companion. At our meeting Steven pulled out a tape he wanted me to listen to of George Fox's song "Clearly Canadian." I was already a big George Fox fan and, thanks to Libby, had been his "date" at the Juno Awards in Toronto the previous Sunday. As we listened to his upbeat celebration of Canada, I agreed that this would make a great entrance theme for the next day. In fact, "Clearly Canadian" became our unofficial campaign theme on the road. We used it as an entrance song, and towards the end of a hard day of campaigning, we would put it into the cassette player in the van or car, turn it up full blast, and let it energize us as we hit whatever highway would lead us to the next event.

I had agonized over my announcement speech. The draft that had been developed by my campaign team was very good. My reservations weren't about the content but about speaking from a text at all. This speech would set the tone of the campaign. I didn't realize then that it would also be one of the rare occasions when I could speak directly to the public, on themes of my own choosing, rather than have my words "interpreted" by journalists. People who had worked with me knew that my best speeches were those I was able to give freely from notes I had put together myself. The only problem with this method was that no text was available for the media until there had been time to transcribe it. I decided to gamble and speak without a text.

March 25 was a beautiful spring day in Vancouver. Diana Lam and Steven Greenaway accompanied me from my house to the Hotel Vancouver. A breakfast reception had begun at 7:30 for the hundreds of people gathered there, and my speech was to start exactly one hour later, when it would be picked up for live national broadcast. Inside the hotel, my supporters were lining the way to the Pacific Ballroom. Co-chairs Pierre Blais and Shirley Martin were gathered near the podium, as were Perrin Beatty, Gilles Loiselle, MP Suzanne Duplessis, and my B.C. caucus supporters. Entering that jam-packed ballroom to the strains of George Fox's song was an incredible experience. Everywhere I looked there were people I knew — former colleagues from the school board and the legislature, high school classmates, law colleagues, friends and acquaintances from all periods of my life. My family was all there, Mum, Alix, Dad, Marg, and Marg's mum, excited and smiling. As I passed by my colleagues from Parliament, Suzanne Duplessis planted a big lipsticked kiss on my cheek, which, unbeknownst to me, showed up clearly on television during my speech. Tom Siddon introduced me and I gave him a hug as I took my place at the podium.

The main theme of my speech was, Who is Kim Campbell and why does she want to be prime minister? I began by addressing the first question, identifying myself as a Vancouverite and a British Columbian. "I think British Columbians in general tend to be visionary, forward-looking, energetic, enthusiastic, very entrepreneurial. We feel that our future is still in front of us, not behind us, and we're willing to try new things. But we also have a sense that from time to time the government of Canada doesn't serve us well, that it doesn't understand us because we are so far away. Perhaps it's that sense of alienation and distance from the centre of power that has often given us an understanding of our compatriots in Quebec, who also sometimes feel a bit alienated from central government."

I spoke about my vision of democracy and of politics. "I think if we want to change the way we do politics, we have to change people's sense of what is in fact possible — people's sense of the possibilities ... To be truly enfranchised you must know that your reality will be considered in the making of public policy, that you count, that those who are making public policy understand who you are, not just that you've given them your vote. And that leads for me to what I call 'the politics of inclusion.' I understand the sense of exclusion as a woman and as a British Columbian."

Drawing on my experience with "inclusive justice" and the Vancouver symposium on women and the law, I explained: "My goal has been not to define one single view of the world as it relates to women, but simply to open the door to women, to say, 'Come on in, be a part of the cut and thrust of resolving issues and contending values in Canadian society. You don't have to agree with me. Come on in the door and fight with me. Tell me what you don't think I'm doing right. But be there as a first-class citizen.' And that is my vision of citizenship in this country."

I described my approach to leadership in similar terms, pointing out that no minister can be effective without the support of his or her colleagues, who represent the diverse realities of this country. When dealing with tough issues, I always asked them to be part of the process, because I believe in treating people with collegiality and respect.

The speech then turned to the economy, and I recalled that it was the Free Trade Agreement that had brought me into federal politics. Canadians want to know, I said, that their government understands the new global economy and its demands. We must "rethink the implications of this new knowledge-based economy for government, what governments can do and what they can't do. I look across the floor of the House of Commons and I see people who are still living in the sixties, who think you can have a purely national economy and put up nice little walls around it, irrespective of what's happening in the world."

Since my arrival in Ottawa, I had been concerned (as had many of my colleagues) that our government had not communicated a broader vision of Canada, one that provided a rationale for the other things we were trying to do. I wanted to link my views on the economy very clearly to my vision of Canada. I spoke of the "social and political culture in this country that is unique to us." I see this culture as a synthesis of the outlooks of people from all parts of this country. "I am devoted to preserving that 'Canadianness,' and I think it is important to understand that if we turn a blind eye to the economic realities of this world, that is a sure recipe for destroying those things that we have built as a country."

On another economic theme — the debt and the deficit — I said that there are, unfortunately, no easy solutions. But the reasons for dealing with the debt and deficit issue are fundamental. Only by restoring the nation's financial health can we restore to future generations "their right to make the same kinds of decisions about the society they want that we think are such an essential part of being in a democracy." Making difficult decisions today gives our society the ability to continue to be what we are, and to have social programs to protect one another.

I spoke about the importance of remembering the human scale of the grand concepts we often speak about in government, and repeated one of my constant refrains: "We're not legislating for abstractions; we're legislating for real people."

I concluded with a simple statement of why I wanted to be prime minister. "I'd like to change the way people think about politics in this country by changing the way we do politics in this country." Switching to French, I elaborated, "In my view, we must reduce the distance between our people and the government. We must create a partnership between citizens and the government because, without that partnership, we cannot do the things necessary to build our future."

My vision of a more open way of governing was not just an idealistic hope, I said, and I stated my belief in the importance of political parties as vehicles for democratic participation. Because of their breadth of membership, they can be very effective in bringing diverse people together to define something approximating the "national interest." I ended with a call to renew the party and make it the vehicle through which Canadians would believe they could build our national future.

I felt very good about the speech and the party shared my enthusiasm. The lack of a text meant that I could reach out directly to my campaign team and to other groups of supporters who were watching in Ottawa and all around the country. I'm sure that a written text would have been more eloquent, but I didn't want anything to come between me and the audience. I wanted people to know that I was saying what I truly thought and believed, not what someone had written for me. I also wanted the freedom to look at my audience and connect with it. On television most of what is communicated is non-verbal, and it felt more important for me to be relaxed and spontaneous than to speak a grammatically or syntactically perfect text. As the leadership campaign unfolded, and the effort was made to script more of it, there would be calls from my supporters to "let Kim be Kim," as there would later be in the election campaign. It wasn't that I couldn't give a decent speech from a text, but the nature of the communication was so different when I spoke freely that those who were expecting that spontaneity felt a sense of letdown when I spoke from a text. This was a problem that would dog me until I left government.

The speech was followed by several hours of meetings with the media, whose change in tone I found interesting. I wasn't to have even a day's grace. Perhaps the worst interview was with Peter Mansbridge and Pamela Wallin of CBC TV's *Prime Time News*. It verged on outright rudeness. Other interviews also had an edge that was a preview of what was to come. In my speech I had remarked on the popular wisdom that I was some sort of media darling, saying that I "expected to be left at the altar" in that particular relationship. I hadn't, however, expected the change to be so immediate. It wasn't made easier by the fact that Brian Mulroney picked that day to announce new appointments to the Senate. He must have realized that I would be questioned about this, as he knew full well how the appointments would be received in the political climate of the time. I was asked my views and I replied honestly that although the prime minister had a perfect right to make the appointments, I would have preferred that he not have done so.

Reflecting back on the early meetings with my closest advisers in Vancouver, David Camp observed that we didn't realize then that we would not be able to get by on my views about changing the political process. Right from the start, a standard of specificity was demanded of me that wasn't demanded of any of the other candidates. A lot of work would be done on policy, and by the end of the campaign, my policy presentations would be more comprehensive and detailed than those of any other candidate and would contain many new ideas. By that time, however, the media had lost interest. Was it naiveté that led us to believe that I could take some time over the three months remaining in the campaign to clarify my positions?

The next day I attended the kickoff of the Quebec campaign in our Montreal headquarters, for which Monique Landry, co-chair of the Quebec campaign, played hostess. The small hall was packed and the atmosphere festive. After a short speech, I made my way slowly through the crowd, handshaking as I went, in a pattern that, together with the crowd of media, would become a typical feature of my days in the weeks to come.

The launch of the National Youth Campaign at our Ottawa headquarters drew an impressive group of young people. We dominated the youth campaign from the start. It always surprised me how many of these young men and women had had considerable political experience. After another round of introductions, a short speech, and a handshaking session with the crowd, I went home to my apartment exhausted but exhilarated.

As soon as I stepped onto the government plane for the trip to Brussels on March 27, I left the leadership campaign behind and began to think of the agenda for the upcoming NATO meetings. Thus began a two-and-a-half-month period in which campaign and portfolio activities ran in counterpoint.

This was no ordinary meeting of NATO defence ministers but a meeting of the North Atlantic Cooperation Council, which included ministers of the former Warsaw Pact countries. I found myself seated next to the Czech defence minister and decided to try speaking a few words of Russian to him. He looked at me in astonishment and said, in perfect English, "You speak Russian without an accent!" (His remark was more gallant than accurate.) As a former Soviet specialist, I was intrigued to be meeting with representatives of countries, including former Soviet republics, that had been our Cold War enemies. Observing a testy exchange between the Russian defence minister and his Lithuanian counterpart about the removal of Russian troops from Lithuania was an experience I could never have dreamed of even two years earlier.

NATO Secretary General Manfred Woerner was a forceful presence as he chaired the meetings. The Vance-Owen plan for peace in Bosnia had just been negotiated and it was estimated that it would require anywhere from 55,000 to 75,000 troops to supervise it if it were accepted. In his private canvass of NATO countries to see what sort of personnel they could commit to this enterprise, Woerner was able to get promises of only 12,000 or so, a reflection of the increasing financial pressures military sectors were feeling.

We departed for London early that evening, where I stayed with High Commissioner Fredrik Eaton and his wife, Catherine. After meeting with the Commonwealth War Graves Commission, I toured the Canadian graves at Brookwood Military Cemetery and laid a wreath at the Stone of Remembrance. A meeting later that day with Malcolm Rifkind, the U.K. secretary of defence, was my main reason for stopping in London. We had serious matters to discuss about the future of our troops in Bosnia. Rifkind also wanted to know about Canada's commitment to the EH-101 helicopter project because the British were also purchasing it. I assured him of my continued commitment.

As we flew home from London on March 30, Cindy Boucher briefed me on the investigation into the death in Somalia of Shidane Arone. It was now complete and the death was being treated as a homicide. What charges would be laid had not yet been decided. It wasn't until we returned to Ottawa that I discovered the full horror of Arone's death.

Once back in Canada, the pace of the leadership campaign picked up again with trips to Toronto, Edmonton, Harrison Hot Springs, B.C., Saskatoon, and Regina. There were now six candidates. Jean Charest and I were the only cabinet ministers. Jim Edwards, an MP from Alberta, had declared, as had MPs Patrick Boyer and Garth Turner, both from the Toronto area. A sixth candidate was John Long, a total unknown who didn't hold elected office. An adherent of the original theories of Social Credit (long since abandoned by the B.C. Social Credit party), he wanted a platform from which to launch his attacks on Canadian banks. Although many party members found his way-out views an embarrassment, he was able to pay the required deposit and so there was no barrier to his candidacy.

In our camp Ray and Ross Reid had been trying to deal with the huge influx of senior campaigners. It was proving impossible to find a job for everyone despite Ray's ingenuity in stretching out the organization chart. Moreover, with no Ontario minister in the running, many of that province's Big Blue Machine people had joined us. These were the very people many of the Young Turks on my campaign wanted to run *against*. The tension was palpable and the campaign was suffering as a result. In our concentration on turning this unwieldy group into a smooth-running operation, we failed to appreciate fully the extent to which the nature of the leadership campaign itself had changed. This is nowhere more clear than in a strategy document for the first policy forum, scheduled for April 15 in Toronto, written by Nancy Jamieson, a political consultant who had worked on the prime-ministerial staff of Joe Clark. (It was Nancy who had warned Clark that he didn't have sufficient votes to survive the confidence vote that toppled his nine-month-old government in 1979.) The party had decided to hold five all-candidates debates, which, in their effort to emphasize the "collegiality" of the campaign, they referred to as policy forums.

Our goal was to communicate my inclusive style of leadership. Concerned about the "increasingly hostile media filter" through which my campaign messages were being communicated, Nancy argued for a strategic approach that would articulate "a difference in both style and substance of the candidate," showing me as "a unique voice in the Canadian political environment." The critical objective was to break the debates out of the usual "win/lose" context and turn them into an opportunity for candidates to be seen collectively defining the problems we face and working together to find solutions. "It will be difficult," Nancy wrote, "to play against the media's perceptions of what these events are all about — traditionally, rancorous shot-taking sessions, and their misconceptions of Ms. Campbell — that she is arrogant and abrasive. It will be similarly challenging to both our own organizers and party members not to rise to the temptation of practising the old school of 'big rally/big mo [momentum]' politics ...

"The challenge is to downplay the very obvious intellectual skills of the candidate without appearing to avoid either specifics or difficult issues, while highlighting her ability to listen and respond sensitively to the concerns and humanity of both potential delegates and Canadians generally. At its best, the policy forum should look and feel like a dialogue rather than a debate."

Much has been written about the first debate in Toronto and what it reflected about my campaign. Much of what has been written misses the point. It is true that there was a lot of last-minute briefing in the afternoon, which probably added nothing to my sense of serenity that evening. A great deal has been made of my turning down the opportunity to go over the site in the afternoon. That was completely irrelevant. I had been appearing on television since I was ten, and there were no significant surprises on the set. The problems I had during the Toronto debate were twofold: first, I quickly became aware that our strategy was completely inappropriate in a context where everybody else was playing by the old rules; second, I was wearing shoes with two-inch heels. By the second hour of standing in one spot in high heels, I was growing distinctly uncomfortable, and it showed. According to Nancy, I needed to appear "serious, thoughtful and relaxed — tough without being difficult, bright without being a 'Jeopardy' contestant, funny without being glib. Ideally, audiences should feel that she is the best of all possible audiences for their concerns — a smart, sensitive listener."

It wasn't just Nancy who thought I could do this. I went into the debate convinced that my biggest liability was the public's perception that I might be "too smart" or "arrogant." By the standards of our strategy, my performance in the debate was on target. However, I quickly realized that I was in trouble. Jean Charest's strategy was to give crisp answers that sounded decisive. The others also took a more traditional approach. Compared to all that crispness, I sounded vague and unfocussed, rather than thoughtful and unwilling to offer up simplistic answers to complex questions. As the evening wore on, my distress increased. The lights were giving me a headache, my feet hurt, and I had a knot in the pit of my stomach.

As I left the stage, I hurried back to my dressing room before anyone could see my dismay. Steve, Cindy, and Ray tried to reassure me, but I knew what a disaster I had been. I also had no illusions whatsoever about what this would mean to the media portrayal of the campaign. This was the turning point the press had been waiting for to make the campaign interesting. There was nothing to do but put on a brave face, forget my sore feet, and go out into the crowd. I brushed my hair, wiped off the heavy TV make-up, and went out with Cindy to smile my way confidently through the media scrums. From the audience's perspective, as confirmed by polling done that night, the result was a draw. However, by the next morning the media spin had altered that to a five-to-one perception that Jean had won.

What we hadn't understood was that as the frontrunner, I was no longer in a position to "redefine" the campaign. The greatest anomaly of the campaign — the absence of the senior ministers as candidates — was illustrated by an abortive attempt by Hugh Segal, who had resigned as Mulroney's chief of staff in April, to enter the race just before the first debate. It was bizarre that Jean Charest and I were the only ministers in the race. Other candidates could experiment with campaign styles, but for our strategy to work, I would have needed to be but one of several strong contenders, and accepted by the press as an "outsider." Once I became the frontrunner, though, I became, by virtue of the support that status attracted, the establishment candidate, and was judged accordingly. We should have seen it coming, but we didn't.

Those few days between the Toronto and Montreal debates were by far the worst of the entire campaign for me. The morning after the first debate, I flew to Montreal for several days of campaigning in Quebec where the use of French would help to prepare me for the Montreal debate on April 21. My personal unhappiness and concern at this point were alleviated somewhat by the careful work of our advance team, who helped make my hectic schedules more manageable. Throughout the country, PC Advance brings volunteers together and trains them to assist visiting ministers and dignitaries with their travel and events. It was in Quebec that I really became aware of what it would be like to be prime minister because the PM spent a lot of time in his home province and so the PC Advance members there who had joined my campaign were Brian Mulroney's team. Elsewhere in the country, we would stay in modest accommodations, with only Cindy, Steve, and our regular advance worker, Dan MacDonald, to coordinate things. In Quebec, the accommodations were always excellent and it seemed like a cast of thousands descended upon us on our arrival in each locale to whisk away luggage, prepare rooms, and ensure we had everything we needed. They were used to serving the prime minister, and it showed.

In addition to meeting me and guiding me through carefully thought out itineraries, the advance people also ensured that anything I might need in the way of snacks and beverages would be in my hotel room when I arrived. At some point I must have indicated a fondness for bagels as a snack food. Everywhere I went across the country I found plates of bagels waiting for me. Sometimes, in a brief stop that didn't even involve my staying the night in the hotel room, there would be a dozen. I began to be somewhat concerned that I was rarely eating the proffered bagels and that money was being wasted. Cindy and I tried to cancel the order but couldn't seem to stop the flow. After a long day in Montreal following the debate, we flew to Quebec City and made our way to the Château Frontenac, where the manager provided me with a lovely suite. I walked into the kitchenette, still devastated from the Toronto fiasco, and started to howl with laughter. Thinking I had finally cracked, Cindy came rushing in, only to burst out laughing herself when she saw me lift up an elegant silver dome to reveal a plateful of — bagels!

Saturday, April 17, looked like it was going to be a day from hell. It wasn't an atypical day, but I woke up feeling nauseated and wondered how I would get through it. I didn't know if it was nerves or if I had eaten something that was upsetting me. My first event was an 8:30 breakfast in the Sainte-Foy riding of Suzanne Duplessis. As we were leaving the hotel, I asked one of the advance people to buy me some Pepto-Bismol. We arrived at the breakfast and in the waiting room, I wasn't sure I could get through the speech without throwing up. Just before it was time to go in, someone rushed in with the pink bottle and I gulped some down. The crowd was wonderful and I tried my best to be lively and inspiring in French at that early hour, without letting on how I felt.

Next we drove to a small airfield to take a charter plane to Mont-Joli. I usually like flying in small planes, but the knot in my stomach was still producing waves of nausea. I sat looking out the window and forced myself to breathe slowly and deeply. Once we were at the Mont-Joli luncheon with delegates from Matane, Rimouski, Rivière-du-Loup, and Gaspé, I began to perk up. The people were warm and as I met with them and went into lunch for the speech, I began to forget about my woes. It helped that nobody was talking about the Toronto debate! A media scrum followed the speech, then we were off in the plane to Bagotville, where I had meetings with media representatives from Chicoutimi and potential delegates from Saguenay–Lac-Saint-Jean. The day concluded with a drop-in reception for about a hundred people from the region. At 7:30 p.m. we were on the plane back to Quebec City, and by 8:45 we were back at the Château Frontenac. Despite the charms of my suite and the beautiful view of the St. Lawrence, I undressed as fast as I could and collapsed into bed.

I continued to feel nauseated the next day. The afternoon was taken up with filming the video to be sent to delegates. I hoped I looked livelier than I felt. Life was made much more bearable by the arrival of David Camp, in one of those great gestures of friendship that can mean so much. Knowing how unhappy I was feeling after Toronto, Cindy had recognized that I needed the company of someone who really knew me, and had called David, who volunteered to keep me company until the Montreal debate was over.

Although I was fond of the people I was travelling with, there was no one in my entourage who could qualify as an old friend. Since I had met David at Ladner Downs, we had developed a great friendship based on our mutual interest in politics. I remember him as one of the volunteers of my 1988 campaign, sitting and chatting about some campaign event. "I wonder if I will ever be in cabinet," I mused. "I think someone with your capabilities could reasonably expect to be prime minister," he said matter-of-factly. Knowing that David had seen that potential in me from such an early date gave his support a special quality. After the election, David became president of my riding association, a position he held for three years. He had now joined the leadership team as a policy adviser.

I always felt it was important to keep morale up on a campaign, so it was difficult for me to convey to the people around me my distress about things that were going wrong. With David I could let my hair down. As the frontrunner, I felt I alone could make or break the campaign, and this responsibility made my errors an agony for me. I wanted so much not to let people down, but I was only human. It was such a relief to be able to share with someone I trusted the anxiety I felt when I hadn't performed well.

I had also asked Ross Reid to come to Quebec City. I told him, "Jean Charest has a clear strategy, and I want a clear strategy."

What had become obvious in the Toronto debate was that Jean's strategy was to go after me. We were going to have to articulate a much clearer picture of me in comparison with the other candidates, especially Jean. Being the frontrunner meant I would have to avoid seeming heavy-handed, but I needed to be more aggressive in setting out my own strengths and experience, as well as ideas.

The Toronto debate was the warning signal that the campaign was in trouble. After discussing the problem with David, I decided to ask Patrick Kinsella to come to Ottawa to see what he could do about it. Patrick had once been a part of the Big Blue Machine in Premier Bill Davis's time. For that reason and because I had watched his skill in motivating the people of Brian Smith's leadership campaign, I thought he might be able to bridge the divisions between those who were BBM people and those who weren't. Bill Davis's Big Blue Machine had come to represent an elite of "old boys" who wanted to run the party and who regarded policy as a necessary evil, rather than a reason for being in politics. The Tories had governed Ontario for forty-two years, and the BBM was not unlike the federal Liberals I had observed, who also reflected the arrogance of a long-term governing party. However, like all stereotypes, that of the BBM was exaggerated. Many of the people associated with it were as eager to change the party as the Young Turks who resented them so much.

Patrick accepted, came into headquarters, and by some miracle got people working together. In fact, within a short time, the anti-BBM types were saying how glad they were he was there. Since I didn't have personal baggage as far as any faction of the party was concerned, I hoped that my campaign could reconcile the hostile camps in preparation for a general election. To a considerable degree that did happen. It was one positive aspect of my lack of deep party roots.

I flew to Ottawa on Monday, April 19, for a day of meetings and to be at Question Period, and left for Montreal late in the evening to prepare for Wednesday's French debate. In addition to sessions to review the issues of the debate and to prepare answers — concise, succinct answers! — I met with a charming woman named France Nadeau, who had been asked to advise me on my television manner and appearance. She arrived with a written

(Photo: ©Julie Paquet, exclusive)

Some members of the victorious team, June 13, 1993. Standing, left to right: Michael Wilson, Cindy Boucher, Jim Ginou, Shirley Martin, Ross Reid, Ray Castelli, myself, Patrick Kinsella, Paul Curley, MP Lee Richardson, Denis Boucher, Jean-Luc Peloquin; kneeling in front: Bob Chant, Pierre Blais, Ginny Richards.

(Photo: Ken Ginn)

June 16, 1993. Replying to the good wishes expressed in the House of Commons after winning the leadership, from my regular second-row seat. I would never occupy the PM's chair. Behind the PM: Jim Edwards, Stan Darling, Marcel Tremblay, Garth Turner. Behind me, clockwise from top: Scott Thorkelson, Greg Thompson, Al Johnson.

(Photo: Ken Ginn)

June 25, 1993, in the cabinet room. After the swearing-in, the members of the new cabinet congratulate one another. Left to right: Senator Lowell Murray, Jean Charest, Tom Siddon, myself, Perrin Beatty.

(Photo: Ken Ginn)

A breakfast meeting at my Ottawa apartment with key members of the campaign team before the cabinet strategy meeting at Meech Lake. Clockwise from my left: Marcel Danis, Patrick Kinsella, Tom Trbovich, John Tory, Jodi White, Allan Gregg.

(Photo: Ken Ginn)

July 3, 1993. Finding time to exercise was always a challenge. Here, Diana Lam and I take a fitness walk on the Stanley Park seawall before my briefings for the first ministers' and G-7 meetings.

(Photo: Ken Ginn)

July 4, 1993. An unexpectedly productive first ministers' meeting in Vancouver (that's a cruise ship in the background). Left to right: Frank McKenna, Robert Bourassa, myself, John Savage.

(Photo: Ken Ginn)

With Perrin Beatty (right) and Gilles Loiselle (back to camera), exchanging pleasantries with Bill Clinton at the G-7 meeting.

(Photo: Ken Ginn)

My final meeting in Tokyo with Boris Yeltsin. My modest attempts to speak a little Russian created consternation among my officials, who didn't know what I might be promising.

(Photo: Ken Ginn)

Ray Castelli has a great sense of humour — essential in the pressure-cooker of politics. Here I am camping it up with the checkered flag before uttering the immortal words "Gentlemen, start your engines!" at the Molson Indy in Vancouver.

(Photo: Ken Ginn)

Campaign, day 2. Out from behind the podium at a town hall meeting in Utica, Ontario. The banner behind me, "A New Breed of Power," refers to a tractor, but my team loved the symbolism.

(Photo: Ken Ginn)

Talking to the employees at the Crayola plant in Lindsay, Ontario (here presenting me with the world's largest blue crayon), was designed to show what the challenges of a new economy meant in human terms. The media weren't sure what to do with this form of campaigning.

(Photo: Ken Ginn)

My compartment at the back of the campaign bus. My chair is semi-reclined because my feet don't touch the floor; David McLaughlin sits on the banquette (which I can't face because my chair is bolted forward), and Paul Frazer sits on the desk's swivel chair.

(Photo: Ken Ginn)

A light moment on the campaign plane as I return a pillow thrown forward from the media section. Left to right: Patrick Kinsella, Fred Loiselle, Mijanou Serré (who looked after a myriad of personal details for me and whose absence from the New York trip led to a near disaster).

(Photo: Ken Ginn)

Flipping through magazines with my stepdaughter Pamela Divinsky during a long ride on the campaign plane. Pamela kept a record in her journal of the private and human side of the campaign.

(Photo: Ken Ginn)

Back behind the podium, attacking the Liberals' "five-hole platform." As a way of illustrating the key omissions of the Red Book it was effective — but too late.

(Photo: Ken Ginn)

The ill-fated meeting with the Globe and Mail *editorial board. Here, an exchange with Hugh Winsor (far left), who would greet with glee my "forty-seven days" gaffe in Saint-Bruno shortly afterwards.*

(Photo: Ken Ginn)

Election night. Last-minute discussion of my speech conceding defeat with Ray Castelli, Paul Frazer, and Patrick Kinsella.

(Photo: Ken Ginn)

Election night. Speech notes in hand, watching the TV coverage with David Camp before going downstairs to meet my supporters and the press.

analysis of several of my television interviews. Basically, she was happy with what she saw, but she gave me a few pointers to keep in mind. She also had some advice on colours to wear on television. Now, it must be said that France is one of those French-Canadian women who make me feel instantly inadequate and frumpy. I wasn't about to dismiss the advice of such an elegant woman, but the kinds of colours that Quebeckers apparently loved to see on TV weren't the colours I had been advised to wear by people in Toronto (bright colours, please) or that I preferred myself. Whereas I always feel well dressed and comfortable when I'm in a navy blue outfit, France advised me that navy wasn't a prepossessing colour for a Quebec audience. My strawberry-blonde hair had faded to a blonde-white colour, but my skin and eyes are still those of a redhead, not a blonde. I loved to wear blue and purple, as well as cream, white and black. Pastels did nothing for me, I thought, but here was France telling me I must wear pale colours. As for my too-blonde hair, could I please have the roots darkened? This was farther than I was prepared to go. Right until the beginning of the election campaign, France tried to advise me on fashion. Although she was never anything but kind and encouraging, I feel that in the end I was somewhat of a disappointment to her.

In spite of the tepid media response, I was satisfied with the Montreal debate. Jean Charest used an opportunity presented by one of John Long's comments to assert his support of minority-language rights. The format made it difficult to speak out of turn and I had already answered the question asked, which was unrelated to the language issue. This was nonetheless interpreted by the media as a softness on my part regarding minority-language rights. I wasn't concerned, though I did take note of Jean's use of the opportunity to make a point that he obviously felt he needed to make. This resulted in a loosening up of the format of the remaining debates to allow for more free exchange and speaking out of turn. As I prepared for the remaining three English-language debates, I paid more attention to putting forward the points I wanted to make, rather than answering the questions exactly as asked. I had been struck by the fact that Jean had nothing new to say in the second debate. I began to feel I could recover the ground I had lost in Toronto because I still had a lot to say. That night

I was in good spirits and the knot in my stomach disappeared, never to return.

On April 23, while campaigning in Halifax, I received word that the Department of Justice was ready to provide me with the advice I had requested about my options in dealing with the Somalia issue. I immediately cancelled the rest of my campaign appearances for that day and arranged to return to Ottawa. That night I met first with my staff, and then with Defence and Justice officials. It was one of the most extraordinary sets of meetings in my entire government career, but no more extraordinary than the events that had brought us all there.

Shortly before I was named minister of defence, members of the Canadian Airborne Regiment had been deployed as part of a UN mission to provide humanitarian aid to war-torn Somalia. The earliest feedback I had received about our troops indicated that they were doing excellent work in extremely difficult conditions. In February, gunfire from a Canadian Forces rifle killed a Somali. An incident report was sent to me describing the manner in which the shot had killed the citizen. I thought the explanation of a ricochet in those circumstances was unconvincing. I sent the note back with the comment, "I find this explanation completely unsatisfactory." Later, our military liaison officer identified that comment as the first "red flag" to be raised about problems in Somalia.

On March 18, Chief of the Defence Staff John Anderson and Deputy Minister Bob Fowler had come to my office for a briefing. Among the items raised was the death of a young Somali, Shidane Arone, at Belet Uen. As the situation was described to me, Arone had been apprehended in our camp in the course of attempting to rob it. Later, he had been found dead in his cell. Although there had been a scuffle at the time of his arrest, his injuries didn't appear to be serious enough to explain his death. It was suggested that some sort of pre-existing condition may have caused his death and I was told an investigation would be carried out. No indication was given to me that there was anything to be concerned about. I asked to be kept informed as a matter of course. I was also advised that Master Corporal Clayton Matchee, a member of the Airborne who was on duty that night, had been detained and had attempted to hang himself. He was in a coma and the prognosis for recovery was not good. At first, no connection was made between the death of Arone and the attempted suicide of Matchee.

The investigative team arrived in Somalia March 23. It wasn't until March 31, the day after I flew home from England, that I learned Arone had been tortured to death and that three soldiers, including Matchee, were under investigation for his murder. The facts of the actual killing were shocking enough, but the revelation that Arone's killers had taken trophy pictures of themselves with his body sent a rocket through my office. What we realized was that people don't take trophy pictures unless they think they are going to show them to someone. What kind of mentality was there among our Forces that would condone this?

As I discussed with Richard Clair, John Dixon, Marianne Campbell, and Peter Lugli what the appropriate response to all this was, I discovered that my hands were tied in ways I hadn't anticipated. I was quickly advised by the deputy and the CDS that I must be very careful about saying anything about these events because, under the National Defence Act, while I clearly had the responsibility for the administration of the Canadian Forces, I also had a position in the military justice hierarchy. As well as giving the minister the power to convene a general court martial, the act provides for appeals to be made to the minister of sentences meted out at courts martial. Accordingly, I instructed the department that everything that could be made public, consistent with the interests of due process and the rights of accused persons, was to be released. Then I called the CDS to register my concern formally and asked to be fully advised of all matters arising out of the investigation.

In the following days, a number of statements by Admiral Anderson led media and opposition members to suggest that I was covering up what I knew about the death of Arone. In a press release, he said that the department knew as early as March 18 of possible "criminal intent" in the death of Arone. No such suggestion had been made in the briefing to me. The question then became, in the minds of many, what I knew and when I knew it. I simply continued to tell the truth, but I was beginning to wonder who had known what and when. Because the circumstances of the death were so horrible, I had difficulty believing that it took two weeks for the truth to get to National Defence headquarters in Ottawa. Then, in an interview with *Maclean's* magazine, Admiral Anderson was quoted as saying that there had possibly been a "complete breakdown in discipline" in Somalia. As the minister of national defence, responsible for the administration of the Canadian Forces, I didn't see why I should first be learning of the CDS's view on the subject from a magazine. Moreover, since I had been advised that the CDS was also a part of the justice hierarchy in Defence, and thus subject to the same constraints as I was, I wondered why he was free to express himself in a way that I had been advised was inappropriate.

Knowing that I was anxious to fulfil my duty relating to the administration of the Forces without compromising the criminal justice process, John Dixon requested a legal memorandum from the office of the judge advocate general explaining the limits imposed on my actions by the National Defence Act. Reflecting that such a request would have been unnecessary when we were in Justice — a memorandum of law setting out my duties, the precedents, and anything else I needed to know to guide my conduct would have been on my desk without asking — he was astonished to receive a reply that suggested he didn't understand the need to avoid political interference in a criminal matter. When I was shown the memorandum, I hit the roof. Nowhere in government was there a staff more fastidious than mine about avoiding impropriety, and I was not going to put up with such shoddy service from the people who were supposed to be advising me. I sent Richard to see John Tait, in his capacity as deputy attorney general, to request from Justice the legal advice I couldn't get from the military's lawyers.

My formal request took the form of a letter asking what my options were for establishing a process that could look into the preparation and training of the Airborne Regiment for their mission in Somalia. I knew there were two sets of constraints. One was my own role in the justice hierarchy of National Defence. Second, in the Patti Starr case in Ontario and the Westray Mine case in Nova Scotia, courts had ruled that a governmental inquiry could not touch on criminal issues. Criminal trials and appeals arising from the killings in Somalia might take another two years at least. I needed information now to help me address my responsibility for the administration of the Canadian Forces. Could I exercise my powers to order a board of inquiry in the present circumstances and, if so, how? That was the question that John Tait and the Justice lawyers were ready to answer when I returned to Ottawa from Halifax on April 23.

The boardroom situated between the deputy's office and my own was full. Around the table were my own staff, the deputy minister of defence, senior officials from the civilian side of DND, the chief of the defence staff and his senior officers, and the judge advocate general and the deputy attorney general, each with lawyers from their respective offices. Along the walls were seated other civilian and military officials. I took my seat in the middle of the table, facing Bob Fowler and John Anderson, and began by expressing my displeasure at the CDS's remarks in *Maclean's*. The CDS made a vague reply, but I was more interested in the advice I had returned to hear, so I didn't pursue the issue. Justice's advice was that I could convene an inquiry so long as the terms of reference were carefully defined and criminal matters were promptly referred to the proper investigative authorities and not pursued by the inquiry. What this meant was that, given the status of the criminal charges, the inquiry would probably have to adjourn at some point to await the completion of the trial and appeal processes. However, there was no reason why an inquiry could not begin work right away. I therefore decided that we would convene the board of inquiry.

We then turned to the question of the make-up of the board. I said I wanted the membership to be half military, half civilian. Civilians could participate only as advisers, I was told.

"Where does it say that?" I asked.

"In the regulations to the National Defence Act," came the reply.

"Fine, we will change the regulations to permit civilians to sit as full members," I said.

I was determined that the inquiry results would be made public, but I feared for the safety of military personnel if they had to testify in open hearings. I thought that the possibility of retribution by other members of the unit or senior officers might discourage members of the Forces from telling the inquiry all they knew. Although my aim was obviously to get at the truth, I didn't know what information would come out. I decided that the testimony would be given in camera but that the report of the inquiry would be made public. This would allow the commissioners to mask the identities of some witnesses if that were appropriate to protect them. No objections were expressed around the table.

When all the details of the inquiry had been worked out, I turned to a matter that had been a source of some irritation to me. During a recent visit to Somalia, the CDS had been quoted as saying that since the minister of national defence was now a candidate for the leadership of the Conservative Party, members of the Canadian Forces should be aware that they would be under serious scrutiny. For some reason, this was taken by the media and the opposition to be a sign that the department wanted to protect me, although I rather thought the warning had another purpose, to alert the listeners to the need to protect themselves. It contributed to the credibility of assertions that I would want to cover up the events in Somalia in order to avoid dealing with them while I was a leadership candidate. The whole notion was preposterous to me and I resented the allegations deeply. After all, *I* was not in Somalia counselling our troops to mayhem. What did I have to cover up? Looking around the table at the senior people in DND, I said, slowly and clearly, "Neither I nor anyone on my staff has ever, or will ever, ask anyone in this department to do anything to accommodate my candidacy for the leadership of my party. If anyone here thinks such a request has been made to them, I want to know about it because it has not been made at my request or with my authorization. I want to be clear on that."

Even without the findings of a board of inquiry, other incidents, beginning with the first shooting I was advised of, led me to believe that our troops were not well enough versed in the rules of engagement, particularly with respect to the use of deadly force. In the absence of a satisfactory explanation of the original incident and the occurrence of several more deaths and woundings, I wrote to the CDS to register my formal concern about this in late May.

The board of inquiry met in the spring, adjourned for the criminal trials, and issued a five-volume preliminary report that was made public in August 1993. Among the interesting revelations was the clear hostility of the military to my office's involvement in investigating the Somalia events. This reflects a remarkable ignorance or resentment of the role of their civilian bosses on the part of some members of the Forces. In early 1995, at the end of the criminal trials and appeals, the minister of national defence convened another inquiry to continue the work begun two years earlier. Even with all the criminal trials completed, the new inquiry agreed to hear testimony from some witnesses in camera.

Throughout the leadership campaign, reporters pressed me with questions about the inconsistency between my statements of what I knew when, and those of the CDS. Even during the election campaign in the fall, candidates campaigning door to door were told by voters that they didn't like Kim Campbell because "she covered up in Somalia." In 1995 the enterprising people at *Esprit de Corps*, a magazine about military issues, obtained through access-to-information legislation a copy of the DND note on which my March 18, 1993, briefing was based. It confirmed what I said I was told at that time. Entitled "Briefing Note for MND [Minister of National Defence]," it concluded: "The death of this Somali national is perplexing. While he did resist apprehension, it is not believed that excessive force was used in effecting the capture. The Medical Officer's initial report supports the assertion that Canadian troops acted properly. The medical history and health of the deceased are unknown, but may have been contributing factors. It is hoped that a pathological examination will shed more light on the incident."

After all we have learned about the murder of Shidane Arone, that such a note could have been written for the information of the minister of national defence is deeply disturbing.

The last week of April through the first week of June appears on my schedule as a blur of travel, punctuated by the last three policy debates. As we moved around the country in small planes and long drives, my small band of road warriors had to deal with breakdowns in communications with campaign headquarters and the vagaries of unfamiliar locations.

Still, in the midst of all the pressure and exhaustion, and the sacrifice of normal life by both the campaigners and the "campaign widows and widowers," the team retained its sense of humour. One day, after enjoying the attentions of a friendly dog, I said to Cindy, "You know, if I win this, I could have a dog." I had been impressed by the Mulroneys' friendly dog, Clover, and reasoned that living in an official residence would make it possible to indulge my predilection for canines. I was much cheered by the prospect. After that, whenever things got particularly rough, Cindy would sidle up to me and whisper, "Bow-wow." Returning from a brief visit home to her husband and two daughters, she brought me a stuffed dog as a campaign companion. In reference to the prime minister's official address, I named it Sussex.

The Calgary debate on April 30 was a major turning point for me. My debate preparation team, consisting of Sharon Andrews, Warren Everson, Lowell Murray, David Camp on substance, and Barry McLoughlin on technique, had finally developed a process for helping me to shine. We practised translating my policy positions into brief, clear, snappy answers to questions. I felt confident going into the Calgary session, a feeling buoyed even more by Bernard Valcourt's declaration of support the same day. The mood of my supporters was jubilant after the debate.

The momentum continued into the Vancouver debate on May 13. There was one glitch, however. In my concluding remarks, I referred to people who tried to tell Canadians that the deficit was not a problem as "not just the enemies of our party but the enemies of Canadians." As soon as the words were out of my mouth, I knew they were a mistake. As a number of commentators would say later, the idea was not particularly outrageous, given my views about the deficit. The problem was that these words appeared to echo Brian Mulroney's use of the expression "enemies of Canada" in a speech he had once given on the Constitution. I did the best I could to modify the comments as soon as they were made — I had been searching for the word "adversaries" but "enemies" is what had come out. It wasn't a huge problem but was indicative of the kinds of things that made headlines. Little did I know that the worst was yet to come.

On the morning of May 18, the day of the Halifax debate, I woke up to the clock-radio in my hotel room to hear the news announcer say, "Kim Campbell says she got converted Anglican to ward off the evil demons of the papacy."

"Holy shit!" I thought, rather appropriately, and tried to reach Ross Reid on the phone. All hell was breaking loose. As we tracked down what had happened, we learned that a column in the *Toronto Star* that morning had taken parts of my interview with journalist

Peter Newman in May's *Vancouver* magazine and either quoted them out of context or completely misrepresented what had been said. The electronic media were running with it, none more so, I was told, than Valerie Pringle and Keith Morrison on *Canada AM*. (Evidently only the weatherman on the show, Dan Matheson, suggested that the remarks didn't sound like me and that perhaps they should be sceptical about the story.) The *Toronto Star* article was written by Patrick Doyle, who we were told had been egged on by a member of Charest's campaign team, former CBC journalist Tim Raiphe.

Peter Newman had interviewed me the previous January. We had met over brunch at the Empress in Victoria for a long talk. At the time, I wasn't at all convinced that Brian Mulroney would step down before the next election. It is clear from the article that Newman didn't miss any opportunity to play up the most unusual or dramatic parts of our conversation, but aside from a tactless comment about the manner of Joe Clark's leadership win in 1976, a remark that I genuinely regretted because it overstated the point I was trying to make, I didn't have any serious problems with the article.

Although there were some vaguely irritating factual errors in the Newman article, I had agreed to its inclusion among the materials our campaign distributed. During the Vancouver debate, the magazine had been in the hotel rooms of all the members of the press corps and no one saw anything in it to create a scandal. Perhaps that is why, in the long run, Doyle's column wasn't as destructive as the Charest people had hoped it would be. In the short run, however, I had to respond to the crazy allegations that were being repeated on all the media.

I was to meet that morning with my debate preparation team. I suggested that the first thing we had to deal with was the Doyle article. We agreed that I would do a media scrum in an hour. Meanwhile, we made the full Newman interview available to all reporters so they could read it first. For an hour the preparation team threw the meanest questions they could think of at me to prepare me. When I arrived at the press conference, the atmosphere in the room was decidedly sheepish.

William Johnson of the Montreal *Gazette* later wrote an article examining Doyle's column in comparison with the Newman profile on which it was based. Johnson's title says it all: "Treatment of Campbell Interview Sensationalistic and Sleazy."

Johnson quoted the context of the "evil demons" remark: "When I went to St. Anne's ... it was in pre–Vatican II days. The nuns still wore habits, the mass was in Latin, and I got confirmed an Anglican the year I was there, I suppose as a way of warding off the evil demons of the papacy or whatever. But I have a lot of respect for spiritual principles." Johnson commented, "In context, it is clear that she was not insulting the papacy. She recalled the more sectarian spirit of the time and suggested her parents had her confirmed in the Anglican church, perhaps as an antidote to the convent. To simply quote 'the evil demons of the papacy' is cruel and unjust, not to say dishonest."

One example of Kim Campbell's "lies" uncovered by Doyle involved my singing. I had quite truthfully told Peter Newman that Nathan Divinsky and I had formed a Gilbert and Sullivan group and that I had sung every mezzo role in Gilbert and Sullivan with the exception of those in *The Grand Duke* and *Utopia Limited.* Doyle wrote that this was obviously false as it would involve "dozens of roles." By my count, it is in fact one dozen roles exactly. (There is no mezzo role in *Trial by Jury*, but in each of *Iolanthe* and *The Gondoliers* I have sung both of the two mezzo roles.) At the press conference, I offered to sing from any of the operettas at their request. I had no takers. The whole situation was so utterly outrageous that there was nothing for me to do but heed Vaughn Palmer's advice from 1986 and take it all in good humour. I soon heard that Peter Newman had been on television himself, defending me and denouncing the hypocrisy of those who argue that politicians should be natural and candid, then crucify them when they are.

Although others joined Johnson in correcting the record, I received no apology for the Doyle article. The press was remarkably silent on Doyle himself, choosing not to enquire into his motivations in writing the piece. Nor am I aware of any disciplinary action against him by his employer, the *Toronto Star.* There was silence from the Charest camp.

I went into the final debate that night in great spirits and did well. I knew the media recognized that Doyle had gone too far and would begin to redress the balance. But the episode taught me an important lesson. It was foolish of me not to have realized that the article could possibly appear in the middle of a leadership campaign. What I came to understand was that being a contender for the prime ministership elevated me to a different level of scrutiny. Giving rein to a sense of irony was risky. Being the frontrunner meant that the natural approach to me of the media was to find the chinks in my armour. It was the only way to make the story interesting over a four-month period.

I had been dismayed by the extent to which the media were hammering me. A memo to the campaign team in early May from Denis Boucher, a former CBC reporter and former press secretary of mine, now working for Gilles Loiselle, suggested that, although I had plenty of contact with the media, it was not of the most effective kind. Perhaps I should be doing more one-on-one interviews with journalists. He pointed out that Charest had been giving about ten times as many one-on-ones as I had, and the press seemed to be giving him a free ride. "You will all have noticed that the Opposition is making sure that Defence issues remain on the front pages. This means that every time the Minister gives a scrum, she has to answer questions on defence rather than on the leadership. Scrums do not allow us to control the questions and the messages ... I do not think that we can go without giving scrums. These are inevitable. But if the Minister gives more one-on-ones then I believe that we could reduce the number of scrums and therefore control our messages a little more."

Our relations with the press were a major source of frustration. Doing more in-depth interviews was one approach, but the problem seemed deeper. In Nancy Jamieson's strategy document, her reference to my new approach to politics was not just an idealistic formulation. On April 19 I had launched "Proposals for Democratic Reform," a document that set out in very concrete terms what I meant by "doing politics differently," at our Ottawa campaign headquarters. It included recommendations under the headings "Party Reform," "Parliamentary Reform," "Government Appointments and Contracts," "A Federal Ombudsman for Canada," "Empowering Canadians," and "Lobbying." After a detailed verbal and written presentation, our communications director, Gail Flitton, was astonished to hear Ross Howard of the *Globe and Mail* asking, "But what does Kim Campbell really stand for?" By the end of the leadership campaign, we had released a significant amount of policy documentation, addressing a whole range of economic issues. But "Proposals for Democratic Reform" clearly expressed the quite radical approach I proposed to take towards the exercise of prime-ministerial power. Just as I felt there was a collective amnesia about everything I had done as a minister, the ideas that were the heart of my reason for wanting to be prime minister just didn't seem to register.

It seemed strange to me that issues that had generated the rise of the Reform Party, namely those relating to the credibility of the political process, seemed unimportant to the press covering the campaign. The question was not which candidate was committed to eliminate the deficit: we all were. What was crucial was who among us understood *why* we Conservatives had been unable to deliver on our promise of the first mandate. Why were the opposition parties, especially the Liberals, so successful in maximizing the political cost of every step we took? Why didn't the voters trust us? I believed that changes in our society had outstripped the ability of our institutions, especially as we currently operated them, to respond effectively and credibly. If we were going to do different politics, we were going to have to do politics differently.

With the debates finally over, I continued the frenetic schedule of meetings with delegates. With three weeks remaining, more time was made for one-on-one interviews with journalists. However, not enough time was scheduled for women's events. Although my victory would make me the first female prime minister in Canadian history, and although many women were drawn into the party as a result of my candidacy, there was remarkably little in the campaign strategy that built upon this important factor. The women who were my key supporters in Vancouver were, in many cases, professional publicists. For example, Marlie Oden, a former partner in McKim Advertising, had volunteered to help oversee the editing of my campaign videos. She was astonished at the "maleness" of the campaign. Not that there weren't women around the table, but their "invisibility" surprised her. It was as if, for the men, the mere fact of my *being* a woman was enough to appeal to women. They couldn't conceive of a different way of strategizing a campaign. Part of the problem was that the women were new and unknown to the many old boys who had gravitated to our campaign. Knowing the pressures on me out on the road, my women friends were reluctant to complain to me directly.

In Vancouver Centre, there was a tradition of strong women. Pat Carney had held the riding for two terms and had attracted other strong women as supporters. I inherited many of these great women and attracted new ones. They were all used to being listened to and respected for their professional expertise. It was a shock to find themselves ignored by the campaign organizers in Ottawa. Their knowledge of how to broaden our appeal to women and their very good idea of how I operated were simply not valued. Part of the problem was that the campaign organizers didn't want to frighten off the anti-feminist elements of the party. But there was also a cultural problem. Ottawa is simply more male and traditional than Vancouver. Unless people told me directly about the problem, there was little I could do. This was just one way in which the wave of campaign support from various people, many of whom had their own agendas, threatened to obscure the candidate herself.

Libby Burnham in Toronto felt the same frustration. The Conservative women's network wanted to set up events for me to meet with women but could never get dates confirmed in time. Finally, on May 27, I was scheduled to speak to a women's breakfast in Toronto, sponsored by the accounting firm Deloitte and Touche. It was a chance to share my vision with an audience of accomplished women. The guests were not just from the business community; writer Margaret Atwood was among those who came up after my speech to say hello. Although we were on opposite sides of many issues, such as free trade, she was very friendly. I wanted so much to reach out and bring together women from all perspectives. I naively thought that what we hadn't done during the leadership campaign, we would begin to do before the election.

Mixed in with campaign appearances across the country were calls to my office in Ottawa for briefings by Richard Clair or Bob Fowler. Cindy, who had top security clearance, was the agreed-upon Defence person on the road, although she was now receiving her salary from the campaign. She was in regular contact with both men and briefed me on Defence issues so that I could respond to both national and international media. I could rely on my cabinet colleagues to substitute for me in Question Period. However, I also made forays back to Ottawa to be in the House and attend meetings.

It sometimes seemed to the small group of us on the road that the campaign was concerned about everything but the candidate. It was not just that speech notes arrived nerve-rackingly late, to give one example. Campaign organizers found it difficult to appreciate the time needed to deal with my portfolio responsibilities, perhaps because this was the first time the Conservative Party had conducted a leadership campaign while in government. These problems between headquarters and the tour were a foretaste of what would happen during the election.

The actual meetings with delegates made up for the irritations. These took place in a variety of venues, from hotel rooms to rec rooms in people's homes. The turnout at meetings was excellent, and given the rough time I was getting in the press, this personal contact was vital. During the month of May, however, a number of delegates whom we had tracked as "leaning" Campbell went to Charest, and many of our firm delegates were getting softer in their support. My success in personal meetings did not entirely compensate for my less than avid performance on the telephone. Despite my good beginning, my habitual shyness returned when it came to calling delegates. Steven worked hard to get me to phone, and I did, but I was no Brian Mulroney in this respect.

We had already had a couple of meetings to discuss my speech at the convention. The weekend of June 5–6 in Vancouver was kept largely free in order to give me time to put together what I wanted to say on June 12. I met with a speech preparation team including Michael Ferrabee and David Camp on Saturday afternoon, to go over the draft that had been prepared. I wanted to try to draft my speech myself and asked David to track down a copy of my speech at Whistler in 1986. I knew I couldn't avoid speaking from a text — the tight timeframe that would govern my speech necessitated a written and timed draft. It had been the same at Whistler, but because the language was my own, that speech had come across as warm and intimate. I hoped to recapture the same feeling in Ottawa.

What I found when I sat down at my desk later that Saturday was that I had hit a wall. I was struck recently in reading a book about Mary Robinson's successful campaign to become the first woman president of Ireland by the similarities between our campaigns. She too ran into trouble for being too candid, and towards the end of the campaign she too felt the pressure of being a frontrunner and hit a wall of fatigue. When I tried to reach down for some inspiring language for my convention speech that weekend, there was nothing there. I was emotionally depleted and mentally exhausted. And I wasn't the only one. Ray Castelli too remembers feeling burned-out at this time.

I had been pouring myself out for almost four months. The strain of trying to avoid errors and the stress of the many I had made had taken their toll. There was so much I wanted this speech to be, but my creative juices were dry. I'd had a great deal to learn in the campaign, but it had been difficult to learn in the full glare of the spotlight. I also felt an enormous frustration. My mistakes seemed to be held against me by the press and my opponents in a way that suggested that I had tricked the other candidates into withdrawing. How dare I be less than perfect in the face of all this support! I seemed to be expected to have all of Brian Mulroney's strengths but none of his weaknesses. But, in fact, I had strengths and weaknesses of my own. As the campaign progressed, my own voice seemed to have got lost in the juggernaut of a process whose rationale seemed somehow disconnected from me. Power was for me a means to an end, not an end in itself. I wanted to communicate that democratic vision in my convention speech, but I just couldn't find the words. I would have to rely on my team to put together the most important speech of the campaign.

CTV correspondent Craig Oliver had told Marjory LeBreton some months earlier that Liberals attending a policy conference had agreed that I was the one person they feared as a Conservative leader, but that they were sure "the Tories would never elect Kim Campbell as leader." If that was the case, then their worst nightmare risked coming true. That certainly explained the extraordinary lengths they were going to in order to discredit me as a minister. I could understand the opposition of other candidates and parties. However, being the frontrunner didn't explain the way I was being dissected by the press. I couldn't help feeling that I was running against a set of expectations that kept changing in a game where the goalposts kept moving. Lysiane Gagnon, political columnist for *La Presse*, wrote an article in the *Globe and Mail* on June 5 that confirmed my sense of what was happening. Under the title "Why Isn't Campbell Judged by the Same Yardstick as Male Politicians?" she wrote:

> The May 17 issue of *Maclean's* magazine featured an eight-page profile of Kim Campbell with the headline: "The Burning Ambition of Kim Campbell ..." "Ambition" is a double-edged sword in egalitarian Canada ... Applied to a woman, it is deadly ... Has the term ever been applied to Jean Charest, the other major Tory contender in the leadership race? In his early 20's, he started a political career in Canada's most conservative party. He is willing to spend the next few years in a job that will virtually cut him off from his children. This, to me, is "burning ambition."
>
> Mr. Charest's political itinerary has been straightforward. He systematically climbed up the Tory ladder with the top job in mind. Ms. Campbell's career followed a typical pattern of women of her generation. It is a winding path, with unexpected opportunities and detours caused by marriage and divorce. So, of course, Ms. Campbell is deemed "unstable" and "unpredictable."
>
> It is a no-win situation. If she tries to convey a different political style, less confrontational and more focused on "inclusion and consensus" she will be judged "flaky" and lacking in leadership. If she tries to play by the traditional rules and lashes out at her opponents, she will be judged "arrogant" ...
>
> Ms. Campbell is a moderate feminist. This will not do either. She is too much of a "liberated" woman for the average PC activist — and radical feminists see her as a sellout. This is a problem male politicians have never to worry about. Mr. Charest is not expected to represent all men or be an advocate for any segment of the male population; nor is he expected to embody maleness. Just like every other male politician, he is judged as an individual ...
>
> Ms. Campbell's gaffes, and there were quite a few, were all exposed and amplified as days went by. Some unguarded remarks she made in an interview with Peter C. Newman were

> deliberately distorted by the media. But Mr. Charest's most spectacular mistake has rarely been rehashed and when it is, it was written off as just a learning experience. (In 1990, as sports minister and a lawyer who should have known better, he contacted a judge sitting in a case involving a track-and-field official.)
>
> If a 34-year-old man wins over a 46-year-old woman next week at the PC convention, this will not come as a surprise to women of my generation. They are used to being upstaged by younger men when the time comes for promotion.

Brian Mulroney's determination to have a "horse race" for the leadership was seriously misguided in the circumstances. Although he is the most manipulative person I have ever met, I hasten to say that this is not necessarily a bad thing. Under some circumstances, manipulation is an important tool of power. At times during the previous four years, after watching the PM orchestrate a cabinet or P&P meeting to avoid a major showdown, I was tempted to applaud. However, being in control is essential to Mulroney's view of himself: he must have a strategic plan for everything. His plan for a four-month, hotly contested leadership campaign that would showcase the party's "stars" and keep it on the front pages was an essential feature of his rationalization for departing when he did. If he could show that his plan would serve to launch the party back into contention, that he had thought of everything and left "the car with the motor running," as he liked to put it, then he could not be accused of having waited too long to take his leave. This view of the departure became an article of faith for Mulroney loyalists. The corollary was that a new leader who could not take the party to victory had only herself to blame.

The situation that unfolded, however, was without recent precedent for any Canadian political party. John Turner contested the Liberal leadership in 1983 as a private citizen. Pierre Trudeau was one of several senior ministers contesting the Liberal leadership in 1968. In neither the 1976 nor the 1983 Conservative leadership campaigns was the party in government. Our campaign guaranteed that I would have the maximum amount of pressure and attack from both within and outside the party. Instead of being a process that raised the profile of the Conservative Party, the leadership campaign threatened to cripple the winner. The last paragraph of Lysiane Gagnon's column concerned me greatly. I was afraid that if I did lose, there would be a serious backlash among women inside and outside the party. Her perception of the media's coverage of me and my campaign was, I knew, shared by many women.

Given the way the campaign had started, for another candidate to win, I had to be discredited and my support shaken loose. This meant that the campaign ran a risk of being seriously divisive and leaving wounds that would be difficult to heal successfully in the short time remaining before a general election had to be called. Perrin Beatty had understood this clearly when considering whether to run. In making his announcement, he had said that he was not prepared to do what would be required for him to win, namely, engage in a campaign to destroy me. A leader who has yet to win an election is always somewhat vulnerable. I worried that the campaign had bruised my credibility, but as events unfolded in that last week I thought it might be worse for the party if I lost, and my determination to win resurfaced with a vengeance.

That Joe Clark and his wife, Maureen McTeer, had decided to support Jean Charest didn't surprise me. There were some in the party who thought that as a former leader himself, Joe should stay neutral in this race. However, given that Jean Charest had backed Joe against Brian Mulroney in 1983, I could understand Joe's loyalty to Jean. His endorsement, like Jean's of Joe in 1983, would emphasize that Jean had support in a key region of the country other than his own.

I had met privately with Joe to solicit his support in early March. At that time Joe said that he put great store in the fact that Jean had weathered a major setback — his forced resignation from cabinet in 1990. It was revealing that he saw the event from the perspective of its effect, rather than its cause. Jean's ability to survive that reversal, as Joe had survived his own very public reversals, was key to Joe's judgment that Jean was the better candidate. I wasn't about to launch into the saga of the reversals in my own life. We parted on friendly terms.

At the beginning of the year, Ray had passed on an observation Joe had made to Steve Greenaway, a Clark supporter in 1983. "He told Steven he had only ever met two people who reminded him of Pierre Trudeau (in terms of intellect, backbone, arrogance, and conviction that they were right): Margaret Thatcher and Kim Campbell. I would take that as a compliment, but I would wonder if Joe isn't nursing some bruises from a previous skirmish with you." Although Joe knew of my misgivings about the process that led to Charlottetown, my complaint against him at the time was not unlike his apparent one against me. I thought he was stubborn and unwilling to accept any criticism. Perhaps the truth is that we are both strong-minded people. Still, I wasn't aware of any residual tension between us.

Maureen McTeer's lack of enthusiasm for me was also understandable. As a member of the Royal Commission on Reproductive Technologies, she had been one of three commissioners who had challenged the chairperson, Patricia Baird. Because I regarded the behaviour of the three dissident commissioners as unacceptable, and because it was I who had convinced Dr. Baird to chair the commission, I took her side in the dispute. The conflict resulted in the three commissioners being removed from the commission by cabinet. Not known for her ability to let bygones by bygones, Maureen had borne me a grudge ever since.

While their reasons for not supporting the female candidate for leader were understandable, both Joe and Maureen had always been strong advocates for women's equality. This is why their remarks about me during the last week of the campaign seemed decidedly out of character. Joe said that it was important for the person chosen as leader to be "stable." I wasn't the only woman to react instantly to that comment with a visceral anger. Here was the old code word for undermining women. Since there was no basis on which to attack my stability, the remark was just offensive. (Given Joe's behaviour before the second ballot at the convention, it would become positively ironic.) This comment was matched by Maureen's claim that my lack of children meant I didn't have a sufficient stake in the future. Aside from being a slap in the face to every woman who had been unable to bear a child, the comment was incredibly sexist and ahistorical, given our country's long tradition of being governed by childless men. Would she have made the same objection about John Diefenbaker?

MP Terry Clifford and Bill McKnight, now minister of agriculture, both Charest supporters, also waded in that week with comments that galvanized the women in my camp. Clifford suggested that Canadians would identify more with Jean Charest because, unlike me, he had a spouse and children. Coming from an MP who was seen as a dinosaur, his remark was taken by women in particular as a dig against my own marital status. Bill McKnight compared my supporters to the followers of Jim Jones at Jonestown, commenting, "I can't believe they are about to drink the Campbell Kool-Aid." These attacks during the last week of the campaign reflected a belief in the Charest camp that victory was possible. Jean had done better than he had originally hoped, and in this final week his support had surged. A major attack was needed to win over Campbell delegates.

Although my campaign had experienced difficulties, many caused by too much success too soon, the convention-week organization under the direction of Paul Curley was superb. A Torontonian associated with the Big Blue Machine, Paul was also the brother of my original Ottawa staffer Sheila Rafter. In November 1992, over lunch in Toronto, he told me that I was, as far as he could see, the only possible candidate who could turn the Tory fortunes around. If Mulroney left, I could count on his support. The convention is critical to a campaign and Paul did not let me down. Visually, technically, and psychologically, our campaign was in top form when it really counted. An important decision was made to give the campaign a new colour scheme for the convention — a combination of hot pink and royal blue. The effect was stunning and fresh. In the arena, hot pink banners and hats made a powerful visual image of our strength. Campbell supporters were instantly visible, and delegates wanted our hats and shirts because they looked so great. A brilliant new technology was used to create individualized campaign buttons. At campaign events, I would go through the crowd, posing for Polaroid photos with delegates. These were then put into a hot pink round frame with the words "Kim met Me/ Kim et moi." More than a thousand of these buttons were created during the convention and people still bring theirs out to show me.

All of my family had come to Ottawa for the convention. Dad, Marg, and Marg's mother, Freda; Alix and her fiancé, David Hambleton; Mum and Pamela. It was so important for me to have them share that time. My mother says it was the most exciting experience of her life. She loved the cheering and the shouting, the tension and the tears of emotion. All around us the mood of our campaign volunteers was excellent. Teenagers, middle-aged businessmen, and women of all ages were decked out in hot pink hats — a great equalizer. We won virtually all the seat rushes for the various events, and the energy from our camp could be felt everywhere.

Aside from the extraordinary pressure on a candidate in a leadership campaign, there is a surreal sensation that comes from seeing your own name and image everywhere. At first it made me feel very awkward to hear chants of "*Kim! Kim! Kim!*" Huge blow-ups of Denise Grant's wonderful photos were everywhere, looking, I knew, rather better than I looked in real life. Sometimes I would look at a huge crowd waving "Kim!" banners and chanting my name and say to myself, "Are they really making all this fuss about *me*?" Rather than taking it too seriously, I came to see all the posters and folderol as simply part of a process that was a necessary step towards what I really wanted to do, which was to govern. Every once in a while, however, I would feel overwhelmed by the responsibility of it. Even now, just thinking about it, that feeling of obligation washes over me.

Technically, our campaign was first rate. John Mykytyshyn's delegate tracking system proved remarkably accurate. Over the period of the convention alone, I met face to face with more than six hundred delegates. These meetings, which often went until 2 a.m., were strategically arranged according to the intelligence that came from our tracking. My caucus colleagues worked very hard to win delegate support. I was deeply honoured when Michael Wilson agreed to support me, because I really respect him. Not only did he give me his endorsement, but he worked the halls energetically to win delegates. Doug Lewis escorted me to delegate meetings into the wee hours, and Pierre Blais was a great crowd leader as well.

When Flora MacDonald gave me her support on the first day of the convention, she announced it at a barbecue rally we held in the courtyard of the East Block, on Parliament Hill. It was so moving for me to be endorsed by the first woman in our party to seek the leadership. Ellen Fairclough, the first woman cabinet minister in Canada, was also a supporter. In the rally I acknowledged how much we all stand on the shoulders of those who have gone before, and I said that I hoped my shoulders would also support women to come. Flora had originally thought she would stay neutral during the campaign, but the anti-woman tone that had started to emerge was enough to convince her to take a position.

The convention itself is largely a blur in my memory, so packed was it with activity. There were policy forums during the day on Friday, June 11, and a carefully organized tribute to Brian Mulroney that night. The affection directed towards the PM and his family as they stood on the stage was strong and genuine. Mila was admired and respected as a dedicated partner to the PM, and the four Mulroney children had made the sacrifices made by all politicians' children, only more so. Not only had they had to endure the intrusion of constant police security, but they had also had to live with almost nine years of press criticism of their father. I often felt that the Mulroneys didn't receive the credit they deserved for having such well-adjusted children under those difficult circumstances.

Since the previous weekend, when I had concluded that I was not going to be able to put my own speech together, my campaign speech team had been working on it. I had provided considerable input, and the political strategists had analyzed the key messages I needed to deliver. As with all creative processes carried out by committee, this one was inefficient and without a clear focus. As each part of the team got hold of the draft, it would add what it considered strategically important. In spite of all that, the speech itself is not bad and, in fact, has some moments of real eloquence.

The speeches were to be delivered Saturday evening, and the voting would start Sunday at midday. Charest had drawn the second-last speaking position and I had the last. His speech was an excellent stump speech, delivered with real force, but short on specifics. The message he was clearly trying to convey was his effectiveness as a campaigner. He spoke of how he would defeat Lucien Bouchard in an election. "The Bloc is a crock!" he assured the delegates. My speech was, by contrast, designed to make me sound prime-ministerial. Unfortunately, because of the constant revisions, I saw the final draft only late Saturday afternoon. David Camp brought it to my room and I practised reading it aloud to him. I think I had time to read it through once before we had to go to the convention centre. I didn't waste valuable emotional energy getting angry about the lack of preparation time. I remembered the story Tuzie used to tell about the great Paganini, who would deliberately break a string on his violin so that he could display his virtuosity by continuing to play on the remaining three. I knew mine would not be a virtuoso performance, but I had no choice. Broken string or no — I had to go out there and play.

Each candidate had exactly thirty minutes for a demonstration, any introductions, and a speech. I was introduced by Ellen Fairclough, Mike Wilson, and two youth delegates. The introductions seemed a bit long, but that wasn't the worst of it. I was supposed to enter the hall to a big laser light display but, unknown to anyone on my campaign team, someone from the CBC plugged something into our power supply and blew it just before my speech was to begin. I waited for the light display, but nothing happened. Finally, I realized something was wrong and that I had better get out onto the stage — not a propitious way to begin a speech! Reading through the text now, I can see many opportunities for a passionate delivery. Unfortunately, I didn't exploit them fully. I did a reasonable job of reading the speech, but it wasn't the type of personal, warm, funny speech I liked to give. Although it was strategically sophisticated, there was no magic in it, unlike the one that had launched our campaign. Some people liked it a lot, others found it disappointing. I fell into the latter category.

By Sunday, voting day, I was feeling tired and fatalistic. My supporters were also exhausted but in great spirits. According to our trackers, our support was holding, and everyone hoped for a first-ballot victory. The hall was hot, so I retired from time to time to my cool dressing room. Bill Neville, a well-respected Tory who was an important member of my speechwriting team, had written two sets of speaking notes, one for either eventuality. I could hardly focus on them. As I went to vote, supporters kept telling me that we would win on the first ballot. But when the results were announced, I had 1,664 votes, 48 per cent of the total cast and 71 votes short of a victory. Charest had 1,369 votes, or 39 per cent. My team were jubilant, declaring that I couldn't lose; the second ballot was a mere formality. I wasn't convinced.

After the announcement, Jim Edwards walked over from his

section next to ours and put on a Campbell button. This sent Charest supporters flooding over from the other end of the hall, across our section, to try to woo Edwards's people. Jim had received a very respectable 307 votes. Patrick Boyer, who had received 53 votes, announced that he would support Charest. Garth Turner released his delegates without declaring his second-ballot support after coming fourth on the first ballot with 76 votes.

I had told Jim Edwards before the vote that I would put him in cabinet. It was the easiest commitment I ever made, since, as I told him before he decided to run, he had already earned a place there. Evidently, he had committed to go to Charest if he had fewer than 500 votes. But the Charest people had assumed they would be no more than five percentage points behind me on the first ballot. In the result, although receiving less than 500 votes, Jim could see that Charest was not within striking distance and came to me.

Charest's campaign had refused the opportunity to be seated in the section of the stadium next to the Edwards campaign, a strategic error for them. In the face of a steady stream of Edwards people moving next door to put on our buttons, Joe Clark came down to try to convince them to go to Charest. I suppose as a fellow Albertan he thought he should have a special claim on Jim's delegates. The ensuing scene was quite bizarre. As one delegate described it, Joe "lost it." As his efforts to draw the Edwards delegates to the other end of the hall were increasingly unsuccessful, he became more and more frantic.

I had retired to my dressing room to cool down again and also to allow for an "entrance" before the announcement of the second-ballot results. I kept thinking that maybe some of my delegates would leave after voting on the first ballot, thinking they wouldn't be needed again. I wasn't going to believe anything until I heard it. Shirley Martin came to sit with me while we waited. The atmosphere in the dressing room was in stark contrast to the pandemonium out in the hall. As a result, our adrenalin levels began to drop off. There was nothing left to do, and we talked quietly about everyday subjects.

At last it was time to go back in. As we moved out of the quiet of the dressing room, Shirley tried to stick close behind me as the advance team attempted to make a path for us through the crowd of reporters, photographers, and television crews. It was frightening to feel them pressing in on us. As one particularly aggressive photographer attempted to get between us, Shirley decided she'd had enough physical buffeting — and hauled off and punched him in the shoulder!

I took my place in the stands feeling nervous and a bit numb. As André Champagne began to read the numbers, I could tell the result in advance: I was watching a wedge of police move down towards our position in the stands. As soon as the number — 1,817 votes — was announced in French, the crowd went wild. After hugging everyone in sight, I reached out for my father, and we began to make our way down to the floor. Someone remarked later how calm and collected I looked. I suspect the only reason I looked that way was that I had learned already that to make your way through a crowd, you had to go slowly to let the escorts clear a path.

Up on the stage, I greeted the other candidates. After Jean Charest moved that the result be made unanimous, I walked to the podium, where my speaking notes had been placed. I spoke of Jean's importance to the future of our party. The notes included the line, "Jean, you are one hell of a tortoise!" This was a reference to his campaign theme — his being the tortoise to my hare. It wasn't a line I would have written for myself, and I hadn't paid enough attention to it when the notes were given to me. I was in a daze. Although no one in the media seemed to pick up any lapse, I was criticized for not being sufficiently gracious to Jean. Bill Neville blamed himself, if that was the case, and was genuinely distressed by the criticism. Aside from his desire to do right by me, he had always considered Jean a friend.

I was moved and overwhelmed by the realization that I would soon be prime minister. I couldn't believe that the long struggle of the last four months was actually over, and that I had won. As we partied later that night, the joy of victory was deepened by the effect of the incredible realization that a woman was going to be prime minister. Paul Curley was in tears at the arena after the vote — "This is for my daughter," he said. Women of all ages were jubilant, many of them crying at this historic moment. A woman was going to be prime minister of Canada, and I was that woman. I put aside all my fears about what was to come, and just savoured it.

14

The Real Thing

THE MORNING AFTER the convention, June 14, I woke up with a sense of urgency. Tired as I was, the adrenalin was pumping because I knew there was so much to do. Arrangements had been made for Jean and me to meet over a private lunch in my hotel suite. Looking back, this wasn't an optimal time for a meeting. Jean had come closer than he had expected to winning the leadership and regarded his showing, 187 votes behind on the second ballot, as a moral victory. I couldn't know then that a "We wuz robbed!" sentiment would linger in the Charest camp for some time. I, on the other hand, was still feeling very bruised by what I considered the no-holds-barred approach of the Charest campaign and Jean's apparent tolerance, if not encouragement, of its tactics. But I wanted to begin right away to forge a relationship with Jean. His participation in the upcoming election campaign would be crucial, and the reconciliation of our two campaign teams was essential to our party's prospects. I needed Jean Charest's cooperation and he knew it.

Jean's demeanour that day revealed very little of what he was actually thinking. I greeted him at the door and we exchanged the usual two-cheek kiss of colleagues. Although he was cordial and correct, I had the impression it was an effort for him. We sat down at the table right away, where a cold lunch of poached salmon and salad had been laid out in advance. I wasn't sure exactly how to conduct the meeting, but my goal was to be conciliatory and communicate to Jean that I regarded him as a valued part of the government and the Conservative team.

I had been advised by a number of old hands not to offer Jean (or anyone) anything specific at that early time, but to ask him what he would like to do. Because the challenge facing both of us was to try to win the next election, I painted a picture of the opportunities I thought we now had, together, to present a new vision to Canadians. I tried to put the leadership result in that broader context. Although of course he was disappointed at not winning, I said the tremendous impact that the result had had on women created possibilities for broadening our voter support, and I mentioned what I had been told of the huge emotional outpouring by women the night before. I also alluded to the potential of gaining back some of the disaffected Conservative vote in the west, not only because I was from the west, but also because Jean was known and liked there. I emphasized the importance of Jean's youth, his talent, and the fact that his support had not come solely from Quebec. I don't remember our conversation word for word, but I do recall saying that I thought that the combination of Charest and Campbell was a very powerful one.

Jean said little and ate even less. I picked up my knife and fork, thinking that if I started to eat, he would have to talk.

"What role would you like to play in the new government?" I asked.

He surprised me by answering quite aggressively that he didn't think being deputy prime minister interested him, but that he wanted to be minister of industry and political minister for Quebec. I wasn't sure how to construe his views on the deputy prime ministership. Did it mean he was trying to distance himself from me? Some people thought the position of deputy prime minister was unnecessary. Certainly my Quebec supporters were not keen on seeing Jean in that position, but although I had not had a chance to think the matter through, I thought it was probably a given for him. I was taken aback by Jean's tone but didn't argue with him. The request to be political minister of Quebec perplexed me. How could I issue such a slap in the face to my own Quebec supporters, who included the most senior ministers in his province? If I delivered such political clout to my leadership rival, I would have a revolt on my hands.

Jean's final comment in response to my question was to insist that all his ministerial supporters who were running again remain in cabinet. I said that I had not yet made any firm decisions about cabinet and would like to reflect on his comments. Jean expressed no objection and told me he was planning to take some vacation with his family. We parted in a friendly way with the expressed intention of being in touch over the coming days. When Bill Neville came in to be debriefed after the meeting, he shared my surprise at Jean's aggressive approach.

At 4 p.m., I called on the prime minister at 24 Sussex Drive. I arrived to see a large scaffolding across from the front entrance that held reporters and photographers. I just waved and smiled on my way in. The prime minister greeted me outside and led me into the house and upstairs to the informal sitting room at the top of the stairs. The main purpose of our meeting was to settle the date for the swearing-in of the new government. He proposed June 25, twelve days away, and I agreed. His plan was to fly to France with his family immediately after his formal resignation. I told the prime minister that I had met with Jean and that he had expressed reluctance about being named deputy prime minister. Mulroney argued strongly that Charest should be named to that position. He thought it was important for our prospects in Quebec. We then discussed mostly practical issues relating to the transition. He invited me to dinner at Harrington Lake the following week so that we would have a chance to discuss the issues of official residences and staff at greater length. "By the way," he added, almost as an afterthought, "the government is going to buy the furniture here, so you won't have to worry about redecorating before you move in."

The remark barely registered. In a conversation a year or two earlier, Jean Pigott, chairperson of the National Capital Commission, had told me that the NCC had adopted a new policy whereby the public rooms of the official residences would henceforth be decorated by the NCC. I assumed that the PM's comment referred to this policy to end the practice of private redecoration of public rooms. In the room where we were sitting, the wallpaper matched the upholstery. It seemed natural to me that the existing decor should be left as it was. What I didn't know was that Jean Pigott had had a falling-out with the prime minister over her refusal to purchase the Mulroneys' furniture. Since I had other, more pressing matters on my mind, it never occurred to me on that day to question the arrangements the PM had described. I had already decided that I wouldn't occupy 24 Sussex Drive until and unless I won an election. For security reasons, I would move into the residence at Harrington Lake. For the brief time I was prime minister, I continued to rent my Ottawa apartment, which I used for meals, appointments, or changing clothes when the thirty-minute drive to Harrington Lake wasn't convenient. I continued to live in my own home in Vancouver when I was there.

At the conclusion of our meeting, the PM escorted me to the front of the house. We said our farewells and he left me to speak to the press. In taking leave of me, the PM gave me a quick hug. I thought little of it, but the image would later be used by those wanting to link me with Mulroney. It was an appropriate gesture of personal goodwill, but had I been a man, it would not have been made in that way. It was an interesting example of the subtle way that gender changes the way the political game is played.

I announced the date for the transition to the new government, answered a few questions, and headed back to the hotel. There, Bill met me with the news that Jodi White, manager of the Charest campaign, had called to say that Jean was very displeased with our meeting. Evidently, he had been particularly insulted by my reference to the "women crying" after the selection of the first woman leader of our party. Even recognizing the sensitivities of our two egos after a bruising campaign, I couldn't fathom how Jean could possibly react so negatively to our conversation. I reluctantly concluded that he was looking for a pretext to quit before the next election. He had damaged himself in the last week of the campaign by his unwillingness to commit himself to running again if he lost the leadership. When asked the question directly, he would only say, "I have to consult with my family." Only at the eleventh hour, when he was persuaded that he was hurting his candidacy by his refusal to commit, did he say that he would run again, no matter the outcome. From my perspective, his comments during and after our meeting looked like an attempt to take the course he had initially indicated while blaming me for his inability to live up to his convention commitment.

For Jean to have quit under these circumstances would have been devastating to the party. I wasn't prepared to let this happen and called Brian Mulroney to enlist his support. He agreed that it would be a disaster for Charest to leave and said he would phone him immediately. Mulroney's direct intervention was the most effective way to head off the problem, and I was grateful for his help. I didn't want to call Jean myself because I didn't want to confront him about the way he had reported our conversation. As the week wore on, Jean's petulance began to be remarked on in the media. When word got out that Jean was planning to be absent from the last national caucus meeting of the Mulroney government, even Mulroney's patience began to wear thin, and he let it be known that Jean had better show up.

Much has been written about that first meeting between Jean and me after the convention. I knew Jean must be feeling very disappointed, a feeling exacerbated by the natural exhaustion and letdown after a leadership race. The last thing on my mind was to gloat or to reproach him in any way. Looking back, I realize how little the two of us knew or understood each other at that time. Of all my cabinet colleagues, Jean was perhaps the one I knew least. My B.C. colleagues and I worked together on a regular basis; the ten western ministers had travelled together during our western ministers' tours and I had entertained them in Vancouver; various cabinet members of Joe Clark's unity committee had travelled the country together and had got to know one another during many a long meeting; other colleagues had invited me to speak in their constituencies, or I had lobbied them because their portfolios touched on some issue of importance to Vancouver or British Columbia. Cabinet committees had provided an opportunity to work with many ministers, but Jean and I had rarely been around the same table. Many of the cabinet debates on the Green Plan had taken place when Lucien Bouchard and then Robert de Cotret were ministers of the environment. Jean's remarks in cabinet and later, when he was named to P&P, had always struck me as intelligent and articulate, but I had no idea what drove him — what passions he brought to the political process. When I asked people who had been close to Jean what his priorities or preoccupations might be, they were unable to enlighten me. Although the issues I had dealt with had made my views well known, Jean had little personal basis on which to feel that he knew what made me tick either.

Another meeting that first Monday was with the transition team led by Bill Neville but also consisting of key people from my leadership campaign. I presented the team with a list of items to be addressed on an urgent basis. Among the first was the swearing-in ceremony. Our first hope was to demonstrate a new, more people-oriented style of governing by having the ceremony at the Museum of Civilization, across the river in Hull. This would have allowed more people to attend. The symbolism of swearing in the new government in a federal facility in Quebec, designed by a native architect, and with a spectacular view across the river to the full sweep of the Parliament Buildings was not sufficient to persuade the governor general to break from tradition. After pressing as hard as we thought was diplomatically advisable, we gave up, and plans were made for the formalities to take place, as was the custom, at Rideau Hall.

Back in April, I had asked Bill Neville to work on a transition agenda for me. As Joe Clark's chief of staff, he had overseen the transition when Joe became prime minister in 1979. Brian Mulroney had asked him to do the same when he was elected in 1984. In the spring of 1993, Bill was undergoing chemotherapy. Because his health prevented him from playing an active role in the leadership campaign (assuming he had wanted to), the job of thinking ahead and mapping out an agenda for the transitional period seemed like a wonderful use of his talents. Bill was well respected by the public service, and would provide some administrative continuity until I could put my own PMO staff in place.

In the days that followed, I was briefed on my new responsibilities and the decisions that needed to be made before June 25. As prime minister–designate I met with the clerk of the Privy Council, Glen Shortliffe, for a series of briefings. In one, I was inducted to the arcane world of prime-ministerial security. As the full picture of what my life was now going to be like began to emerge, I kept thinking of that song "You'll Never Walk Alone." While being driven by the Mounties one day, I heard them refer to me as "Redwood." Yes, they confirmed, it was the custom to use the names of trees for prime-ministerial code names, and because I was from British Columbia, they confided proudly, I was to be designated by a western tree. They seemed nonplussed when I told them that, except for a redwood seedling that my father once brought back from California and planted secretly in a West Vancouver park, I was unaware of any redwoods in B.C. — cedar, arbutus, Douglas fir, dogwood, pine, I suggested, but no redwoods.

The party and its organizational and financial health were also of concern to me. David Angus, recently made a senator by Brian Mulroney, came to present me with his resignation as chairman of the PC Canada Fund, the party's fundraising arm. His report on the financial state of the party indicated that we weren't in as good shape as I had been led to believe by Brian Mulroney. Of the $5 million in the party coffers, $3.3 million was in the form of a trust fund that couldn't be spent. Clearly, appointing a new chairman was a priority if we were going to have the resources to fight an election. I also had a meeting with Allan Gregg, our party pollster, and John Tory, campaign chairman, to hear their perspective on our campaign preparedness. Clearly, there was a great deal to do.

Prime Minister Mulroney convened his last cabinet meeting on Thursday morning. Each minister was presented with a leather-bound volume entitled "Promises Made — Promises Kept" as a record of the Mulroney government. We started passing them around the table to get one another's signatures, like kids at graduation. For many of the ministers, it was their own swan song, too. Mike Wilson, Don Mazankowski, Barbara McDougall, John Crosbie, Joe Clark, and others wouldn't be running again. It was a poignant meeting. There was no question that the people there felt a strong sense of gratitude towards the PM. By leading the Conservatives to power on two occasions, he had enabled us all to do jobs that were perhaps the most exciting and meaningful we would ever have. I was grateful to Brian Mulroney for giving me my big chance.

Being outside the political arena for the first time in fifteen years, I see now how much simpler the political process appears from that vantage point. The reality is much more ambiguous, gut-wrenching, and frustrating. Because his cabinet colleagues admired the Mulroney they had often seen at his best, a strong and far-sighted leader, they genuinely regretted that he evoked such hostility that he had become a political liability. The negative feelings towards him seemed so disproportionate to his actual shortcomings that on occasions such as this, his colleagues tended to try to compensate with outpourings of appreciation.

I felt a bit strange at this last cabinet meeting. I was excited about the challenges facing me, but this was still Brian Mulroney's show. Despite my earlier rancour over his hostility to resignations in order to contest the leadership, I was caught up in the mood and praised the PM for the way he had prepared the groundwork for his successor. When the afterglow of all the emotional leave-taking had worn off, I would come to a more realistic assessment.

The previous day, at national caucus, a similar scene had occurred, with heartfelt tributes to the PM. I spoke as well and was warmly welcomed by caucus colleagues. We then went into the House, where I received the congratulations of other parties. I still occupied my ministerial seat, and because the House was to rise before the swearing-in of the new government, I never did sit in the PM's front-row chair.

Throughout that first week I talked to all the other leadership candidates and began to touch base with my own supporters and Jean's key supporters. It was important to bury any hatchets. I had congenial conversations with Bill McKnight and Joe Clark, among others. Joe wrote me two very thoughtful letters about the situation facing the party as he saw it. He was candid in saying that, for the first time in his life as a Conservative, the party was led by a stranger. What he meant, I hope, was a stranger to him, someone he didn't know well. I understood that, but couldn't help reflecting that someone who had been a minister in a Conservative government for almost five years could hardly be a "stranger" to the party. The comment reminded me of the constant references to my being a "rookie" MP when I was running for the leadership. Finally, I asked Michael Ferrabee to do a little research. It turned out that ten of the eighteen men who preceded me as prime minister had had less cabinet experience than me.

In his letter Joe went on to speak candidly about the party. Like me, he believed that it had to become more democratic. His comments were instructive on the natue of leadership. He had more than a few scars, including those inflicted by Mulroney. Nowhere had Mulroney better demonstrated his capacity for ruthlessness than in his relations over the years with Joe Clark. His public declaration of support for Joe's leadership at the same time he was organizing to depose him was ancient history. That Joe was able to overcome what must have been enormous resentment of Mulroney and serve with distinction in his cabinet was something I admired. Although my leadership win wasn't the personal defeat for him that Mulroney's had been, Joe's graciousness and constructive help was a gesture of reconciliation that I valued highly. It was a reflection of his commitment to democratic processes, no matter what he thought of the outcome.

I received many congratulatory calls that first week from other political leaders. I remember Ontario Premier Bob Rae advising me that if I was going to downsize cabinet I should do so right away. His tone suggested this was a lesson he had learned from hard experience. It was a pertinent comment, because the biggest challenge facing me was the restructuring of the government and the creation of the cabinet.

During the leadership campaign, I had committed myself to reducing the size of cabinet to about twenty-five ministers from thirty-five. A growing public concern about the cost and efficiency of government had led to attacks on the historically large Mulroney cabinets. In fact, Mulroney had reduced the size of cabinet from thirty-nine ministers to thirty-five in the January 1993 shuffle and had commissioned retiring Treasury Board Secretary Robert de Cotret to prepare a report on the restructuring and streamlining of the federal government.

When I received the briefing books on the various issues requiring my action before and immediately after the swearing-in, four options for restructuring were presented to me: a smaller government with a cabinet of twenty-nine; a moderate restructuring with a cabinet of twenty-five; "reorganize for the nineties" with a cabinet of twenty; and a proposal from de Cotret for a cabinet of seventeen senior and eight junior ministers. In the end, I borrowed ideas from a number of these proposals, added some of my own, and "reorganized for the nineties" but with a cabinet of twenty-five. Getting there was an agonizing process, but I couldn't begin to put together a roster of ministers until I knew how many would be in my cabinet. At the end of the week I moved back to my apartment and set aside the weekend for the restructuring process. Ginny Richards remembers my confiding to her that weekend my concern about making such important decisions when I was so tired. Nonetheless, I think the result was reasonable.

The restructuring of cabinet was the most radical since Confederation. I departed from all the recommended proposals in a number of ways; for example, all had suggested the continued combination of Defence and Veterans' Affairs. I knew the commemorative function was expected by veterans to become more low-key after the celebrations of the fiftieth anniversary of the end of World War II. I decided to appoint a full-time minister for Veterans' Affairs who could be a presence at these important commemorations but who could also work with veterans on the process of redefining and reallocating the work of the department.

As a leadership candidate I had emphasized the need for Canadians to know more about one another. Since the provinces jealously guard their jurisdiction over education, the possibilities for a federal role must be found elsewhere; thus, the suggestion to form a Department of Canadian Heritage appealed to me. All of the ceremonial, commemorative, symbolic, cultural, representational, and educative functions of the federal government could be combined in this department with the specific mandate to foster a greater knowledge and understanding of the country among all Canadians. Although there was little public enthusiasm for a renewal of constitutional discussions, the issues that Meech Lake and Charlottetown had attempted to resolve remained. The fragmentation of education led to a strongly regional tinge to the teaching of Canadian history, especially in Quebec, but elsewhere as well. In addition, our very high rate of immigration meant that many adult Canadians were not educated in Canada. Given the strains on Canadian society, the federal government needed to rethink its role in this area.

With the end of the Cold War, the world order as we had known it for fifty years was turned upside down. During the spring I had met our former ambassador to Washington, Allan Gotlieb, at a luncheon in Toronto. Although probably doing better financially than he ever had during a distinguished career in government, he obviously missed the excitement of being at the centre of things internationally. "The first two years are awful — then it gets worse!" He told me that when Trudeau had become PM, he had prepared for him a memorandum with his views of the international situation and its implications for Canadian foreign policy. Would I be interested in receiving such a memorandum? "Indeed I would," I replied.

The Gotlieb paper corresponded in many points with my own view of Canada's post–Cold War positioning. I was particularly taken with his idea that while Canada was not a great power, with the end of an era where power was measured by military might, Canada should see itself as a major power. My experience in both Justice and Defence had convinced me that Canada had a unique contribution to make to the post–Cold War reconfiguration of international institutions and the support of democratic development in the world. To allow us to maximize that contribution, I wanted separate ministers responsible for Defence, Foreign Affairs, and International Trade.

The creation of the Department of Human Resources reflected another major theme of my leadership campaign: the need to have greater coordination between the policies of income support and those relating to workforce development and training. There would always be people who would need income assistance because they were unable physically or mentally to join the labour market; however, given the extraordinary changes occurring in the workplace, we had to look at how we could enable displaced workers to re-enter the labour force. The new department would keep the employment responsibilities of the old Employment and Immigration Department, and that part of Immigration that dealt with the criteria for selecting and admitting immigrants into Canada. It would also incorporate the Department of Labour and the welfare part of the old Health and Welfare. The minister would thus be strategically positioned to lead the process of reforming our social policies as they relate to employment and income security.

Hiving off the welfare responsibilities from Health and Welfare left a smaller but very strategic Department of Health. Since reform in this area was becoming crucial and would involve intensive work with the provinces, it made sense to give Health its own full-time minister.

Other changes included a Department of Industry, expanded to take over the functions of Consumer and Corporate Affairs, with a separate minister responsible for science and small business. Public Works and the Department of Supply and Services would be combined into a Department of Government Services. Forestry and Energy, Mines and Resources would be amalgamated into a new Department of Natural Resources. The Department of Solicitor General would be renamed the Department of Public Security and be expanded to include all the law enforcement functions of the federal government, including customs and the enforcement of immigration laws.

After reaching my goal of a twenty-five-person cabinet, I could begin to address the question of who would be in it. What followed was an exercise like solving a jigsaw puzzle as I tried to take into account experience, along with region, gender, and other factors. The most significant of the "other factors" was who the person had supported during the leadership campaign. Obviously, I couldn't appoint only people who had supported me; however, because most of the ministers seeking re-election had been on my team, that complicated my options.

Trying to meet the expectations of cabinet hopefuls and loyalists with just twenty-five positions was a frustrating task. It was particularly hard for Alberta MPs: the smaller cabinet left me with only two ministerial slots for the province, but a large caucus of very able people, many of them my supporters. On Sunday night, David Camp came over with some take-out Chinese food for a quick dinner. "I'm not sure I really want this job," I joked. Careful to stay only long enough to eat, offer some encouragement, and clean up, David left me to complete my first draft of a ministry and cabinet.

Bill Neville and Glen Shortliffe were both very positive about my presentation the following Monday, but it was too soon to finalize anything. As a courtesy, I wanted to consult with Jean Charest about my proposals for Quebec. The appointments there were troublesome for several reasons. First, with a reduced cabinet, I proposed to appoint seven ministers from Ontario and seven from Quebec. Although more ministers from Ontario could be justified by population, given the relatively equal sizes of our Quebec and Ontario caucuses, an equal number from each seemed fair. The problem was that more Quebec ministers were staying on than there were places. To make matters worse, the split between Campbell and Charest supporters was particularly bitter in Quebec. Almost no matter what I did, my own supporters were going to feel cheated.

During my meeting with Jean the previous Monday, he had told me he would like his ministerial supporters, Pauline Browes from Ontario and Pierre Cadieux and Jean Corbeil from Quebec, to remain in cabinet. But keeping both Cadieux and Corbeil would have required me to fire one of my own ministerial supporters from Quebec. Since this was impossible, my preference was for Pierre Cadieux, not only because I knew him better but also because I was impressed with the efforts he had been making since the convention to bring the warring sides together. Jean Charest drew to my attention that Jean Corbeil was from the strategic and heavily populated island of Montreal. I knew Pierre's riding had less regional significance and could see that it might be more important to have a francophone from Montreal for geographical balance. This view was supported by responses to my discreet inquiries of those more knowledgeable about the region than I was. I was disappointed, and when I eventually called Pierre to tell him I wouldn't be able to include him in the cabinet, so was he.

Before I finalized my cabinet list, I met with the ministers who had indicated they were retiring, to confirm their intentions and as a courtesy. Fisheries Minister John Crosbie and Elmer MacKay, minister of public works, were the first to arrive to confirm their resignations. Barbara McDougall, who had already announced publicly her intention not to seek re-election, came by and we discussed the upcoming G-7 meeting. She arrived with her deputy minister, Reid Morden, who would be serving as my sherpa, or chief official, at the summit. Barbara had supported Jean, and I think she found it strange to be meeting with me as the PM-designate, but we both tried to be as conciliatory and constructive as possible.

I liked and respected Barbara McDougall, but we never became close. She represented the Toronto constituency of St. Paul's and returned to Toronto on the weekends, and while I was married to Howard, I didn't go out with colleagues on my own during the week unless absolutely necessary. So there was little opportunity for us to socialize and we didn't see each other often at work, particularly after she became secretary of state for external affairs and began a life of considerable travel. Also the chemistry between us wasn't compelling enough for either of us to go to great lengths to overcome the logistical barriers. However, when Howard and I separated, Barbara very kindly invited me to dinner in her Ottawa apartment on a Sunday evening. It was a warm gesture, and I appreciated it very much.

In November 1992, I encountered columnist Allan Fotheringham at a Toronto brunch. He was an old friend of Barbara. Out of the blue, he began telling me that Barbara thought she was a decade too old to be prime minister. I didn't know what to say — I thought it was preposterous. Clearly, however, Barbara must have been feeling that, despite the hot speculation about her future from 1984 to 1988, her moment of opportunity had come and gone. She had been a very credible minister and was as entitled as anyone to have ambitions for the top job.

I quickly realized after winning the convention that as long as I was prime minister I would never know what my colleagues (with very few exceptions) really thought about me or what I was doing. Even people whom I knew to be less than keen on me were unfailingly "correct." It was something in the eyes — a guarded expression that I had not seen before. It is no accident that leaders gravitate to those whom they've known for a long time and whose frankness they can count on.

I took my cabinet list with me the night I went to Harrington Lake to dine with the Mulroneys. They came out to greet me as the RCMP car drove me to the front door. The house, which stands on a hill overlooking the private lake, is large but feels like a home. Behind it are buildings housing the RCMP security staff, and on another part of the property there is accommodation for the household staff. Beyond the house, across a lawn, can be seen a wooden fence surrounding the vegetable garden created by Margaret Trudeau, which still provides fresh produce for the household.

As at 24 Sussex Drive, Mila Mulroney had done a wonderful job of decorating Harrington Lake. From the front door I was ushered into the living room. We sat around a low table set in front of the large stone fireplace. I pulled some papers from the small portfolio I was carrying, and showed Brian (as I now called him, somewhat uncomfortably) my cabinet list for comment. He seemed impressed, and his only remarks were in agreement with specific choices. I wasn't looking for approval, but after the Cadieux/Corbeil issue, I wanted to make sure there was nothing that an experienced PM would identify as a problem.

We then talked about the domestic and personal life of a prime minister. At one point, Brian noted that in all the years he had known Margaret Thatcher, whether he had seen her early in the morning or late at night, she had always been perfectly groomed. Mila mentioned that her hairdresser, Rinaldo, would come to 24 Sussex at 6 a.m. if necessary and added that she was sometimes up until 2 a.m. doing her nails. Were they telling me I needed improvement in the grooming department? I was getting my nails done professionally on a regular basis, and I thought my hairdo was pretty muss-proof. I resolved to take it all seriously, but not too seriously.

Dinner was an informal meal with just the three of us in the sunporch adjoining the living room. Its small round table would become my regular eating place when I lived there, except for the few occasions when more than two guests stayed for a meal. The room has a wonderful view and gets the late-afternoon sun. After the meal I followed the Mulroneys into the kitchen to meet the people who served the household. When I took office, I had to reduce the number of household staff because there was only one of me, as opposed to six Mulroneys. Those wonderful people were what made it possible for me to have any private life at all. In no time they organized my life, and they kept me fed, clothed, pressed, and packed for the next four months.

The last thing on the evening's agenda was a tour of the house. Brian and Mila showed me the five bedrooms upstairs, plus a small room where the children were watching TV and a den used by the PM. The master bedroom looked out over the lake. I was beginning to think it would be paradise in the summer until Mila warned me about the blackflies and mosquitoes. Oh well, I thought, I'm not going to have much time to sit around anyway. I took my leave of the Mulroneys that evening, carrying a gift of a hand-knit cardigan with Canadian symbols on it, and wished them bon voyage for their trip to France.

After the 1993 election, a friend asked me if Brian and Mila Mulroney were the first people I had ever met who were "professionally charming." I was struck by the expression. I suppose in public life we are all "professionally charming" to a degree. Certainly people would find it unacceptable if public figures expressed their dislikes openly. The problem with professional charm is that it masks the real person and makes it hard for people to feel they really know him or her.

I think the Mulroneys are good "professional charmers" because they both genuinely like people. I have been told that Mulroney favoured Jean Charest by the end of the leadership campaign, but that night at Harrington Lake gave me no inkling of whether this was true. Like Joe Clark, I would never experience Mulroney's enmity directly, if it existed. Of course, some would say that "professional charm" is simply the manifestation of the maxim "If you can get someone else to stick the knife in, don't do it yourself!"

It was obvious that Mulroney's respect for his wife was real, and there is no question that Mila is intelligent and effective. In a private conversation with me, he once compared her with the well-known wife of another colleague, who, he suggested, would egg her husband on if he came home fuming over some behaviour that had angered him. In his case, Mulroney said, if he came home fuming, Mila would try to calm him down and often force him to look at the other side of the issue and be more reasonable. It was an interesting insight into the dynamic between them.

Once I had finalized my cabinet list, it was time to appoint the ministers. Cabinet-making has traditionally been shrouded in secrecy, and there are practical reasons for that. If last-minute changes have to be made, the confidentiality prevents embarrassment. Since I did not have the use of an official residence yet, my staff set up an elaborate system of rooms at the Westin Hotel for meetings and allocated code names to all the ministers and MPs who had been called. They called the exercise "Operation Cat in the Hat" and gave the prospective ministers code names from that Dr. Seuss story. The rooms were arranged in such a way that people entered on one floor but left from another. It was all designed to prevent ministers from knowing who else was there. Each meeting had its own character, but perhaps the most fun were those with the first-time appointees. There is nothing quite like the thrill of that first confirmation that you are going into cabinet. Bobbie Sparrow, Peter McCreath, Ross Reid, Jim Edwards, Garth Turner, Larry Schneider, Rob Nicholson — almost a third of the cabinet were new. Unfortunately, with the decision to reduce the size of cabinet, the hopes of some very worthy candidates had been dashed. Beyond regional and gender balance, my decisions were based on a need to combine stability in the short period available before an election with new energy and ideas. With the smaller cabinet, I could only maintain the same proportion of women as before. I hoped that after an election we would have a larger percentage of women MPs. (Well, we did — 50 per cent, in fact!)

The final make-up of cabinet reflected the many factors I had worked to balance as well as my goals for the new government. In British Columbia, Tom Siddon and Mary Collins would remain in cabinet, Tom in Defence and Mary in Health. As an engineer, Tom, I hoped, would be able to deal with the technical issues related to military procurement. Mary, who would also retain the status-of-women portfolio, had worked on health policy in the days when she was the first woman appointed as a cabinet secretary in Ontario. I wanted to facilitate a major initiative on women's health issues, an interest that I knew Mary shared and was well equipped to lead.

In Alberta it was important to have representation from both Edmonton and Calgary, which the appointment of Jim Edwards and Bobbie Sparrow accomplished. Jim was delighted to be appointed as president of the Treasury Board, a position that would enable him to spearhead reforms to goverment spending and management, important issues in Alberta. With her background in the energy industry, Bobbie was a natural for the new Natural Resources Department. She would be running against Preston Manning in her riding and the cabinet profile was important to her.

Saskatchewan and Manitoba had lost two senior ministers with the retirement of Bill McKnight and Jake Epp. Larry Schneider was the first minister from Regina in sixty years. In the western economic diversification portfolio, with responsibility for Canada Post, he would have clout on both urban and rural issues affecting the west. Charlie Mayer became the minister of agriculture and agrifoods and minister responsible for the government's strategies for small towns and rural areas.

Ontario's seven ministers included two newcomers: Garth

Turner, who in National Revenue could exploit his history as an advocate for taxpayers in working to make the tax collection system function better; and Rob Nicholson, who, as my parliamentary secretary in Justice, had impressed me enormously with his skill in steering measures through the House. Rob would become minister for science and small business, working within the Industry Department. Pauline Browes, MP for Scarborough, who had first joined the cabinet in the January 1993 shuffle, went into Indian Affairs, where experience had shown that urban ministers fared better. Among the veterans, Perrin Beatty, a seasoned performer, went into External Affairs. His supposedly safe seat made the travel required less of a detriment than it might have been for others. Tom Hockin's base in London, Ontario, and his Harvard Ph.D. gave him the right background and profile for the international trade portfolio, a key one for Ontario. Doug Lewis took on the enlarged Public Security Department from his former position as solicitor general, and Paul Dick's good ideas about rationalizing government functions and attacking efficiency issues would find a useful outlet in the new Department of Government Services.

Quebec's seven ministers also reflected that province's clout in our caucus. Jean Charest had graciously agreed to be deputy prime minister and minister of industry. Monique Landry, who had been vice-chair of my leadership campaign in Quebec, became political minister for Quebec as well as minister of Canadian heritage. Jean Corbeil remained in Transport, and Gerry Weiner, an anglo-Montrealer and our only Jewish minister, remained minister of multiculturalism, working within the Heritage Department. Pierre H. Vincent, only recently promoted to cabinet by Brian Mulroney, went into Environment. Pierre Blais remained in Justice and became president of the Privy Council. He was my preferred choice for political minister but was not a wise choice at this early date because he had ruffled a few feathers as co-chair of my national leadership campaign. Gilles Loiselle became minister of finance.

With the smaller cabinet, there were only three ministers from Atlantic Canada, but they were an impressive trio. Bernard Valcourt from New Brunswick took on the enhanced Human Resources Department, where his experience as minister of employment and immigration gave him a head start. First-time minister Peter

McCreath, from Nova Scotia, took over Veterans' Affairs and the political responsibility for Prince Edward Island as well as for his own province. A historian with a naval background, Peter was well suited to seeing the department through the upcoming commemorations, then rethinking its constitution. From Newfoundland, Ross Reid, manager of my leadership campaign and widely admired, joined cabinet in the difficult fisheries and oceans portfolio and took responsibility for the Atlantic Canada Opportunities Agency. In the Senate, Lowell Murray kept his cabinet post as government leader. Geographically, Lowell was a "twofer" since, despite his deep Maritime roots, his Senate seat was in Ontario.

A day or two before the swearing-in on June 25, Glen Shortliffe told Bill Neville that he would like to change the deputy ministers at the same time because the deputies would need to know what departments they would be leading. Bill told him to draw up a list for my approval. We were so pressed for time that I didn't give the list of proposed deputies more than a cursory glance. I should have studied it more carefully. I hadn't noticed that a number of the women deputies were put in minor portfolios or ones that required them to move from Ottawa. The unhappiness of the women deputies was not drawn to my attention until Jodi White joined my staff right after the swearing-in.

Inviting Jodi White to head up my office was one of the steps I took to heal the divisions of the leadership campaign. I had known Jodi before the leadership and thought we would be able to work well together. Some in my leadership camp were unhappy with my choice, but others were enthusiastic. I was confident of Jodi's integrity. I didn't believe she would accept the position if she couldn't serve me comfortably. She had served as Joe Clark's chief of staff at External Affairs in the first mandate and had been regarded then as the best chief of staff in the government. Jodi's appointment was also a clear indication to Jean that I had no intention of shutting him or his supporters out of the government. Ray Castelli, who was thirty-three, didn't think he was ready to take on the job of chief of staff to the prime minister and became deputy chief of staff. Jodi's experience with the senior public service over a long period of time would prove valuable for both efficiency and stability. I also liked the idea of a woman chief of staff, for personal and political reasons.

After spending Saint-Jean-Baptiste Day in Valleyfield, Quebec, in Jean-Guy Hudon's riding, I met with Governor General Ray Hnatyshyn the afternoon before the swearing-in ceremony so that I could present him with the list of the new cabinet. My relationship with Ray Hnatyshyn was one of the delights of my brief time as prime minister. It was wonderful to feel I could talk openly to him with complete confidence in the confidentiality of everything I said. He has a great sense of humour and a talent for putting people at their ease. We confirmed all the details for the swearing-in ceremony, and the governor general looked over the cabinet list with great interest, to see not only the names but also the reorganization of the government. He was impressed by the reduction in the size of the cabinet.

June 25 was a beautiful day and I felt very upbeat as I put on the lovely suit — navy skirt and white jacket, trimmed with navy — that Lee had made for me. Mum and Alix had returned to Vancouver after the convention, but Dad, Marg, and Freda had stayed on in the east so that they could be at the swearing-in. The four of us were ushered into a small sitting room to meet the Hnatyshyns prior to the ceremony. Finally, when everyone else had been seated, I was shown to my seat and the ceremony began. Although it wasn't the first time I had taken an oath in Rideau Hall, it was a moving experience. It wasn't just that I was being sworn in as prime minister, but that I was making history by being the first woman to take that oath.

In many ways, the events of the day were familiar. There was even a certain naturalness to it all. But there was also a sense of being on auto-pilot because of the pace of the past few months. I hadn't had time to look forward to the occasion and reflect on its significance. Hearing myself addressed as "Prime Minister" by the media after the ceremony startled me. Taking my place in the PM's chair at the cabinet meeting that afternoon and looking around at the new faces at the table was more effective in bringing the change home than even the congratulatory phone call from President Clinton that followed.

This was a significant day not only for the government but, just as important, for the party. I spoke by conference call to our campaign chairs in each province. A campaign college was in session in Ottawa, and I had my picture taken with the candidates for use in election materials. It was almost 8 p.m. when I arrived at a "Party for the Party" on Parliament Hill. The mood was euphoric. The downsizing of cabinet was wildly popular, being seen as an important sign that I would make changes and live up to my promises.

I returned to my apartment, where a private party was in progress with my family and closest friends and associates. All three of my Divinsky stepdaughters were there (Judy with her husband, Neil Kornfeld, and their two young daughters), as were Ginny and John Richards. Ross Reid spoke on behalf of all the participants in my leadership campaign, and I responded with my own message of thanks and love. After the incredible ups and downs of the campaign, we all felt happy that the new government had got off to a good start. There were few illusions in the group, but lots of optimism. Tired as we were, we cherished the moment.

My first clear reminder that from now on I was never to be off duty occurred the next day in Vancouver. After a euphoric "Welcome Home, Kim" reception at the Plaza of Nations, I was entering the studios of radio station CKNW for an interview when I was asked by the press about the attack by American missiles on Baghdad. I had been alerted about this only moments before but had no details. The staff at the station remember that I took a call from President Clinton in their boardroom.

Wherever I travelled as prime minister, an office was set up, usually in the hotel where my party was staying, to provide a secure communications link to Ottawa. That night I spoke from the Pan Pacific Hotel to Secretary of State for External Affairs Perrin Beatty about events in Iraq and his discussions with his American counterpart, Warren Christopher. Neither of us was happy about the lack of prior warning of the attack. Finally, I went home and dropped like a lump into my own bed.

The next day we flew back to Ottawa, and around 10 p.m. I arrived for the first time at Harrington Lake as a resident rather than a guest, to be greeted by Ginny and John Richards. I had invited them to stay with me for the June 26 weekend before they went back to Vancouver. The only antidote for loneliness was to have houseguests, I found, but I soon learned that I was destined to be a negligent hostess. Not that anybody really minded, since the staff were ready to spoil anyone who came within range. They were so used to looking after a family of six that I think they considered the residence virtually deserted during my tenure.

The next morning I showered and dressed for the first time in my new home. I felt very strange. The beauty and peacefulness of the surroundings in some ways only added to the air of unreality. I would never feel entirely at home there — perhaps just as well!

Jodi White was on duty now as chief of staff and had begun the task of reorganizing the office. It had become the custom to second a senior official from External Affairs to serve as press attaché to the PM, and Jodi recommended Paul Frazer, who had been our ambassador in Prague. I liked him immediately and would enjoy his company during our many travels together over the next four months. No one, least of all Cindy, objected to this change, but it was another example of the people closest to me finding themselves put just outside the circle of direct access. Ray assured me that Cindy would be found a position in the PMO, and I was upset later to learn that this had not been done.

One of our first priorities was to address the dissatisfaction being expressed by our MPs from Metro Toronto and by Premier Rae, who felt that I had slighted Toronto by including only one Toronto minister — Pauline Browes — in the cabinet. In particular, Bill Attewell and Barbara Greene, two Metro MPs who had given me wonderful support, were very upset. So was I. Although Garth Turner, who represented Halton-Peel, was from the Toronto region, he was not seen as a Metro MP *per se*. Nor, in the eyes of some, was Pauline, who represented a Scarborough riding. Perhaps because Garth had been a journalist for the *Toronto Sun*, I thought he was well connected in Toronto. Moreover, there had been a compelling reason of party solidarity to appoint Pauline and Garth. Garth spoke for the fiscal conservatives, who were otherwise not strongly represented by Ontario ministers, and Pauline was one of only two Charest supporters in the cabinet. In a cabinet of twenty-five, I didn't have much room to manoeuvre, and the Metro situation hadn't been spotted by any of the Ontarians who had seen the cabinet list, nor by Brian Mulroney. In the short term, the only thing I could do was name Bill Attewell as my parliamentary secretary.

The election campaign team met at 7:30 a.m. on June 26. Campaign chair John Tory, pollster Allan Gregg, Quebec co-chair Marcel

Danis, national director of the Conservative Party Tom Trbovich, Jodi White, and Ray Castelli arrived to discuss the presentation that the team was to make later that morning to a cabinet planning session at Meech Lake. After breakfast, we all drove out there together in a van. When the awaiting press saw me get out of the van with the campaign team, there was a flurry of excited speculation that I was going to call the election that very day. John and Allan gave a review of our political situation, which was bleak but not hopeless. It was a fair enough appraisal given the as-yet-unknown impact on our prospects of the change in party leadership. When Allan described our challenge — "to do right-wing policies for left-wing reasons" — he was identifying a contradiction that was more fundamental than any of us understood. The same briefing was given to national caucus that evening. Allan had identified an interest in the new Conservative leader that would be key to making the voters, who had written us off, give us a second look. The next few weeks would be crucial for establishing my credibility as prime minister.

Facing me were three pressing priorities: Canada Day, a first ministers' meeting, and G-7. The idea of a Canada Day marathon started with my expression of regret that, as prime minister, I would be expected to be on Parliament Hill, meaning the end of my practice of spending the national holiday in my own riding. Someone figured out that I could do both if I were content to arrive in Vancouver at the end of the day. Ross Reid mentioned that in St. John's, Canada Day is celebrated with a sunrise ceremony. With the time difference, I could attend the St. John's ceremony but also make it back in time for the wonderful pomp and circumstance of the Ottawa celebrations, with a side trip to Hull. And so I began Canada Day 1993 on Signal Hill in St. John's, Newfoundland, at 5:30 a.m., participated with the governor general in the ceremony on Parliament Hill at noon, and closed the day at Canada Place in Vancouver. It was truly magical.

The weather was cold on Signal Hill as we listened to a choir of beautiful young voices singing "O Canada" and the haunting "Ode to Newfoundland" as the sun came up on the country. As the music swelled to the words "We love thee," in homage to Canada's newest province, I was struck by the way strong regional loyalties can co-exist with a love of country in Canada. In that sense,

B.C. resembles Newfoundland and Quebec much more than Ontario, where a sense of entitlement has made the provincial identity much less marked. My St. John's hosts presented me with a cape of warm Grenfell cloth. Normally, I receive gifts of clothing with thanks but leave them in the box. Not this time — I was freezing.

After the celebrations in Ottawa, I was confronted by media asking me about the government's purchase of the Mulroneys' furniture. I was taken by surprise, having no idea why it would be an issue. Since all I could think of was the unnecessary expense that would be incurred in changing the perfectly acceptable decor, I said that I had no objection to having second-hand furniture at 24 Sussex Drive. I didn't realize what an issue the furniture question would become, so my pleasure in Canada Day was undimmed as I proceeded to Vancouver. It was a heavenly evening as I arrived at Canada Place at about 7 p.m. By the time I got home to bed, it was 11 p.m., twenty-three hours after I had arisen in St. John's.

Because I had been in Vancouver during the 1984–88 Conservative mandate, I was largely unaware of all the controversy surrounding the redecoration of 24 Sussex Drive and the question of who had paid for the furnishings: the Conservative Party or the Mulroneys themselves? Of course the issue was reported in Vancouver, but it was very much an Ottawa story. The Mulroneys said they had borrowed money from the party and repaid it. It never occurred to me that the NCC would buy the furniture without proper documentation. However, I was now astonished to learn that in fact there were no receipts, and there was some difference of opinion as to the actual value of the goods. Finally, there was the question of whether a sitting MP (which Brian Mulroney still was) or a member of his family (the transaction was with Mila) could do business with the government in this way. It appeared not.

After discreet entreaties from my office and the party, the deal was cancelled and Mila Mulroney mailed back the cheque, but not without a self-justifying letter that generated another round of hostile letters to the editor. It was another indication of the widespread resentment towards the Mulroneys and what were seen as their "imperial" and big-spending ways. I suspect the Mulroneys were genuinely puzzled by this reaction. They took pride in doing things well and with style on behalf of Canada. The problem was that there was a great deal of cynicism about who, in fact, was the ultimate beneficiary of this largesse — Canada or Brian Mulroney. Also, Canadians seem to resent public figures who take obvious pleasure in the trappings of wealth and power, as the Mulroneys appeared to do. I remember during one meeting with Mulroney, we got to talking for some reason about the style of party events. He quoted a party member as saying that before he became leader, the party had entertained with "Styrofoam cups." "Now," said the PM proudly, "we do things first class."

During the leadership campaign, I had said I would work with the provinces to develop a national fiscal plan that would address not only the federal debt and deficit, but those of the provinces as well. Otherwise, the efforts of the two levels of government were likely to continue at cross purposes, as when a Mazankowski budget reduced federal taxes to stimulate economic activity only to have the provinces raise their own taxes to fill the "tax room" left by the federal budget. Moreover, because the provinces had constitutional jurisdiction over the design and delivery of social programs, there couldn't be reform in that area without close cooperation between the two levels of government. Because I had served at all three levels of government, I understood the challenges facing provincial governments and had considerable sympathy for them. I believed that a clear demonstration that the federal government would no longer act unilaterally in ways that heavily affected provincial areas of responsibility could make for a fairer federalism. For all these reasons, one of my top priorities now was to develop a relationship of trust and cooperation with the provinces. As soon as I was elected leader, I invited the provincial premiers to a meeting in Vancouver to be briefed on the upcoming G-7 meeting in Tokyo and to begin discussions of the country's financial situation. I was well aware that concrete results would be unlikely until my government had received an electoral mandate. However, I wanted to set the stage and feel out the premiers on their thinking.

All the premiers except Ontario's Bob Rae, who decided it was just a photo op, accepted the invitation, as did the two territorial leaders. Unfortunately, Newfoundland's Clyde Wells missed the plane connection because of bad weather and was unable to attend.

I entertained the premiers at a working dinner on July 4, the day before I was to depart for Tokyo. We gathered around a large square table in a dining room of the Pan Pacific Hotel, with a magnificent view of Vancouver harbour. Premier Bourassa, whose battle with skin cancer had raised serious concerns about his health, sat on my right looking relaxed and energetic despite the long flight. His constructive and supportive attitude contributed greatly to the consensus that emerged. The G-7 briefing was not just a courtesy. Premiers had particular ideas about some of the issues. Even when they didn't have jurisdictional responsibilities, such as over the deployment of Canadian troops in the former Yugoslavia, they brought the views they were hearing from their constituents and helped to provide a corrective to an overly "Ottawa-centred" perspective. Because a discussion with President Clinton about his plans for the ratification of the North American Free Trade Agreement by the U.S. Congress would be on the agenda for our private meeting, the discussion of American intentions was particularly interesting. The premiers shared their insights from the meetings they had had with governors of the U.S. border states. This active exchange between provincial governments and the governments of neighbouring states is often overlooked by Ottawa as a source of political intelligence.

After the G-7 discussion, we began to talk about domestic issues, particularly the ongoing discussions on duplication and overlap between the two levels of government. My concern was that, in view of the uncertainty of my own government's mandate, the provinces would be inclined to let those processes, which had only recently been put in place, lapse until after an election. In my opinion, there was an urgent need to continue the work of the various committees and task forces, no matter what party formed the next federal government, and they agreed to keep going.

As we continued the discussion of the fiscal pressures being felt by all governments, I was struck by the consensus among the premiers present, who represented all three major Canadian political parties. As I drew them out on how we might approach the challenge of health care funding, for example, I was inwardly very encouraged that there was, indeed, an opportunity to "de-partisanize" the issue. Most surprising, and gratifying, to me was that they didn't gang up on me, but talked constructively about the problems.

I'm not naive about the politics of federal-provincial relations. I come from a province where running against Ottawa is common in provincial campaigns. But we all knew how tough the challenges facing us were, and I could see that the premiers recognized the political credit that a more consensual approach could now bring. The positive mood of expectations exceeded was reflected in the comments the premiers and territorial leaders made to the press. As I walked out of the meeting, Alain Gourd, the one federal official who attended to keep a record of the meeting, smiled delightedly at me — pleased and surprised at how well it had gone.

On July 5, before flying to Tokyo, I called Premiers Rae and Wells to brief them. Fortunately, I had seen Premier Wells on Canada Day, so we had already had an opportunity to break the ice. I was determined not to let Bob Rae use me to build on the Ontario-versus-Ottawa theme he had been developing in recent months. For the first time, a premier of Ontario was beginning to question the province's role in Confederation and, quite aside from my inherent scepticism as a British Columbian about protestations of Ontario's weakness or lack of political clout, I thought it was a dangerous road. The well-being of Ontario, economically and socially, was of vital importance to all Canadians. I can't imagine a greater foolishness for a federal government than to neglect Ontario. Aside from the political value of a province with 40 per cent of the country's population, the economic performance of Ontario is key to the achievement of any redistributionist policy we might have as Canadians. Three provinces are net contributors to equalization as of this writing: British Columbia, Alberta, and Ontario. No one would dispute that Ontario's is the lion's share of that contribution.

If I occasionally had to pinch myself to be sure that I really *was* prime minister of Canada, I knew it for certain when I found myself sitting practically alone in a room with Bill Clinton. It was Friday, July 9, and we were meeting in a small sitting room in the American embassy in Tokyo, with just one official from each of our governments in attendance. When I had first been introduced to the president two days earlier at the opening talks of the G-7 summit, my reaction was that this was a highly intelligent man who had the confidence to be simple. The president of the United

States has no need to put on airs; he carries with him just by virtue of his office an enormous stature. It seemed to me that Bill Clinton understood this well.

Having spent most of 1994 in the United States, I now find it difficult to separate my initial and personal impressions of President Clinton from all the gossip and controversy that have increasingly surrounded him. In the summer of 1993, he was still fairly new in the job. As we spoke that day, sunlight was streaming through the window and onto the president. Even though I was looking directly at him, I remember thinking that his face had a slightly blurred quality, perhaps a result of fatigue and the huge burden of his office. As we completed the discussion of our bilateral concerns, I said that I thought this was a particularly difficult time to be president of the United States. The U.S. was now the only superpower, and defining just what America's role was to be in the new post–Cold War world was a challenge. I offered Canada's help and support in that process of redefinition.

The G-7 summit is the most high-profile gathering of world leaders in the year. With the end of the Cold War, the presence of the Russian president for meetings at the end of the regular agenda had further heightened international interest in the gathering. How I fared at the summit would be a crucial factor in my credibility as a prime minister. In a note to me entitled "The Summit, Media and Canadian Politics," communications adviser David McLaughlin wrote, "The media politics for Summits are relatively simple: Find or create a mistake." He went on to say that the media "are cynical about the process and substance of summits and hence, will seek to magnify any perceived 'mistake'. Their focus will be on process as much as policy; on details of protocol arrangements (i.e. snubs and order of precedence) as much as the broader sweep of the communiqué." He concluded that our goal should be "error-free ball … No mistakes, a tight focus and exceeding low expectations."

Perhaps nothing did more to convince the Canadian press that I could be a serious player on the international stage than the success of my participation at the G-7 and, in particular, my meeting with President Clinton. When I objected to Canada's not receiving prior notice of the cruise missile attack on Baghdad two weeks earlier, Clinton apologized. A vigorous defence of Canadian "cultural protectionism," which the president asked me to repeat over lunch with his and my senior cabinet officials, also made the news. Oblivious to some of the finer nuances of international summitry, I realized only later that Canada had been singularly honoured when the president not only gave me a lift back to the summit in his limousine after lunch but also instructed that the Canadian flag be flown from the flagstaff on the right front fender. The meeting helped to establish that my relationship with the president would be cordial but not subservient.

Many months later, I answered a query about whether I had ever been to Japan in the negative, then suddenly corrected myself, remembering my visit to Tokyo. It's not surprising, in a way, that I don't have the feeling of really having "been" in Japan. On our arrival, Perrin Beatty, secretary of state for external affairs, Gilles Loiselle, minister of finance, and I were whisked through empty streets that had been cleared for security reasons. (Trade Minister Tom Hockin had preceded us there for the delicate discussions that would determine the success or failure of the Uruguay round of the GATT talks.) None of the teeming street life of the Japanese capital was visible to us. Our hotel was like a new international-class hotel anywhere in the world. Only the television programming indicated that we were, in fact, in Japan. The G-7 meetings were held in the Akasaka Palace, modelled on the palace of Versailles. Nothing could have evoked Japan less than its gold leaf, rococo decoration, and heavy draperies. Even the banquet hosted by the emperor and empress was in a pavilion that appeared to have been purpose-built for such occasions, with little to identify it as Japanese. We sat down to European cuisine eaten with Western silver cutlery. Prime Minister Kiichi Miyazawa entertained at a traditional Japanese lunch, but we could have been in a good Japanese restaurant in Vancouver or Montreal. Ironically, the most "Japanese" of the places we visited was the new Canadian embassy building.

G-7 summits consist of a number of sessions with the leaders alone, including a dinner with no officials other than translators. Finance ministers and foreign ministers have separate meetings. Then a large, combined meeting is held to finalize the communiqué. I enjoyed meeting the other participants. John Major was delightful, and his wry interpretations of François Mitterrand and

Helmut Kohl in the context of Europolitics were both funny and informative. Whatever one might think of the specific policies they and their governments had supported, Mitterrand and Kohl were moving figures, the last Western European leaders with a direct connection to World War II. As the prime mover of German reunification, Kohl had also put his stamp on the shape of post–Cold War Europe. In contrast to the enormous bear-like Kohl, Mitterrand had a cadaverous quality, with his skin pulled tight against his skull, a result of both age and the cancer from which he was suffering. Our host, Prime Minister Miyazawa, had huge political problems as the G-7 establishment descended upon him. Unfortunately, his excellence as a host and the unexpected successes of the summit would not help him with his domestic problems. He was out of office not long after the meetings. (An observation he could equally make about me!)

The summit proper started that afternoon with a reception and the taking of the official photo. Then began the first three-hour session among the leaders. We met around a circular table, just big enough for us all to sit comfortably. Each leader had one official or sherpa present, seated somewhat behind the leader at a desk equipped with telephone and fax, enabling the sherpa to be in contact with the rest of the delegation in case information was needed. The electronic equipment was of the quietest kind, and the sherpas for the most part kept their conversations hushed. The result was a surprisingly intimate atmosphere around the table. I spoke about the need to explore the serious problem of unemployment in our economies through the possibility of greater cooperation on structural and labour-market issues. President Clinton proposed an employment summit, to be hosted by the United States.

Our meeting over dinner that night was even more intimate. No officials were present, although Mitterrand and Kohl had their translators with them. The mood of the discussion was serious but warm. The opportunity to meet informally really does enhance the personal connection among leaders. We were all facing the same pressures, and I felt my shyness melt away in an atmosphere of collegiality. The working dinner was billed as a political discussion, as opposed to an economic one, and I had been asked to lead it off. I proposed that we talk about how we were going to deal with the urgent need to find a new framework for international intervention and, in particular, whether the United Nations could be made to function effectively as an instrument to deter aggression in the post–Cold War world. The cloud of Bosnia hung over us all. I was particularly struck by Helmut Kohl's concern about the dangerous precedent being set of altering European borders by force.

Our working sessions continued the next day, followed in the evening by the state banquet at the Imperial Palace. I lay down for a quick nap before getting dressed and awoke to discover to my horror that I had ten minutes to get ready. I moved as fast as I could, but I was obviously going to be late. I dressed in a navy blue outfit with long sleeves, having been advised that, according to imperial court etiquette, my arms should be covered. When I arrived, slightly out of the order required by the strict protocol of who should arrive when, I was amused to see that the empress and the crown princess were both in short-sleeved gowns. A comment by Prime Minister Miyazawa led me to believe that perhaps I had been given advice that applied to the late Emperor Hirohito's time. After all the heads of government had arrived, we assembled for a formal portrait. The spouses (all wives, as it happened) sat in the front row and the heads of government stood behind. The empress sat and the emperor stood behind her. Miyazawa was shocked that anyone would sit in the presence of the emperor while he was standing. "That would never have been allowed with the old emperor," he muttered disapprovingly.

The cynical Canadian press had to concede that the summit had gone well for me. Trade ministers had made a welcome breakthrough in the GATT talks. I had made no gaffes and had clearly defined a friendly but independent posture with respect to the United States. I could link my government restructuring, especially the creation of the new Department of Human Resources, to the ministerial-level meeting on employment proposed by President Clinton. I could point to the opportunity I had seized of addressing bilateral and multilateral issues of importance to Canada, such as our trade disputes over softwood lumber and wheat with the U.S. and the east coast fisheries agreement with the European Community. I had been asked to lead the important political discussion, which I had turned to an issue of great importance to

Canadians, the future of the peacekeeping role of the United Nations. From the media perspective, we had succeeded in playing the all-important "error-free ball."

My last event before departure was a bilateral meeting with President Boris Yeltsin. Meeting Yeltsin was a memorable experience for me. As much as anyone there, I understood the political milieu from which he had arisen and the huge challenges facing his country, politically, socially, and economically. Trying to create democracy and a modern economy in Russia was a dangerous voyage into the unknown. Notwithstanding my fascination with the political histories of Mitterrand and Kohl, Yeltsin, in my opinion, was the giant in that company.

It was almost 9 p.m. when I arrived at the meeting place in the hotel. To Yeltsin's surprise, I began chatting with him in Russian, explaining that I had spent three months in the Soviet Union in 1972 and that since that time my spoken Russian had slipped somewhat. After the obligatory photos, we began the formal discussion through our translators. He invited me to visit Russia, and I said I would be delighted to come, but "no hunting." Yeltsin felt it necessary to launch into a tirade blaming Prime Minister Mulroney's photographer for distributing the infamous "dead boar" picture to the media. (Mulroney's photographer claimed it was Mrs. Yeltsin's photographer who was responsible for the leak.) The meeting concluded amicably, after a discussion in which I pressed for payment of our outstanding wheat account and communicated a number of concerns relating to the uncertainty of Russian banking procedures and regulations. Later I discovered that my brief chat with President Yeltsin in Russian had thrown my officials into confusion, because they didn't know what I was saying. Perhaps they thought I was making commitments they didn't understand — "The cheque is in the mail, Boris" — I don't know. My Russian was far too rusty for me to get into much trouble!

The next morning I had breakfast for the last time in the dining area of my small but elegant suite under the watchful eyes of the enormous Daruma doll, a large head in traditional Japanese style, which our delegation had presented to me on my arrival. It is the Japanese custom when beginning a major undertaking to paint one eye of the Daruma doll, and then, when the project is completed, to paint the other. I had duly painted in the first black dot, and all week this one-eyed creature had kept an eye on all my comings and goings. My officials and staff had been exuberant as we convened back in my suite Friday night to paint the Daruma's second eye. What had promised to be an inconclusive meeting had proved unexpectedly substantive and successful.

The first phase of the post-leadership whirlwind was now complete. Restructuring, cabinet-making, first ministers' meeting, and G-7 were now all successfully behind me. So far, I was enjoying being prime minister!

15

No, Prime Minister

FOR THE LEADERS of the 1993 election campaign team, front-page pictures of Prime Minister Kim Campbell dancing the twist provided one of their most gratifying moments of the summer. If the goal was to communicate that I was different from my predecessor, I had certainly done that! The occasion was a reception at the Art Gallery of Ontario following the July 22 showing of Ron Mann's film *Twist*, and the media solemnly compared the significance of my demonstration of this dubious accomplishment to that of Pierre Trudeau's somersaults off a springboard when he first became prime minister.

The summer of 1993 was a summer of contradictions. While my political stock rose dramatically, strengthening my hand in a number of areas, in others I was unable to do what I wanted to do. The power of a party leader derives fundamentally from the belief of others that he or she can gain or keep political power for the party. Power is the ability to influence events in such a way as to achieve your desired outcomes. During the time that I was leader of the Conservative Party, I learned a great deal about the reality of political power.

In my first month as PM, my political strength grew considerably. I had emerged from the leadership campaign weakened by the onslaught of criticism and the unavoidable failure to meet expectations. The change in my fortunes was a reflection of two things: the success of my early actions as prime minister, and the apparent willingness of the media to turn the page once I had, in fact, won the leadership. Whether they were just tired, or whether they had simply decided that Kim Campbell as prime minister was a new and different game from Kim Campbell as leadership candidate, the media appeared to be giving me a fresh start. The decisiveness of the restructuring and the success of my first international venture seemed to have removed any doubt about the wisdom of the Tories' choice. In the course of the summer, I would attain the highest approval rating for a prime minister in thirty years. This increased my ability to get cooperation from people who now assumed that I might be prime minister for some time. All of this, however, was of little use to me in winning the battle over how I would spend my time during the less than two months that remained between my return from Tokyo and the last date on which I could call an election.

Although my goal was to demonstrate that I represented change, one area where I deferred without demur to the knowledge of my predecessor was with respect to running a national campaign. Brian Mulroney knew the party inside out and had led two national campaigns. I, on the other hand, was relatively new to the party, and my experience in the last election had been as a new candidate, confined to my own constituency. The formal leadership structure of the party was not something I had the power to change; the officers were elected by the party in convention. I also knew from reading about other leadership changes that every leader must recognize that those who may have been instrumental in winning the leadership campaign do not necessarily have the skills to run a general election campaign. I knew my limitations, although time was to show that perhaps I should have trusted my own instincts and placed more value on the abilities of my closest associates.

The leaders of the campaign team were John Tory, the chairman, and pollster Allan Gregg. Who were these people to whose greater campaign wisdom I felt I should defer? A Toronto lawyer, the aptly named John Tory had for years been a key player in the Ontario Conservative establishment. He is an extraordinarily nice person, a true boy scout in the best sense of the word. This gives him a certain Teflon quality. Ignoring his role in directing the disastrous 1987 Larry Grossman campaign in Ontario, Mulroney had called on him to take on the upcoming federal campaign. Later, as our own campaign began to falter, resentment about John's role in the Grossman campaign would surface, but I heard only vague murmurs about it during the summer of 1993.

Allan Gregg had originally been brought into Tory election planning by Joe Clark, but Mulroney was impressed by him and kept him on as the party pollster. With his long hair, earring, and trendy clothing, Allan had created an incongruous image for a Conservative adviser, but his role in two successful election campaigns had won him considerable loyalty in the party. By 1993, however, he was tiring of the public opinion research business and had announced his intention to sell his interest in his company, Decima Research. He was increasingly turning his attention to the entertainment world and, in particular, the management of the successful rock band The Tragically Hip. There was another, sadder preoccupation vying for Allan's attention and emotional energy that summer, the grave illness of his wife, Marjory, whose breast cancer would finally claim her life in early 1995.

Looking back now, it's easy to speculate on what I might have done differently. As soon as I was sworn in, I could have gone to John and Allan and said, "If I'm to have any hope of winning this election, I have to have a campaign team that represents a clear break from the Mulroney era, run by people who know me and understand what I'm about. It's a huge risk, but I believe it's the only hope I have of convincing voters that I really am new and different." This would have been an enormous gamble, and I don't see how I could have taken that step. Coming out of the leadership campaign, the party had divisions that needed to be overcome if we were to run an effective campaign at all. I think such a move would have been interpreted as arrogant — Kim Campbell rejecting all that savvy help for her band of relative neophytes.

The truth was, I didn't yet know who could replace the existing team. Certainly Ray Castelli wasn't willing to take on the direction of a national campaign. Asking Norman Atkins, who had chaired the 1988 campaign, was an option, but it would have angered the critics of that campaign. I needed time to get a sense of who the experienced campaigners were and their strengths and weaknesses. Even knowing what I know now, I don't think finding new people to lead the campaign would have changed the outcome for me, although it might have for the party. If I had made major changes, and if the party had held together for the campaign and won, say, thirty to sixty seats, the conclusion of the Mulroney loyalists would have been that Kim Campbell had rejected the advice of her much more experienced predecessor and led the party to disaster!

Although I wasn't an experienced campaign organizer or strategist, I was a sufficiently experienced campaigner to know that I needed to rest and devote time to the policy message of the upcoming election. I had been very fit in the fall of 1992 at the beginning of the referendum campaign. In September 1992, I had told Ray Castelli that I had a feeling I would be campaigning nonstop for the next year. In fact, it was to be fourteen months to the date of the 1993 election. As the Charlottetown referendum campaign progressed, my exercise time began to disappear, a process that continued throughout the leadership campaign. Although my stamina had been legendary among my ministerial staffers, by the summer of 1993 I was tired mentally and physically.

When I returned from Tokyo on July 10, the integration of the campaign planners and the Prime Minister's Office was a fait accompli. John Tory and Allan Gregg were now intimately involved in the development of my schedule. The battles began. Already it had become apparent that my presence in public generated excitement. John and Allan argued that I must travel around the country meeting Canadians before the election campaign, and they proposed a gruelling schedule of community events and barbecues. I, on the other hand, thought it was crucial for me to spend time in Ottawa, leading the policy process and building myself up physically for the ordeal of the campaign. John Tory and I had knock-down, drag-out fights about this. "There are two reasons why I must get some rest," I argued. "First, my French deteriorates when I'm tired, and second, people who are tired make mistakes." I had no illusions about the kind of exposure and scrutiny I would be under once the campaign began. I had had a foretaste during the leadership race and knew the election would be worse. Fatigue is a great enemy of patience and judgment.

So why didn't I win the battle? As John and Allan put it to me, "Unless you are prepared to travel, we're not even in contention!"

John promised that my schedule would make room for exercise. Every week, when I received the schedule with no time set aside, he would promise on his honour that the next week's would resolve the problem. It never did.

It wasn't just my physical condition that suffered. Because I was away most of the time, the campaign team didn't have a chance to get to know me. I got along well with John Tory, our battles aside, but he had very little idea of what I was about. Because Mulroney had named him campaign chair before the leadership campaign, John had felt he should remain neutral during that race. He confided to me during the summer that he had originally accepted the job as a last gesture of support for the PM, but without any hope or expectation that the Tories could win. Perhaps that is why he apparently felt no need to understand the person who would be the standard-bearer in the upcoming election. After I won the leadership, the clerk of the Privy Council showed me documents and papers prepared on the basis of the positions I had taken during the contest, and I assumed similar efforts had gone into familiarizing the senior public service with the views of Jean Charest. But what the public service took as a natural obligation appeared never to have occurred to the campaign leadership.

My absence from Ottawa also meant that there was little time to sit with colleagues, advisers, and staff to consider the basic messages of the campaign. Shortly after the convention, my former student Andy Stark ("become a star"), now the holder of a Harvard Ph.D. and a position in the University of Toronto's Faculty of Management, presented me with a series of policy papers prepared by thinkers and academics across the country. In response to my request to begin the process of reaching out beyond the normal sources of advice to a prime minister, Andy had asked experts in a variety of areas to prepare advice for action by a new prime minister. In addition, all during the leadership I had urged my colleagues to prepare policy advice for me. Many backbenchers were extremely knowledgeable about various public policy issues. Here was their chance to get in on the ground floor of a new government's agenda, and they took up the challenge with gusto. Cabinet colleagues did the same. The papers filled two large binders. My own policy booklet from the leadership was of necessity somewhat general in nature; I was determined not to commit to anything that I couldn't deliver as prime minister. Still, it indicated my priorities and the direction of my thought. Following a two-day session of caucus to consider policy issues, we developed a strong consensus.

On my return from Tokyo, I had told John Tory that I wanted to spend time in Ottawa to drive the policy process. His response had been that others could do that for me — my job was to get out and meet the voters. And so a policy team was drawn together under the direction of Lowell Murray. Unfortunately, the results were meagre. Time was short, and without the direct intervention of the prime minister, it was difficult to get the kinds of information and ideas we needed out of the departments. In many cases, the ministers were trying to get a handle on new issues and responsibilities. I never understood what use, if any, was made of the policy suggestions I had received. One meeting to consider Andy's proposals ended indecisively. In my absence, the meetings tended to err on the side of caution. Knowing that my approach to consultation was central, Cindy Boucher offered to develop detailed proposals on consultation for the election platform, but received no response.

A series of speeches was planned by the policy team for the summer. The first, on the theme of integrity in government, was actually quite good. I delivered it in Vancouver on August 9. The firm commitments to reform MPs' pensions and to open up many patronage positions to Canadians in general were well received. In an unprecedented move, we advertised in the *Canada Gazette* for about a thousand positions that had previously been filled by a closed political process. I did not disavow patronage; on the contrary, I said that where the positions involved *making* policy as opposed simply to implementing it, it was appropriate for an elected and accountable government to appoint like-minded people. In my observation, however, the use of patronage is no guarantee of loyalty. In Stalin, it led to paranoia, and in Brian Mulroney, a lesser but still formidable practitioner of the art, anger and disillusionment at those who, having "got theirs," were not averse to biting the hand that fed them.

Meanwhile, the campaign team was taking its own look at government policy and forming its own positions. I will never forget a meeting I had with members of the team in Toronto on August 20. John Tory, Allan Gregg, Pat Kinsella, Lowell Murray, and Jodi White were there. The subject was helicopters. The government's decision to purchase new EH-101 shipborne and search-and-rescue helicopters had become a political football, and the campaign team's proposal was to cancel the purchase. I was stunned. How could I perform such an about-face? Moreover, if we did that, all the people who understood the issue would be on our backs. It was bad public policy, pure and simple, and I wasn't having any part of it. The atmosphere in the room was decidedly unpleasant. Lowell was the only other person who seemed to see the peril in a change of direction. What struck me was the underlying mood of threat. The suggestion, carefully put, was that if I was not prepared to take the committee's advice, perhaps I should find someone else to run the campaign. I didn't care what the polls said: I thought they were wrong, and I refused to budge. They didn't resign and that was that, or so I thought.

Reflecting on the summer of 1993, David Camp believes that while I may have been ready to be prime minister, I was not yet ready to lead the party into a campaign. I didn't know the campaign operatives in the Conservative Party, and I hadn't had adequate time to develop a message that would communicate my vision of change. However, shortly after the convention, John Tory told me that we were ready to fight an election at any time I might wish to call one, although "We'd be readier on September 8 than on August 11," the two dates being considered. I would discover later that John's idea of "being ready" was not what I thought "being ready" meant.

Travelling constantly kept me in a bubble, and my sense of not being completely on top of things made me anxious. I had to rely on Jodi back in Ottawa before she and I had really had a chance to build a comfortable relationship. Whenever the pace slowed down enough for me to reflect on the big picture, a nagging sense of worry overtook me. Out on the road, I enjoyed what I was doing and the frenzy of activity served to distract me from my sense of doubt. As it did when I was a minister, my work followed me wherever I went; there were always memos to read and decisions to make.

Nor did political crises elude me. At the end of July, I was faced with the necessity of making a quick decision about whether three Quebec MPs who had been charged with separate offences relating to their conduct in public office would be permitted to run on the Progressive Conservative ticket. It was a tough issue because they had not yet had their day in court. In the past, when an MP had been charged with an offence of any kind, he or she withdrew from caucus until the matter was resolved. That seemed to me to be the appropriate principle to apply here. I decided I couldn't sign their nomination papers under the circumstances. I knew that if they ran as Conservatives, all our candidates across the country would have to answer for them in a campaign. It wasn't fair to our other 292 candidates. I discussed the problem with Jean Charest; he wasn't supportive because one of the MPs, Gilles Bernier, had backed him. The other two, Carole Jacques and Gabriel Fontaine, had supported me. After my decision was announced, other Quebec MPs thanked me; they had been getting an earful on the doorstep. It was, however, a painful decision and didn't improve my relations with the Charest loyalists in Quebec.

Throughout July, the response to my public appearances was enthusiastic, but this in itself had the effect of throwing my schedule off. In Charlottetown, for example, with the city full of tourists and an unusually large number of people on the streets, what should have been a fifteen-minute stroll one day turned into a mob scene for an hour and a half. The effect was to kill the time set aside for rest and reading. I love meeting people, but the energy required to connect and respond is enormous. I became more and more concerned about my ability to keep up the pace through an election if I didn't have some time off during the summer.

I met with Premier Bob Rae in Toronto in late July. He seemed determined to do most of the talking and went on at some length about the problems Ottawa was creating for Ontario. At the press conference following our meeting, his tone became more aggressive and hostile. I think in the end it served him poorly. When I later joked that Premier Rae seemed to have "sucked on a lemon" before meeting the press, there were knowing nods from some of the media people.

My meeting with Premier Robert Bourassa in early August was more conciliatory and more fruitful. The manpower training agreement between Ottawa and Quebec had expired in March

1993, a year earlier than those with other provinces, so there was both an urgency to negotiate a new arrangement and the opportunity to create something better than we'd had before. Not surprisingly, since education is a provincial jurisdiction, Quebec's position was that it should have a monopoly on training. The federal government's position was that because it was responsible for unemployment insurance and other aspects of economic policy, it had to play a role. The question of labour-market training was fundamental to my vision of the future of the Canadian economy. As I saw it, the issue was not primarily which level of government could keep which powers, but rather, how to serve Canadians most intelligently and effectively.

In anticipation of taking over the responsibility for labour-market training, Quebec had created a body, the Société québécoise de développement de la main d'oeuvre, known as SQDM. Because our government wasn't prepared to abandon its role in labour-market training, Bernard Valcourt proposed instead that the federal government join this consortium of government, employers, trade unions, and educational institutions. In this model, the federal government would continue to administer unemployment insurance, but the services of both governments would be offered from one location and be designed on the basis of the most complete and up-to-date knowledge of the labour market. Other provinces, in particular B.C. and New Brunswick, were interested in the model, and if we could get it up and running in Quebec, we could then look to use it in other provinces the following year. Although Quebec had wanted control over the whole area, Bourassa responded favourably to our approach.

Many of my activities as I travelled communicated a sense that I was new and different; for example, I took the subway in Toronto, and could actually give the price of a litre of milk on a national open-line radio show. There was some grumbling about my "barbecue circuit" being a form of taxpayer-paid campaigning, with the public events garnering most of the media attention, not the business meetings. However, our plan to give a number of major policy speeches proved too ambitious in light of the capacities of the policy team. A second speech in Kitchener on August 16 took up the theme of education. Although I could announce several substantive steps I had taken since becoming PM, there was a built-in limitation to what could be said about this primarily provincial responsibility. The speech was less successful than the one in Vancouver, resulting in a loss of momentum.

The development of a policy platform is a twofold process. First, you must determine the positions you want to take. Then you have to find the language that most directly and effectively communicates them. These decisions cannot be made at one sitting. Ideas need to be mulled over. None of this was possible in the short time available. Instead of staking out half-baked policy positions in speeches, I would have been better occupied hammering out those positions in a way that would withstand the stresses of an election campaign. As it happened, the positive parts of my policy speeches would be forgotten by the end of the summer, but the mistakes would stick like glue.

The pressure of time and my absences from Ottawa meant that I wasn't able to be hands-on in making sure that the government and the party reflected the changes I represented. Bill Neville and I had both been distressed to realize that we hadn't picked up on the lower status given to some of the women deputy ministers. Jodi White proposed that I invite the women deputies to lunch at Harrington Lake to discuss the matter with them, and I hastily agreed. We went ahead with the planned luncheon in August. I expressed my frustration at the oversight and listened carefully to the women, all very accomplished and experienced government managers, discuss their own views. The meeting was a success. I learned a great deal, and the deputy ministers were assured of my commitment to address the situation after the election.

But it wasn't just in the bureaucracy that women were upset. On August 12 I met with leading Conservative women in a roundtable discussion in which their anger at being excluded from the campaign planning was forcefully expressed. They had not worked to support a woman leader to be shunted aside by the old boys. Jocelyne Côté-O'Hara, Linda Oliver, Stella Torontow, Elizabeth Rosco — these women and the others present were experienced campaigners. Had I been able to re-make the campaign team, many of them would have been on it. Still, I was irritated to hear of these women's exclusion because when I had spoken to John Tory earlier in the summer about complaints I was hearing from experienced campaigners who felt shut out, he had assured me that they would be welcome to participate. Jodi and I agreed that there needed to be more input from women. Jodi undertook to follow this up and I undertook to speak to John. At least I had had the chance to hear these concerns directly. I would later find out that others had been unable to speak to me that summer.

As August progressed, a feeling of fatalism overtook me. While my approval rating was now over 50 per cent, the highest for a prime minister since the early 1960s, the party support numbers weren't following suit. On the one hand, I found the public enthusiasm gratifying. On the other hand, I was under no illusion about the extent to which it was the office itself that conferred a good part of the magic on my presence. Yes, my own personal style and accessibility were factors, as was the special pride felt by women. But I also knew that the response I was seeing would not necessarily be translated into electoral support.

Even at his lowest ebb in the polls, Brian Mulroney could generate excitement in a crowd. I had seen teenagers mob him as if he were a rock star. There is, at any given time, only one person who is the prime minister of Canada. That, and the fact that constant TV appearances have a way of conferring an aura of celebrity, make the opportunity to get close to the prime minister exciting for most people, regardless of their partisan loyalties. The excitement generated by my public appearances was certainly important in ensuring that people would be prepared to take a look at the Conservatives again. I knew full well, however, that it would not be enough to overcome the anger that had led to the change in its leadership in the first place.

A profound change had taken place in the Canadian electorate, one that had eluded many of the key players in our campaign. The Yes side of the referendum campaign had been unsuccessful in winning the confidence of Canadians, not seeming to understand the depth of their resistance and scepticism towards what they saw as elite processes designed to make fundamental changes to their government. The underlying disaffection was masked to some degree because, for the most part, the media were part of the elite that had supported the Charlottetown Accord. Although the Yes campaign had brought together the top campaign organizers from all three national political parties, the anti-government sentiment was most strongly directed towards the Conservatives, as the governing party. My call to do politics differently was a response to that deep disaffection and cynicism.

My approach to the use of power was dramatically different from what was customary in the federal government. I had already tested some of my ideas as a minister, and as prime minister I had taken several steps — the dismantling of parts of the patronage system, for example — to show my sincerity. My commitment to involve the provinces in making policy that affected their responsibilities and my proposal for an open budgeting process were designed to make it possible to create the support necessary to tackle the deficit both seriously and sensibly. But issues of process are difficult to translate into campaign imagery. Whereas I and those who had been closest to me in the leadership campaign believed that we needed some dramatic examples of a new way of doing things, the seasoned pros were reluctant to take risks.

In addition to a lack of time to hammer out more concrete proposals, part of the problem was an ambivalence on the part of some members of the campaign team about the Mulroney legacy. John Tory had, after all, been appointed to head the campaign by Mulroney and had supported his first leadership bid in 1976. Once Mulroney returned from Europe, he was in regular phone contact with John. Several times John begged me to phone him myself to receive his advice personally. But, although Mulroney had been most helpful when I had called on him for assistance after the leadership, I felt it would be harmful to our prospects if I answered yes when the media asked me if I had been speaking regularly to my predecessor. I was fastidious about not criticizing him, even when I was declaring my intention to do things very differently. The whole point of the leadership campaign was to put the party under new management. Any sense that Mulroney was still calling the shots would be the kiss of death. Sheila Copps had already taken to calling me "Brian Mulroney in a skirt."

The line was a delicate one to walk. After all, I was a Conservative, and my general approach to policy was consistent with the direction our party had been following since 1984. If anything, my goal was to get us more firmly on the track of what we had undertaken to do in 1984 — namely, to put the country on a firm financial footing. But Mulroney was very protective of his image and reputation, and the campaign team erred on the side of caution if any policy appeared to open the door to a criticism of him.

By the end of August, I had decided to call the election on September 8 for an October 25 polling day. Technically I could have delayed the election call for a few more weeks, which would have enabled us to call Parliament back and have a Speech from the Throne before going to the voters. However, an election after October 25 would have required a new enumeration of voters. This would have opened us up to charges of "desperately clinging to power at great and unnecessary expense to the taxpayers," and the effectiveness of Speeches from the Throne as a way to announce policy is marginal outside the Ottawa milieu. Without the opportunity to push some legislation through, the Throne Speech would be just as much a campaign promise as any other. Besides, we didn't have one to present. In spite of Brian Mulroney's claim to have left a draft Throne Speech for ready use, all there was in the cupboard was a collection of generalities.

As we approached the Labour Day weekend, a third policy speech on the economy was scheduled before the Edmonton Chamber of Commerce on August 30. It was overshadowed by one of the most extraordinary lapses of good taste I ever encountered in public life. The man appointed to introduce me launched into a long disquisition on the failure of my parents' marriage and other details of my personal life. There was a stunned, disbelieving silence in the room. As I rose to speak, I could see expressions of acute embarrassment on the faces in the hall as people wondered how I would respond. The only way to deal with such an offensive introduction was simply to ignore it. I still meet Edmontonians who feel the need to apologize for the incident, which I'm told led to a much overdue shake-out of the leadership of the Edmonton Chamber of Commerce.

After the Edmonton fiasco, I tried to focus on the small amount of free time that had survived in my schedule. In addition to being tired, I was lonely. In the eight and a half weeks between my return from Tokyo and the election call, I slept at Harrington Lake a total of only twenty-eight nights, eight of them in the last days before the campaign. Often I arrived around midnight and had little opportunity to enjoy company. Alix and her fiancé, David, accepted my invitation to fly out from Victoria to spend the

Labour Day weekend with me. I had recently begun to see Gregory Lekhtman, an inventor and manufacturer of medical electronics and fitness equipment, from Montreal. After being introduced in early August, we had had dinner together a couple of times in Toronto and Montreal. He was just back from Argentina, so I invited him and Pamela, who was now living in Toronto, to make up a house party for the weekend.

It seems odd to say that I felt lonely that summer. I was seldom alone. Although the members of the security detail took great pains to be unobtrusive, I still hadn't adjusted completely to their presence. During a brief July visit to see my sister in Victoria, I had learned that even a fitness walk required prior notice so that the Mounties could wear the appropriate clothing needed to precede and follow us without looking like police. When Gregory flew to Toronto to have dinner with me, my staff arranged a table in the restaurant of my hotel. I couldn't understand why Gregory seemed to be delaying our departure until finally he said, "Aren't they ever going to bring us a bill?" I explained that I had looked after it already (since he had flown in from Montreal just to see me, I thought I should pay for dinner), and so we got up to leave. I remember thinking as I looked over at another couple, "Well, at least we aren't the last ones in the restaurant." Just then, the other couple rose from their table; they were my RCMP security detail.

The campaign team had planned one final policy speech to be given in Ottawa on September 2. After the date had been announced, the policy team realized that the speech wasn't ready; nonetheless, we were committed. The schedule was being driven by the schedule, rather than by what we had to say. In addition, we were now planning for a September 8 election call, and I had been promised a week off to rest up, beginning August 30. As the date approached, I watched the week fill up with other events. I found it hard to object since I could see the importance of the various meetings. I felt very conflicted between my duty to meet these obligations and my concern about being ready to campaign. We had yet to hold a thank-you gathering for my leadership supporters. As other meetings and briefings were slotted in, my week's holiday dwindled to Saturday, Sunday, and Monday, with a television interview Sunday afternoon and a session with my French teacher each morning.

Unbeknownst to me, the August 20 meeting about the helicopters had not been the last word on the issue. John Tory kept lobbying for some sort of action around the PMO. Jodi White accepted his view that something should be done and approached DND. I was astounded when I was told that Defence had agreed to reduce the number of helicopters to be purchased by seven. In all my speeches on the subject, I had pointed out that the main costs were in the research and development, and that reducing the numbers bought would lead to marginal savings at best. Now Defence itself was suggesting just such a plan.

I was advised on August 31 that the announcement was to be the key part of the September 2 speech. Defence Minister Tom Siddon had apparently been persuaded to agree with it, and I was now being told that we could announce savings of $1 billion with a cut of seven aircraft. This was to be a compromise between outright cancellation, which I had stated clearly was a non-starter, and a commitment to cut government expenditure, even in areas of high priority. I was highly sceptical but I had no supporters — everyone insisted the helicopters were a terrible political liability. There was no time to argue the issue; the speech was set. Against my better judgment, I put the best face on it I could. It was a disaster. As I built up to the announcement, the audience expected a reaffirmation of my commitment to keep the helicopters. The announcement came as a surprise, and not a particularly pleasant one. The numbers that had been hastily put together weren't persuasive. From that point on, I was just another politician doing politically expedient things.

The September 2 speech was a preview of what would be wrong with our campaign. As Allan Gregg had clearly stated, the challenge we faced was to convince Canadians that Kim Campbell represented change. But for the campaign team, change meant doing the twist and knowing the price of milk. For the public, change meant not being an old-style politician. It meant integrity and not being subservient to public opinion polls. It meant leading a party that was not still controlled by the old boys.

Power, as I learned that summer, is much more than holding a formal position. If no one will support you, it matters little what your title is. I understood instinctively where I could push and where I couldn't. Reading the memoirs of Margaret Thatcher in

1994, I realized how unrealistic it had been for me to expect to be able to get my own way so soon after the leadership race and before winning an election. Having led her party for four years in opposition and trailed her party in popularity at her first win, it was not until after her second, post-Falklands electoral victory that the Iron Lady could finally put her own stamp on her government. As she herself says, leaders serve "on sufferance" until they have won an election, and I had yet to pass that test.

Alix, David, Pam, and Gregory were all at the party for my leadership-campaign volunteers held the evening of September 2. There was food and dancing on the outdoor patio at the National Arts Centre, and my house guests took the opportunity to get acquainted while I was mingling with my supporters. Finally, we made our way by motorcade out to Harrington Lake, where I deserted them for much of the next day for a final stint of work before the weekend.

Saturday was blissful. I went rowing on the lake with Gregory (under the eyes of the Mounties) and lounged by the dock talking to my sister. Gregory had brought several pairs of his Exerloper running boots and we all tried them out, leaping about on the lawn on powerful springs mounted on the soles. The boots so intrigued the ever-present Mounties that one of them actually came over to ask if he could try them himself. (The sight was particularly incongruous since, in order not to reveal the gun he was carrying, the bouncing officer kept on his suit jacket.) For entertainment that evening, I arranged for some women to come out from Ottawa to teach us line dancing. It was hilarious. On Sunday the weather turned stormy and I did a television interview at Meech Lake between bouts of thunder and lightning. Pamela headed back to Toronto that afternoon. Before she left, I asked her to accompany me on the campaign tour since I would have no other family with me. Because she is a professional historian, I suggested she could do what I regretted not having done during the leadership campaign: keep a journal.

That evening we had a concert. When Alix and I had attended the interfaith service at the leadership convention, we had both been thrilled by the voice of Floralove Katz, a lay cantor. As a surprise for my sister, and in honour of Gregory's birthday, I invited the couple who had introduced us, Bella and Jan Fooksman, to dinner and asked Floralove Katz to sing for us. For more than an hour, she enchanted us. The music went right into my core, leaving me soothed and relaxed for the first time in months. After a break for champagne and birthday cake, we continued to make music. Alix and I sang and Jan played his saxophone. It had been years since I had enjoyed such a musical evening, and for a few hours the burden of anxiety I had been carrying was lifted.

Monday was the last day of our idyll. In lovely weather we lazed about, savouring the last opportunity to talk. David, with his wonderful architect's eye, worked on a watercolour sketch of the living room. Dinner that night, just the four of us, had a poignant quality. Alix, David, and Gregory would all head home on Tuesday, leaving me to the final day's preparation for the election call.

16

THE ELECTION

Question: "Why did you lose the election?"
Answer: "Because we didn't get enough votes."

CAUTIOUS OPTIMISM WAS my frame of mind as I walked out of Rideau Hall into the sunshine the morning of September 8, 1993. The formalities of resigning my government concluded, I approached the microphone before a large group of reporters to make it official: Canadians would be going to the polls on October 25. Although our party support had lagged behind the Liberals' numbers for most of the summer, our own polls showed us now six percentage points ahead of them among decided voters — 35 per cent to 29 per cent — and in other public polls we were neck and neck. What increased our optimism was that my personal support as leader was 57 per cent, 10 per cent higher than the level of support for Liberal leader Jean Chrétien. Despite my misgivings about the way my time had been allocated, I had to admit that the polls were encouraging. The slow but gradual upward movement of our party support led me to wonder if perhaps I had been wrong and Allan and John had been right. I knew that the forty-seven-day campaign would be a tough fight, but if we got any breaks at all and if we could avoid serious errors, we might be in contention. Those were bigger ifs than I ever could have imagined that day.

Like the proverbial elephant being described by a group of

blind men, an election campaign looks very different from different perspectives. My perspective was that of the campaign events themselves. Images of long hours on buses and planes, exuberant crowds, interviews by sceptical journalists, press scrums, question-and-answer sessions with voters in town hall meetings or on open-line radio, and an endless succession of speeches and podiums constitute my campaign memory. Like me, the media experienced campaign events directly, but the perspective from which they viewed those moments could not have been more different. Our campaign organization saw and heard the campaign through the media, in images that didn't always correspond with what they were trying to achieve, and through the daily tracking of voter opinion. The voters, too, got their main impressions of the campaign through the media. Later, when it was all over, political scientists would provide yet another perspective, a perspective based on an analysis of the events set in the broader context of public opinion and Canadian history.

If I cannot entirely explain the outcome of the 1993 election, I can certainly share what it was like to be in the middle of it as party leader and prime minister. I can also share some of the things I have learned since then that make some sense of events that seemed so confounding to me at the time. A fellowship at the Joan Shorenstein Center on the Press, Politics and Public Policy at Harvard in 1994 gave me a chance to study the media coverage of the election. In the process, I read what political scientists had written about the election and gained a better appreciation of the daunting challenge facing the Conservatives in 1993. Pamela Divinsky's diary is also a valuable record of the mood of our campaign on the road and of my own frame of mind throughout that period. Because of the central role I played in the 1993 election, I cannot possibly distance myself sufficiently to be totally objective in analyzing it. My perspective is simply one of many.

As Allan Gregg studied the polling results at the end of the summer, he had concluded: "The propensity of people to vote Progressive Conservative is directly related to their belief that Kim Campbell is new and different." The campaign's purpose was to illustrate this. The challenge was to figure out how. There seemed to be two important aspects of the task: one was to avoid traditional rhetoric and the empty promises that generate so much voter cynicism, and the other was to come out from behind the podium and meet with voters in an intimate, unstructured, interactive manner that would inspire confidence. In my view, speaking realistically to the electorate was a matter of respect, but my desire to be straightforward created the first controversy of the campaign and almost derailed us on that first day.

After announcing the date of the election, I read a statement that contained the following words: "But there is more to economic success than bringing the deficit down. We will carry the cause of an active government that will work hard with Canadians to expand economic opportunity to create more and better jobs, to take advantage of trade abroad, to encourage small business, and to do better at education and at training. Jobs and greater opportunity are the key priorities for Canadians in the 1990s. And they will be our central priorities as a government."

During the question-and-answer period that followed, Edison Stewart of the *Toronto Star*, prefacing his question with the remark that Canadians wanted results and clear answers, asked, "I wonder if you can tell us realistically: how long do you think they'll have to wait before the unemployment rate is below 10 per cent?"

I responded by pointing out the problem of structural unemployment that was bedevilling all of the industrialized countries, and said, "So I think, realistically, all the developed industrialized countries are expecting what I would consider to be an unacceptable level of unemployment for the next two, three, or four years." I then noted some of the things I thought favoured Canada in this situation, namely, a system of government that could act decisively and a high level of natural and human resources. Since I had already reaffirmed my commitment to eliminate our budgetary deficit by the 1998–99 fiscal year, I concluded, "And I would like to see, certainly by the turn of the century, a country where unemployment is way down, and where we're paying down our national debt, and there's a whole new vision of the future opening up for Canadians."

Two things happened to these remarks. First, I had said that I saw unemployment falling to an acceptable level in "two, three, or four" years — that is, by 1997 at the latest, an estimate consistent with government and private-sector forecasts. But these words were "spun" by Jean Chrétien to imply that I had said there would be no reduction in unemployment until the year 2000. Second, a debate started in the media over whether my remarks constituted a "gaffe" or a new form of political integrity. The debate was complicated by the fact that it was based on Chrétien's distortion of what I had said. It became conventional wisdom that I had said there would be no new jobs until the year 2000! Initially, there was some tentative praise for my honesty, but the ensuing argument was not over whether the "2000" statement was true, but over whether it made strategic sense. The statement dominated the coverage, and my commitment to making economic growth and job creation central priorities of my government was completely ignored.

Finally, on September 14, the *Globe and Mail* carried an editorial entitled "A Gaffe Is When You Tell the Truth." It began: "Let's see if we've got this straight. Kim Campbell says something that everyone acknowledges to be true, and it's a 'gaffe.' Jean Chrétien vows to do something that everyone knows will accomplish nothing, and is said to offer 'hope.' It is any wonder the public thinks the press are out to lunch?"

After quoting the correct version of my words and confirming them with an analysis of the current unemployment prospects, the editorial concluded: "By our own, unscientific reading, the public's view of things is quite different. We don't sense much popular resonance in the media's 'gaffe' verdict. Indeed, we suspect the voters rather appreciate the Prime Minister's candour."

The *Globe*'s editorial was correct in identifying a minimum of negative reaction from the public on the issue. Although the controversy resulted in a brief drop in our support, by the end of the first week we had bounced back.

We knew before the Liberals unveiled their Red Book of policy on the eighth day of the campaign that the centrepiece of their policy was a job creation program based on $6 billion of spending on infrastructure. It was astonishing to me that anyone could take such a program seriously, because it involved an enormous expenditure of borrowed money to create a minuscule number of jobs. Moreover, it didn't begin to address the problem of unemployment created by changing or disappearing industries. Our approach to job creation was indirect, but ultimately more effective. We wanted to focus on retraining workers, promotion of small business, promotion of the commercialization of Canadian innovation in Canada, reducing the administrative and financial burdens of government on business, and promoting export markets.

The campaign events of the first week consisted of a bus tour in southern Ontario and Quebec, designed to translate these macroeconomic concepts into practical measures that could readily be understood. The first stop was an elementary school in Perth, where I talked to young children about books to mark International Literacy Day. A visit to a school in Pickering, where a course in computer-assisted design is offered as early as grade ten, was followed by a visit to Trenton Industries, where this design technique is used to create containers for an international market. The aim was to illustrate the different factors that would lead to future prosperity in Canada. The problem was that, however meaningful the approach was from our perspective — in this case, illustrating the importance of giving young people the skills that are needed in new industries — the media didn't appear to know what to make of it.

On the second day of the campaign we held a town hall meeting in the rural community of Utica, Ontario. The point was to show that we were responding to the real concerns that Canadians were facing, that issues like training and regulatory reform were not just abstract concepts but practical concerns for people in that agricultural community. Sensing that somehow the media weren't getting our overall message about a plan for economic growth and jobs that responded to the realities of today, I tried to reiterate the theme and the specifics of the approach in a long answer to a question in the press scrum following the meeting.

My answer concluded with the comment: "I am extremely optimistic about our ability to create jobs and opportunity for Canadians. But it requires making the right decisions. And one of the reasons why it's so important to get out and listen to Canadians is that it reminds you of where the problems are, so that we're solving today's problems, not the 1960s' problems. And the Canadian people have every reason to hope. This is a country that can thrive in the modern economy."

After this answer, I was somewhat astonished when Robert Fife of the *Toronto Sun* asked me: "Prime Minister, we've just come out of a bad recession, and as we did in 1984 when Prime Minister Brian Mulroney was running and he promised jobs, jobs, jobs, Mr. Chrétien has torn that same page out, he's promising jobs, jobs, jobs. He's offering hope to Canadians. I haven't heard — it's only day two, but — what kind of hope you are offering to Canadians who are out of work, who are on welfare?"

It seemed to me as if Fife had not heard a word I'd said, and had only been waiting to see my lips stop moving so that he could ask his question. In my irritation I replied, "Well, maybe you need a hearing aid. I *am* offering hope to Canadians, I'm offering Canadians a solid economy. I'm saying to Canadians that I'm going to put them back to work."

The "hearing aid" comment was seized upon and rightly criticized. I shouldn't have allowed myself to get so testy, but I was becoming frustrated at the surliness of the journalists who were travelling with us. As minister of justice, I had enjoyed a courteous and open relationship with the media. A number of beat reporters covered justice issues, and I had found it a pleasure to talk to journalists who understood the broader context of the stories they were covering. That openness had continued until the early days of the leadership campaign. But the phenomenon of "pack consensus" became frighteningly evident during the election campaign. The media, of necessity, travel in packs on campaign buses and airplanes. This creates a dynamic whereby the interpretation of events becomes uniform among them. Still, I sensed something else at play those first few days — an edge that I hadn't felt before. Much later I discovered that this was not a figment of my imagination.

It wasn't until the day after the election that I learned of a problem that had beset our relations with the media that first week of the campaign. For some reason, our campaign planners had decided to offer only the most spartan accommodation and facilities to the media corps travelling with us. It took almost no time for the journalists covering our campaign to learn that their colleagues on the Liberal leader's tour had access to cellular telephones on their buses, enabling them to file their stories en route, as well as amenities such as cappuccino machines. Several days into the campaign, my press attaché, Paul Frazer, mentioned to me that our press buses would be retrofitted with cellular phones, but I didn't know the whole story. It was a stupid mistake. To annoy the press corps deliberately was, to put it mildly, counterproductive. Had I known of the problem, I could have apologized for the oversight and tried to make amends. As it was, I didn't understand the barely veiled hostility of the reporters, and my sharp reaction only confirmed their view that our treatment of them was deliberate and condoned by me personally.

This unnecessary alienation of the press reflected our lack of a proper communications plan. When John Tory had told me in the summer that we were "ready" to fight a campaign, I certainly assumed that such a plan would be central to that readiness. The Liberals, on the other hand, had their communications plan worked out superbly. It was conventional wisdom among Tory campaign planners that the Liberals were making a big mistake in putting out their Red Book. There was great glee over the prospect of beating the Grits over the head with their own campaign promises. Unfortunately, just how we were going to do this was left somewhat vague. The Liberal plan was perfectly designed to capitalize on the strengths of their leader. What the Red Book did was make it unnecessary for Jean Chrétien to talk about policy. Whenever he was asked a question he didn't want to answer in detail, he could just say, "It's all in the Red Book." The Liberals were smart enough to know that few people would actually read the book all the way through. It was the perception of having a plan that worked in their favour. Few would know that a number of the Red Book promises were already completed Tory government policies! Even the silences of the Red Book worked for the Liberals. While I hammered away at the omissions — NAFTA, the GST, etc. — the Liberals could avoid the tensions and disagreements that would inevitably have been generated within their own party by more specific positions on these issues.

Where the Grits were superb in the campaign was in the area of "spin doctoring" — influencing the interpretation that the media would put on a particular statement or event. They were able to respond incredibly quickly to statements made by me because they had allocated a worker to follow our campaign on the road. Thus, on the first day of the campaign, that person relayed my remarks to the Chrétien tour right away, so that Jean Chrétien could create the "no new jobs till the year 2000" impression while the media were still trying to figure out what to make of my comments.

During those first weeks, the campaign strategy was clearly designed to show that I was very different from other leaders and my predecessor. Our public meetings showed that I understood the challenges of the economic transformation that was upon us and that I could deal with policy questions in a spontaneous way in direct discussion with the voters. Looking back, I am struck by how naive we were in thinking we could single-handedly change the dynamic of the campaign from the traditional "glib answer" approach to one of thoughtful dialogue. We hadn't fully appreciated the difference between the media's calls for a new way of doing politics and their ability to recognize it and cover it when they saw it. At one point, Edward Greenspon of the *Globe and Mail* remarked to Paul Frazer, "New politics, old media."

One of the places we visited that first week was the Crayola factory in Lindsay, Ontario. Since most Canadians had grown up with Crayola crayons, it seemed like a good place to talk about some of the changes taking place in the economy. Throughout the campaign, I tried to disabuse people of the notion that the "new economy" required everyone to become a computer operator. Some of the new skills were skills of organization and management, rather than of technology. Crayola had switched to high-velocity manufacturing, in which, instead of simply building up inventory, manufacturing is done to order. Because this type of production requires teamwork, the employees had had to learn new interpersonal skills. The workers talked about how they took pride in solving their own problems and brainstorming with their teams to resolve difficulties rather than turning to management. At the end of the discussion, the manager said, "We are just ordinary people, but together, we can do extraordinary things." I thought this summed up the challenge we faced as Canadians — to understand that the demands of the new economy were not beyond us if we understood what we needed to learn and do.

I began to take some good-natured ribbing from journalists over my continued use of the manager's comment in my speeches. A major problem with the relationship between candidates and the media lies in the need for the former to give the same message over and over. Journalists get bored hearing the same policies, jokes, or inspirational stories, and this leads them to look for something out of the ordinary to write about. If the campaign itself cannot satisfy that search for novelty, the media depiction of it strays farther and farther from the reality.

The two press buses on our campaign came to be known as "Smoke," for those journalists who smoked, and "Mirrors," for the well-groomed TV reporters. Our campaign bus didn't have a name, but our plane was christened "Helicopt-air" in honour of the controversy over the EH-101. The front of our bus was equipped with desks and electronic equipment, a washroom, and a place for food. The campaign team and staff rode up front in this section. Patrick Kinsella, Paul Frazer, my executive assistant, Frédéric Loiselle, personal assistant Mijanou Serré, and Pamela were regulars, supplemented by combinations of policy adviser Sharon Andrews, David McLaughlin, speechwriter Paul Therien, principal secretary Jean Riou, and later Jodi White and Wendy Waite.

At the back of the bus was the leader's compartment, with a washroom in one rear corner and an L-shaped couch in the other. Between the end of the couch and the dividing wall was a small desk with a chair and a cellular telephone. On the opposite side, next to the windows, sat a large recliner chair. I used the cellular phone with some caution, because the Mulroney cabinet had been severely lectured on the lack of security in cellular conversations. (Lest we ministers have any doubts, Perrin Beatty, communications minister at the time, brought a scanner to cabinet one day to demonstrate how easy it was to listen in on conversations.) Mostly I spent my time on the road reading briefing papers or trying to rest and collect my thoughts between engagements. Sometimes, if there was room, I moved up front to avoid the loneliness of sitting alone in the back.

When I first saw the compartment, it looked like a comfortable place to work and rest. That it wasn't was clearly demonstrated early on when we were travelling from Montreal to Ottawa and had two guests on the bus: Gregory, who was coming up to Ottawa to have dinner with me, and Robert Foster, chairman of the PC Canada Fund. Since what Robert wanted to talk about wasn't particularly confidential, Patrick Kinsella, who was in charge of the tour on the road, suggested that Gregory ride in the leader's compartment. The three of us tried to arrange ourselves as comfortably as we could. When I sat in the recliner chair, my feet couldn't touch the floor, so I tended to sit in a semi-reclining position. Unfortunately, the chair was bolted to the floor facing forward, making it difficult to talk to people sitting on the couch. Robert took the chair at the desk, which at least swivelled, enabling us to face each other. Gregory sat at the end of the couch, which was also too high for me to sit on with my feet on the floor.

The motion in the back of the bus was like riding in a Cuisinart. When I tried to sit at the desk and write, I couldn't read my writing. Because it was so dangerous to stand in the back while the bus was moving, Patrick would sit on the floor with his back to the dividing wall. We finally had grab bars installed so that people could stand safely and talk to me.

Pamela had arranged a leave from her job to help out and make a record of the campaign from the perspective of the PM's tour. Having a family member on the campaign was important to me, although since access is the name of the game in politics, her privileged access occasionally caused resentment. She and Patrick were my only confidants on the road. Pamela's record of what I really thought of our prospects during the campaign is a reminder to me now of how often my campaign optimism was at odds with my realism.

Pamela had an intimate view of the logistics of the campaign and how they worked or didn't work for me. On the long flight from Ottawa to Vernon, B.C., on September 14, she made her first journal entry, including a section entitled "Personal Issues." It is worth quoting at length because the issues she raised on this, the seventh day of the campaign, would continue to be problems for the next forty.

> The personal time is being eroded; there is not enough time carved out for personal rejuvenation. The PM is not sufficiently informed of scheduling. To be really effective, that is, authentic, passionate and committed, and to produce the personality of trust and connection to the public requires giving of the self in a substantive way. That takes energy, and it takes learning the issues. What is then needed is time to reload one's energies and that time is not being allotted. Down time does not necessarily mean time to do hair and nails ...

> Clothing is another issue. Packing: this is done by PM staff, but the PM still needs to make decisions about what to take and that requires forward knowledge of what events, locations and climate are going to be. The PM advisors are slow in getting this information to her. Again, inadequate forward planning. With men, presumably this is not an issue — three suits, four shirts and four ties, socks and two pairs of shoes do one for all occasions. Women's clothing requires more planning and co-ordination ...
>
> Speeches are extremely late getting to her. The speech she is meant to give in Vernon tomorrow to a class of political science students is being rewritten on the flight west. Kinsella does not like the speech and suggests to PM — on the plane — that perhaps she speak from notes rather than from text ... Schedule for the next day is also delivered on the plane, with no schedule of further days. This is a source of concern, and frustration. PM feels she needs more prep time. Excellent performance requires a certain comfort level, and while PM is adept at "winging it" — perhaps better than most — the gruelling pace and expectations, not to mention stake, of the campaign trail require more prep time. She is, after all, the creative centre — the quarterback — and she needs to be protected for the team to win the game.

Because the campaign headquarters' view of the campaign was based on the media coverage, by the second week of the campaign, friction was developing between the central office and the tour. The reality of what was happening on the road — happy crowds and good interaction — was different from the "reality" that the strategists at HQ saw in the press. Part of the problem was our slow response to what the other campaigns were saying and the lack of people on the tour who could spin the media messages. From the perspective of the tour, the strategic organization from HQ often seemed woefully inefficient. This included campaign events whose rationale was incomprehensible.

This confusion was apparent during my first visit to the Maritimes on September 18. During the leadership campaign, I had set out policy proposals to address some problems specific to Atlantic Canada. The original plan was that I would present these proposals in a policy speech during the summer, but the speech never appeared. When it arrived barely twenty-four hours before the September 18 deadline, it lacked any local colour or politically sensitive content. Like most of the draft speeches we received, it had to be rewritten on the road, requiring, as was not unusual, that the staff stay up all night to do it. The speech itself was delivered at Saint Mary's University in Halifax on a cold, rainy day. Initially, the audience wasn't overly friendly, but by the end, I was awarded a standing ovation. Unfortunately, the impact of the speech was diluted, first by the fact that I was delivering it on a Saturday, a notoriously bad media day, and second by the question-and-answer session that followed; media coverage of the more contentious questions displaced coverage of the speech. Finally, it was almost another three weeks before the Atlantic Canada strategy was available to our candidates in the form of a brochure they could share with their region's voters.

Although I tried to deal with the rough spots on the campaign as best I could, I was perplexed as to why they occurred at all. For example, on September 21, after a long day of Ontario events that took us to Wiarton, Owen Sound, and Walkerton, I was scheduled to fly out of Walkerton with four members of the campaign team in a small plane. On the way to the airport, we got lost, and the same thing happened when we arrived in Sarnia. The second time we were rescued by a scoutmaster in a mini-van who led our RCMP car to the Canterbury Inn. A partisan crowd of at least six hundred people were attending what was billed as a karaoke event. As it was about 9 p.m., past the time to expect a "media hit," my instructions were to speak briefly, then circulate through the crowd. Although I took my time going through the room, shaking hands and signing autographs, the organizers were angry because they had expected me to "perform." As uninhibited as I am, I would not have sung at such an event — and besides, I had been fighting a cold and needed to conserve my voice. Patrick was furious, seeing no apparent point to the event.

In her diary entry for that day, Pamela wrote: "In Sarnia the PM is distressed. She doesn't think that the team is on her side. Part of the problem is that the team members are not 'her' people, but rather from the Charest team or from the Mulroney team. She feels isolated and alone. At the same time she is not Mulroney and continues to be treated as if she were. (For example, everywhere we go the temperature in autos, buildings and planes is very cold which was Mulroney's desire. It is not hers. In general she is not accommodated as Kim Campbell, but rather is treated as a second-place Mulroney.)"

The whole organization of the campaign seemed designed for Mulroney, not me. Pamela was told that the reason the speeches and briefing notes arrived so late was that my predecessor had done things that way. Supposedly, he was handed speeches just before events and then read them without vetting them. I had always been told that he took considerable care about his speeches, so I found that hard to believe. The thinking behind the selection of events also took little or no account of how I was different, and there were virtually no women involved in the strategic planning. Those who were there, like Nancy Jamieson and Jodi White, were ignored if their views varied from the larger consensus. A campaign team that couldn't find a date until the last week for an event focussing on women put enormous importance on my opening the Indy car race in Vancouver!

Mulroney travelled with Mila during a campaign. She was an advocate for his comfort, a smoother of ruffled feathers, and a constant source of loving encouragement. At the end of her first journal entry, Pamela had written, "Exercise, clothing, maintaining healthy ego and battling exhaustion are issues I foresee will be of continuing concern." She talked with Patrick, who shared her concern, about ways of alleviating the stress of the campaign. Although eager to help, she did not have the status of a spouse, nor did she have the political experience that would have enabled her to intervene forcefully on my behalf.

Although I would occasionally express my exasperation over the logistical problems, if Patrick and John Tory couldn't sort them out, it was too late to allow myself to get upset. I had been spoiled during my four and a half years as a minister, working and travelling with people I knew and who understood my needs. Knowing what I know now, I should not have allowed the situation to deteriorate. Unfortunately, I didn't know then to what extent Ray was out of the loop. Many people forgot just how much of what they took for granted had been put in place to meet the needs of Brian Mulroney.

By the beginning of the third week of the campaign, it was clear that while the people who attended our town hall–type events liked the interactive format we were using, the media couldn't relate to it. On September 20, the policy team met with me to discuss the changes we needed to make in our strategy. A week earlier Allan Gregg had reported on focus groups he had been conducting. On the list of important issues, jobs were top, with 50 per cent, the deficit commanded 10 per cent, and free trade, 1 per cent. The Liberals' simplistic "public works" scheme was proving easier to communicate than our more complex approach to job creation.

I was open to a new strategy, even though we had recovered from a dip in support to be tied with the Liberals again. I agreed that it was appropriate to go on the offensive against the Liberal platform. The plan was for me to set out clear distinctions between our approach to jobs and the economy and that of the Liberals in a lunchtime speech on Wednesday in London, Ontario.

Although we had very few opportunities to see each other, Gregory and I were in regular contact by phone. Gregory had taken it upon himself to monitor the TV coverage and give me his sense of how my message was coming across. He also conducted his own informal surveys among people he met to see if they understood what I was trying to communicate. He wasn't encouraged by what he heard. On September 22 he stayed home in Montreal to watch the London speech. I hadn't liked the original draft of the speech, which, happily, I had seen on Monday. However, the final version was fine and I was able to deliver it forcefully, looking straight at the camera. Minister for International Trade Tom Hockin, who was the MP for that constituency, was enthusiastic about the speech, and my new, more combative tone received good reviews, no doubt because it was a form of political communication that journalists knew how to cover. When I spoke to Gregory before we left London, he was ecstatic. He loved the delivery, but more important, thought the message was punchy and to the point. As we headed into Quebec, spirits were high. Finally, we were setting the agenda for the campaign. Little did I know I was about to shoot myself in both feet.

The Quebec campaign organization operated completely independently of the national HQ and in 1993, it was a disaster. Despite my efforts to bring Charest supporters into the government and campaign, bitterness between the two leadership campaigns in Quebec remained strong. Every plus for a Charest supporter was seen as a negative by the Campbell camp. There was grumbling about who had really won the campaign. Many of Jean's supporters had not accepted the convention result, although Jean himself had been very careful to be supportive and our Quebec campaign kickoff had been a great success and demonstration of solidarity.

The tension between Campbell people and Charest people came on top of the customary division in the party between the Montreal and the Quebec City groups. I had named Charest supporter Pierre-Claude Nolin from Montreal as co-chair, with Marcel Danis, of the Quebec campaign. Nolin had been one of Brian Mulroney's last appointments to the Senate. My key supporters Pierre Blais and Gilles Loiselle were in the Quebec City group, which added to the tension with the Montreal-based headquarters. But it wasn't just a matter of inter-city rivalry. After the election, I encountered Montreal MP Gerry Weiner, who was minister of multiculturalism in my cabinet and a Campbell leadership supporter. He could barely contain his bitterness at what he felt was a total lack of support for his campaign from the Montreal HQ. Later in the campaign, there was speculation in the French-language press that Charest and his followers weren't really campaigning very hard for the party. Whether this was true I cannot say, but the accusation was fed by the deep divisions in the Quebec wing of the party that, as far as I know, still persist.

If there is one day in the campaign that I would like to wipe off the calendar, it would be September 23, 1993. The people on my tour couldn't see the rationale for an event that took me that morning into a riding we had no chance of winning, into the midst of a group of students who were ardent separatists. The location was the National Aerotechnical School in Saint-Hubert, a training facility designed to support one of the most important and growing industries in Quebec. After touring the school, I met with a large group of students in an open area surrounded by balconies draped with banners supporting separatism and the Bloc Québécois. I was relaxed and in good form and could feel the audience begin to warm to me as I dealt seriously but forcefully with their questions. Although it was hardly the sort of event designed to make me look good, I came out better than anyone expected.

From there, I went on to Saint-Bruno to tour a private-sector aerospace facility. Afterwards, a brief press scrum had been scheduled in the lobby to give me a chance to respond to a story that had been featured for the last two days in the *Globe and Mail*. The paper claimed it had a leaked document showing that the Conservatives had major plans for reforming social programs. I had made the commitment that the federal government would not act unilaterally to change social programs. While the national government contributes financially to these programs, they are the constitutional responsibility of the provincial governments. I knew first-hand how frustrating these governments found it when the federal government imposed changes upon them, usually as conditions of financial transfers, without a clear idea of the impact on service delivery. Reform of unemployment insurance was being discussed, but in conjunction with a re-examination of other income security programs. Bernard Valcourt had briefed cabinet in the summer about some of the work being done in his Human Resources Department, but no decisions had been reached, in deference to the need to engage the provinces in a dialogue. The NDP claimed to have a "secret document" that "proved" we had a "secret agenda." The cabinet briefing document in question was authentic, but it certainly did not indicate a secret agenda. If anything, it confirmed that our plan was to engage the provinces in a post-election dialogue about the reform.

During the press scrum in Saint-Bruno, Hugh Winsor asked whether the federal government "plan" referred to in the *Globe*'s stories existed. I replied that I knew of no document that answered the description, and I went on to restate my views on the need for discussion. "The first budget of the new government would be in February of '94, and Parliament will come back this fall — I think that there is ample opportunity to engage Canadians in a serious dialogue and to work with the provinces to find the best way to deliver those services."

I was then asked if I didn't think it was possible to have that dialogue during the election campaign, and I replied, "I think that's the worst possible time to have that kind of dialogue."

When Winsor asked my why, I explained, "Because I think it

takes longer than forty-seven days to tackle an issue that's that serious. It's a very important policy issue. Now, I've stated very clearly that I'm fundamentally committed to preserving quality social programs in this country, to preserving our health care system. But the issues are much too complex to try and generate some kind of blueprint in the forty-seven days that's available in an election campaign."

Later in the scrum, Winsor came back to the topic and asked me about some studies on social policy that I hadn't seen, and that I was pretty sure he hadn't, either. When he tried to get me to state a commitment to the study results, I said, "Well, I can tell you that it's not government policy. I don't know about it. This is not the time, I don't think, to get involved in a debate on very, very serious issues."

This would be the crucial statement, and despite my several lengthy exchanges with Winsor, the context was lost. Because of the other detailed remarks surrounding these comments, it wasn't immediately obvious just how badly I had "stepped in it." Since I had been trying to conduct serious discussions with the voters from the beginning of the campaign, I didn't see how anyone could claim that I was saying elections were not the time to discuss serious issues. That, of course, is exactly what the press took my comments to mean, although not, I understand, without some debate. I was told of a rancorous argument on the press bus with Leslie Jones of CTV arguing that they all knew I didn't mean elections aren't the time to discuss serious issues, and others arguing in favour of the Hugh Winsor line, which he gleefully said would crucify me.

Some of the people on our tour thought I should take steps to clarify my comments at that evening's event in Drummondville. Campaign HQ was not so sure. Remarks that were drafted to make the clarification did not fit naturally into the text of the speech I was to give, and I wondered if I would just be making the problem worse by drawing attention to it. There were no stories on the wire about my remarks ahead of the Drummondville event, and I decided not to say anything. I take full responsibility for this decision. It was a disastrous error of judgment on my part. The next day I met the press and tried to clarify what I meant, but by that time it was too late — the media were full of reports that I had said elections were not the time to discuss serious issues.

Knowing what I know now, I cringe at my naiveté in thinking I would not suffer for my remarks at Saint-Bruno. I wasn't exactly inexperienced in dealing with the media, but this was the first time I had run in a general election as a party leader. There is simply no comparison between the degree and the significance of the media scrutiny that come with that role, and the media exposure of a candidate running in a constituency. The repercussions of a party leader's remarks can kill a campaign. Even knowing this, I couldn't understand why I was never getting the benefit of the doubt from the media; why, for example, the distortion of my opening-day comments had taken such flight, beyond my capacity to set the record straight. What I came to understand in 1994, when I had an opportunity at Harvard to explore the literature on the press and politics, was that there was indeed an underlying dynamic driving the approach of the media, the nature of which I did not fully understand. I should have had it more in mind.

The most insightful book I found on the role of the media in election campaigns, *Out of Order* by Thomas E. Patterson, was published around the time of the 1993 election. Patterson, a political science professor at Syracuse University, brings together the results not only of his own research but also of a wide range of scholarly examinations of the media. As I read his explanation of the fundamental clash between journalistic and political values, I saw how wrong I had been to assume that simple honesty and candour would serve me well. According to Patterson, the basis for this conflict resides in the fundamentally different approaches that voters and candidates, on the one hand, and journalists, on the other hand, take towards an election campaign. Voters and candidates have a "government" framework, based on policy problems, leadership qualities, and policy debates, while journalists bring a "game" framework to the task, one that sees politics as a strategic game.

The game framework doesn't refer just to an emphasis on the "horse race" aspects of an election campaign, but also to an attitude that assumes everything that candidates do is designed primarily to manipulate the voters. In this view, candidates seek office for personal gain and power. It is a cynical approach that treats the election campaign itself as the single most important political phenomenon rather than as simply one part of a broader democratic process. It means that while politicians are trying to communicate messages about policy, and voters are trying to glean the positions of candidates, what journalists are interested in is the "real" story behind the campaign, which cannot possibly be understood by simply reporting on what people say and do. Elections, in this view, are not about issues: they are about elections. While I already knew much of this, it was not until I read Patterson's analysis that I fully appreciated all the ways this conflict between journalistic and political values affects the way messages are perceived by the media in a campaign.

The game framework, according to Patterson, becomes the dominant characteristic of election coverage and is central to the way a candidate is portrayed in the media. Basically, the better the candidate and his or her party are doing, the more likely the candidate is to be described in positive terms. The same candidate will be ascribed negative personal qualities in a campaign where he or she is losing.

Treating an election as a game works against in-depth or constant coverage of issues and policies. Once a candidate's position has been discussed, it is no longer news. Policy positions are often too nuanced to make interesting stories. However, mistakes or gaffes in a campaign do.

Patterson argues that there has been a dramatic shift to the game framework in election coverage over the past twenty years. This is shown not only in the relative decline of issues as a subject of coverage but also in a change in the way issues themselves are dealt with when they are discussed. For example, rather than let the candidates speak for themselves, journalists tell the viewers what they think the candidate was saying. The decline in the length of a television sound bite of a candidate from an average of forty-two seconds in 1968 to less than ten seconds in 1992 has been mirrored in the print press.

The view that "politics is essentially a game played by individual politicians for personal advancement, gain or power" creates a cynicism towards the political process among those journalists who cover it. As candidates insist on repeating their key messages, journalists become frustrated at the lack of "news." "Not surprisingly, the press becomes increasingly hostile toward the candidates as the campaign wears on." Patterson comments, "Negative campaigning is as old as politics itself. Negative news is the new element."

The final aspect of the game framework, as Patterson describes it, is the tendency it creates to explain election outcomes in terms of personalities or events. Other factors, such as the state of the economy, regional and ideological considerations, or incumbency, are neglected in favour of an interpretation that rests entirely on the candidate and the campaign.

I had never seen such a comprehensive analysis of the media coverage of elections before the 1993 campaign. Patterson's study is based largely on American sources, but the same phenomenon is readily apparent in Canadian journalism. For example, with respect to the increasing negativity of election coverage, the analysis of the TV coverage of the campaign conducted by Lydia Miljan of the National Media Archive at the Fraser Institute concluded that of the party leaders, only Preston Manning received more favourable coverage than negative, reflecting his steady climb in the polls.

As Miljan points out in her analysis of the TV news, the September 23 "gaffe" was given enormous significance by journalists in the strategic context of the campaign: "Various media personnel have described Kim Campbell's September remarks ... as 'the defining moment of the campaign.' Probably no other incident best illustrates the power of the media. After all, it was the media who dubbed Campbell's statement as 'defining' and it was the media who emphasized those remarks throughout the remainder of the campaign to ensure that they in fact did define the campaign. The role of the media in identifying these 'defining moments' and in ignoring others is best illustrated in the comparison of Kim Campbell's 47-day remark to one Jean Chrétien uttered a few weeks later.

"On October 7 Jean Chrétien stated to reporters: 'Let me win the election and after that you come and ask me questions about how I run the government.' While Kim Campbell tried to emphasize the statement, not only did the media fail to emphasize Chrétien's comments as they had Campbell's earlier remarks on revamping social welfare, but they only provided scant information on the statement Campbell was attempting to highlight."

Accepting that the game framework leads reporters to look

for gaffes, how do we explain why I got nailed and Jean Chrétien didn't? Part of it has to do with Patterson's observation that where a candidate sits in the horse race can affect his or her treatment by the media. During the first week of the campaign, the Liberals and the Conservatives were roughly equal in the polls, and I led the leadership stakes. By the time of my comment in Saint-Bruno, the Conservative Party had started its decline. Although many would attribute that decline to the Saint-Bruno remark, a more serious analysis suggests another factor also at play.

I think we were all less sensitive than we should have been to the potential for certain issues to trigger negative associations with previous Conservative positions or controversies. Although we realized it was essential to communicate Kim Campbell's "newness," this could be undone by reminding voters of what they didn't like or trust about Brian Mulroney's government.

Shortly after my return to Harvard in the fall of 1994, I ran into Richard Johnston, one of the leading authorities on Canadian elections, who had arrived to take up the Mackenzie King Chair in Canadian Studies. Dick was eager to share with me the analysis he had done on the 1993 election. In particular, he wanted to assure me that my September 23 statement was not responsible for our drop in the polls; the free fall had actually started two days earlier. This was small comfort to me!

However, Johnston wrote in his paper, "the general controversy that the remark encapsulated does seem to be the key to the campaign. It had simmered for a few days before the remark and its structure echoed the Mulroney style. At issue were the social programmes that the former Prime Minister had described as a sacred trust and yet had sought to alter. The 'threat' to the programmes was secret and thus partook of the 'hidden agenda' so often attributed to Brian Mulroney. The Conservatives' denial of a secret plan simply was not credible and may only have reminded voters of a theme that the Liberals emphasized in 1988: 'say one thing, mean another.'"

Patterson's analysis and the search by the media for "hidden agendas" help explain why my comments were so devastating. So much of the newness of my approach was a question of process. We had no hidden agenda on social programs because I wanted to open up the process of public discussion and debate and call on the provinces to bring their expertise to the table. But process as an issue is difficult to make exciting in an election campaign. It needs to be demonstrated.

I found later that scholars who examined the 1993 campaign had clearly understood my remarks — *all* my remarks — at Saint-Bruno. But the sort of position that seems clear to political scientists is not necessarily seen as policy by journalists. There is no sense in arguing that the press *should* have seen it that way. Our campaign should have presented our policy in a way that would have dispelled any fear of a hidden agenda. For that, we needed a fuller discussion of policy over the summer. Although we tried to defuse the issue by including some basic principles that would guide our deliberations on social policy in the Blue Book, which we finally produced in response to the Liberal Red Book, the damage was already done. Dick Johnston may be right that the controversy over a hidden agenda was the real trigger for our collapsing vote, but I believe my failure to appreciate the importance of counteracting my comments immediately made things much worse. Because there was a serious argument on the press bus about how my comments should be reported, a timely intervention by me might have staved off some of the worst of the fallout.

Even in the midst of all this media turmoil, the campaign continued on its hectic pace of speeches, interviews, and pressing the flesh. Election campaigning involves an incredible amount of physical contact. Wading through crowds shaking hands is, in fact, one of the best parts of this strange ritual. At the International Ploughing Match in Walkerton on September 21, I felt my hand again and again being enveloped in the strong callused hands of farmers. Unfortunately, it's easy to pick up other people's colds and flus while campaigning, as I did during the third week of the campaign. Before we left for Vancouver on the 24th, my secretary Wendy had already been on the phone arranging for me to see a doctor when I got home. On Saturday morning, armed with a bagful of medication, I tried to get some rest before I had to start campaigning again the next day. I was astonished to hear of media reports, after the election, that I had supposedly spent this weekend in some sort of getaway with Gregory!

Sunday was jam-packed with events, starting with a walk around

Stanley Park in support of AIDS causes. Although the event was meant to be nonpartisan, NDP MP Svend Robinson launched into an attack on the government, saying that the money for helicopters should be spent on AIDS research. This kind of simplistic rhetoric is great for making cheap political points, but not very helpful. We had finally removed the barriers to full participation of gays in the military. Did we now want them to risk their lives in ancient aircraft?

That evening, I began to review the major speech on the deficit I was scheduled to make the next morning. Unknown to me, two officials from the Privy Council Office had flown out from Ottawa to advise me on the proposals for expenditure cuts. We were preparing to announce these cuts in response to the pressure to demonstrate the credibility of our commitment to eliminate the deficit by the 1998–99 fiscal year. Because I didn't see the revised speech for the first time until late that evening, the officials weren't summoned. The next day, not having seen me, they were sent back to Ottawa, guaranteeing that they were incommunicado on an airplane should I want their help before the late-morning address.

The spending cut proposals were hastily put together by the PMO with help from the PCO, and while they brought us close to our goal, they were still $1.5 billion short for the final year. What they did demonstrate was that it was not necessary to go to the social policy envelope for most of the savings. We could make them realistically without devastating our social programs. I was determined that the actual priorities for expenditure cuts should be set only after a broad public process in which all the options could be clearly identified and discussed.

September 27 started with an early-morning appearance on the Rafe Mair program on CKNW. My relationship with Rafe had deteriorated from one of respectful sparring to simple antagonism as a result of our disagreements over Meech Lake and Charlottetown. Pamela's journal entry describes the confrontation: "Mair is objectionable, combative, antagonistic. Only male callers are taken — no female callers are taken. In response to his attacks the PM clicks off — this is her personal response to being attacked. What is required actually is the response of a public person — that is, to rise to the attack. Instead of the calm, aloof response, she needs to be passionate and animated when attacked. Herein rests one example of the tension between the personal and the public personalities and the problem with them residing in the same body. The callers are cruel — even one call about her being divorced twice."

I don't know if it was my cold, or whether I had simply decided that a more animated response would be taken as shrill, but I'm surprised to see myself described this way. If anything, I have had to learn to keep my cool when baited. Perhaps, given my recent history of confrontations with Rafe, I had overdone the self-control.

The deficit speech was scheduled for Earl Marriott Secondary School in Surrey. I was trying to show the generation that would suffer the most from a lack of action on the deficit and debt what it all meant. The speech went reasonably well. Charts and graphs clearly illustrated the danger of continuing to run the country in the red. Afterwards, we headed straight to the airport to fly to Toronto, not knowing that campaign HQ had scheduled a meeting the next day with the editorial board of the *Globe and Mail* to discuss the spending cut proposals. There was no time for serious briefing for this encounter, since I had a 9 a.m. interview with Peter Gzowski on CBC Radio, followed by a major luncheon address.

Editorial boards can be a real problem for a politician. Jean Chrétien did not do one during the 1993 campaign. However, John Tory thought I should meet with the *Globe and Mail* board because it appeared to be leaning towards the Reform Party. In light of what happened at the meeting, I regard this with a certain bitter irony. At one point, when asked whether a figure relating to expenditure cuts referred to cumulative or annual cuts, I mistakenly said annual, then corrected myself when one of my staff pointed out the error. For that, the *Globe* concluded that I did not have a good command of the issue. I was not the minister of finance; my proposals were not a budget. But they were as credible as any that had been put forward. Nevertheless, the *Globe and Mail* decided that I had been vague and unclear, and compared me unfavourably with Preston Manning. Because the Reform figures for eliminating the deficit were clearly bogus, a matter easily determined by a simple reference to Statistics Canada data, I found the *Globe*'s position strange. Serious economic commentators had warned that Manning's proposals would throw the economy into a tailspin and result in massive unemployment. Yet the Reform

Party proposals were greeted with an approval bordering on sycophancy by the *Globe and Mail*'s editorial writers.

I interrupted campaigning to fly to New York on September 29. I had agreed to give Canada's speech at the opening session of the UN General Assembly. It was an opportunity to set out Canada's views on peacekeeping and the administration of the UN at a crucial time for that organization. However, it had not been my intention to advocate fiscal restraint by appearing half-dressed on the podium.

My staff decided that because this was prime-ministerial business, not a campaign appearance, campaign worker Mijanou Serré wouldn't accompany me. She had joined the tour to ensure that I ate regularly and sensibly and to keep my clothes organized. Ray Castelli had told me I'd be on my own, but I was too preoccupied to think much about it. I arrived at the hotel with a little time to spare before I had to change and decided to check on my clothes. My heart stopped. The bag with my suit was there, but not my blouse, pantyhose, and shoes. Fred Loiselle was quickly dispatched back to the plane to get the missing garments, but a few moments later, he called to say that the plane had returned to Ottawa.

I was beside myself. I could make do with the shoes and stockings I had been wearing, but my suit wasn't the sort that could be worn without a blouse unless I wanted to draw attention to my speech in a way unrelated to its content. Fred offered to go out and buy me a blouse, but I didn't think he would be able to get me what I needed in such a short period of time. It's not like buying a man's shirt, where you just ask for a 16/34, or whatever. In desperation, I called our ambassador, Louise Frechette. I knew she was about my size and that her residence wasn't far from the hotel, so I asked her if she could possibly lend me a blouse. She hurriedly looked through her closet and had three sent over within the hour. Although everything turned out all right in the end, and the speech went well, I kept thinking, "This would never have happened to Brian Mulroney!"

At the midpoint of the campaign, two televised leaders' debates had been scheduled: the first in French, for Sunday, October 3, and the second in English, for the following evening. Preparation began on Friday, October 1, at Meech Lake. Allan Gregg, Nancy

Jamieson, Sharon Andrews, David McLaughlin, and I began by looking at some real-time analysis Allan had done of videos of the leadership debates. Members of focus groups use a mechanical device as they watch a debate to indicate their approval or disapproval of what they are hearing. Their signals are then transferred to the video in the form of a moving line, indicating the response to what is being said at any given moment. In those places where I had positioned myself as a reformer and as sympathetic to people's problems, the increase in the positive response was immediately evident.

The preparation on that first day was primarily for the English-language debate. The main themes I was to bear in mind are recorded in Pam's journal.

> Be real and tangible. List answers. Different realities demand different solutions. Right-of-centre initiatives for left of centre reasons.
>
> Establish different perspective, motive and approach. Ethics, deficit, meeting the people, responsiveness, consensus and co-operation — these are the features that distinguish Campbell from Mulroney. This plays the gender card without actually playing it. Different ways of making decisions lead to better results. Plus it shows she has the political will and strength to do what she says she will.
>
> Avoid references to Tory record. Focus on the future. We will do things differently.
>
> Real problems with real faces deserve real solutions.
>
> Tone is all-important.
>
> Higher deficits and higher taxes will kill jobs and this kills social safety programs.

What was interesting to me during the debate preparation was the clear acknowledgment for once that Brian Mulroney was a political liability and that we were carrying a lot of political baggage. Brian Mulroney spoke to John Tory by telephone often during the campaign, and John had continued to urge me to call him. I did speak to him on September 17, when I was in Regina. It was a friendly and supportive call, and I chatted with both Brian and Mila. What I couldn't seem to get across to John was that the press were constantly asking me if I had been speaking to Brian Mulroney. Associating me with Mulroney was still one of the main ways to attack me. "Kim, Kim, you're just like him!" was a favourite chant of demonstrators. We did speak by telephone again before the French debate, and when I acknowledged this publicly it created a small media flurry. Mulroney urged me to charge Chrétien and Bouchard with having a vested interest in each other. Because Chrétien was disliked by the nationalist elements in Quebec, his presence would keep them out of the Liberal ranks. Similarly, if Bouchard captured the Conservative vote in Quebec, he would enhance the Liberals' chances of forming a government. However, I couldn't see how making this point would induce either Liberal or Bloc Québécois supporters to switch to the Conservatives.

On Saturday, we began preparation for the French debate with a team from Quebec. Jean Charest was there to help. No one could identify an argument or debating point that would shake loose Bloc votes, except the prospect of Quebeckers' being excluded from government by voting for a regional party.

The format of the debates was the same awkward one we had used in the leadership campaign. Rather than the traditional series of one-on-one confrontations, which enabled leaders to argue without struggling to be heard, the debates would involve discussions among all the participants, which would make it extremely difficult for one leader to contradict or question another if it was not his or her turn to speak. In theory, there was to be a certain amount of open give and take, but in reality, it meant we would often be talking over one another. If I wanted to respond to an attack — and I was to be the recipient of the lion's share of the attacks — I ran the risk of appearing too aggressive, and aggressiveness is seen as less attractive coming from a woman.

The conventional wisdom among our campaign strategists was that a campaign didn't really begin until after the debates. In 1984, Brian Mulroney had scored a major hit on Prime Minister John Turner when, attacking his appointments using Trudeau's patronage list, he had skewered him with the line, "You had a choice, sir; you could have said no!" In 1988, John Turner had got his revenge when he attacked the Mulroney government's negotiations for the Free Trade Agreement, saying, "I believe you sold us out!" There were no such exchanges in the 1993 debates. The reviews were all over the map. Supporting Patterson's thesis, Lydia Miljan's analysis of the TV news states, "Coverage of the debates focused on the preparations made by the leaders and assessments of their performance rather than on what the leaders had to say."

The questions were initially posed by journalists. I was somewhat startled when I saw that the French panel included Denise Bombardier, who had lived for a time with Lucien Bouchard when he was ambassador to France. I had no idea whether this would be good or bad for Lucien, although Bombardier has since written a book entitled *Nos Hommes* that suggests she takes a benign and sentimental view towards her old loves.

The initial responses to the French-language debate were that I had done rather well. At an upbeat reception in my Langevin Block office after the debate, Pierre-Claude Nolin joked, "If I'd known you were that feisty, I'd have supported you in the leadership!" The French-language press seemed evenly divided between those who, like André Pratte of *La Presse*, thought I was too aggressive, and others like Lysiane Gagnon, also of *La Presse*, who thought I had looked the most comfortable. "After their first presentations," Gagnon observed of the four of us, "they all, except Kim Campbell, had the air of people condemned to die," adding, "Her French flowed well."

In the English-language press, francophone Michel Gratton suggested that the debate had been like a "good, old-fashioned French family dispute" and that in that kind of argument, "[Campbell] can match any Quebecker, any day ... Her previously noted weaknesses in the language were seldom, if ever, apparent and she certainly can go to bed knowing she put to rest the doubts many francophones had about her ability to communicate when the chips are down."

But the *Toronto Star*'s verdict was "PM Lost Round 1, Pundits Say," according to Robert McKenzie. "Almost all agreed on one thing: Campbell bombed ... Campbell's hesitant French, which led her to thrash her arms while searching for the right expression, probably contributed to the impression she was more excitable than Bouchard, who expressed indignation without losing control."

I couldn't win with the anglophone press. Whereas the French-language journalists had found my French quite adequate, the anglophones thought it could have been better! A little later, on October 5 at a campaign rally in Repentigny, I argued that Quebeckers should not consign themselves to the impotence of opposition by supporting the Bloc. Putting my text aside, I exclaimed, "N'acceptez jamais d'être deuxième dans le pays que vous avez fondé!" (Never accept being second place in the country you founded.) The crowd went wild at this heartfelt cry, but the English press the next day assumed that I must have been fed the line by Brian Mulroney.

The back-to-back schedule for the debates schedule couldn't have been worse. By the time of the English debate, the night after the French one, we were all tired. Preston Manning, on the other hand, was fresh as a daisy because he hadn't been a participant in the French debate. I stood next to the Reform leader and was amused to see a crib sheet encouraging him to be cool, to smile, etc.

The worst moment of the English debate came when Lucien Bouchard accused me of hiding the real figure for the deficit. He demanded to know the figure for the last fiscal year. I didn't know the exact figure, but suddenly wondered if I should, in fact, have known it. I seemed evasive although I knew I wasn't hiding anything. After the debate, Sharon Andrews, who had worked for former finance minister Don Mazankowski, told me that the answer involved "Finance arcana" that I could not be expected to know. The official figure for the deficit can be given only by the auditor general. Although for a number of years when Michael Wilson was finance minister, an interim estimate was given in August, pending the final figure in November, two years earlier the auditor general had insisted that, since the August figure could be misleading, only the November figure be published.

The English-language debate received similarly mixed reviews. Carol Goar of the *Toronto Star* wrote, "Campbell Didn't Win — or Lose": "Prime Minister Kim Campbell showed poise under fire in last night's election debate. She did not ignite her faltering campaign, but she may have stabilized it enough to buy herself a second chance with the Canadian voters ... Campbell ... was not dazzling or personally appealing. But she ... showed steady leadership and avoided the kind of gaffe that can sink a campaign. None of the five party leaders shone in last night's verbal slugfest."

Not all the reviews were so favourable. In the *Ottawa Sun*, Sean Durkan gave "Round 2 to Chrétien," but in Vancouver, the *Province*'s Brian Kieran declared, "Carping Campbell, Chrétien Both Lose: Only Manning Managed to Avoid Bickering and Address Issues." In the *Sun*, Lisa Fitterman declared me the winner but only "by default." The paper's voters' panel, she wrote, was "not impressed" with the contest.

Several days after the debates, the *Toronto Star* reported on a scientific study of the English-language debate conducted with panels of undecided voters in five Canadian cities. Using hand-held continuous response measurement devices, the voters rated the debate. As Antonia Zerbisias reported, "Kim Campbell won the debate, tying Manning for first place. Chrétien came in next with Bouchard and McLaughlin bringing up the distant rear."

According to the *Star* article, such techniques often show a difference between the opinions of voters and what the pundits say. But that independence of opinion doesn't last forever. "After a few days, the people start believing what the pundits say. They think, 'Oh yes, I must have been wrong. So I'll start believing what the media are saying.' It's what psychologists describe with children in a classroom, a state of learned helplessness. It's not that the public is stupid. It's what you call the power of the media."

As we moved into week five of the campaign, our strategy became even more directed at attacking the Liberal Party. In the two days after the debates our support had risen slightly, although we remained at least ten points behind the Liberals. Our campaign slogan was changed from "It's Time" to "Think Twice." The original slogan had been the subject of great disagreement within the party. Allan Gregg insisted that of all the slogans tested before focus groups, "It's Time" tested better than *any* other slogan he had ever seen. That didn't make it any more comprehensible to our candidates or the voters. It was easy for our opponents to complete the thought with "It's time for a change." Now, the idea was that voters should consider the strategic implications of a protest vote or a vote for the Liberals.

I had been frustrated since the beginning of the campaign with our failure to generate the kind of language and catchy phrases that would make our message memorable. That week I received some help, not from the pros but from Ray Castelli. He had taken one of the Liberals' Red Books and found someone who could drill holes in it. He passed it on to Jodi, who had joined the tour in an effort to improve communications. I tried it out on October 6 in Charlottetown.

The campaign team had given me five questions to pose to Chrétien in my speeches. They were designed to point out what was *not* in the Red Book, namely, positions on key issues such as NAFTA, the future of the GST, and the deficit. That night I brandished the altered Red Book, which I referred to as Chrétien's "five-hole platform." It was an effective visual aid and allowed me to use that most powerful of political weapons: ridicule. Since I'm comfortable with that kind of humorous attack, it fit my speaking style. The audience loved it, and needless to say, it got great media coverage. It struck me that all our professional communications consultants had not come up with anything nearly as effective. Used quickly after the Liberals had issued the Red Book, it could have seriously limited the Red Book's usefulness in their campaign.

It seemed that every time our campaign was gaining some steam, something went wrong. On October 5, Jean Chrétien decided to launch an attack on the government's agreement to lease Terminals 1 and 2 at Toronto's Pearson Airport to a private consortium, which would renovate the terminals and run them for the period of the lease. The arrangement was similar to the one that had created the beautiful Terminal 3 at Pearson, although in that case the land had been leased and the private-sector developers had built the new terminal from scratch. The attack took us by surprise because announcements of previous stages of the deal had generated little or no negative comments from the Liberals. The basis for the attack was the presence in the consortium of Don Matthews, a well-known Conservative fundraiser, who was also the father-in-law of the former Liberal premier of Ontario, David Peterson.

The project had involved competitive bidding, and a close inspection of the participants in the successful consortium revealed strong ties not to the Conservatives but to the Liberals. In fact, I read later that Chrétien's campaign team had warned him that the attack could backfire on that account. These were the same Liberals who had attended a $1,000-a-plate fundraiser for Chrétien in Montreal. The Pearson deal would inject $700 million of private money into the refurbishment of two terribly outdated terminals at Canada's most important airport. The immediate result would be the creation of 14,000 construction jobs.

The campaign team was concerned about this issue and wondered if I ought to delay the completion of the transaction. The terms of the various agreements had been approved by Treasury Board at the end of August, and by the time of Chrétien's attack, the documents had been signed by Jean Corbeil, the minister of transport. All that was left for me to do was approve taking them out of escrow on October 7, the date agreed upon early in the summer for the exchange of documents. Senator Lowell Murray, the only one of my ministers who did not need to seek election, was holding the fort in Ottawa. He was assured by senior public officials that the deal was "clean" and that, moreover, a failure to complete it at this stage would leave the government liable for significant damages. In fact, on August 27, I had received a memorandum from Clerk of the Privy Council Glen Shortliffe saying, "The selection of the developer followed a competitive process which is entirely transparent." And further, "We can assure you that officials have reviewed the file and can confirm that due process has been followed at every stage."

When Jodi asked Glen in October if it would be possible to delay the final steps of the project, his horrified response was, "Do you understand what you would be doing?" Although some would claim, much later, that I exceeded my constitutional authority in authorizing the release of documents during an election, I am sure that if there had been such a constitutional restraint, alarm bells would have gone off all through the Privy Council Office. Moreover, we would have welcomed a fair reason to take this issue off the table during the election. Not a whisper of any such advice was given, and in fact, court decisions support the view that the government could not use an election as an excuse to fail to complete a transaction when it had already indicated a clear intention to contract.

I regarded Chrétien's attack as a political ploy designed to exploit the willingness of journalists and many Canadians to believe the worst about Brian Mulroney. I knew how overdue this project was and, having been confronted by demonstrating construction workers in Toronto over our failure to fund a new convention centre there, I knew how important the jobs at Pearson would be to that industry. Even putting it on hold might not have defused the issue, because, presumably, we would remain committed to going ahead if we won. At that point Chrétien was promising to review the project, not cancel it, and I had no concerns about that. I could see no legitimate reason for the government to renege on its agreements, beyond political expediency at considerable expense to the public. I instructed that all relevant documents be made public to answer concerns that had been raised. This was not easy to do on short notice, but valiant efforts were made.

At the time of writing, there has been no substantiation of any irregularity in the bidding for the Pearson lease. Sworn testimony at a Senate inquiry by public servants with no vested interest in protecting their former Conservative bosses has refuted every single allegation. Unfortunately, the scandals of the first Mulroney mandate had created fertile ground for such allegations, and the Liberals understood that perfectly. It was ironic that the only real, verifiable commitments for jobs coming out of the 1993 election were the 14,000 for Pearson and the 45,000 from the EH-101 helicopter contract, both of which were cancelled by the Liberals once they were elected.

On Thursday, October 7, I spent the morning in St. John's, Newfoundland, with Ross Reid, who held the difficult fisheries portfolio. I was enormously fond of Ross and respected his political judgment and integrity. His calm presence was encouraging in view of the devastating Southam poll we had been told to expect the next day. The campaign events went well, including an excellent hour on open-line radio. But somehow, I knew it was all too late.

With only two and a half weeks to go until election day, the Southam poll showed the Liberals at 40 per cent, Reform at 20 per cent, Conservatives at 19 per cent, and the Bloc Québécois at 16 per cent. Our own new numbers from Decima, which we received the next day, were more encouraging. They showed the Liberals at 34 per cent and the Tories at 25 per cent. The *Globe and Mail* misreported an Angus Reid poll, giving the numbers as Liberals, 41 per cent; Reform, 20 per cent; Tories, 19 per cent; and BQ, 12 per cent. The true numbers were Liberals, 37 per cent; Tories, 22 per cent; Reform, 18 per cent; Bloc, 12 per cent; NDP, 8 per cent;

and 3 per cent for other parties. Showing us behind Reform was very detrimental to the psychology of our support. Although the *Globe* had egg on its face because it took the false numbers from a Liberal spin doctor, the reality was that we were in deep trouble.

Sometimes when things are really bleak, the only thing to do is laugh. As we prepared to fly out to Vancouver on Sunday, October 10, I discovered that everyone on the plane was in costume for a pre-Halloween Masquerade flight. As I approached the plane, there was Scott Munnoch, the very large person who headed up our advance team on the tour, dressed as a cow. He was wearing a black-and-white body suit and a little cap with yellow horns on it. I broke up. The crew were all dressed as Catholic clergy of various ranks. Among the best costumes in the media section were Leslie Jones and Laura Lynch, who were dressed as Crayola crayons in the obsolete "flesh" colour.

If I thought we had hit rock bottom, I was disabused of this notion by the misery that unfolded over the weekend beginning Friday, October 15. The stage was set on Thursday evening by two events. First, I received a telephone message from John Tory advising me that we would be airing new TV and radio ads starting that night. Because the ads were critical of Chrétien, John wanted to forewarn me so that I wouldn't be spooked by any negative reaction to them. He told me that the picture used in the TV ads was not flattering, but certainly no worse than a recent photo of Chrétien that had appeared on the cover of *Maclean's* magazine. I'm not sure if John had seen the ads himself when he spoke to me. At any rate, he was following the instructions of Tom Scott and Allan Gregg to make sure that I would defend them. Tom was in charge of our advertising, and when I'd spoken to him earlier in the campaign about possible negative advertising, he had emphasized that any negativity would be in the message, not in the visual images. He had explicitly said that any pictures of Chrétien would be "neutral."

The other gateway to trouble on Thursday was a conversation I had with my principal secretary, Jean Riou, regarding a meeting I was to have with the editorial board of *La Presse* in Montreal the next day. Since it was to be early morning, he told me, the people at *La Presse* had suggested I do the interview in English, to make discussion go more quickly. "Is it really their idea?" I asked. Assured it was, I foolishly agreed that it might make sense and reduce the fatigue level of a demanding day.

When I arrived at *La Presse* the following morning, I discovered that no one seemed aware of the suggestion to do the interview in English. Jean was not with us, so I had no idea to whom he had spoken. I was angry and embarrassed. The interview proceeded mainly in English, with some French. Then one of the reporters began to question me about the new ads. Not having seen them, and having been carefully primed by John Tory, I replied that I understood the picture was no worse than that on the cover of *Maclean's* magazine. The mood in the room grew distinctly chilly. I was offended when André Pratte, who had written a scathing column after the English debate accusing me of deliberately hiding the truth about the deficit figures, conceded that he had verified the truth of my explanation about the auditor general, but had not passed on this news to his readers.

The conversation that followed enabled *La Presse* to write a story in Saturday's edition in which I apparently managed to insult Jean Charest, Brian Mulroney, and Don Mazankowski in one fell swoop. I was devastated because the comments weren't intended to be offensive at all. I was being pressed to explain how I was different from my predecessor and how my approach to the deficit was any different from that of Mazankowski. When taxed about our slowness in releasing specific policy initiatives during the campaign, I said that it was not unusual to release policies throughout a campaign and said, by way of example, that although Jean had put forward more policy earlier, by the end of our leadership campaign I had a more fleshed-out policy platform than he. Particularly galling was the notion that I had criticized Brian Mulroney because I said I would do some things differently. The only reason I was leading the party at all was that Mulroney had become the most negatively regarded prime minister in Canadian history, and the only message that gave us a chance of winning was that, under Kim Campbell, the Conservatives had something fresh to offer. Notwithstanding all that, I had bent over backwards to avoid saying anything negative about Brian Mulroney.

There had been many attempts by reporters to draw me into such conversations, but I had always sidestepped them. Now, under pressure from yet another editorial board to explain what I was about, my answers were cast as repudiations of my colleagues. I blame myself because I allowed myself to get tied up answering the questions put to me instead of being careful to say what I wanted to say. Part of the cause was my profound frustration at my inability to gain recognition of the importance of what we were proposing. On September 23, the *Globe and Mail* had published, under the title "Worth Repeating," a speech by John Cleghorn, president of the Royal Bank. In this excerpt entitled "Governments Must Listen to Stakeholders," Cleghorn basically set out my proposal for bringing Canadians into the discussions about attacking the deficit and working with the provinces on social and fiscal reform.

> Government must adopt a new approach to consultation with Canadians.
>
> Take, for example, the matter of the federal budget. There has never been a greater need to co-ordinate fiscal strategies across levels of governments or to generate broad consensus about the tough choices required to bring deficits and debt under control. Yet the budget is still drawn up in isolation from Parliament, the provinces and the public. Clearly, a much more open process could be developed without creating opportunities for speculation.
>
> We must also increase public awareness. Many of the tough issues we face — the debt and deficit, or improving health care and education while making them more cost effective — are extremely complex. If Canadians are ill-informed, they cannot participate in any meaningful way in the answers.
>
> Our problems are not going to be resolved without a broader understanding of the trade-offs that are needed and a sustained effort that will take more than a few years. What it all comes down to is listening to our stakeholders, and moving ahead as a team with confidence that we can exceed their expectations.

This could have been taken from any one of dozens of my speeches or interviews, going back to the leadership race. It was the reason I didn't want to present specific proposals for budget cutting ahead of public consultation and debate. What drove me to distraction was why this was "worth repeating" when articulated by the president of the Royal Bank, but not worth mentioning when the prime minister of Canada pledged it as government policy.

The delights of the weekend were only beginning. After my meeting with the *La Presse* board, I departed for Quebec City, where I met the full force of the protests over the ads that had been aired the night before. Campaign HQ was insisting that they must run, while across the country there was a revolt in Conservative ranks. I had a luncheon speech but told Patrick I wanted to see the ads as soon as they were available. I felt I had to make a decision on the ads before my scheduled meeting with the editorial board of *Le Soleil* that afternoon. Meanwhile, we were taking calls from all over the country. I spoke personally to Steven Greenaway in British Columbia, whose judgment I trusted, who insisted we had to pull them.

When we finally received the video and ran it in my hotel room, I was mortified. The ads were stupid and offensive. If our goal was to show that Kim Campbell was "new and different," this was hardly the way to do it. Experts on negative advertising warn that such an approach should be used only as a last resort. Even assuming that our situation warranted such a desperate tactic, these ads were completely unintelligent as negative advertising. The key to negative advertising is figuring out how the other side will try to get your ads off the air and forestalling their objections. Although John Tory and Allan Gregg claimed that there had been no intention to make fun of Chrétien's disability, it was hard to believe they were so obtuse as to think that the Liberals would not seize on this line of attack instantly. Not only were the ads unsustainable, but we gave our opponents a huge club to beat us with. To use the football metaphors so beloved by John Tory, I realized that we were losing with seconds left in the game, but Allan and Tom's "Hail Mary pass" was neatly intercepted by Chrétien's line, "God made me this way." I was disgusted. I instructed that the ads be pulled as soon as possible. John and Allan were furious, but no more so than I. All across the country, public-spirited men and women were campaigning for us, putting their hearts and souls into a campaign that it was now clear to everybody we couldn't win. The "experts" at headquarters had managed to give those nice people a collective kick in the stomach.

To the very end, Brian Mulroney would reassure me that this campaign team was the best there was.

I went to *Le Soleil*, where I announced the cancellation of the ads. The meeting with the editorial board (in French) went much better than the one at *La Presse*, although the paper was strongly supporting the Bloc. I returned to my hotel and prepared to meet the press. I was still extremely upset. I had intended to confirm the cancellation of the ads and apologize to Jean Chrétien and to Canadians. My mind was racing because I had begun to wonder if the ads had been a deliberate attempt to sabotage what was left of the campaign. It seemed unthinkable, but I had been astonished at John Tory's uncharacteristic rudeness in response to my instructions to cancel them. I keep thinking of one of my favourite sayings, "Just because you're paranoid doesn't mean they're not really out to get you!" In my confusion, I forgot to apologize and had begun to turn back to the elevators when someone in the scrum called out, "Aren't you going to apologize?" Of course I did, but the circumstances made it seem grudging, which it certainly wasn't.

As if all this weren't enough, I returned to my room to be told by Patrick that my desperately needed rest time on Sunday was to be cancelled. It had already been cut back to the afternoon and evening. Now there was an important breakfast in Orillia Monday morning, and to get there, I had to fly out of Ottawa Sunday evening. Orillia was the riding of Doug Lewis, who had been a co-chair of my Ontario leadership campaign, was in my cabinet, and had a strong claim on my loyalty — how could I say no to the event in his riding?

For the first time in the campaign, I lost my temper. Pam wrote in her journal: "Scheduling problem … PM is furious. She thought she had a sense of her schedule, needs the time to get her [chipped] tooth fixed, get her nails done, get laundry and bills sorted out. She explodes, and part of this is about being manipulated, not informed sufficiently, not adequately prepared, being handed speeches ten minutes before the event, being the last to see schedules, being ruled by guilt, and being exhausted. She is tired, she is worried about her performances and how she may really blow it in front of the media the more worn she gets. Patrick listens, is supportive and lets her unload. After her anger subsides we discuss ways to deal with the new schedule that will allow her to get all things done. Things calm down somewhat and then Patrick admits that he, too, is angry — about the ads."

That Friday evening, Pamela joined me for a quiet dinner in my hotel room. Over the past few weeks I had spoken to her about my doubts, wondering what I could be doing differently. I felt totally frustrated; so many of our campaign events were truly wonderful, but they didn't seem to make any difference. On October 14 in Toronto, CTV News anchor Lloyd Robertson had interviewed me at length. He let me talk and I set out my vision of the country. When he asked me what I would do differently, I answered that perhaps I had overestimated what people knew about my program at the outset. I should have spent more time reiterating and explaining it. It was a great interview, and when it was over, Robertson said, "Everyone should have this kind of time with you." Well, it was too late now. I knew the ads were absolutely the last straw. We were dead.

This didn't mean that no one would kick the corpse. After the article in *La Presse* came out on October 16, Jean Corbeil called to express his concern over my remarks. Jean Riou spoke to him, but his conclusion that the matter had been resolved was contradicted by the receipt of a stinging letter from Corbeil attacking me. To make a long story short, the letter, which could only have had a vindictive purpose, was made public. That evening, at a press conference in Montreal, I tried to clarify my remarks and defuse the Corbeil issue. There was some call for me to fire him from cabinet, but I decided that was counterproductive. His conduct was unacceptable, but I wasn't prepared to make a martyr out of him and his days as a minister were numbered anyway. I thought wistfully of Pierre Cadieux.

At this point I felt about as low as I had ever felt in my entire public career. I blamed myself for the campaign and felt sick about my own screw-ups. On Sunday, October 17, I did a television interview in Montreal before heading back to Ottawa. Just before leaving the Radio-Canada building, I took a call from Bernard Valcourt, who had been speaking to some of the other ministers and felt we needed some sort of dramatic step if we were to salvage anything from the campaign. He wanted me to fire the campaign team and bring the ministers together to create a strategy for the last week. Bernard's remarks crystallized my own frustration and anger, and I said his suggestion was a good idea. I stormed back to the campaign bus, avoiding the media who were expecting to talk to me, and said I wanted to meet with the campaign team that night in Ottawa before leaving for Orillia.

Ray Castelli later told me that he had stifled his doubts about our strategy over the summer, thinking, "Well, these guys have done this before and I've never run a national campaign." But we were both mesmerized by the mythical stature of Allan Gregg and by Mulroney's assurance that this team was "the best there was." I had suspected we might well be heading for disaster but had felt helpless to change things. Now I realize I should have been much more intrusive in the campaign planning. I have a hard time forgiving myself for not trusting my own judgment when it really counted.

Gregory accompanied me on the drive up to Ottawa and listened sympathetically to my concerns. He kept me company at the dentist's while my chipped tooth was patched, then joined me for a quick bite at my apartment before returning to Montreal. By this time I had cooled down. Pamela had come up to Harrington Lake earlier in the day with my clothes so that fresh ones could be packed for the coming week. I didn't have time to go to Harrington Lake myself, but at least I got my laundry done, which was more than some of the others on the tour could do.

After dinner I met with the campaign team in Ottawa, with John Tory on the speakerphone from Toronto. I realized it was too late to do what Bernard was suggesting. It would only add to our image of desperation. John had no new ideas. New ads were being prepared. Since we couldn't cancel our media buy, we had to use the time. John, Allan, and Tom would never forgive me for cancelling the Chrétien ads. They claimed that the night the ads were shown we had our best tracking in weeks. The *Globe and Mail* poll on Saturday had shown the Liberals at 40 per cent and Tories at 20 per cent, yet John insisted we were only eight points behind the Liberals. From the perspective of the tour, any improvement was the result of some good events and days on the road. None of the campaign team could accept that there had been problems in the campaign strategy.

When I was finally shown the new ads in Toronto two days later, the atmosphere in the room was decidedly hostile. The new ads were also aggressively critical but the images were more neutral. Two were aimed at Chrétien and one at Reform. When I asked if any focus groups had been done on the ads, I was told there had been no time. The messages were pointed, but a far cry from the "new and different" image we had wanted to convey. "Well," I said, "I don't have any choice, do I?"

I concluded that the best strategy for the last week was simply to try to do the best I possibly could. After six weeks, I was finally scheduled to do an event for women in Toronto on October 18, Persons' Day. Among women, young, middle-class "workers" supported me. A more difficult group for us was middle-aged, highly educated professional women, who, perhaps because of their own experiences, worried about my ability to take on the old boys' network. My experience during the leadership was that once I had talked with these women directly, they frequently came on side. The town hall meeting at the O'Keefe Centre was sponsored by several organizations of business women. I felt relaxed and in my element, and the meeting was a great success. I was happy at the reaction but sad, too, knowing that there could have been so much more of this. These women could have been great ambassadors if they had had a chance to meet with me sooner.

As the week progressed, the days were filled with riding events at which I gave a speech setting out the details of what the initial days of the new Kim Campbell government would look like. This was our new strategy, and even the media acknowledged that it was a good and important speech. Too late.

On October 19 there was another small crisis as my friend Isabel Bassett, one of the Toronto candidates, wrote me an open letter of encouragement that included the admonition to ignore the boys in the back room and stick to my own judgment and plans. Of course the media picked up on this. Poor Isabel, her campaign chairperson had fallen into the oldest trap in the book. In desperation to salvage the seat in a losing campaign, she had encouraged Isabel to separate herself from the main campaign. Still, I didn't have the heart to criticize; after all, my errors had been borne by all the other candidates.

On Friday, October 22, a three-hour open-line stint on *Canada AM* had been scheduled for the morning. I had a cough, and in the last hour of the program had a coughing fit. The station went to a commercial and I asked Frédéric to grab my cough syrup. I took some swigs and was able to get through the program. I was sitting in the make-up room preparing to remove my make-up when one of the hosts, Keith Morrison, came in, and in a gesture that revealed his sense of his own status as well as the imminent change in my own, gave me a thwack on the back and said, "Great to see you, Kim." My staff just stared in stunned disbelief.

I was scheduled to give a speech at the Canadian Club at noon. I had decided it would be my "vision of Canada" speech. Because the speech would be televised live, I wanted to put on the record my goals for this country. I put together my own notes, not a written text. What I hadn't realized was that on an empty stomach, the cough syrup was going to make me high! I hadn't paid much attention to just how much syrup I was guzzling. On the way to the luncheon speech, I started to feel light-headed, and by the time I arrived, my head was reeling. Isabel Bassett was chairing the meeting, and as she invited me to the podium I wondered, "Can I get through this without falling over?" Amazingly, the speech went well, and I received a standing ovation. Apparently what felt like being semi-comatose to me came across as serene and low-key to the audience.

We flew to Winnipeg that afternoon for an amazing rally where Premier Gary Filmon made a wonderful speech of introduction. Among the best lines: "Hope is not a strategy." After I took the stage, the applause and cheering continued for a full four minutes. I laughed. It was all so incongruous. There was a valedictory mood about it all. We knew we were going down, but we were quite unrepentant.

On the flight from Toronto to Winnipeg, I had talked to Pamela about our situation. Her journal entry says: "She is sad this morning — somewhat downtrodden and defeated, angry and frustrated … She knows the Tories have lost, and the plans will depend on how badly the party is defeated. She is leader of the party and is committed to that. She plans to regroup, take control of the party, re-establish it both intellectually and financially. There will be a leadership review in 1994; she will take six months to decide what she wants to do about it all. Perhaps she will decide she doesn't want to be leader, or perhaps she will take control and place the Tories back on the map. We will see what Monday's results are."

What I didn't know then was that after the ads, my own seat was lost. When I asked David Camp in the last days of the campaign if I was going to win in Vancouver Centre, he told me, "We think you're going to win." In fact, he was sure I would lose but didn't think it would do any good to say so. Earlier in the week, when support for me began to plummet, he had decided against trying to persuade me to return home to save my own seat (I would lose by 3,821 votes). In making that decision he had come to feel that defeat in Vancouver Centre was probably for the best, because it would reduce the conflict and trauma of a change in the leadership of the party.

I was angry not to have been consulted and given a chance to review all the options. But he was right. Jean Charest could devote the last two weeks of the campaign to winning his own riding. As party leader, I couldn't. As long as there was a chance to win other seats, I had to act for the party as a whole. So although I didn't know it that day, my life support system had already been unplugged. I would breathe on my own, or not at all.

Saturday, October 23, was the last day on the road, taking us from Regina to Medicine Hat, Williams Lake, Victoria, and finally Vancouver. The events were surprisingly well attended and upbeat. In Medicine Hat, I retired to a local motel after our event while the media filed their stories. British Prime Minister John Major called to wish me well. He was at the meeting of Commonwealth heads of government in Cyprus and wanted to remind me that his own party had been down eight points right before the last British election. "You have replaced St. Jude as the patron saint of lost causes, at least for politicians," I joked. It was a remarkably kind and thoughtful gesture from a man who had also had his share of naysaying and who knew what it meant to be an outsider. I was touched.

Williams Lake was in the riding of Cariboo-Chilcotin, home of my great friend Dave Worthy. I felt terrible about not having been in his riding before. For some reason, the campaign organizers had not capitalized on my strength in British Columbia. Although I had made a point of featuring my B.C. roots after becoming prime minister, during the campaign I had to be a "national" figure. But no one had ever thought Brian Mulroney shouldn't spend lots of time in Quebec! The neglect showed. We were in bad shape in B.C.

The final event of the day was an evening rally near the Victoria airport at Cordova Bay Elementary School. The school gym was packed. As I waited for my entrance cue, I looked at the posters the children had created to welcome me. They described the various things that government does, and many featured drawings of me. One said, "Thank-you for taking care of our country." Perhaps I should have felt discouraged, but I didn't. I thought to myself, "Democracy matters; these people matter." As I made my way to the podium to the beat of our campaign music, I saw the faces of many old friends and supporters. No one in this crowd would be surprised by my exuberance or my sense of humour — these people knew me. The three women candidates were upbeat and proud. I gave a speech that some later described as the best of the campaign. I didn't have to explain myself here or cut through layers of cynicism. I had only to reach out to inspire and motivate people who took for granted the genuineness of my affection for them. By all rights I should have been exhausted, but I felt refreshed. As I looked out over the crowd and saw the smiling faces of Alix and David, I felt an emotion I hadn't felt in weeks — perfect trust.

Alix and David wanted to see me privately before we left, and so the lights were turned off on the bus to thwart the cameras. As Alix asked me if I was okay, I could see the worried expression on her face. I knew my family was in agony for me. I reassured her and, after hugs all around, she and David stepped off the bus as it began to make its way to the airport.

The short flight to Vancouver was more eventful than expected because our plane hit a wind shear that sent it bouncing all over on take-off. Our pilot, a flying instructor, said it was the most turbulent take-off he had ever experienced and radioed back to Victoria airport to have it closed. Sitting up front, I wasn't too bothered. It didn't seem any worse than my first flight to Victoria more than thirty years before. Maybe it was just that after enduring the previous seven weeks it was hard to become frightened over something as swift and painless as death by plane crash.

How much did I know about the reality of our situation? Because I felt I couldn't reveal my doubts and worries openly, even to the campaign staff, many people have wondered about this. I talked to Pamela a little at first, but mostly I kept my concerns to myself. I knew we weren't going to win, and I knew a real disaster was possible, but I wasn't sure what would happen on election day. We weren't totally lacking in support; after all, we finally wound up receiving almost the same number of votes as the Reform Party, and more than the Bloc Québécois. I could feel that support out on the campaign trail, so my hope that the numbers might break in a way that gave us some seats wasn't completely unrealistic. On the other hand, it had been clear to me from the first week of the campaign that we were unprepared for the very tough fight ahead of us. It wasn't just that our organization wasn't everything it should have been. We didn't really comprehend what had happened to the Conservative vote since the last election.

We often speak of the electorate that put the Tories in power in 1984 as a coalition of the west and Quebec. Dick Johnston puts it somewhat differently: "The combination that Brian Mulroney created and Kim Campbell inherited was deeply incoherent: 'francophones and francophobes'... This incoherence may have been the price of power but it always lurked in the background as a threat to the Conservatives' own aspirations. One way to contain the incoherence was to emphasize an issue on which Conservatives were agreed and which distinguished them from other parties' supporters." Finding such an issue was the challenge of 1993.

In 1984, the nationalist francophone vote in Quebec was deeply hostile to the Liberal Party, primarily because of Pierre Trudeau's patriation of the Constitution. In the west, anti-Trudeau sentiment had been reflected for some time in electoral support for the Conservatives. What Mulroney brought to the mix was a native-son appeal in Quebec that was able to move that accessible francophone vote to the Conservatives. In 1988 there was some restiveness in the Conservative coalition, especially in the west. Initially, the Tory campaign strategists had sought to avoid making the Canada-U.S. Free Trade Agreement a defining issue of the campaign. That it became one turned out to be a blessing in disguise. Free trade was the one issue on which the western Conservatives and their Quebec counterparts agreed. Furthermore, it was important enough to drive voting behaviour, because a victory by the Liberal Party appeared to mean certain abrogation of the agreement. The Reform Party had been gaining support in the west, but it also supported the Free Trade Agreement. When the Liberals took the lead after the 1988 debates, Reform Party supporters were faced with a strategic decision, and many supported the Conservatives in order to assure the ratification of the FTA.

The day after the 1988 election, Senator Lowell Murray asked Allan Gregg, "What will be our 'free trade' issue in the next election?" The answer was that we didn't have one. Our Quebec vote had followed Lucien Bouchard to the Bloc Québécois in 1990 after the failure of the Meech Lake Accord and barely budged from that time. With no overarching issue to create a commonality of interest between the francophones and francophobes, the contradictions became more significant. As Johnston describes it: "Compared with 1988, attitude to French Canada was clearly a more important factor in the [1993] outcome; a modest relationship became a stark one … Reform thus did two things at once. First, it increased the system's overall polarization on this dimension. In doing so, it must have attracted francophobes across the board, not just from the old Conservative bloc. But the Conservative bloc was, in fact, where francophobes were disproportionately to be found. The second thing Reform did, then, was hollow out the Conservative base."

So who remained with the Conservatives? Johnston says that defection by voters who rejected forms of ethnic accommodation, in the context of either language or multiculturalism, "was so complete that by the third-last week in the campaign the only Conservatives left were those who positively favoured" such accommodation. "At this point, for the first time in living memory, the Liberals and Conservatives were actually occupying the same turf … In the end, Tories who favoured ethnic accommodation — especially, we suspect, accommodating French Canada — went over in serious numbers to the Liberals; indeed they may have contributed the bulk of the late Liberal surge."

While this analysis describes the major factors at play in dismantling the Conservative coalition, other issues played a role, such as the "anti-politician" sentiment that constituted some of Reform's appeal. Without an overarching issue, the Conservative campaign faced an impossible task. Attempts to win back our Quebec support — which, by virtue of its strong nationalist leaning, would only respond to a strongly accommodative appeal — were guaranteed to alienate the francophobes. On the other hand, attempts to articulate a position that would appeal to voters who opposed ethnic accommodation would destroy any attraction the party had in Quebec.

The Conservative campaign did not face this profound contradiction squarely for a number of reasons. First, Mulroney and many others did not believe that Quebeckers would, in the end, vote for a regional party that would deny them the power of being in government. The view that Quebeckers always vote primarily for the party that will form the government had been a truism of Canadian election punditry. In 1993, they strongly supported a party that could not form a government. Second, Reform's appeal was underestimated. Even Preston Manning thought his party might have peaked in the fall of 1992 after the Charlottetown referendum. But clearly the importance of sentiment against ethnic accommodation in the Canadian electorate was also underestimated. Although these miscalculations were shared by strategists in most parties, they were fatal only for the Conservatives. The Conservative campaign made the assumption that if voters could be persuaded that Kim Campbell was new and different, most of the 1988 voting coalition (though not all) could be retained, supplemented by some newly accessible voter groups, such as working women. But however different I was from Brian Mulroney, I was not different on the issues that affected the voters who opposed ethnic accommodation, and if the Conservatives under Mulroney couldn't pull back the Bloc Québécois voters, they were unlikely to be dislodged by me.

For the first time in a long time, the political right in Canada outside Quebec is divided, while, with the collapse of the NDP, the left is consolidated. Moreover, as long as the question of the accommodation of Quebec remains unresolved, that division of the right will not easily be overcome. That will happen only if the importance of the issue declines because it is formally addressed in some way (through Quebec separation or a constitutional change), or if an issue arises that is seen by both sides as more important, as free trade was.

There tends to be twenty-twenty hindsight in evaluating political campaigns: the successful ones are seen as well conducted, and losing ones as disastrously run. Our organization in 1993 left much to be desired, but the underlying incoherence of the Conservative campaign had much to do with the incoherence of the voting coalition to which we were attempting to appeal. By the end of September, in a memo to John Tory, Allan Gregg admitted that we had been "outmanoeuvred on two fronts simultaneously," but there was no obvious way to overcome the problem.

The role of economic conditions in elections has not been as well demonstrated in Canada as it has in the United States. However, in 1984 the economy was poor, usually a factor favouring an opposition party, whereas in 1988, the economy was strong and unemployment low, a factor usually favouring the incumbent party. In 1993, Canada was in a recession, and the Conservatives were in government.

In 1988, particularly when it looked as though the Conservatives might lose the election, we had the support of nonpartisan groups, especially the business community, who wanted to protect free trade. There were no such efforts on our behalf in 1993, even though we did retain significant support among Canada's business leaders.

There were other factors as well. The tone of the media's coverage of the Tories during the last two weeks, when we were clearly losing, was negative to the point of gratuitous cruelty. At the same time, however, there was recognition in the press that the coverage of our campaign had not been fair. Even relatively early on, journalists were identifying a double standard in the coverage. Although it didn't seem to affect what happened on their news pages, the *Globe and Mail* editorial of September 28, "Liberally Adjusted," deplored "the media's apparent willingness at every turn to give the Liberals the benefit of the doubt. Just as the figures from Statistics Canada are seasonally adjusted, so party pronouncements are 'Liberally adjusted' to correct for their obvious failings. Thus a document pledging, in effect, to do nothing is described as 'prudent' while a promise merely to refrain from increasing the deficit — from near-record levels — is hailed as 'frugal' on the curious grounds that the party would have proposed much worse in the past."

Ron Collister, writing from Edmonton for the *Ottawa Sun* on October 11, said: "Now that Kim Campbell is not the front-runner, it's time for us to examine the kind of Canada we'll have if any of the others win. That is the challenge of the second half of this campaign. The first half has been devoted to a kind of public vivisection of Campbell, the incumbent with the presumption of success. The game has changed and, quite properly, it's time to give all leaders the same treatment. In that process, there may yet be a hope — maybe the only hope — for a Campbell revival, as the best of the worst."

These are just two examples of a number of media criticisms of media. With very few exceptions, however, there were no attempts to explain why this unfairness had occurred. October 1 saw an article in the *Ottawa Sun* by Doug Fisher entitled "Self-interest" that claimed actual bad faith and conflict of interest by the CBC in the coverage of the election. A respected Ottawa journalist, Doug Fisher had been an MP for many years as a member of the NDP before joining the press gallery. Fisher focussed on the CBC's having assigned Brian Stewart, a reporter well known for his criticism of my handling of the Somalia affair, to do a feature debunking the "fixation" on debt and deficit. He said, in part: "Let me turn to the line we've heard since 1984 from CBC officials and friends of the CBC about the cultural harms and the ruination ahead for the CBC from cuts in funding by the Mulroney government. Usually the 'friends' see this slow strangulation of the CBC as calculated neo-conservatism. Whatever ... it's obvious the CBC and those who work for it have a huge interest in the scale of future government funding. The two bleakest hopes for more money are the Campbell Tories and the Manning Reformers ...

"It's wrong that a Crown company, the largest, costliest news force and interpreter of ourselves to ourselves (though not the most watched) is reality-busting those likely to sustain or increase the company's funding."

Lyn Cockburn of the *Toronto Sun* addressed the question of sexism in some of the language of campaign coverage and of how the double standard applied: "Everything stuck to Kim ... Campbell was criticized for gaining weight, for daring to paint a less than optimistic employment picture, for continually wearing a gold lapel pin, for pointing her finger during speeches, for not presenting the electorate with specific programs. The media ignored Chrétien's body, clothes and hair; they let him wave his red policy book about as if it were the staff of life and rarely questioned its vague premises …

"Explain to your kids that Canada has a fine tradition of choosing women leaders in no-win situations. Never has a woman been permitted to lead either a provincial or federal party in circumstances that were sure to lead to election victory. That scenario has always been reserved for men."

Most journalists shied away from attempts to explain the bias. They tend to refer to "media manipulation" as if it is something beyond their control. George Bain, in his book *Gotcha! How the Media Distort the News*, does suggest some reasons why the coverage of the 1993 election took the form it did. He argues that there is an anti-Conservative, pro-left bias in the media. Bain details a number of occasions in the 1993 campaign when comments made by Jean Chrétien that could be thought of as serious candidates for "gaffedom" were, in fact, ignored by the press. In one case a journalist told Bain, who had asked if he was going to make anything of a particular comment, "I think I'll give him the benefit of the doubt."

Whatever the reason, there was something amiss in the media coverage of the 1993 election, as journalists themselves have identified. The following question posed by Alan Frizzell and Anthony Westell, authors of a paper called "The Press and the Prime Minister," deserves serious consideration: "Journalists might well pause to reflect on whether they would really be open to 'the new politics' for which they so often call. For example, what if a woman leader — or a man for that matter — brought to political campaigning qualities said to be feminine, such as gentleness, peacemaking, compassion, conciliation, the ability to listen, and comfort? Could traditional news values adjust to report fairly such an eccentric approach to politics?"

The role that hostility to Brian Mulroney played in the 1993 election result is difficult to assess. Anecdotally, it would seem to be significant. When writing about this hostility in the introduction to the report of the Citizens' Forum, Keith Spicer spoke of a "fury in the land" against the prime minister. The ghost of

Brian Mulroney still haunted the Conservative Party in the fall of 1993, and I had not been leader long enough to exorcise it.

For better or for worse, the campaign was now almost over. Sunday was beautiful and sunny. After a walkabout at the McDonald's near my house, I went to the post-race awards ceremony for the Run for the Cure, in support of breast cancer research. I spent the rest of the day until early evening visiting the campaign headquarters in the ridings around Vancouver. In her journal entry for Sunday, October 24, Pamela notes: "Boy, was she ever spunky and lively this morning. She is out there fighting for her political career and her dreams of Canada ... giving it her all ... But I don't know what she is really thinking or feeling."

In fact, my heart was very heavy. Perhaps it was the very magnitude of the pain that made it impossible for me to think about it as long as there was a job to be done.

Monday morning I voted early and then went home until it was time to go down to the Pan Pacific Hotel to await the results. British Columbia law prohibits the broadcasting of election results from the rest of Canada before the polls close in B.C. With the Newfoundland polls closing at 3:30 p.m. Vancouver time, we began to get the results at the hotel by phone. They weren't good, and as the results moved west, the full nature of the disaster began to appear. Only Elsie Wayne in Saint John, New Brunswick, and Jean Charest in Sherbrooke would be elected. I felt so bad about Elsie. The popular and effective mayor of Saint John, she had become a candidate at my direct request and seemed to share my hope for a new politics. Now she was half of a caucus that wouldn't receive official recognition as a party in the House.

I couldn't keep up with all the phone calls as candidates went down like ninepins. I called Brian Mulroney and Joe Clark, who had anticipated the loss but were supportive. What else could they be? As my family and close friends and close aides watched the TV in shock, I couldn't help joking that at least the windows in the hotel room were too small to jump out of. When the result was clear, I spoke to a teary John Tory and found myself comforting him. "We should have done better for you, Prime Minister," he lamented. I don't know how well John was prepared for our rout, although I'm told he had access to a more accurate prognosis than I was given. Libby Burnham once told me of a conversation she had had with John in the summer of 1993. Explaining to him that she wanted to speak to me and was having difficulty getting through, she then received a lecture on how one is supposed to talk to a prime minister. In his view this involved a great deal of building up of the prime-ministerial spirits and ego. Libby was astonished because this didn't correspond to her experience with me at all. Hearing the story led me to wonder just how much I had been "built up" as opposed to "levelled with" by the chairman of my campaign and others.

The magnitude of our defeat, which included the loss of my own seat, made the speaking notes that had been prepared for me unsuitable. My exhausted team put together a revised version that was dignified and graceful. I had brought a red suit to wear that evening, since I wanted to look anything but sombre. After I had changed, I telephoned Jean Chrétien to congratulate him and to offer my full cooperation for the transition. I advised him that he could take occupancy of 24 Sussex Drive at his convenience since I had never moved in. He graciously told me that there was no hurry for me to vacate Harrington Lake, but I assured him that I wouldn't need to stay past the transition date because I had kept my apartment in Ottawa. Then it was time to make my way downstairs to meet the media and our party supporters in the Trade and Convention Centre adjoining the hotel.

As I approached the backstage area, I stopped to hug and comfort devastated friends and supporters as Ray Castelli came up. We began exchanging bits of black humour. Ray joked that at least I still had my car. David Camp went to the podium and introduced me to the crowd. As I walked up onto the stage in the full glare of the television lights, I could see so many faces that had been part of my life for so long. The cheers were heartfelt — sad and affectionate and defiant. I realized that if I was ever going to lose it, it would be in front of this group. I had to break the tension. "Gee, I'm glad I didn't sell my car," I began. The crowd roared with laughter and delight. It wasn't just the joke. This was the Kim Campbell they all knew and had seen disappear during the campaign.

I delivered the remarks that had been prepared, adding some of my own sentiments. As I congratulated Mr. Chrétien on his victory, there was a rumble in the audience. Few knew better than I, I insisted, the dramatic changes that would now take place in the lives of the Chrétiens, and they would need the support and goodwill of all Canadians in their new responsibilities. I also felt I needed to say something more to the members of our party. I expressed the consternation I knew they must be feeling that even though our vote was virtually the same as that of Reform and the Bloc, we had only two seats while each of them had more than fifty. I joked that perhaps we would be the first national party to support proportional representation. I reminded them that many great leaders and parties and movements have spent time in the wilderness. Our moment in the sun would come again. Then, knowing I could not wade into the crowd before me that night, I concluded my remarks with Dad's expression, "Consider yourselves hugged."

17

AFTERMATH

SEVERAL DAYS BEFORE the election, Jodi White had returned to Ottawa to begin the process of transition. As she remarked, no one would be returning her calls the next week. Arriving back in Ottawa on October 26, I met that week with cabinet and caucus. Before the cabinet meeting, I had breakfast with Jean Charest in my office. I congratulated him again on winning his seat. As always, I couldn't tell what he was really thinking. I told him that although I hadn't made any definitive decision about my future yet, it seemed to me that it probably made more sense for the party to be led from the House if he was willing to become interim leader. I said I was willing to stay on for as long as the party wanted me to, but that I wasn't prepared to become a pincushion. Of course, much would depend on what his plans were. Jean indicated an interest in becoming interim leader but said he wanted to go away with his wife for two weeks to think about things. We agreed that we would talk again on his return. The cabinet meeting was subdued. The consensus was that there should be no change in the leadership in the immediate future. As Charlie Mayer put it, we needed to go through a grieving process.

Caucus was also in a state of shock. I was dismayed to learn that a large number of our candidates wouldn't be eligible for the publicly funded rebate on their campaign expenses because they hadn't received the required 15 per cent of the vote. Many had borrowed money to finance their campaigns on the assumption that the rebate would be there to pay off the loans. The threshold had been set to discourage frivolous candidacies, and it seemed ridiculous that candidates running for the governing party should be penalized in this way. I discovered, however, that quite a number of Liberal candidates had encountered the same problem in the 1984 election, and the Conservatives had refused to agree to change the rule. This didn't bode well for getting the cooperation of the Liberals to address our problem. It was a good example of the expression "What goes around comes around." We had been jerks in 1984 and now we would pay for it.

After I made my concluding remarks, Toronto MP John Bosley stood up to say that he was damn mad, and wasn't I mad? Yes, I replied, I was mad. There seemed to be a collective sigh of relief with that declaration. I realized that my colleagues needed to see an expression of the deep anger I felt.

I was certainly on my own as far as taking responsibility for the campaign was concerned. The papers were full of stories of how I had done everything wrong and the campaign team had performed valiantly. An interview given by Allan Gregg, in which he was critical of me and disavowed any responsibility for a losing strategy, made party members particularly angry. Not only did they see it as unprofessional — a betrayal of client confidence — but they were mindful of the rewards Allan and his company had claimed in dollars and recognition over the years that they were the Conservative Party's official pollsters.

Meanwhile, I was dealing with the question of what my tenure as leader should be. From my own self-interested perspective, it made sense for me to go. However, I wanted to make sure that it didn't seem as if I was just cutting and running. If it made sense for me to stay on for a while, I would. However, it was clear to me that many in the party leadership wanted me out as soon as possible.

Two things concerned me. First, I had heard rumours that Jean Charest was under considerable pressure from his wife and family to return to private life. I could certainly not have blamed him if that had been his decision. If I resigned immediately, however, it seemed to me that this would have made it harder for him to go. If Jean were not available to take over the leadership, the party would have to be led from the Senate, which seemed an unappealing idea.

The other thing that concerned me was that the House was scheduled to return on January 17. I felt the party had to announce some sort of rebuilding process before that date if it wanted to get any publicity. After January 17, the media weren't going to be interested in the Tories. We needed to communicate to our members and, more important, to potential contributors that the Conservative Party was alive and well. The major fundraising event, which with a much happier election result would have been billed as the annual Prime Minister's Dinner, was scheduled for Toronto on November 25, exactly one month after the election. I agreed to speak and decided that the dinner might be a good place to announce a process to put together a strategy for rebuilding the party.

I needed some rest and relaxation before making serious decisions. The previous November, at Endeavour '92, a charity auction in support of arts and social organizations in Vancouver, Ginny Richards and I had successfully bid on a five-day stay at a California spa. We had all but given up on being able to use it as 1993 unfolded, but now we could go, and the mild California weather combined with healthy food and exercise was truly refreshing. Before going to California on November 13, I had joined Gregory for a couple of days in Chicago, where he was attending a trade show. One day, returning to the hotel, I was approached by a man who reached out to shake my hand. He said he was a Canadian and a great admirer. "The next time you run for election," he boomed at me, "just lie through your teeth!"

After returning from California I met with Jean a second time, on November 22, again for a private, one-on-one meeting, this time over lunch. I found him less forthcoming about his intentions than he had been during our first meeting. As I tried to find out whether he planned to stay, he kept saying, "Surely your decision doesn't depend on my decision." Well, in fact it did. I left the meeting disconcerted because I was less clear about what he had in mind than before.

The afternoon of the Toronto fundraising dinner, party president Senator Gerry St. Germain visited me in my hotel room. Gerry and I had never been close although we were both from British Columbia. He was a true Mulroney loyalist. I knew he would be one of the custodians of the Mulroney reputation, which meant that the sooner I threw myself on the funeral pyre, the happier he would be. He paced up and down my room, explaining that when he lost his seat in 1988, he "wasn't rational" for at least two years afterwards. Watching him, I wondered about his current state of mind. As he kept assuring me that I could count on him to tell me the truth, I remembered all the reports I had heard of his badmouthing me over the past few years, all the while professing friendship in person, and assumed it was business as usual.

I opened my remarks at the dinner that night by saying I took full responsibility for the campaign and also took responsibility for rebuilding the party. What I had worked out with my advisers was an approach that would be very grassroots-oriented. A commission would draw suggestions together and present a strategic approach to rebuilding no later than June 1994. Since the question of my resignation had not been determined, I wasn't sure whether to say that the report would be presented to "the leader" or to "me." I chose the latter, not realizing the consternation it would cause. I suppose in a way it was not a bad thing, because it precipitated a resolution.

That night after the dinner, which had turned into a successful reunion of party members, three of the Montrealers who had been close to Brian Mulroney and had ostensibly supported me in the leadership came up to my hotel room to tell me they had it "on direct authority" that "Charest wants it now." "Well," I replied, "he's an adult — why can't he tell me himself?" I suppose Jean had decided, or had been advised, that whatever happened, he mustn't be seen to push me out of the leadership. Telling me he would be prepared to accept the interim leadership in response to my own query hardly constituted pushing in my mind. I wondered whether Charest or his advisers were so Byzantine that they didn't know what to make of someone who didn't have a hidden agenda.

The upshot was that the process of my departure was accelerated. Unfortunately, certain members of the party executive ensured that my departure would reflect badly on the party. A report had begun circulating that the executive had refused to vote me a salary, which would have been necessary if I were to stay on. I had never asked for a salary and was offended at the gratuitous insult. I received calls from angry people in a number of ridings who were embarrassed by the ham-handedness of the party leadership and said that if the party executive was not prepared to give me a salary, they would raise the money at the riding level.

In the period after the election, I needed to reassure myself that I was not abandoning ship if I resigned. Not only did I want to be sure I wasn't letting down my supporters, but I was anxious to see the party's rebuilding process begin as soon as possible.

After the Toronto fundraiser, I spent a weekend with John and Isabel Bassett at their country home in Caledon. Their unreproachful friendship warmed me. John was dismayed by the recent election result but philosophical. He also knew exactly what I would face if I tried to stay on as leader. "You don't owe anybody anything," he said forcefully. "Get on with your life."

Ross Reid led the effort to work with Jean and his people on the details of the restructuring framework I wanted to put in place before the House came back. Finally, I came to see that the original plan I had worked out with my advisers — in which I would step down around January 15, leaving the plan in place as a parting contribution — would not work. If I was going home for Christmas, they suggested, it made more sense for my future to be clear at that time. I agreed. I was as much in shock as anyone, and concerned not to make serious, irrevocable decisions without careful thought. I had wanted to show the party that I cared about its future and had not lost interest just because I had ceased to be prime minister. However, that was not to be. It would be up to Jean to take advantage of the pre–January 17 window if he could.

Over several weeks, I spoke to my closest supporters to be sure that they were comfortable with my itention to resign sooner rather than later. I finally decided that what I owed to all the people who had worked so hard to support me for the leadership was not to debase myself. Staying on, even if the party executive agreed it was appropriate, would be a non-stop process of pulling knives out of my back. This was made particularly clear after the Toronto dinner. The *Globe and Mail* carried a vicious editorial about me that actually asserted that Jean Charest had *really* won the leadership! *Toronto Star* columnist Dalton Camp probably called it right when he accused the *Globe and Mail* of being Brian Mulroney's mouthpiece, referring to Mulroney's close relationship to its editor-in-chief, William Thorsell. From time to time Thorsell would write columns that carried some idea that came from Mulroney. People who knew Mulroney could always detect his distinct diction in the way the ideas were expressed, and this editorial was a classic example of the kind of hyperbole Mulroney uses when he wants to make a particularly hostile point.

During that post-election period, I also became aware of another problem — I owed the party money. At the conclusion of the leadership campaign, the PC Canada Fund had offered to lend the leadership candidates the money to pay their campaign debts. The reason for this unusual offer was that, being so close to an election, we didn't want to find that companies and tradespeople would not accept orders from the party because they were owed money from the leadership campaign. I took advantage of the offer. My campaign then arranged just enough fundraising activity to cover the debt, and I was told my account was settled. After the election I discovered that, unbeknownst to me, other bills had been paid on my campaign's behalf by the party. My leadership fundraisers were angry because they had raised exactly the sum they were told was owing and could easily have raised more if they'd known it was needed.

As if that weren't bad enough, I began to hear of rumours in the party that not only did I owe the party money, but I was making my resignation as leader contingent on my debt being written off. This was completely untrue, since I insisted that the party *not* say it would pay my debt. Given the enormous debt the party was facing, the rumour was designed to turn party members against me. I told Robert Foster that my debt had to be paid and, thanks to his quiet efforts, it now has been. Robert had the distinct feeling that events were, in his words, "being orchestrated from Montreal." He told me about a conversation he'd had with a psychiatrist friend who had said he hoped the party understood the need to go through a period of shock and grief and not make important decisions right away. An insight that had certainly been shared by cabinet and caucus, it was ignored by Gerry St. Germain and others who seemed to take my continued presence at the helm of the party as a personal affront. In their view, all our problems were my fault, and the party would never be able to raise money or recover as long as I was there.

As a matter of courtesy, I had kept in touch with all of the previous Conservative Party leaders. Joe Clark was in California, but Robert Stanfield and his wife asked me to dinner with Dalton Camp and Norman Atkins to discuss the situation and what I should do. Suspecting that Brian Mulroney was implicated in the goings-on behind the scenes to hasten my departure, I was curious to see what his comportment would be when I went to pay him a courtesy call before announcing my resignation. He invited me to meet with him late one afternoon at his elegant, sumptuous home in Westmount. After greeting me warmly, Mulroney took me to a den on the second floor of the house for our meeting. I sat on a chair facing my host, who was seated on a couch, beneath the large portrait of Mila that I had last seen at 24 Sussex Drive the day of my shuffle into Defence.

"Well," began my former boss, "the party let you down. The party did not serve you well."

Ah, I thought, so that is the line.

There was a strange unreality to our meeting. We chatted amiably. I told him that I had been offered a fellowship at Harvard, which I now thought I might take up in the New Year. Good idea, was his response. Harvard had offered to make him a "full professor" but he couldn't take up the offer because he had "four small children" to support.

I said that I was planning to resign the leadership. Being very careful not to tell me what I should do, Mulroney said that what he would do under the circumstances would be to announce on December 15 that he was resigning effective January 15. We met for about an hour, and as it was getting time for me to go, the man who had spoken to me several times during the election and to John Tory regularly suddenly blurted out, "You know, I was talking to one of your great supporters at a cocktail party last week, one of your great supporters in Montreal. He said to me, 'You know, when I saw last August who was doing our campaign ads, I knew we were in trouble.' And I said, 'Yes, I did too. And I bet you didn't phone Kim either.'"

Hullo, I thought, what planet are we on? At that moment, Brian Mulroney became entirely opaque to me. When I had first met him, five years earlier, I had taken him at face value — his charm, his anger, his humour. Gradually, during the intervening years, I became aware that he wasn't always what he seemed. Now I realized I didn't know him at all.

"An Irish rogue," one old acquaintance described him to me. As I took my leave of Brian Mulroney and climbed into the car, I wasn't angry, just bemused. "How does he do it?" I marvelled at the former PM's ability to portray himself as a mere bystander in the saga of our party's electoral defeat. His aplomb reminded me of a line from Edith Wharton's *The House of Mirth*: "She had the art of giving self-confidence to the embarrassed, but she was not equally sure of being able to embarrass the self-confident."

On December 13 I announced my resignation as leader of the Progressive Conservative Party of Canada in the National Press Theatre in Ottawa, exactly six months to the day after I was elected. Gerry St. Germain sat beside me as I made my announcement. Afterwards he read a statement accepting my resignation with the obligatory regret. I tried to be upbeat and positive, but Gerry's expression confirmed everything that had been rumoured about the shabby treatment I had received from him and others. It was in particular contrast with the gracious way Prime Minister Chrétien had behaved. In providing me with an office and small staff for a year, he had not only made it possible for me to deal with the continuing large volume of correspondence I received after the election and the challenge of organizing my papers, but had also enabled me to accept the invitation of a fellowship that January at the Institute of Politics at the Kennedy School, rather than immediately find some place to hang my hat that could supply my secretarial needs. The PM's courtesy was widely discussed as evidence that the Liberals were treating me better than my own party. The shortsightedness of the national executive created considerable resentment against the party, particularly among women, which could only hinder the rebuilding process. Watching the frenzied activity of those individuals after the election was like watching a group of pygmies running around in a tizzy (no offence intended to pygmies). At times like that I would remind myself that these few people were not the party. The party was all those great people I had met across the country who are the real guarantee of its future.

The day after my resignation, Jean Charest was named interim leader of the party, and he was confirmed as leader by a party convention in April 1995. At that meeting, I joked to Jodi White, "I can't believe I'm voting for Charest on the first ballot." I did, and I wish him well.

During the election, a high school student asked me what I would like my legacy as a politician to be. I answered that I would like to contribute to the belief that public life is a noble calling. Many people tell me that I will always have my own place in the history of this country because I was the first woman to be prime minister. What pleases me more is knowing that my being there has changed the sense of what is possible for a lot of young women and girls in Canada. Several teachers have told me that girls in their classes are taking a greater interest in politics, and young women themselves have told me that they are going to be prime minister. To be a model for that ambition is truly gratifying. About a year after the election, a visiting friend described watching a mother checking on two little girls playing in the basement. "What are you up to?" asked the mother. "We're playing Kim Campbell and Hillary Clinton," answered the daughter. "Why are you doing that?" inquired the mother. "Because," came the reply, "they're the women who can do the most to change things."

On the other hand, my sense of personal disappointment remains. I had a dream, a vision about how democracy could be transformed in Canada, and the prime minister had given me the opportunity to begin to test my ideas by putting me into the cabinet. As I grew more experienced and confident, I had tackled difficult issues in my own way and seen my ideas vindicated. My faith in the ability of people to work constructively together when given the chance had been proven right. But after the election my dream was dead. It seemed as if my whole life had been leading to this opportunity, and it had slipped through my fingers. For the people close to me who understood and shared the vision that had brought me to the leadership, this was a disappointment almost too great to contemplate. But there was nothing to do but carry on with life. It was only a year and a half later, writing these pages in the summer of 1995, that I was able to reach down into that deep well of sadness I had been carrying around since the election and, finally, shed my personal tears.

I will always be haunted by questions of what I could have done differently that fateful summer of 1993. Still, I regard my time in public life positively. For every example of pettiness, self-serving, or narrowness I encountered in people, there are ten examples of courage, broad-mindedness, and generosity of spirit. I am much more worldly-wise than when I started. For every devastating failure, there are real accomplishments in which I take pride. Not only do they give me some comfort, they confirm my belief that individuals can make a difference.

INDEX

G

H

I

J

M

N

O

P

Q

R

S

T

U

Y

Z